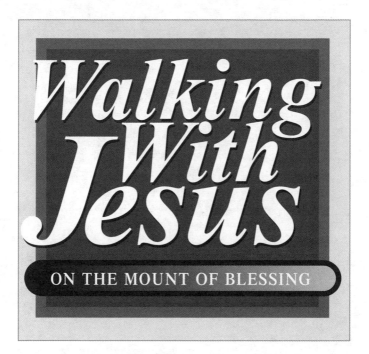

Walking With Jesus

ON THE MOUNT OF BLESSING

Walking *With* Jesus

ON THE MOUNT OF BLESSING

Daily Meditations for Adults

GEORGE R. KNIGHT

REVIEW AND HERALD® PUBLISHING ASSOCIATION
HAGERSTOWN, MD 21740

Copyright © 1996 by
Review and Herald® Publishing Association

This book was
Edited by Raymond H. Woolsey
Cover design by Helcio Deslandes
Cover photo by Green Directory/Masterfile
Typeset: 10/12 Janson

Printed in U.S.A.

00 99 98 97 96   5 4 3 2 1

Library of Congress Cataloging in Publication Data
Knight, George R.
    Walking with Jesus on the Mount of Blessing / George Knight.
        p.   cm.

    1. Sermon on the mount—Meditations.   2. Bible. N.T. Matthew V
-VII—Meditations.   3. Devotional calendars.   I. Title.
BT380.2.K57   1996
242'.2—dc20   96-9263
                                                                          CIP

ISBN 0-8280-0965-1

DEDICATION

To Cleone Bond,
a wonderful mother-in-law,
a woman who exemplifies the teachings
of the Mount of Blessing
in her daily life.

A WORD TO MY FELLOW TRAVELERS

W elcome aboard. This year we will spend 365 days walking with Jesus on the Mount of Blessing. We will progress through the Sermon on the Mount, spending a week on this text and a couple of days on the next. Unlike the general practice of devotional books, which take their texts from all over the Bible, this year's volume confines itself to a progressive exposition of the 111 verses of Matthew 5-7. But while the exposition progresses through those three chapters, the need for a new Bible verse for meditation every day means that on most days verses from outside Matthew 5-7 have been selected. However, the message of those verses is tied directly to the ongoing exposition of Jesus' presentation in the sermon.

The Sermon on the Mount provides an excellent basis for a year's daily study because it covers nearly every aspect of Christian belief and living. Beyond that, it places those doctrinal and lifestyle issues in the framework of the gospel.

Books on the Sermon on the Mount are legion, but I found the work of four authors to be especially helpful for devotional purposes: Ellen White's *Thoughts From the Mount of Blessing*, D. Martyn Lloyd-Jones's two-volume *Studies in the Sermon on the Mount*, Frederick Dale Bruner's *Matthew: The Christbook*, and the various works on the Sermon on the Mount by William Barclay. For those with an interest in further study in the first Gospel, I would like to recommend my *Matthew: The Gospel of the Kingdom* in the Abundant Life Bible Amplifier series.

The preparation of this volume would have been impossible without the skilled help of my secretary, Bonnie Beres.

George R. Knight
Berrien Springs, Michigan

An Overview of the Journey

Step 1
A Christian's Character (Matt. 5:3-12)
January 1-March 5

Step 2
A Christian's Influence (Matt. 5:13-16)
March 6-March 25

Step 3
A Christian's Righteousness (Matt. 5:17-48)
March 26-June 22

Step 4
A Christian's Piety (Matt. 6:1-18)
June 23-August 17

Step 5
A Christian's Goals and Priorities (Matt. 6:19-34)
August 18-October 11

Step 6
A Christian's Relationships (Matt. 7:1-12)
October 12-November 13

Step 7
A Christian's Commitment (Matt. 7:13-29)
November 14-December 31

THE UPSIDE-DOWN KINGDOM

Blessed are the poor in spirit, for theirs is the kingdom of heaven. Matt. 5:3, RSV.

This doesn't seem like a very good way to start a sermon. I mean, it is not very politically astute. It lacks the finesse and insight of a public relations expert.

After all, who wants to hear about poverty of spirit? This preacher is obviously not in tune with the world. To be "successful," you have to give people what they want; you have to present them with the words and ideas they want to hear.

And anyone with ears to hear knows that people are overjoyed with such messages as "Blessed are the rich" or "Blessed are the rich in spirit."

Now, if Jesus really wants to draw a crowd, He will have to wise up to the ways of the world. With a message such as "Blessed are the poor in spirit," He will never get beyond first base with most people. He will never achieve the kind of success that is respected by the larger culture.

But that's exactly where the rub comes between conventional values and Jesus. He is not concerned with the admiration of the world around Him. His concern is to be in tune with God.

As a result, His message is the opposite of that of the larger culture. It is a message counter to the wisdom of the world. In the eyes of the world, Jesus is preaching a countercultural message. In effect, *this first beatitude sets the world's value system on its head*. It turns it upside down.

Jesus' kingdom is a radical kingdom, and its citizens will be radical also. That is the startling message of the Beatitudes, the Sermon on the Mount, and the entire New Testament.

"Blessed are the poor in spirit." That is one of the world's most radical sayings. Yet it stands at the foundation of Jesus' Christian message.

And that message is for me personally. It is for you. We have to make a choice between Jesus and the world—between its values and His. In the Beatitudes, Jesus sets forth the central principles of His radical kingdom.

JESUS' ATTACK ON "HUMANITY"

Is not this the great Babylon I have built as the royal residence, by my mighty power and for the glory of my majesty? Dan. 4:30, NIV.

Nebuchadnezzar is the successful human par excellence. He was top man, and he knew it. He was proud—proud of who he was, proud of his accomplishments, proud of his dignity. He was anything but poor of spirit. He was proud of spirit and glad of it.

Nebuchadnezzar's spiritual stance is at the very center of the sin problem. Sin is misdirected love. The core of sin is redirecting our love from God and our neighbor to our self. It is putting our personal little self at the center of our universe and being proud of it.

That was the problem with Lucifer. "I will ascend into heaven," he mused; "I will exalt my throne above the stars of God: I will sit also upon the mount of the congregation, . . . I will ascend above the heights of the clouds; I will be like the most high" (Isa. 14:13, 14). In short, Lucifer became the god of his own life. In so doing, he became Satan, the adversary of God and Christ.

Adam and Eve followed a similar path when they chose their will and way above God's will and words in Genesis 3. That rebellious sin has resulted in all the misery that has since infected Planet Earth. Pride and self-sufficiency stand at the very center of the sin problem. That is why Jesus began expounding the principles of His kingdom with "Blessed are the poor in spirit." He needed to hit immediately at the heart of the problem. Nothing could be done until the heart of the problem had been exposed.

The greatest need of human beings is a heart transplant. God wants to take my selfish, self-centered life and transform it into a life of outgoing love toward both Himself and my fellow humans.

The first step in God's heart surgery is to diagnose the problem. Then it must be confronted in each of us. Thus Jesus' "attack" on our "humanity"—our "normal" self-centered ways.

He wants me (and you) to see that the first step toward entering into His kingdom is poverty of spirit.

The question is Am I willing to be poor for the kingdom?

PROUD OF MY GOODNESS

I thank you, God, that I am not like the rest of mankind—greedy, dishonest, adulterous—or, for that matter, like this tax-collector. I fast twice a week; I pay tithes on all that I get. Luke 18:11, 12, REB.

Well, you may be thinking by this time, *I am not so stupid as some people think. I know that it is wrong to desire worldly power and possessions. I have given up that way of life. My life is focused on spiritual things. I am not like those other people out there. I have my act together.*

Wait! Hold on! Don't go any further! I think you've missed the point. I am not sure if you have tumbled off the spiritual cliff yet. But if you haven't, you are teetering on the very brink.

After all, the man in our Scripture reading today was a "good" man. He also had given up the ways of the world and focused his life and thoughts on spiritual things.

But he didn't go deep enough. He cleaned up his surface act, but he hadn't become "poor in spirit." In fact, he was still proud in spirit. He had merely transferred his pride from worldly things to so-called spiritual things. As a result, he still had the same disease. But he now had it in a more subtle form—he was proud of his goodness.

There is nothing more dangerous to true Christianity than spiritual pride. As Ellen White puts it: "There is nothing so offensive to God or so dangerous to the human soul as pride and self-sufficiency. Of all sins it is the most hopeless, the most incurable" (*Christ's Object Lessons*, p. 154). That is true because "pride feels no need, and so it closes the heart against Christ and the infinite blessings He came to give" (*Steps to Christ*, p. 30).

The tax collector is the true hero in Luke 18 because he knew he was a mess and needed help. "God, be merciful to me a [*the* in the Greek] sinner" (verse 13, RSV) was his prayer. Because he was poor in spirit, God was able to forgive him.

Lord, help me this day to see the extent of my need for You. Help me to be willing to be poor in spirit.

THE POVERTY MAKER

Nevertheless I tell you the truth; It is expedient for you that I go away: for if I go not away, the Comforter will not come unto you; but if I depart, I will send him unto you. And when he is come, he will reprove the world of sin, and of righteousness, and of judgment. John 16:7, 8.

One of the most wonderful things about Christianity is that we are never alone. Because of God's infinite love, each of us has the ministry of the Holy Spirit in our personal life.

The Holy Spirit in our text for today is characterized in various translations as not only "the Comforter" (KJV), but as "the Helper" (NASB) and "the Counselor" (RSV). In actual fact, He is all of these and much more. Of all people, Christians are most blessed because they have a Member of the Godhead working actively with them every day. We need to praise God more for the Comforter.

But not all of the Spirit's work in our lives seems to be comforting— or at least not right away. Sometimes His work is initially annoying. It even hurts. For, you see, it is the work of the Spirit to convict us of sin. It is the work of the Spirit to tell us that something is wrong in our lives; that we are not what we should be; even that we are selfish, mean, or proud. He is always poking around in areas of our life that we would like to keep secret.

But that work is actually one of mercy. It is like that of the physician who probes us on the physical level to determine if we have a dangerous disease.

Listen to the Holy Spirit. He has a message we need to hear. It is a message that we are messed up from birth. He convicts us of our spiritual poverty. But His work is much more than that. The Comforter also points us to the solution to all of our problems—Jesus Christ, His sacrifice for us on the cross, and the boundless righteousness that He wants to supply us with.

Praise God for the work of the Comforter. He points out our poverty that we might become rich in Jesus.

HEROES OF POVERTY

Woe is me! for I am undone; because I am a man of unclean lips, and I dwell in the midst of a people of unclean lips: for mine eyes have seen the King, the Lord of hosts. Isa. 6:5.

The Bible is a strange book because it repeatedly features people as heroes who admit their weaknesses and needs.

On the shelves of my library I have many volumes about "great" people—of presidents, intellectuals, socialites, and military commanders. The most accurate of these volumes point out the weaknesses of the individuals they treat, but they go on to emphasize that they were great because they overcame their weaknesses through heroic and sustained effort.

The Bible paints a totally different picture. Its heroes are great because they recognize that their most important weaknesses are beyond overcoming through human effort. They admit that they need God's help. In short, they are poor in spirit.

Again and again the Bible's heroes express their unworthiness. Such was the case of Isaiah in today's Scripture reading. Upon being given a vision of God's magnitude and glory, he fully confessed his weakness. He realized that he was as nothing by comparison. He became poor of spirit.

Moses shared the same spirit. He felt deeply unworthy of the task God laid upon him. He was acutely conscious of his inadequacy. The same can be said of David and Gideon and a host of other Old Testament heroes.

The same truth is found in the New Testament. The example of the apostle Peter comes to mind. Peter the natural man was aggressive, self-assertive, and self-confident—a typical man of the world. He was anything but poor in spirit. But that would all change at the cross and beyond, when he got a fuller glimpse of his weakness and his need of Jesus.

Peter's new life began at the foot of the cross when he became poor in spirit. So it is with each of us.

It is no accident that Jesus begins His discussion of the principles of His kingdom with poverty of spirit. It is that sense of our spiritual helplessness that forces us to look to Jesus for the priceless blessings He wants to give each of us.

CITIZENS OF THE KINGDOM

In those days came John the Baptist, preaching in the wilderness of Judea, "Repent, for the kingdom of heaven is at hand." Matt. 3:1, 2, RSV.

Jesus began His preaching with the exact same message as John (see Matt. 4:17). The kingdom arrived with the initiation of Jesus' ministry. And in the first beatitude the poor in spirit are called blessed because "theirs *is* the kingdom of heaven" (Matt. 5:3, RSV).

Note that in the first beatitude the blessing is a present reality. That same truth is repeated in verse 10, whereas many of the intervening blessings are stated in the future tense.

What does that mean? Doesn't the kingdom arrive at the second coming of Jesus? The answer is both yes and no.

The New Testament has a twofold view of the kingdom of heaven. The kingdom arrived with the public ministry of Jesus, but it will not be established in its fullness until Jesus returns in the clouds of heaven. The first of those aspects of the kingdom might be thought of as the kingdom of grace, while the second may be viewed as the kingdom of glory.

Thus believers are *already* citizens of God's kingdom, and they *already* have eternal life (John 5:24; 6:47). It is a current possession.

How did this happen? How did we become citizens of the kingdom? Ellen White puts it nicely. "All who have a sense of their deep soul poverty," she writes, "who feel that they have nothing good in themselves, may find righteousness and strength by looking unto Jesus. . . . He bids you exchange your poverty for the riches of His grace. . . . Whatever may have been your past experience, however discouraging your present circumstances, if you will come to Jesus just as you are, weak, helpless, and despairing, our compassionate Saviour will meet you a great way off, and will throw about you His arms of love and His robe of righteousness. He presents us to the Father clothed in the white raiment of His own character" *(Thoughts From the Mount of Blessing,* pp. 8, 9).

Praise God today, because if you are poor in spirit, you are already a member of the kingdom of heaven. Praise God today for His infinite blessings in Jesus.

BLESSED OR HAPPY?

What happiness there is for you who are poor, for the Kingdom of God is yours! Luke 6:20, TLB.

Each of Jesus' beatitudes in Matthew and Luke begins with the Greek word *makarios*. That word can be translated in several ways, including "blessed" (NIV, KJV, RSV) and "happy" (Phillips and TLB).

There is a sense in which believers in Jesus are happy and have a right to be happy. After all, as we noted yesterday, they are already members of God's kingdom.

But by and large, "happy" is an inadequate translation of *makarios*, because most of us see happiness as a subjective state. That is, happiness is how we feel. We feel either sad or happy.

But the Christian life is not based on a subjective feeling. Once a young man came to my office all upset because he didn't feel happy. Those feelings had led to deep spiritual discouragement. After all, didn't Jesus say repeatedly that if he was a Christian, he would be happy? Therefore, since he wasn't happy he must not be a Christian. Something must be wrong with his life, but he couldn't figure out what it was. As a sincere person he had been living in the pit of despair.

I explained to my student friend that he had it all wrong. Our acceptance with God is based not on subjective feelings of happiness or sadness, but in the *objective fact* that Jesus died for our sins and that all who accept His sacrifice in faith have *already* been forgiven and adopted into the covenant family, and have become citizens of the kingdom.

In other words, he was blessed no matter how he felt. The good news is that our salvation is an accomplished fact.

Thus even though I may not feel happy about being "persecuted for righteousness' sake" (Matt. 5:10), I can still have peace because I have been blessed by Jesus. That is a fact. And while there is a sense in which I can be happy about that peace of heart, blessedness is more than happiness. "Blessed," said Jesus, "are the poor in spirit, for theirs is the kingdom of heaven" (RSV).

JESUS GETS IT BACKWARD AGAIN

Blessed are they that mourn: for they shall be comforted. Matt. 5:4.

L ike the first beatitude, this one stands over against the wisdom
and ways of the world. "Normal" non-Christians regard such a
statement as utterly ridiculous.

The motto of the world is not "Blessed or happy is the mourner,"
but "Blessed and happy are those who have escaped any need to
mourn." Mourning is one thing the world seeks to avoid with all its
heart. The philosophy of the world is "Forget your troubles"; "Do your
best to escape from problems."

The vast entertainment industry is aimed at helping people avoid
the necessity of mourning, of spending much time contemplating the
stupendous problems we face as a world culture and as individuals.

The cultural pleasure mania is in many ways an escape mechanism
from serious mourning. The TV is by and large a visual narcotic or
tranquilizer. It presents relatively meaningless programming as an escape from a relatively meaningless daily existence. The same can be said
for organized sports. They help us tune out of the real world and into a
world that is not nearly so threatening. Mass entertainment is too often
an escape from life rather than life itself.

People desperately want to be happy. Providing happiness is
America's largest industry.

But such "wisdom" is not that of Jesus. "Blessed [or happy] are they
that mourn." Luke, in his parallel passage to the second beatitude, has
Jesus making the point even more clearly. "Woe to you who laugh now,
for you will mourn and weep" (Luke 6:25, NIV).

As in all the beatitudes, Jesus challenges the conventions of the world.
He presents the Christian ideal as the opposite from that of the unconverted world. The Christian person is unlike the world at the deepest level.

While Christians have a deep joy in their salvation, they are not of
those who seek out empty, meaningless happiness. They are impelled to
take life seriously and to mourn in a manner that eventually leads to
blessedness. In fact, according to Jesus, the route of mourning is the
only way to lasting happiness.

Lord, please help me to understand better what it means to mourn
as Christ mourned.

THE NEGATIVE BEFORE THE POSITIVE

What a wretched man I am! Who will rescue me from this body of death? Rom. 7:24, NIV.

The word for mourn in Matthew 5:4 is the strongest word for mourning in the Greek language. It is the word used of mourning for the dead. As such, it is a passionate lament for a loved one. In the Greek Old Testament it is the word selected to express Jacob's grief when he believed his son Joseph was dead (Gen. 37:34). It reflects deep grief. Thus William Barclay amplifies the second beatitude as "blessed is the man who mourns like one mourning for the dead."

Yet while mourning for the dead catches the intensity of the experience of Matthew 5:4, it does not reflect its meaning. The deep experience of the second beatitude is caught in today's scripture—"O wretched man that I am! who shall deliver me from the body of this death?" (Rom. 7:24). That cry tells us something of what is meant by mourning. It reflects a person so grief-stricken that he or she cries out in agony of spirit. Christians know the experience of feeling utterly hopeless because of their failures.

"For I know that in me (that is, in my flesh)," cried the apostle Paul, "dwelleth no good thing: for to will is present with me; but how to perform that which is good I find not. For the good that I would I do not: but the evil which I would not, that I do" (Rom. 7:18, 19).

Christians mourn because of their deep sense of unworthiness. It is no accident that the very first word of Jesus in Matthew is "repent." To repent is to recognize my sinfulness and disown it. It is to mourn that I am a sinner and to turn to God for forgiveness.

This is no surface experience. It is heartfelt. It is like mourning for the dead. But with the mourning comes hope. After all, "if we confess our sins, he is faithful and just to forgive us our sins, and to cleanse us from all unrighteousness" (1 John 1:9).

Thus mourning brings victory. The negative comes before the positive. I am convicted of sin so that I can experience the joy of salvation.

MOURNING AT THE CROSS

Christ died for our sins according to the Scriptures. 1 Cor. 15:3, NIV.

Have you ever hurt another person through some carelessness of your own?

I have a picture in my mind that I am unable to erase. It took place one spring evening in Houston, Texas. My 6-year-old daughter, Bonnie, was always very glad to see me after my long absence at work.

One day as I carelessly and heedlessly gunned the car up the driveway, she rushed around the corner of the house to greet me with outstretched arms.

The next thing I saw was her head hitting the hood as I plowed into her fragile body. The impact knocked her several feet through the air. The next few seconds were fraught with rapid thoughts. Had my carelessness destroyed her life? Had I caused her irreparable physical injury? How could I have been so stupid? so thoughtless? so irresponsible?

Fortunately, Bonnie was uninjured. But I was devastated and totally exhausted by the experience. Self-recriminations filled my mind. I was in a state of deep mourning for my actions. My carelessness had threatened the life of my only daughter.

As Christians we experience a similar emotion in our relationship to Jesus. Our sin, our rebellion, our thoughtlessness, put Him on Calvary's cross. He died for our sins. No! No! No! It is more personal than that. He died for *my* sins.

As we look at the cross we need to come to the full realization of what sin can do. It took history's loveliest life and smashed it on a cross.

One of the great functions of the cross is to open our eyes to the immensity and horror of sin. When we see what sin has done to Christ, we can't help experiencing deep sorrow for our sin. Thus we mourn not only for our personal sins but also for what those sins have done to Jesus.

Christianity begins with a sense of sin. But it doesn't stop there. After all, those who mourn will be comforted. God takes essentially bad things and brings ultimate good out of them.

JESUS ALSO MOURNED

He is despised and rejected of men; a man of sorrows, and acquainted with grief. Isa. 53:3.

Jesus never had any sins to mourn over, but He still mourned over sin and its effects. At the tomb of Lazarus we read that "Jesus wept" (John 11:35). Again near the end of His earthly sojourn we read of His sentiments for the Jews. "O Jerusalem, Jerusalem, you who kill the prophets and stone those sent to you, how often I have longed to gather your children together, as a hen gathers her chicks under her wings, but you were not willing. . . . Your house is left to you desolate" (Matt. 23:37, 38, NIV). The next verse goes on to discuss the destruction of Jerusalem.

Some Christians seem to imagine that if they are right with God they will be perpetually grinning and continuously bubbly. That perspective is unbiblical. According to Jesus, the Christian life is not all joy and laughter.

Not only do Christians mourn over their sins that put Jesus on the cross, but they, like their Lord, mourn for a lost world—a world pictured daily in the news media as lost and torn by violence.

Jesus wept over the sins of the world and the church, and so should we, as did the biblical prophets. "My eyes," cried the psalmist, "stream with tears because your law goes unheeded" (Ps. 119:136, REB). Ezekiel heard God's faithful people described as "those who groan and lament over abominations practised" in Jerusalem (Eze. 9:4, NEB). And Paul wrote of his sorrow over the false teachers troubling the churches of his day. "Many, of whom I . . . now tell you even with tears, live as enemies of the cross of Christ" (Phil. 3:18, RSV).

Christians are mourners. They mourn as over the death of a loved one for their sins that put Jesus on the cross. And they mourn over a sin-sick world that needs God's love and salvation.

But the paradox of the gospel is that mourning is the route to joy. Those who mourn are comforted daily by Jesus; they will find even more comfort when they meet their beloved Lord in the clouds of heaven.

PRESENT COMFORT

Blessed be the God and Father of our Lord Jesus Christ, the Father of mercies and God of all comfort, who comforts us in all our affliction, so that we may be able to comfort those who are in any affliction, with the comfort with which we ourselves are comforted by God. 2 Cor. 1:3, 4, RSV.

Comfort comes in many forms. Little children are often comforted by a special toy or their favorite blanket. Older folks are comforted by fond memories of places, people, or events that have special meaning for them. And people of all ages seem to be comforted by an endearing touch from a loved one and by words of kindness.

Human comforts are good, but the comforts of God are even better. Some of His comforts for us are present realities, while others are yet future.

Among the present comforts available to Christians are God's forgiveness and assurance of salvation.

Those who mourn over their sins and freely admit their need are fully and completely forgiven by God. God's forgiveness is both instantaneous and free. It costs us nothing. Through His death, Christ makes it available to all who believe in Him.

A few years ago I stopped by a grocery story in Virginia. A tabloid headline at the counter caught my eye. "Hubby Crawls 900 Miles to Beg Forgiveness." That, I mused, is the way some people think about God.

But God is not that way. He doesn't make us earn His forgiveness through life in a monastery. He doesn't suggest that we wear hair shirts or place dried peas under our knees as we kneel for prayer.

No, He loves us. And because He loves us, He is more than eager to forgive us. All He asks of us is that we truly repent of our sins and accept the sacrifice of Jesus. The result is instantaneous. We are forgiven.

That is where mourning comes in. Heart sorrow for sin drives us to Jesus for cleansing. "Blessed are they that mourn: for they shall be comforted" (Matt. 5:4). And what greater comfort could there be than to be right with God?

FUTURE COMFORT

But I would not have you to be ignorant, brethren, concerning them which are asleep, that ye sorrow not, even as others which have no hope. 1 Thess. 4:13.

Above-ground entombment," read the newspaper ad, "in a garden mausoleum constructed of time-defying granite, bronze, and reinforced concrete provides a peace of mind that comes only with knowing that the precious remains of loved ones are protected from the unfriendly elements of the earth."

Is that so? Does safe entombment provide peace of mind concerning our deceased loved ones? I think not. As I read this advertisement, Paul's remark about those who have no hope beyond the grave came to my mind. I find no comfort or hope in the promise of the ad.

But that does not mean there is no hope for the Christian. "Blessed are they that mourn," reads the second beatitude, "for they shall be comforted." Note that while the promise of the first beatitude is in the present tense, this one is in the future. Believers *already have* the kingdom of heaven, but they *"shall be"* comforted.

As we noted in yesterday's devotional, the promise of the second beatitude has been somewhat fulfilled in the sense that those who mourn over their sins have been forgiven. But the verse's future tense suggests much more than that.

The real comfort of the Christian takes place at the second coming of Jesus—that event described by Paul as the "blessed hope" (Titus 2:13). In reaching out to the bereaved Thessalonians, the apostle wrote: "The Lord himself will come down from heaven with a mighty shout and with the soul-stirring cry of the archangel and the great trumpet-call of God. And the believers who are dead will be the first to rise to meet the Lord. Then we who are still alive and remain on the earth will be caught up with them in the clouds to meet the Lord in the air and remain with him forever" (1 Thess. 4:16, 17, TLB).

Now there is hope, there is the fullness of comfort for those who mourn.

STILL MORE COMFORT

Behold, I shew you a mystery; We shall not all sleep, but we shall all be changed, in a moment, in the twinkling of an eye, at the last trump: for the trumpet shall sound, and the dead shall be raised incorruptible, and we shall be changed. 1 Cor. 15:51, 52.

The future comfort for those who mourn is almost boundless. Praise God that this life is not all there is to existence. Praise God that the grave is not the end for those who believe in Jesus. Paul put it nicely when he penned that "if being a Christian is of value to us only now in this life, we are the most miserable of creatures" (1 Cor. 15:19, TLB). The great truth is that Jesus won the victory over death and the grave—the strongholds of Satan and his kingdom of death.

That victory is the significance of the Lord's raising of Lazarus in John 11. Jesus has power over death. He demonstrated that power when He brought His friend from the grave.

Dwight L. Moody used to say that Jesus had been very careful to put Lazarus' name before the words "come forth" because if He didn't, all the tombs would have opened at His command. But someday that very thing will happen for all who have accepted the sacrifice of Jesus on their behalf.

Lazarus' resurrection, however, was only a milestone on the way to victory. It was the resurrection of Jesus Himself that sounded the death knell on death and paved the way for the resurrection of each and every one of His followers.

The grave could not hold Him, and because it could not hold Him, it will not be able to hold us. His resurrection guarantees ours. Paul calls Jesus the "first fruits of those who have fallen asleep. . . . As in Adam all die, so also in Christ shall all be made alive" (1 Cor. 15:20-22, RSV).

Part of the glorious comfort of the gospel is that someday the "last enemy," death, will be completely and finally destroyed (verse 26).

EVERLASTING COMFORT

And God shall wipe away all tears from their eyes. Rev. 7:17.

Those who love Jesus and those who have mourned over their sins and the sins of the church and the world receive comfort on several levels. There is present comfort in forgiveness for sins and adoption into the family of God. There is future comfort at the Second Coming and resurrection. And there is everlasting comfort in the Bible's promises of heaven and the new earth.

"We, according to his promise," penned Peter, "look for new heavens and a new earth, wherein dwelleth righteousness" (2 Peter 3:13). That new earth experience is the ultimate hope and the ultimate comfort for those who mourn for sin and its results in this present earthly epoch.

The comfort of all comforts will be the setting up of the saints' eternal home in the earth made new. The revelator gives us a glimpse of the future comfort of Jesus' followers when he penned that "God shall wipe away all tears from their eyes; and there shall be no more death, neither sorrow, nor crying, neither shall there be any more pain: for the former things are passed away" (Rev. 21:4).

"Blessed are they that mourn: for they shall be comforted" (Matt. 5:4).

I don't know how you feel, but such promises make me want to get right with God; they make me desire to make the kingdom the first priority in my mind and heart.

God has not left us on our own. And that is good, because we are helpless, hopeless, and poor in spirit. Realizing our true condition leads us to mourn for our sins and our sinful world. But mourning is not the end. That is the negative side. Of a more positive nature will be a hungering and thirsting for the things of God.

Lord, help me today to realize more fully the hopelessness of my world and my life without You. I look forward with all my heart to Your coming kingdom. I look forward to the joys of heaven and the earth made new. Help me this day to have a closer walk with You. Amen.

THE "UNNATURAL" PERSON

Blessed are the meek: for they shall inherit the earth. Matt. 5:5.

Like the previous beatitudes, this one is entirely opposed to the thinking of what the Bible calls the "natural man." The world thinks in terms of power, self-assurance, aggressiveness, and conquest. But Jesus uplifted such unpopular character traits as poverty of spirit, mourning, and now meekness.

Jesus is truly a revolutionary of the revolutionaries. He has truly turned the value system of the dominant culture on its head.

The very radicalness of Christ's teachings implies a totally different way of life for His followers. It is no accident that Jesus referred to a person's becoming a Christian as a new birth (John 3:3, 5). As Paul puts it: "If any one is in Christ, he is a new creation; the old has passed away, behold, the new has come" (2 Cor. 5:17, RSV).

The born-again Christian belongs to an entirely different kingdom than the larger culture, and even, unfortunately, much of the church. As a result, he or she has a new set of values.

Jesus' teaching in the third beatitude once again stands over against the acceptable wisdom of our world. According to Him, it is not the pushy, the violent, the aggressive, or the selfish who will inherit the earth. Rather, it is the meek. It is those who have seen their helplessness (and thus possess poverty of spirit), who have mourned over their shortcomings, and who have committed themselves to the way of the meek who will eventually end up inheriting the earth. That teaching is not one that can be gained from the lessons of history or by reading the daily newspaper.

The words of the third beatitude should not be read lightly. They are deep words, full of insight. They are words that are impossible for us to live up to in our own strength. As we continue to work through the Beatitudes, we will come to an increasing understanding of our need for the transforming power of the Holy Spirit in our lives.

Today we need to pray that God will not only give us insight into the way of Jesus, but that He will give us power to walk in that way.

MEEKNESS IS NOT WEAKNESS

Love is patient and kind; love is not jealous or boastful; it is not arrogant or rude. Love does not insist on its own way; it is not irritable or resentful; it does not rejoice at wrong, but rejoices in the right. Love bears all things, believes all things, hopes all things, endures all things." 1 Cor. 13:4-7, RSV.

The Greek word translated as meek means "gentle," "considerate," and "courteous," and implies the exercise of a self-control that makes these qualities possible. Thus *The New English Bible* is quite in harmony with the thoughts of Jesus when it translates Matthew 5:5 as "blest are those of a gentle spirit." The meaning of meekness overlaps many of the character traits in Paul's masterful definition of love found in today's scripture reading.

Biblical meekness should not be confused with indolence. Some who appear to be meek may merely be lazy. Nor should it be confused with weakness of either personality or character. As we shall see in our next two readings, those whom the Bible calls meek had great strength of character. The meek person may be so firm in standing for truth that he or she is willing to die for it if necessary. The martyrs were meek but not weak. Biblical meekness is compatible with great power and authority.

Undergirding meekness is a correct view of one's self. When I finally see myself as a hopeless sinner and come to mourn over that fact, I will be ready for meekness. I will be ready to lay aside all pride.

Because they have a realistic view of themselves, the meek are not enslaved by defensiveness or retaliatory motives. Ellen White helps us on this point when she writes: "It is the love of self that destroys our peace. While self is all alive, we stand ready continually to guard it from mortification and insult; but when we are dead and our life is hid with Christ in God, we shall not take neglects or slights to heart." Again she notes: "Far better would it be for us to suffer under false accusation than to inflict upon ourselves the torture of retaliation upon our enemies" (*Thoughts From the Mount of Blessing*, pp. 16, 17).

One of the great needs of our world, our church, and our families is meekness.

THE SHOCK TREATMENT GOES ON

Not by might, nor by power, but by my spirit, saith the Lord of hosts. Zech. 4:6.

Blessed are the meek: for they shall inherit the earth" (Matt. 5:5). That statement must have come as a major shock to the Jews of Jesus' day. After all, they were looking for a Messiah who would break the power of Rome over them through force of arms.

The Messiah, they believed, would be like David the warrior king. After all, didn't the Psalms of Solomon (written during the period between the Old and New Testaments) claim that the anointed Son of David would be a king who would arise from among the people to deliver Israel from its enemies? He would "shatter all their substance with an iron rod; to destroy the unlawful nations with the word of his mouth" (Psalms of Solomon 17:26, 27).

The last thing the first-century Jews wanted was a meek Messiah. They wanted a leader who could and would give Rome its just desserts. Jesus was the opposite from the type they desired and were looking for.

Now, it is easy for us Christians to see that the Jews were wrong. But are we not guilty of the same type of thinking at times? Don't we also tend to lionize the successful and glorify the accomplishments of the "great" preachers and leaders of the church as if the battle will be won by human words and effort? And are we not also tempted, as was David, to look to organization and numbers for strength? As good as these things may be, they are not the source of Christian success.

God has a thousand ways to finish the gospel commission and bring in the fullness of the kingdom of which we know not. From time to time we need to reread the story of Gideon. In his case God went on reducing the numbers rather than adding to them before supplying the victory.

In Christ's kingdom meekness rather than human might stands at the foundation of success. We need to remember that victory in both our personal life and in the church at large comes "not by might, nor by power, but by [God's] spirit."

MEEK IN SPITE OF THEMSELVES

Now the man Moses was very meek, above all the men which were upon the face of the earth. Num. 12:3.

Meekness didn't come naturally for Moses. He had been trained as an Egyptian prince and undoubtedly had a pretty high estimate of himself as a young ruler. In that frame of mind he killed an Egyptian he caught abusing an Israelite (Ex. 2:12). He thought he knew how to care for God's people and fight God's battles.

That killing led to the young prince's fleeing for his life to the desert. It was there that his education was completed. Moses had to unlearn many of the lessons taught him in the elite track of the University of Egypt. It was in that 40-year intermission from the seat of power that he learned meekness as a herder of sheep.

It was that meekness that qualified him to become the founding leader of God's new nation of Israel. It was that meekness that made Moses a representative of Christ to God's people (see Deut. 18:18).

The new Moses was far from weak or vacillating, but he was meek. He had largely lost his pride and uncontrolled anger, but he was not spineless. To the contrary, he was a forceful and fearless leader under God's guidance. But his strength, power, and authority were now tempered by meekness. Because he had been transformed, he was chosen to lead God's people.

The Bible is full of meek heroes. Take David in his relationship to Saul. David knew he was to be king, yet how he suffered under Saul's unjust and unkind treatment of him! He exemplified meekness to an extraordinary degree.

And in the New Testament we have the example of Paul, who had been converted to Jesus while on a mission to persecute Christians. Paul also had a desert education between his roles as a leader in Judaism and as a leader in Christianity. Paul became an example of meekness to those who misused him both inside and outside the church. At the foundation of his strength was a gentle meekness that was far from his natural self.

And then there are you and me. We also need to be transformed; we also need to learn the lessons of meekness so that we can be used by God.

THE ULTIMATE MEEKNESS

Take my yoke upon you, and learn of me; for I am meek and lowly in heart: and ye shall find rest unto your souls. Matt. 11:29.

The lives of Moses, David, and Paul are helpful, but it is the example of Jesus that is of utmost importance for the Christian. Christ's life was the example par excellence of meekness. We find it everywhere in the Gospels. We find it in His reaction to other people, especially in the way He suffered persecution, scorn, and derision. "Father, forgive them; for they know not what they do" (Luke 23:34), He was able to say of those who crucified Him. Being God, it was in Jesus' power to retaliate against those who mocked Him as He was dying. But He chose not to. He chose to die even for those who were despitefully using and abusing Him.

While Jesus' meekness is seen in relation to other humans, it is even more evident in His submission to the Father. Behold Him in Gethsemane when He had at last come face-to-face with the crisis of the cross. Three times He prayed to stay submissive to His Father's will. Although a fearless Man of great strength of character, Jesus was submissive to God. His meekness was evident in all He did and said.

Especially helpful in understanding Jesus' meekness is Philippians 2:5-8, where Paul tells us to follow the example of "Christ Jesus, who, though he was in the form of God, did not count equality with God a thing to be grasped, but emptied himself, taking the form of a servant, being born in the likeness of men. And being found in human form he humbled himself and became obedient unto death, even death on a cross" (RSV).

That passage presents each of us with a staggering example to emulate in our daily lives. Jesus was God, yet He consented to pass through earthly life not as a king who demanded homage, but as one who had a mission of serving others.

That, my friends, is what Christianity is all about. God wants to free us from pride and self-sufficiency so that we might become His servants and the servants of our fellow humans.

AN IMPOSSIBLE COMMAND

Dearly beloved, avenge not yourselves, . . . for it is written, Vengeance is mine;
I will repay, saith the Lord. Therefore if thine enemy hunger, feed him; or if
he thirst, give him drink: for in so doing thou shalt heap coals of fire on his
head. Be not overcome of evil, but overcome evil with good. Rom. 12:19-21.

What would the world be like if people took Paul's injunctions about vengeance to heart? What would it be like if people chose to live by the principle of meekness rather than the principles of pride and self-protection?

The conclusion is obvious. It wouldn't be our world. It would be heaven. And while we will never see that world in its fullness before the second coming of Jesus, each of us can begin to experience it here and now. The beginning point is me.

For too long we as Christians have waited for the new reformation to start elsewhere. Many of us are waiting for the reformation to start at the General Conference or in some other important body.

That whole approach is wrongheaded. Biblical reformation does not start with the General Conference, union conference, local conference, or even the local church. It begins with individuals who surrender their hearts to God and dedicate themselves to living out the principles of the kingdom of God in their daily lives here and now. Reformation begins with *me*.

Well, you may be thinking, *that's impossible. I can't feed and care for my enemies. Such a command is beyond me.*

You're right. You can't do it. But God can do it if you are willing to let Him live out His life within you through the power of the Holy Spirit.

Oh, how He wants to bless you today. How He wants to free you from your natural self and bless you with Christlike meekness.

Dear Father, today I want You to come into my life and do for me what I cannot do for myself. Help me not to strike back at those who treat me wrongly. Give me the power to share Your kindness with them. Give me the grace to overcome evil with good.

HEIRS OF THE EARTH

For the Lord taketh pleasure in his people: he will beautify the meek with salvation. Ps. 149:4.

Earthly economics is based upon security and power. There is not an infinite amount of wealth. As a result, men and women everywhere struggle to obtain their share—or to put it more honestly, more than their share.

The results of human selfishness and aggression are seen everywhere. Nation strives against nation on the international scene, while individuals struggle for position on the corporate ladder.

It hardly looks like the meek inherit much of anything worth having. Jesus' final reward was a cross. And many of His faithful followers have been persecuted, imprisoned, and put to death.

The daily newspapers seem to flatly contradict the dictum of Jesus that the meek will inherit the earth. The earthly view of success seems to be stacked in favor of the Darwinian law of the jungle: the survival of the fittest.

But apparent short-run realities are not the only realities. Nor are they the ultimate realities.

The promise of the third beatitude is a future promise. "The meek . . . *shall* inherit the earth" at the end of all things (Matt. 5:5).

But it will not be the earth as we know it now, with its destruction, selfishness, and pollution. It will be an earth restored to its Edenic condition. It will be an earth in which there are no more broken hearts, funerals, or hospitals. It will be an earth truly worth having.

As Isaiah puts it:
> "Then the eyes of the blind shall be opened,
>> and the ears of the deaf unstopped;
> then shall the lame man leap like a hart,
>> and the tongue of the dumb sing for joy.
> For waters shall break forth in the wilderness,
>> and streams in the desert;
> the burning sand shall become a pool,
>> and the thirsty ground springs of water" (Isa. 35:5-7, RSV).

Not only will the physical characteristics of the earth be different, but so will be its citizens. Meekness will be a characteristic of all. *Only* those characterized by meekness will inherit the earth.

A DEEPENING CHRISTIAN EXPERIENCE

Blessed are they which do hunger and thirst after righteousness: for they shall be filled. Matt. 5:6.

The order of the Beatitudes is not random or accidental. Far from it. It is a well-thought-out sequence that represents "an advancing line of Christian experience" *(Thoughts From the Mount of Blessing*, p. 13).

An examination of the first four beatitudes demonstrates that point. The beginning of the Christian life is feeling our need of Jesus. Without that conscious sense of need there is no desire for change or filling. Thus the first step in a person's Christian walk is to be poor in spirit, to realize one's utter hopelessness in and of himself or herself.

The second step is to mourn over our helplessness and hopelessness. At this point we have begun to recognize our wretchedness, but are not yet certain as to the solution.

That realization leaves us with a humble view of our condition that the Bible refers to as meekness. We are stunned by the depth of our problem.

The fourth beatitude represents a major shift in our advancing line of experience. Whereas the first two beatitudes exemplified a *turning away from* our human weakness and sin and the third expressed our humility in light of that weakness, the fourth is a *turning toward* the positive aspect of Christianity. It is a hungering and thirsting after righteousness and Godlikeness.

Thus the fourth beatitude moves the focal point from the problem to the solution. In the list of beatitudes the fourth forms a bridge that links the first three with the last four.

Whereas the first two beatitudes represent the human needs that lead to salvation, the last four flow out of a saving relationship with Jesus and are of a more active nature than the first three. Being merciful, pure in heart, and so on are the fruits of having met righteousness in Jesus.

We need to remember that the Christian life is a balanced life that grasps the whole message of the gospel in all its parts. That lesson Jesus set before His followers in the first segment of His great sermon.

THE GOSPEL UNVEILED

Come, all you who are thirsty, come to the waters; and you who have no money, come, buy and eat! Come, buy wine and milk without money and without cost. Isa. 55:1, NIV.

The fourth beatitude is one of the greatest promises of the Bible. Those who hunger and thirst after righteousness shall be filled. This is a definite promise. It does not say "may be" filled, but "shall be." That is the good news that stands at the focal point of the New Testament.

Righteousness is a word with many meanings. In this context it implies the lofty height of being right with God in relationship and of being like Him in character.

Humans have failed dismally in those endeavors. Paul puts it succinctly when he notes that "all have sinned, and come short of the glory of God" (Rom. 3:23). Recognition of that fact in our personal experience is what poverty of spirit and mourning are all about. Those being led by the Spirit have a deep sense of unworthiness about which they are powerless to do anything.

And yet the last thing we want to do is to openly admit our spiritual poverty. We want to be worthy and righteous on our own. That desire led the Jews of Jesus' day on an ego trip of works righteousness. If they just tried hard enough and had enough dedication, they believed, they could become not only right with God but like God. The same line of thought drove the monks of the Middle Ages into a frenzy of activity. That same misguided notion is still alive and well in the 1990s. "How can we be good enough?" is the question that drives people on. The answer is that we cannot ever be good enough of ourselves.

God knew that. That's the reason He sent Jesus to die in our place. Righteousness is a free gift to those who recognize their hopelessness (the first two beatitudes) and hunger and thirst after it (the fourth).

Ellen White puts it nicely when she writes: "The righteousness of God is embodied in Christ. We receive righteousness by receiving Him. Not by painful struggles or wearisome toil, not by gift or sacrifice, is righteousness obtained; but it is freely given to every soul who hungers and thirsts to receive it" *(Thoughts From the Mount of Blessing,* p. 18).

MORE ON RIGHTEOUSNESS

All thy commandments are righteousness. Ps. 119:172.

There is more to righteousness in Matthew's Gospel than merely being right with God. It also implies being like God in character.

Therefore, even though in the fourth beatitude righteousness is primarily something to be received by faith in God's free grace rather than something to be achieved, the achievement aspect is not completely absent. After all, the righteous are to be merciful (the fifth beatitude) and pure in heart (the sixth beatitude).

In short, the righteousness with which those who hunger and thirst are to be filled is active as well as passive righteousness. In other words, it is righteousness related to sanctification as well as righteousness related to justification.

The gospel of Christ not only saves me from the penalty of sin but also from the ruling power of sin in my daily life. In place of being a gossiper and hateful, God wants to make me into a peacemaker. In place of lust, He wants to infuse me with purity of heart. In place of selfishness and petty (and not so petty) meanness, He wants to transform me into a merciful Christian. In short, God wants each of us to become like Him in character.

Thus the word "righteousness" in the fourth blessing spans both halves of the Beatitudes. Jesus promises both to freely forgive us of our sins and shortcomings and to transform us into His image.

But that transformation, it must constantly be emphasized, is not our transformation of our own selves. To the contrary, it is God filling us with His Holy Spirit so that we will be empowered to live the Christian life.

Both God's forgiving grace and His empowering grace are reflected in the fourth beatitude in the word "righteousness." Both come through faith in the God who so loved the world that He gave His only Son to save helpless and hopeless human beings.

Praise God for the good news!

A LESSON IN DESPERATION

O God, my God! How I search for you! How I thirst for you in this parched and weary land where there is no water. How I long to find you! Ps. 63:1, TLB.

Very few of us have ever faced life-threatening hunger and thirst. We think of thirst as having to wait an hour on a hot day for a cold drink, and of hunger as missing a couple of meals in a row. That is not the kind of hunger and thirst that Jesus is talking about in Matthew 5:6. He is referring to a starvation hunger that cannot be satisfied with a midmorning snack, the desperate thirst of people who feel they will die unless they drink.

E. M. Blaiklock tells the story of a large force of Allied soldiers in World War I. As they pursued the retreating enemy across the Arabian Desert they outdistanced their water-carrying camel train. When their water ran out their heads ached, their mouths got dry, and they became faint and disoriented. They began to see mirages. All they could think of was water as their companions died in the desert.

They were literally fighting for their lives as they drove the Turkish forces from Sherish and its life-giving wells.

As water was distributed, thousands of the more able bodied were required to stand aside as the wounded and others received their ration. It was four hours before the last man had his drink. Yet during that time they were within yards of thousands of gallons of the very substance that had been at the forefront of their thought in the days of their desert march.

One of the officers is reported to have remarked, "I believe that we all learned our first real Bible lesson on the march from Beersheba to Sherish Wells. If such were our thirst for God, for righteousness, and for His will in our lives, a consuming all-embracing, preoccupying desire, how rich in the fruit of the Spirit would we be."

Jesus said, "Whoever drinks of the water that I shall give him shall never thirst" (John 4:14, NASB), and "I am the bread of life; he who comes to Me shall not hunger, and he who believes in Me shall never thirst" (John 6:35, NASB).

A MATTER OF PRIORITIES

He got to the point of longing to stuff himself with the food the pigs were eating, and not a soul gave him anything. Then he came to his senses and cried aloud, "Why, dozens of my father's hired men have got more food than they can eat, and here I am dying of hunger! I will get up and go back to my father." Luke 15:16-18, Phillips.

How bad does it have to get? How bad does it have to get before I recognize my poverty for what it is? How bad off do I have to be before I turn to the riches of my heavenly Father?

John Darby wrote, "To be hungry is not enough; I must be really starving to know what is in God's heart toward me. When the prodigal son was hungry, he went to feed on the husks, but when he was starving, he turned to his father." That is the hunger of the fourth beatitude.

As a pastor-evangelist I often had people come to a few of my meetings or Bible studies and then back off. Some of those people wanted to be religious, but not too religious. They had a little hunger for the things of God, but not a famishing sort of hunger. Too many people want to pick and choose, to nibble around the edges of religion. They are basically happy with the way they are. They feel no deep need of poverty of spirit. They have not yet, as did the prodigal, come to their senses.

Such miss the blessing that God has for them. As Mary the mother of Jesus put it: "He has filled the hungry with good things, and the rich he has sent empty away" (Luke 1:53, RSV).

We are dealing here with a matter of priorities. Each of us fills our life with something every day. But that something varies greatly from person to person.

We need to realize this day that it is *only* those who desperately, with all their hearts, hunger and thirst after *God's righteousness* who will be filled.

Today is the day to put daily Bible study and heartfelt prayer at the top of your list of priorities.

DESIRE HAS MANY FACES

And they heard the sound of the Lord God walking in the garden in the cool of the day, and the man and his wife hid themselves from the presence of the Lord God among the trees of the garden. But the Lord God called to the man, and said to him, "Where are you?" And he said, "I heard the sound of thee in the garden, and I was afraid, because I was naked; and I hid myself." Gen. 3:8-10, RSV.

All the trouble in the world today results from the fact that humanity is not right with God. All our hungers and frustrations stem from that realization.

Hungering and thirsting after righteousness ultimately means to desire to be free from sin in all its forms. Consequently, that hungering and thirsting is a desire to be right with God.

D. Martyn Lloyd-Jones helps us catch the point when he writes: "The man who hungers and thirsts after righteousness is the man who sees that sin and rebellion have separated him from the face of God, and longs to get back into that old relationship, the original relationship of righteousness in the presence of God. Our first parents were made righteous in the presence of God. They dwelt and walked with Him. That is the relationship such a man desires."

Hungering and thirsting after righteousness also means desiring to be free from the power of sin in our daily lives, a power that leads us into bondage to bad habits and dysfunctional relationships.

But hungering and thirsting after righteousness is more than that. It is a desire to be set free from the very desire to sin. Even Christians must deal with the horrible fact that they still want to sin even after they recognize its destructiveness.

In the long run, hungering and thirsting is the desire to be free from self and self-centeredness in all its variations. It is the love of self that makes us and those around us miserable.

Lord, help us today to hunger and thirst after those things that we need most, those things that will truly fill us.

TESTS OF SPIRITUAL HUNGER

At night my soul longs for Thee, indeed, my spirit within me seeks Thee diligently. Isa. 26:9, NASB.

Christians need not be in doubt as to where their priorities lie. Each of us is able to ascertain in the privacy of our thoughts what we are hungering and thirsting after, what we most diligently seek, and what is of most value to us. Today we will do a little exercise in self-examination.

Of utmost importance is the test of heart. Along this line, I have found a statement in *Steps to Christ* to be especially penetrating. "If we are Christ's, our thoughts are with Him, and our sweetest thoughts are of Him. All we have and are is consecrated to Him. We long to bear His image, breathe His spirit, do His will, and please Him in all things" (p. 58).

That quotation raises a second test of our priorities—that of doing God's will. After all, honest outward actions are an extension of the values of the heart. Of course, not everyone's thoughts and lives are straight. The false prophet Balaam said, "Let me die the death of the righteous, and let my last end be like his!" (Num. 23:10). But while Balaam wanted to die the death of the righteous, he had no desire to live the life of the righteous. He hungered and thirsted after the wrong things.

That brings us to a third test. If I am truly hungering and thirsting after the things of God, I will not be spending all my time in slavery to earthly things. In fact, I will be free from dependence on earthly things for my satisfaction.

Last, if we are truly hungering and thirsting after God, we will be freed from false views and attitudes toward our self. "A view of our sinfulness drives us to Him who can pardon; and when the soul, realizing its helplessness, reaches out after Christ, He will reveal Himself in power. The more our sense of need drives us to Him and to the Word of God, the more exalted views we shall have of His character, and the more fully we shall reflect His image" (*Steps to Christ*, p. 65).

FILLED BUT NOT FULL

As the hart panteth after the water brooks, so panteth my soul after thee, O God. My soul thirsteth for God, for the living God. Ps. 42:1, 2.

Water and food are the stuff of life. Without them all other things pale into insignificance. After all, what meaning has a new car or home if the owner is perishing of hunger or thirst?

And yet there is something quite remarkable about food and water. We can eat and drink to the full, but the next day we always need more. We are filled, but never full in a permanent sense.

The same is true in our experience with God. We can be filled, but we always want more. So it will be throughout the ceaseless ages of eternity. We will always desire more of His love and His fellowship, and we will always desire to become more like Him. One of the joys of the universe is that we can be filled without ever being permanently full. Heaven has already started for Christians in the sense that the joy of God's filling has already begun in their lives.

While it is true that God's children will always hunger after His loveliness, it is also important to recognize the magnitude of their present fullness. When we read that those who hunger and thirst after righteousness "shall be filled," we are reading the whole of the gospel.

The filling is both a present and a future promise. It is God who does the filling for those who desire Him. Here is the gospel of grace. The filling is God's free gift to every one who comes to Him. "Him," said Jesus, "that cometh to me I will in no wise cast out" (John 6:37). That is an absolute promise. *All* who are hungering and thirsting after righteousness will be filled.

Today they will be filled with God's justifying righteousness as they are rescued from the penalty of sin. Daily they will be filled with God's sanctifying righteousness as they are given victory over the power of sin in their lives. And at the Second Coming they will be filled with glorifying righteousness as they are rescued from the presence of sin.

SHIFTING THE FOCUS

Blessed are the merciful: for they shall obtain mercy. Matt. 5:7

The fifth beatitude presents us with a turning point. The first four dealt with our relation to God. The fifth begins to deal with our relationship to other people. The same is true of the last three. Thus the simplest division of the Beatitudes is to divide them in the same manner as the two tables of the Ten Commandments.

There is a profound truth at the foundation of this arrangement. Christianity is not merely a matter of loving and caring about God. Far from it. Both Testaments picture Christianity as loving both God and other people. We are not dealing with an either/or but a both/and.

In fact, it is impossible for me to love God without loving other people. Likewise, if we really think it through, it may be impossible to *genuinely* love other people without loving God. Too much of what passes for brother or sister love outside of divine love is merely a more subtle form of human selfishness. That is, I love you because of what you can do for me.

Our Lord chose the order of the Beatitudes carefully to represent the order of salvation. Each beatitude follows logically from the previous one. Thus when I realize that I have no righteousness of my own and am truly poor in spirit, I mourn over my utter helplessness. I cry out for deliverance, and my understanding of my true state makes me genuinely meek rather than high and mighty. Having seen my desperate condition, I naturally hunger and thirst after God's forgiving and empowering righteousness.

At that point the God of all mercies jumps in and accepts my repentance, declares me forgiven, and implants a new heart within me. I have been redeemed, saved by His mercy toward me. That is the promise of the first four beatitudes.

But how shall I respond? That is the topic of the "second table" of the Beatitudes. I will be merciful, pure of heart, a maker of peace, and patient when treated unjustly. In short, through God's power I will become more and more like Jesus.

TURNING A BEATITUDE ON ITS HEAD

The Son of man is come to seek and to save that which was lost. Luke 19:10.

One of the easiest things in the world is to get things backward. That is especially true of the fifth beatitude. Many read it as if it said, "If I am merciful and forgiving toward others, God will be merciful and forgiving toward me." In short, if I am merciful toward others, God will then, but not until then, be merciful to me.

The problem with that approach is that it flies in the face of all of Scripture. It fails to account for how lost I really am, how hopeless I am. It fails to account for the depth of the sin problem.

The Bible picture is one of God in His mercy always taking the initiative to reach out and help the lost in their lostness—even before they know they are lost.

Thus it is God who searches out Adam and Eve in their nakedness after the Fall. It is God who takes the initiative to search out the lost sheep and the lost coin in Luke 15, and it is the Father who goes out to speak to the hopelessly lost older brother of the prodigal son in the same chapter.

God so loved the world that He took the initiative to give His only Son, and that Son came "to seek and to save" those under the sentence of death.

Ellen White puts it nicely when she writes, "God is Himself the source of all mercy. His name is 'merciful and gracious' (Ex. 34:6). He does not treat us according to our desert. He does not ask if we are worthy of His love, but He pours upon us the riches of His love, to make us worthy" *(Thoughts From the Mount of Blessing, p. 22)*.

Thus I am not merciful because I want to be saved. No! As a Christian I am merciful because I *already have been saved*. I have been rescued from the pit of sin and death by the God of all mercy.

The result? I have a heartfelt desire to be merciful in my daily life. I want to pass on God's gift.

THE MEANING OF MERCY

The Lord, the Lord, a God merciful and gracious, slow to anger, and abounding in steadfast love and faithfulness, keeping steadfast love for thousands, forgiving iniquity and transgression and sin, but who will by no means clear the guilty. Ex. 34:6, 7, RSV.

It is all too easy to confuse mercy with an anything-goes attitude. But the merciful person is not one who smiles at transgression or sin.

Our text today pictures a careful balance in the character of God between gracious compassion and a firmness that refuses to tolerate rebellious sinfulness. Here we are dealing with the God who is both loving and just, the God who stands for principle, yet is willing to be merciful toward those who hunger and thirst after a better life.

"As many as I love," says Jesus, "I rebuke and chasten: be zealous therefore, and repent" (Rev. 3:19). God loves us too much to let us lead destructive lives that not only impact upon our own happiness, but are disruptive to the larger community.

He wants the very best for us. He cares enough to rebuke us for our wrongs. But that rebuke is a function of His mercy. It is people who don't care enough who let their kids run wild. It is people who don't care enough who don't warn their friends of the unhappy consequences of their course of action.

Such care-less-ness must not be confused with mercy. Mercy is being care-full, or full of care for those around us. Thus in our mercy we reach out to others in Christian concern.

In one sense mercy is a state of mind—one that represents cares about other people; it is an attitude that cares enough to be both forgiving and loving, even when that means having to confront problems and wrong actions in the spirit of Jesus.

Lord, help me today to imbibe the merciful attitude that stands at the heart of God's character. Help me to approximate the balance in my life that You exhibit in Yours.

MERCY IS MORE THAN AN ATTITUDE

Truly I tell you: anyone who gives so much as a cup of cold water to one of these little ones because he is a disciple of mine, will certainly not go unrewarded. Matt. 10:42, REB.

The story is told of Jacob Bright coming home from town and finding a poor neighbor in great trouble on the road. His horse had met with an accident and had to be killed. People were crowding around the man, saying how sorry they were. To one who kept on repeating this most loudly, Jacob said, "I am sorry $50. How much are you sorry?" He then passed round the hat to buy the man another horse.

Being merciful is more than an attitude. It is also an action. Mercy is outgoing love.

But before love can become *outgoing* it must be *outlooking*. As William Barclay puts it: "Mercy is the reverse of self-centeredness. . . . It is the antithesis of selfishness."

One theologian has suggested that "the church is the fellowship of the dead-to-themselves and alive for Christ." Mercy comes when love of self is replaced by love of God and love of other people.

Mercy is an attitude of the heart that gives birth to specific attitudes toward specific individuals. Thus Ellen White can truthfully say that "kind words, looks of sympathy, expressions of appreciation, would be to many a struggling and lonely one as the cup of cold water to a thirsty soul. A word of sympathy, an act of kindness, would lift burdens that rest heavily upon weary shoulders. And every word or deed of unselfish kindness is an expression of the love of Christ for lost humanity" (*Thoughts From the Mount of Blessing*, p. 23).

Why put it off! This very morning, why not begin with an unexpected kindness to your husband or wife? Why not start the workday with a kind deed for a colleague? Why not surprise your parent or child? *Today* is the day to pass on God's mercy. Not at noontime or after work, but now—and then, too.

RELIGION THAT HARDENS

Woe to you, scribes and Pharisees, hypocrites! for you tithe mint and dill and cummin, and have neglected the weightier matters of the law, justice and mercy and faith; these you ought to have done, without neglecting the others. You blind guides, straining out a gnat and swallowing a camel! Matt. 23:23, RSV.

Not all religion is religious. Not all religion is Christian. Not all religion is helpful. Some people would be better off without religion, or at least, the kind they have.

That is particularly true of those that religion makes more severe. One thinks of health reformers who become upset with family members or friends who are not quite as rigorous as they are. Or take the people who explode when their "thoughtful hour" of meditation on the life of Christ is interrupted. Again we can picture the doctrinal purist who becomes less than loving when someone differs with him or her on a point of belief or biblical interpretation.

Such people have become hardened by their so-called religion. They are heading in the wrong direction. They are moving away from Jesus.

Now, don't get me wrong. Health reform, a faithful devotional life, and correct doctrine are important.

"Why?" I hear someone say.

Because sick people are grouchy and find it hard to be merciful to others to the fullest. The very purpose of health reform is to prepare us better to live the life of merciful love. The same can be said for devotional study. Those who walk with Jesus should be those who act most like Him. And doctrinal correctness should help us understand the love of God better so that we can experience it more fully.

But when any of our so-called religious experiences in lifestyle harden us so that we become less merciful and more severe, we have missed the Christian boat—not partially, but *totally*.

The religion of Jesus will make us more merciful, not more severe. If it is not having that effect, we are plugged into the wrong experience—whatever we have it is not the religion of Jesus.

RELIGION THAT SOFTENS

By this all men will know that you are my disciples, if you have love for one another. John 13:35, RSV.

B y this all men will know that you are My disciples, if you keep the Sabbath."

"By this all men will know that you are My disciples, if you pay tithe."

"By this all men will know that you are My disciples, if you eat the right things."

Some years ago I read John 13:35 this way at a conference lay advisory meeting in Ohio. Immediately after my presentation I was confronted by a zealous new convert. He wanted to know exactly where that text was. His Bible, he claimed, didn't read that way.

What he really wanted, in his excitement, was the ultimate Adventist proof text. Some might be tempted to think that it would be absolutely wonderful if we had a verse from Jesus claiming that we could identify His real followers beyond the shadow of a doubt by ascertaining if they kept the seventh-day Sabbath.

And Jesus could have given us such a text. But He didn't.

But He did give us the *one* and only way we can identify His genuine followers. They will really care for one another from their hearts; they will love one another.

It cannot be said often enough that true Christians are lovers—lovers of God and other people.

Christianity will make you a kinder person. Christianity will make you more thoughtful of others, more merciful, and more careful of how you speak to and about others. Christianity will transform your life.

The mean or harsh Christian is an impossibility, a contradiction in terms. We have to be one or the other—Christian or unthoughtful, Christian or harsh. We cannot be both. Christianity softens both our attitudes and our actions. It informs them with love.

Lord, today we pray that You will help us to love and to be the real thing. Help us to internalize the great principle of Your character, help us to be more like Jesus. In addition, show us someone to whom we can express Your loving care today.

MERCY ON "THAT" DAY

May the Lord show mercy to the household of Onesiphorus, because he often refreshed me and was not ashamed of my chains. On the contrary, when he was in Rome, he searched hard for me until he found me. May the Lord grant that he will find mercy from the Lord on that day! 2 Tim. 1:16-18, NIV.

The reward of the merciful is that they will obtain mercy. The fifth beatitude is the only one in which the reward is the same as the virtue. The beatitude could easily have said that they will find "more mercy" or "additional mercy," since these faithful ones have been already experiencing God's mercy. After all, it was responding to God's merciful grace that inspired them to be merciful in the first place.

Their reward: more mercy. There is something especially beautiful about the sequencing of this promise. With God life gets better and better, and it will continue to do so throughout the ceaseless ages of eternity. What a promise!

The reward of mercy comes at two stages. First, those who are merciful on this earth often receive mercy from other people in their daily lives. It is generally true that we feel more kindly toward a merciful person who has made a mistake than to those who are hard-nosed. Those who are cruel are more apt to receive cruelty in return. But that is not always so. The sad fact is that kind people are sometimes treated poorly on this earth.

And that brings us to the second stage of the promise of mercy. That stage takes place at the second coming of Jesus. All who have been merciful in their life will find unfailing mercy from God on "that day."

At that time all the injustices of earth will be put right. The merciful will receive God's mercy in the fullest sense of the word.

As Christians we look forward to "that day" above all days. And one of the grand truths of the Bible is that the way we live now will determine how we will live then.

THE DARK SIDE OF THE BEATITUDES

For judgment will be merciless to one who has shown no mercy; mercy triumphs over judgment. James 2:13, NASB.

All is not rosy about the Beatitudes. They have a dark side, just as the gospel has a dark side for those who reject it.

God can only invite us to the gospel table; He can't force us to partake. And even though Jesus invites every individual to accept His salvation, He will not compel anyone to accept.

Likewise, Jesus has set forth the wonderful blessings of the Beatitudes, but we must individually choose to accept or reject them. To those who do accept, the promises are clearly spelled out.

But to those who refuse the good news and the blessings, the result is just as sure. For example, those who refuse to be merciful will often fail to receive mercy here on this earth and will certainly miss out on mercy in the final judgment.

That last point is not just an arbitrary decision on God's part. He wants everyone in His eternal kingdom to be happy, to feel at home there. But if I have not imbibed God's characteristics, I will not be at home in His eternal kingdom.

Let me illustrate. I remember the first time I had dinner with a preacher. The invitation came in advance, and it worried me all week long. I was living on a ship in San Francisco Bay at the time, and I was definitely out of harmony with his principles.

Most things are worse in anticipation than in reality. Not so with that dinner. I was uncomfortable in the extreme the entire time.

After I was converted some years later, I concluded that the worst thing that could happen to an unconverted person would be for him or her to have to spend eternity in the presence of the God of love, who not only knows our every action but also our very thoughts. Such an existence would be worse than hell. Nonexistence would be preferable.

The blessings of the Beatitudes are for those who internalize the characteristics set forth. All others will be outside the kingdom.

EVERY GOOD SERMON HAS A PLAN

Blessed are the pure in heart: for they shall see God. Matt. 5:8.

Every good sermon has a plan. That is certainly true of the Sermon on the Mount in general, and the Beatitudes in particular.

We earlier noted how each beatitude leads to the next. Thus those who realize their spiritual poverty mourn over their shortcomings and truly come to the place where they feel sincerely humble and meek.

Those realizations lead them to hunger and thirst after something better—the righteousness of God as both forgiving grace and life-changing, empowering grace.

This fourth beatitude (hungering and thirsting) forms the center of the Beatitudes. The three that go before have dealt with a person in relation to God. Those that follow deal with an individual's relationships to other people.

The reward of the hungering and thirsting ones is that they will be filled. But filled with what, one might ask? The righteousness that they seek! They are both forgiven and transformed into persons who have a new outlook on life.

Part of that filling is made explicit in the "second table" of the Beatitudes. They will become merciful, pure, and peacemakers. What a blessing! What a transformation! What a gift! Praise God from whom all blessings flow!

There is another thing that is important about the plan of the Beatitudes. Beatitudes 5, 6, and 7 correspond to 1, 2, and 3, with the fourth forming the center point. It is like going up one side of a mountain in the first three, arriving at the peak with the fourth, and then going down the other side with the fifth through the seventh.

Thus the merciful are those who truly recognize their poverty of spirit. It is only when we have a correct view of ourselves that we can have a right view of others.

Likewise, the pure in heart are those who have earlier mourned about the impurity of their hearts. In a similar vein, the peacemakers are those who have become meek.

The great truth is that not only does Jesus have a plan in the Beatitudes; He also has a definite plan for my life.

Help me, Father, to grasp Your plan.

THE HEART OF THE MATTER

Watch over your heart with all diligence, for from it flow the springs of life.
Prov. 4:23, NASB.

When Sir Walter Raleigh was led to the execution block, his executioner asked him if his head lay right. Raleigh answered, "It matters little, my friend, how the head lies, provided the heart is right."

In like manner, when I go to my physician to have an operation on my leg, the first thing my doctor does is to check my heart. After all, if my heart is not right, there is no use getting my leg fixed up. Without a healthy heart, the best leg in the world will do me no good.

In the physical realm the heart is at the center of life. It is the pumping of that muscle that spreads life to the rest of the body.

It is the same in the realm of the spirit. Thus the biblical emphasis on the importance of having our hearts right with God.

Jesus pronounces His blessing on those who are "pure in heart." It is significant that He does not commend those who are intellectual. He does not say "Blessed are those who understand correct doctrine, for they shall see God." His focus is on the heart.

Now, don't get me wrong. Correct doctrine is important, but it is not at the center of the matter. You can have a correct doctrinal understanding and be meaner than the devil. A person can be "straight" on doctrine, yet be a curse to the church and a false representative of his or her Lord.

As in the physical life, the core of Christian existence is the heart. A heart right with both God and other people sets the stage for both a correct understanding of doctrine and a correct expression of one's faith in daily living. Without a healthy spiritual heart you are spiritually dead, no matter how well you understand theology or how much of the Bible you have committed to memory.

It is the pure in heart who shall see God.

Lord, help me today to get my priorities right. Help me today to surrender my heart to You. Help me today to start seeing You better.

THE CONTROL CENTER

Listen and understand: it is not what goes into the mouth that defiles a person, but it is what comes out. . . . What comes out of the mouth proceeds from the heart, and this is what defiles. For out of the heart come evil intentions, murder, adultery, fornication, theft, false witness, slander. Matt. 15:10-19, NRSV.

In the world of first-century Palestine the heart was thought of as much more than a physical organ that pumped blood. The Greek *kardia* translates into English as "heart." It is the word from which we get cardiac and similar terms.

Throughout the Bible the *kardia* is the seat of a person's motives and attitudes as well as the center of personality. It also includes both the mind and the will. Thus Jesus could ask, "Why do you think evil in your hearts" (Matt. 9:4, RSV), and the wise man can note that "as [a man] thinketh in his heart, so is he" (Prov. 23:7).

The Bible sets forth the heart as the control center for the mind and will as well as for the emotions. The heart is the spring from which all else in a person's life flows.

As a result, it is of the utmost importance that the heart be pure. An impure heart leads to an impure life, but a pure heart results in a life in harmony with God's principles. The control center is all-important. "Blessed are the pure in heart."

Jesus gave His teachings about the heart in a world in which people's spirituality was judged by exteriors. How they washed their hands, how they dressed, and whom they ate with became points by which they were judged. Religion had become exterior in the minds of the Jews.

It is not so much different today. Too many professed Christians are still evaluating other people by their outward actions. And their yardstick is too often the yardstick of human tradition and human perspective used by the ancient Pharisees. That even happens among Seventh-day Adventists.

Jesus' teachings put an end to all such evaluations. His concern is with my control center. If things are right at the center, they will also be right at the periphery of my life.

PURITY IS IMPORTANT

And there shall in no wise enter into it any thing that defileth, neither whatsoever worketh abomination, or maketh a lie: but they which are written in the Lamb's book of life. Rev. 21:27.

The basic meaning of *pure* is "freedom from such things as dirt, filth, and contamination." The Greek term is often used of metals that have been refined until all impurities have been removed, leaving only the pure metal.

Thus purity in this sense means unmixed, unadulterated, unalloyed. When this thought is applied to the heart, we think of the pure motive or, better yet, of single-mindedness, individual devotion, a person who is totally dedicated to God and His principles.

The opposite of purity in the spiritual realm is to be double-minded. A person who is double-minded seeks to follow the Lord and the world at the same time. The impure heart is a divided heart. It is a heart that seeks to achieve two incompatible goals at the same time.

Jesus says that that is impossible. "No one can serve two masters; for either he will hate the one and love the other, or he will hold to one and despise the other" (Matt. 6:24, NASB). James says much the same thing when he writes that "to be the world's lover means becoming the enemy of God! Anyone who deliberately chooses to be the world's friend is thereby making himself God's enemy" (James 4:4, Phillips).

God wants us to get our act together. He wants us to decide who will truly be the God of our life—the things of this earth or the Lord Jesus. Those two realms represent two kingdoms built upon two different sets of principles.

When Jesus tells us that His followers must be pure of heart, He means more than merely cleaning up the outward things that defile our lives. He also means that we need to understand that we live on a spiritual battleground and that we need to choose our allegiances with care. To be pure of heart is to totally give our lives, minds, and wills over to God and His principles. Such people will have their names in the book of life and will see God.

SEEING GOD IN THE HERE AND NOW

No man hath seen God at any time. 1 John 4:12.

There shall no man see me, and live. Ex. 33:20.

Happy are those whose hearts are pure, for they shall see God. Matt. 5:8, TLB.

What does the Bible mean when it says that the pure in heart shall see God? Is this a present experience of something that will take place in the future? The answer is both.

Moses is a good example of that point. After the tragic experience of the golden calf and just before God gave Moses the Ten Commandments a second time, the prophet asked to see the glory of God. God in His graciousness placed Moses in the cleft of a rock and promised to let Moses see His back: "You shall see my back; but my face shall not be seen" (Ex. 33:23, RSV).

That is kind of how it is with us. Even though there will come a time when we "shall see him as he is" (1 John 3:2, RSV), at the present time, so to speak, we only see His back—we only see Him partially.

But that partial glimpse is a present reality. After all, Jesus said that if we have seen Him we have seen the Father (John 14:9). Jesus came to reveal the Father to the world. As a result, when we study the gospel story we get the best glimpse of the Father currently available. Of course, what is true of the four Gospels is true also of the rest of the Bible to a lesser extent. All of Scripture is merely a partial glimpse of God.

Not only do Christians catch glimpses of God in the Bible, but through the understanding eye of faith they see the touch of God in nature, in the events of history, and in His daily dealings with them. And even though we enjoy our fleeting glimpses of God, we wait with eager anticipation for that time when we can see Him face-to-face in the world made new. The glimpses of His glory and love permitted us here are only a faint glimmer of what is to come for those who have single-mindedly dedicated their lives to God.

SEEING GOD IN THE THEN AND THERE

Beloved, now are we the sons of God, and it doth not yet appear what we shall be: but we know that, when he shall appear, we shall be like him; for we shall see him as he is. And every man that hath this hope in him purifieth himself, even as he is pure. 1 John 3:2, 3.

Yesterday we noted that in this present world we catch glimpses of God from time to time, but that we never see Him in the fullness promised to the pure in heart. That will change. As Paul puts it: "Now we see through a glass, darkly; but then face to face: now I know in part; but then shall I know even as also I am known" (1 Cor. 13:12).

In this life we see only the beginnings of the fulfillment of God's promises to the pure of heart.

Think for a moment of what it will mean to stand in the presence of the King of the universe. You and I are being prepared to enter into the very presence of the King of kings and Lord of lords. Grasping that thought will revolutionize our lives.

Now we see through a glass darkly, but then we shall see Him face-to-face. Think of it. Meditate upon it. Read of the throne room of God in such places as Revelation 4 and 5 and Ezekiel 1.

Then read some of the great anthems of praise in Revelation. "Then I looked," John reports in Revelation 5:11-14, "and I heard around the throne . . . the voice of many angels, numbering myriads of myriads and thousands of thousands, saying with a loud voice, 'Worthy is the Lamb who was slain, to receive power and wealth and wisdom and might and honor and glory and blessing!' And I heard every creature in heaven and on earth . . . saying, 'To him who sits upon the throne and to the Lamb be blessing and honor and glory and might for ever and ever!' And the four living creatures said, 'Amen!' and the elders fell down and worshiped" (RSV).

Someday you will be before that throne! "Blessed are the pure in heart: for they shall see God" (Matt. 5:8).

WHICH WAY TO PURITY?

Create in me a clean heart, O God; and renew a right spirit within me. Ps. 51:10.

If we confess our sins, he is faithful and just to forgive us our sins, and to cleanse us from all unrighteousness. 1 John 1:9.

How do our hearts become pure? Men and women have grappled with that question across the ages. Some have thought the answer lies in segregating themselves from the world as hermits, monks, nuns, or in some other form of a "pure" community.

One such ascetic was Simeon Stylites (c. A.D. 390-459). Simeon, after having been buried up to his neck for several months, next decided that his way to holiness was to sit on top of a 60-foot pillar, where he would be removed from all temptation. For 36 years (until his death) "Saint" Simeon remained atop his pole. Not only did his body "drip" with vermin, but he performed excruciating exercises far above the desert floor. Once, for example, he is said to have touched his feet with his forehead more than 1,244 times in succession.

Other ascetic athletes for God incarcerated themselves in cells so small that they could neither lie at full length nor stand at full height. Many of them gave up bathing and wore hide garments, with the hair next to the flesh. And still others are reported to have subsisted largely on grass, which they cut with sickles.

Such men and women were desperate to get right with God. They sought after purity of heart with all their might.

Unfortunately they were following the wrong path. They had not come to grips with the power of sin in their lives. Jeremiah accurately set forth the human predicament when he asked, "Can the Ethiopian change his skin, or the leopard his spots? then may ye also do good, that are accustomed to do evil" (Jer. 13:23). The answer is obvious. We are indeed hopeless in and of ourselves. No matter what we do, we still have the same unclean heart.

Our scriptures for today put it right when they note that it is God who cleanses our hearts and makes us pure.

Thank You, God, for helping us in our great need.

IS THERE NOTHING WE CAN DO?

Therefore, my beloved, as you have always obeyed, so now . . . work out your own salvation with fear and trembling; for God is at work in you, both to will and to work for his good pleasure. Phil. 2:12, 13, RSV.

To put it bluntly, there is nothing we can do to purify our hearts. That is God's work. He is the great cleanser and purifier. It is His power that gives us a new heart, a new mind, and a new outlook on life. All we can do is to accept the divine gift. But that acceptance is crucial. God will not force His salvation upon us.

Yet once God has made us into new creatures with new values, there is something we can do as He progressively seeks to purify our lives. We can cooperate with Him. As Paul put it so nicely in today's scripture reading, God works within us, through the power of the Holy Spirit, to progressively purify our daily lives so that our actions will match up with our new hearts. We "work out" our salvation through the dynamic power of God.

Some people seem to have the idea that all works are wrong. That is true if you are trying to become saved. The Bible is against all attempts to earn salvation—it is the gift of God.

But once a person is saved in Jesus, he or she will naturally and joyfully want to live his or her new life in harmony with God's principles. Purity of heart will lead to a desire for purity in everything one does.

Thus Paul can talk of "faith working through love" (Gal. 5:6, RSV). He commends the Thessalonians' "work of faith and labor of love" (1 Thess. 1:3, RSV). And part of his task was to call the Gentiles to "the obedience of faith" (Rom. 1:5; 16:26).

Perhaps Paul's clearest picture of the sequence of salvation is found in Ephesians 2:8-10: "For by grace you have been saved through faith; and this is not your own doing, it is the gift of God. . . . We are his workmanship, created in Christ Jesus for good works, which God prepared beforehand, that we should walk in them" (RSV).

Purity of heart leads naturally to purity of life.

SURPRISED AGAIN

Blessed are the peacemakers: for they shall be called the children of God. Matt. 5:9.

L ike the other beatitudes, this one ran against the grain of Jewish thinking.

From his very first chapter Matthew has set forth Jesus as both the Messiah and the Son of David. In the Jewish mind both titles had political overtones. The two titles come together in the vision of an earthly king. David had been an illustrious conquering warrior, and first-century Jews expected their Messiah-King to carry out the same program. The Messiah (or Christ) was to be a national deliverer.

For example, in the Psalms of Solomon (a Jewish book written in the period between the Old and New Testaments), the anointed Son of David is a king who will arise from among the people to deliver Israel from its enemies. This Davidic king is to be endowed with supernatural gifts. "With a rod of iron he shall break in pieces all their substance, he shall destroy the godless nations with the word of his mouth." Likewise in 4 Ezra (a first-century A.D. apocalypse) the Messiah reigns over a temporary Messianic kingdom for some 400 years.

There had been three great bondages in Israel's history: the Egyptian, the Babylonian, and now the Roman. The first two had had political solutions, and the same was expected for the third.

For first-century Jews, a Messiah who did not at least deliver the nation politically could hardly be considered a genuine Messiah.

It is in the light of that expectation that we see Jesus' revolutionary proclamation that it was the peacemakers who would be blessed rather than the Zealot who left his dagger in the side of a Roman soldier.

As usual, Jesus has it backward. His kingdom is of a different order from earthly kingdoms. It is of a different order from that expected by the Jews.

Of course, Jesus did come as a conqueror. He came to defeat the forces of evil. He came to conquer the principles of Satan's kingdom and "to save his people from their sins" (Matt. 1:21).

MEEKNESS LEADS TO PEACEFULNESS

For to us a child is born, to us a son is given, and the government will be on his shoulders. And he will be called Wonderful Counselor, Mighty God, Everlasting Father, Prince of Peace. Isa. 9:6, NIV.

Blessed are the peacemakers." This blessing corresponds to "Blessed are the meek" in the first table of the Beatitudes. Those who are humble and gentle will also be peacemakers.

These characteristics indicate the radicalness of Jesus' explanation of a Christian's character. By nature we are not normally either meek or peacemakers. That shows up in the troubled world around us and in troubled homes and families. We are dealing here with the principles of a kingdom in opposition to the principles of the kingdoms of this world. And the citizens of this new kingdom will have to have new natures.

It's not that we are altogether bad. After all, as Ellen White puts it: "A perception of right, a desire for goodness, exists in every heart" (*Education*, p. 29). But that desire struggles in our hearts with the tendency to choose the evil that we inherited from Adam.

In many ways, life would be much simpler if we were either all good or all bad in our individual selves. As it is, our lives are the scene of the controversy on a microcosmic scale, for we daily stand in tension between the principles of Christ's kingdom and the principles of the kingdom of evil.

Studdart Kennedy captured the core of the problem when he noted that there is a bit of saint and a portion of sinner in each of us; that part of us is from heaven and part from earth. Kennedy also phrased it nicely when he said that every person is nothing but a "great beginning."

That is the essence of the problem. A great beginning is not enough. God wants to come into our lives and finish the job. Part of that will be to make us into peacemakers so that we might become more and more like the Prince of peace.

THE WHY OF WAR IN THE WORLD

He that is of a proud heart stirreth up strife: but he that putteth his trust in the Lord shall be made fat [prosperous]. Prov. 28:25.

Every government has its army, police, judges, courts, and penal system. The history of the world is full of wars and aggression, and the daily news constantly presents us with stories of crime. Why? Why must we live in a world of war and crime?

The answer is simple—sin. Undergirding every human problem, whether between individuals or nations, are the sinful characteristics of lust, greed, selfishness, and self-centeredness.

We cannot even begin to understand the problems of our world until we come to the biblical doctrine of sin. It is sin and its nasty offspring that make it so difficult to maintain peace in the world. It is sin that has led to the breakdown of all the great plans for peace that have filled the corridors of diplomatic history.

The basic problems of our world are not political, economic, or social. No! The real problem is an attitude of nations and individuals that puts personal wants and desires above everything else.

As a result, if I am big or strong enough, I will take whatever I want, right now, by force. Of course, if I am not strong enough for that, I will take it when you are not looking.

If peace is ever to rule, new hearts and minds and attitudes will be needed.

The story is told of two deeply religious men who had lived in isolated peace with each other for years in a mountain hideaway. One day they decided to break the boredom by acting like the rest of the world.

That meant quarreling. To get things started, one brother suggested that the other take a stone and place it between them, claiming that it was his and his only.

Willing to accommodate his friend, the second brother said, "This stone is mine."

Pausing for reflection on their years of friendship, the first man concluded, "Well, brother, if the stone is yours, then keep it." And that ended the quarrel.

Such is the peacemaking spirit needed by our strife-filled world.

THE WHY OF WAR IN THE CHURCH

Don't be selfish; don't live to make a good impression on others. Be humble, thinking of others as better than yourself. Phil. 2:3, TLB.

Martin Luther liked to tell the story of the two goats that met upon a narrow bridge high above a deep valley. "They could not go back; they dare not fight. After a short talk, one of them lay down and let the other go over him, and thus no harm was done."

"The moral," Luther would note, "is easy: Be content if thy person be trod upon for peace's sake." Luther hastened to add that he was speaking of a person's pride or dignity, not their conscience.

Such an attitude would solve a great deal of the difficulty that we face in both the world and in the church.

But why, you might be asking, do we have such problems in the church? Haven't we left the world to join the church?

The answer, once again, is simple—sin! But haven't Christians given up sin for Jesus? Yes, Christians have, but being a church member is not the same as being a Christian. And being a Christian does not mean that self does not sneak in from time to time and pridefully demand its own way in the church and in a Christian home.

It would be wonderful if every church member obtained full and perfect holiness at the moment of signing on. But such is not the case. Not only are some members not converted; but even the truly converted face the fact that sanctification is the work of a lifetime.

That truth, however, is no reason for not becoming more humble, caring, and loving today. God wants to take *you today* and make you into a peacemaker for His kingdom.

There is a quip that goes:

"To live with the saints in heaven will be bliss and glory,

But to live with the saints on earth is often another story."

God is calling *you today* to make the church different from the world. He is calling you individually to become a peacemaker in the likeness of Jesus.

A Peacemaker Is Not a Pansy

Do not think I have come to bring peace on earth; I have not come to bring peace, but a sword. For I have come to set a man against his father, and a daughter against her mother. . . . He who loves father or mother more than me is not worthy of me; and he who loves son or daughter more than me is not worthy of me; and he who does not take his cross and follow me is not worthy of me. He who finds his life will lose it, and he who loses his life for my sake will find it. Matt. 10:34-39, RSV.

One of the great paradoxes of Christ's life is that even though He is the "Prince of Peace" (Isa. 9:6), accepting Him brings a sword that cuts so deeply that converts often find their closest relationships disrupted.

That paradox finds its basis in the fact that the principles of Christ's kingdom are diametrically opposed to those of the kingdoms of this earth.

Thus when some members of a family or community operate on one set of principles while others operate on another, animosity is the inevitable result. Jesus argues that in such cases a Christian's greatest loyalty must be to Him and His principles, even though such a position may bring trouble.

While Christians often have peace of heart in this life, for them the fullness of external peace will not arrive until the Second Advent. Until that time God's children are obligated to exist in the kingdoms of this earth while seeking to live according to the principles of the kingdom of heaven.

Their dual citizenship brings its own tensions. But in Jesus' strength Christians do not give up their principles. After all, the blessing is upon peace*makers,* not peace *lovers.*

The road to ultimate peace is in being firm to God's principles. If a person loves peace in the wrong way, he or she may succeed in making trouble rather than peace. Such a person, for instance, may allow a threatening or dangerous situation to develop without saying anything. William Barclay notes that "the peace which the Bible calls blessed does not come from the evasion of issues; it comes from facing them, dealing with them, and conquering them."

PEACEMAKING
DEMANDS A NEW ATTITUDE

If anyone would come after me, he must deny himself and take up his cross and follow me. For whoever wants to save his life will lose it, but whoever loses his life for me will find it. Matt. 16:24, 25, NIV.

Peacemaking, as we noted a few days ago, is not a normal human activity. The "normal" person in this world is first and foremost concerned with his or her own pride and privileges.

How are people treating me? Am I getting my due share? Do people show me proper respect? These are the questions of central importance. Such are also the questions that destroy peace and generate strife.

In reply to all such thinking, Jesus points to the cross.

Most of us will never have to endure a physical cross, but each Christian must crucify the willful nature that above all wants to put itself first and do its own thing.

To understand Jesus' meaning in today's scripture, we need to remember that sin, in its most basic sense, is putting our self and our will, rather than God and His will, at the center of our lives. Sin is rebellion against God in the sense that our self becomes the point of focus and control.

It is the self-centered life principle, so natural to human beings, that must die. Thus Dietrich Bonhoeffer spoke to the heart of what it means to be a Christian when he wrote that "when Christ calls a man, He bids him come and die."

When I come face-to-face with the claims of Christ, I must either crucify Him or let Him crucify me. There is no middle ground. Fortunately, after the cross in a person's life comes new birth in Christ.

Becoming a peacemaker begins with that crucifixion and new birth. Without that experience we will be merely a nasty, grouchy, or selfish church member—a disaster in the pew. But with that experience we become servants of the living God and lovers of our fellow beings. With it we are on the road to becoming peacemakers.

Help us today, our Father, to find the cross that is the beginning of the path of true Christian peacemaking.

THE PRACTICE OF PEACEMAKING

Let every man be quick to listen but slow to use his tongue, and slow to lose his temper. For man's temper is never the means of achieving God's true goodness. James 1:19, Phillips.

Ideals are good and wonderful, but they are just a great deal of nothing unless they are accompanied by practice.

Perhaps one of the most important skills for the peacemaker is knowing how to be quiet. If people had control of their tongues, there would be much less discord in the world.

Our text for today suggests that we should be quick to listen, but slow to speak. But I am afraid that all too many of us are quick to speak and slow to listen.

A world of discord and sorrow could be saved if we merely refused to repeat things when we know they will do harm. A major function of peacemaking is being silent even though we may be mightily tempted to pass on this or that tidbit of gossip. The "natural man" is strong in us, but for the sake of peace Christians hold their tongues. Remember, it is never good to say unkind or unpleasant things.

James likens the tongue to a little match that can start a whole forest afire. Once out of our mouths, words cannot be recalled. They move from one person to another—often with a great deal of exaggeration and distortion.

The temper is closely related to the control of speech. "Keep your temper!" wrote one preacher. "Nobody else wants it!" When under attack, how easy it is to lose our cool and give people a piece of our mind. That results in a lack of peace for them and for us.

Fortunately, the tongue can be used for peace as well as for war, as we note in the following item:

"A careless word may kindle strife,
A cruel word may wreck a life;
A bitter word may hate instill,
A brutal word may smite and kill;
A gracious word may smooth the way,
A joyous word may light the day;
A timely word may lessen stress,
A loving word may heal and bless."

MORE ON THE PRACTICE OF PEACEMAKING

But the fruit of the Spirit is love, joy, peace, longsuffering, gentleness, goodness, faith, meekness, temperance: against such there is no law. Gal. 5:22, 23.

Holding my temper and my tongue might be thought of as passive peacemaking. But passivity is not all there is to the topic. Equally important is active peacemaking.

The following prayer sets forth some of the active aspects:

"Lord, make me an instrument of Your peace.
Where there is hatred let me sow love;
where there is injury, pardon;
where there is doubt, faith;
where there is despair, hope;
where there is darkness, light;
and where there is sadness, joy.
O divine Master, grant that I may not so much seek
to be consoled as to console;
to be understood as to understand;
to be loved as to love.
For it is in giving that we receive;
it is in pardoning that we are pardoned;
and it is in dying that we are born to eternal life."

Peacemaking is a many-faceted activity. To be a peacemaker I need to evaluate every situation in the light of the gospel. I must ask, What are the implications of this? After all, there are more involved than just me. How will my actions affect them? What effect will they have on the good name of Christ? on the church? on my community? A peacemaker walks in the light of the gospel message.

A peacemaker is also an evangelist. A peacemaker is involved in helping people come to a saving relationship with God through Jesus Christ. A peacemaker is a minister of reconciliation. He or she is an underminister to their Lord in helping people find peace with God.

To be a peacemaker is to be a blessing to the world. Let us never forget that in this world we are either a part of the solution or a part of the problem.

CHILDREN OF GOD

Let this mind be in you, which was also in Christ Jesus. Phil. 2:5.

The reward of the peacemakers is that "they shall be called the children of God" (Matt. 5:9). That is no small privilege. To be a child of God is to be as high as can be.

But it is not only a privilege; it is also a responsibility. To be a child of God means to be like Him. It is commonplace that children resemble their parents.

Similarly, Christians are called to be like God. We are to have, as noted in our scripture today, the mind of Christ. And what was Christ like? Our passage goes on to point out that He humbled Himself and became obedient even unto death. He became a servant for us.

In another place we are told that "God so loved the world, that he *gave* his only begotten Son, that whosoever believeth in him should not perish, but have everlasting life" (John 3:16).

That is what we are to be like. We are to be servants not only of God, but of our fellow humans. We are to give of ourselves as Christ gave to us. We are to be like God because we are His children.

Peacemakers will not only be like God in passing on His peace. They will also be filled with God's peace in their daily lives.

We read in *Thoughts From the Mount of Blessing* that "there is no other ground of peace" (p. 27) than making peace in our own lives with God through renouncing sin and opening our hearts to the love of Christ.

The passage goes on to claim that "the grace of Christ received into the heart subdues enmity; it allays strife and fills the soul with love. He who is at peace with God and his fellowmen cannot be made miserable. Envy will not be in his heart; evil surmisings will find no room there; hatred cannot exist. The heart that is in harmony with God is a partaker of the peace of heaven and will diffuse its blessed influence on all around. The spirit of peace will rest like dew upon hearts weary and troubled with worldly strife" (pp. 27, 28).

Such is the blessing of being a child of God.

THE LAST BLESSING

Blessed are those who are persecuted for righteousness' sake, for theirs is the kingdom of heaven. Matt. 5:10, RSV.

With verse 10 we have come to the last beatitude. The promise of this beatitude is identical with the promise of the first beatitude—"theirs is the kingdom of heaven" (Matt. 5:3, 10). Thus Jesus started and ended with the same promise. The promise of the first and the last beatitudes forms an inclusive verbal pocket, with Matthew 5:11, 12 providing a commentary on verse 10.

Into that pocket Jesus packed some of the most important counsel of His ministry. In it He described the essence of *every* Christian's character.

The fact that Jesus bracketed this most important segment of His teaching with mention of the kingdom of God is highly significant. The center of both His message (Matt. 4:17) and that of John the Baptist (Matt. 3:2) was that the kingdom was at hand.

The significance of the Sermon on the Mount is that it sets forth the principles of Jesus' kingdom at the beginning of His ministry. And those principles, as we have noted repeatedly in the past two months, are extremely different from the principles of the world and even the principles of the religious world of Jesus' (and our) day.

The Jews expected a kingdom of power and glory, but Jesus said that before that kingdom arrived His followers would exist in a kingdom of poverty of spirit, mourning over sin, meekness, hungering and thirsting after righteousness, mercifulness, purity, peacemaking, and persecution.

To put it mildly, Jesus' kingdom was not the one expected by the Jews. That kingdom will come in fullness at the Second Advent. In the kingdom of power and glory the ways of the world and worldly religion will have no place. To the contrary, meekness, peacefulness, mercifulness, and so on are its ways.

That means for me that the present era is the time to begin living the principles of heaven. My character will not change at the Second Advent. I will continue to be what I have been. Now is the time for me to let God change my heart and life so that I might be prepared for the fullness of the kingdom.

JESUS NEVER PROMISED US A ROSE GARDEN

If the world hates you, keep in mind that it hated me first. If you belonged to the world, it would love you as its own. As it is, you do not belong to the world, but I have chosen you out of the world. That is why the world hates you. John 15:18, 19, NIV.

Christianity as Jesus presented it is something less than a peaceful picnic. Of all the world's great teachers, perhaps He is the most brutally honest. Again and again Jesus emphasized the fact that His followers would be persecuted *because* they were like Him, *because* they would live according to principles diametrically opposed to those of the larger culture.

Christianity has resulted in persecution in every area of Christians' lives: in their work because of such issues as Sabbath observance, in their family because of new allegiances and priorities, and in their social life because of new lifestyles.

The plain fact is that true Christianity changes people. It makes them out of harmony with "normal" (that is, "sinful") human culture. The result is persecution.

And that persecution has not always been gentle. The emperor Nero, for example, wrapped Christians in pitch and set them afire to serve as living torches to light his gardens. He also sewed them in the skins of animals and set his hunting dogs upon them to tear them to death. Other Christians were sewed into fresh animal skins and then put out in the sunlight to dry and die as the shrinking skins slowly choked and crushed their helpless bodies. Still others had parts of their bodies cut off and roasted before their eyes, or had hissing molten lead poured upon them.

The list of atrocities goes on and on. Even Jesus was not exempt. He died the excruciating and humiliating death of the cross.

And persecution and discrimination aren't at an end yet. The Bible tells us that they will continue up to the end of time.

But such things have not crushed the spirit of Christ's followers, because they know that this world is not their home. They know that those who are "persecuted for righteousness sake" inherit the kingdom of God.

PERSECUTED FOR WHAT?

Persecution will indeed come to everyone who wants to live a godly life as a follower of Christ Jesus. 2 Tim. 3:12, REB.

All kinds of people who claim to be Christians are persecuted. Does their persecution mean that they are Christians?

The biblical answer to that question is a categorical no! Jesus did not say "Blessed are those who are persecuted," but "Blessed are those who are persecuted for righteousness' sake."

There is a big difference between those two ideas. I have a friend who belongs to a religious group that believes that the persecution it receives is a sign of the rightness of its doctrine and way of life.

At this point we need to read our Bible carefully. It does not say "Blessed are those who are persecuted because they are objectionable or difficult." Nor does it promise blessing on those who are persecuted because they are foolish and unwise in the manner in which they give their testimony.

Let's face it. Some people bear their testimony in ways that rightly anger sensitive people. It is their foolish notion of witnessing that brings persecution upon them. Such persecution may have little or nothing to do with what Jesus is talking about.

The same can be said for those who are overzealous or fanatical. Fanaticism and extremism are never commended in the New Testament.

Our passage in the final beatitude is quite specific. It reads: "Blessed are they which are persecuted *for righteousness' sake*" (Matt. 5:10). They are deemed blessed because they have been living the principles of Jesus, the principles of the Beatitudes. As a result, they have found themselves out of harmony with the larger culture and even religious groups that have bought into the principles of the larger culture.

As our text for today puts it, persecution in one form or another will come to *every person* who seeks to live a godly life in Christ Jesus. The world is unable and unwilling to accept the radical principles of the gospel. True Christianity is out of harmony with culture because it is based upon a radical set of principles.

THE DIFFERENCE BETWEEN GOOD PEOPLE AND CHRISTIANS

Woe to you, when all men speak well of you, for so their fathers did to the false prophets. Luke 6:26, RSV.

M any of us find today's text to be perplexing. After all, shouldn't Christians be the best citizens, the friendliest neighbors, and the most helpful fellow workers? Why does Jesus pronounce a woe rather than a blessing on those who are spoken well of by all people?

We need to remember here that the blessed ones are not those who are persecuted for being good or for being noble or for being self-sacrificing. These are traits that are generally appreciated by the non-Christian culture. As D. Martin Lloyd-Jones puts it: "You will probably not be persecuted for being good . . . [or] noble. The world . . . generally praises and admires and loves the good and the noble."

Lloyd-Jones goes on to suggest that the good and noble are seldom persecuted because even non-Christians feel that such people are just like themselves at their best. It is not the good who are persecuted, but the righteous, those who are living the life of Jesus as set forth in the Beatitudes. True Christian righteousness makes mere human goodness and nobility look self-centered and shabby.

It is one thing to be good; it is quite another to be humble and meek. It is one thing to be proud of our noble accomplishments; it is quite another to have poverty of spirit and a deep hungering for that righteousness and goodness that only God can supply.

We might as well face it. The Beatitudes draw the battle line between the principles of Satan's kingdom and those of Christ's kingdom. And every conversion to Christ's way is an act in the drama of the great controversy between the forces of good and evil.

Ellen White puts it nicely when she writes: "When one presents the love of Christ and the beauty of holiness, he is drawing away the subjects of Satan's kingdom, and the prince of evil is aroused to resist it. Persecution and reproach await all who are imbued with the Spirit of Christ" *(Thoughts From the Mount of Blessing, p. 29)*. Therefore, we need to take stock of ourselves when "all men speak well" of us.

PERSECUTION'S HALL OF FAME

Blessed are ye, when men shall revile you, and persecute you, and shall say all manner of evil against you falsely, for my sake. Rejoice, and be exceeding glad: for great is your reward in heaven: for so persecuted they the prophets which were before you. Matt. 5:11, 12.

We noted a few days ago that these two verses do not form a new beatitude. Rather, they are an extension and commentary on the eighth beatitude. As such, there are several things that we should note about verses 11 and 12.

The first is that down through history God's prophets have been persecuted. In fact, in the Old Testament it was generally the false prophets rather than the true who were better accepted by people, by the political authorities, and often even by the religious leaders. That was because they had a smooth, pleasing message. As God put it to Ezekiel: "They have misled my people, saying, 'Peace,' when there is no peace" (Eze. 13:10, RSV).

People would rather hear smooth things than the call of God for repentance and reform. It was that straightforward call that has brought rejection and persecution to God's messengers across time.

Persecution's hall of fame is filled with the names of those who have followed God down through history. Abel was persecuted by Cain because he offered "a more acceptable sacrifice." Noah was mocked as a fanatic and an alarmist. David was persecuted by Saul, and Elijah by Ahab. Daniel spent time in the lions' den, and Paul was persecuted at every turn by those outside and even inside the church.

The status quo never likes to be challenged by God's truth when it is truly God's truth. Those who are rejected for Christ's sake have an unparalleled heritage. We must always be on guard "when all men speak well" of us (Luke 6:26, RSV). It was not so with God's prophets. Nor was it so with the greatest of God's people—Jesus. He died on a cross because of what He taught and lived.

Father, help us today to take courage from the history of Your people when trouble comes our way. Help us to live Your principles in spite of difficulty.

LEAPING FOR JOY
IN THE FACE OF TROUBLE

Blessed are you when men hate you, when they exclude you and insult you and reject your name as evil, because of the Son of Man. Rejoice in that day and leap for joy, because great is your reward in heaven. Luke 6:22, 23, NIV.

That's wild!

Who wants to "leap for joy" because they are hated, excluded, insulted, and rejected? I have found this to be one of the most difficult of Jesus' commands to put into practice.

My first reaction when insulted is to insult back, when rejected to reject back. That is human, but Christ's way is divine, and He claims there is a blessing in it.

Just a few days ago I had an opportunity to leap for joy at being treated wrongly. My family and I had built a nice fire for a Sabbath evening picnic in a fire pit in the Smoky Mountain National Park. But after the fire was blazing nicely I was told by a ranger that I had to move on because that fire pit wasn't open for use yet.

I had used that pit several times before early in the season with no problem. But this time I was "kicked out." My first thoughts were not altogether pleasant. But I kept my mouth shut and moved on to a picnic ground some seven miles downstream.

There we had an excellent "veggie dog" roast, a lively song service, and an uplifting devotional.

At 10:00 p.m. we were ready to head back to our lodging. At that point a car drove up to our lonely fire. Its occupants told us the car was out of gas. They were glad to see us because the nearest open gas station was 15 miles away and the nearest people other than us at that time of night were about five miles away.

We soon discovered that our new acquaintances were two theological students from Southern College of Seventh-day Adventists. It was our privilege to help them and to make some new friends. Without our knowing what was happening, God had placed us at the right spot at the right time. All of us leaped for joy at His providential care, even though it seemed at first that we had been unjustly treated.

SHOULD CHRISTIANS BE CONCERNED WITH REWARDS?

Henceforth there is laid up for me a crown of righteousness, which the Lord, the righteous judge, shall give me at that day: and not to me only, but unto all them also that love his appearing. 2 Tim. 4:8.

Some people seem to have the idea that Christians shouldn't be concerned with their final reward. That is, they should live above thoughts of the heavenly promise or the fear of hell. The true Christian, so the thought goes, lives the Christian life from the sheer joy of being a Christian.

Now, it seems to me that there is an element of truth in that line of thought. After all, no one will be saved because they feared hell. Nor will people be in God's everlasting kingdom merely because they see it as the ultimate goodie. Beyond that, people receive an intrinsic blessing just because living the Christian life is a better way than the alternatives.

But such truths are not the whole truth. The Bible is not backward in talking about rewards and punishments at the Second Advent. Matthew 5:12, with its talk of great rewards in heaven for the faithful, is merely one of many texts on the topic. James talks about "the crown of life, which the Lord hath promised to them that love him" (James 1:12). And Paul left little doubt in today's scripture that he looked forward to receiving his "crown of righteousness" at the Second Coming.

God loves His children. He wants to bless them more abundantly than they can even imagine. Part of His blessing is their future reward in the earth made new.

That thought runs from Matthew to Revelation. "Behold," we read in the last chapter of Revelation, "I come quickly; and my reward is with me, to give every man according as his work shall be" (Rev. 22:12).

While our primary motivation is not hope of rewards and fear of punishment, we need to move beyond the less-than-biblical idea that these are not motivators. God wants us to covet the best things. He wants us to desire and look forward to heaven as we make our pilgrimage through this less-than-ideal world.

ANOTHER GLIMPSE OF HEAVEN

For, behold, I create new heavens and a new earth: and the former shall not be remembered, nor come into mind. Isa. 65:17.

Before moving away from the Beatitudes and the idea of God's rewards to faithful believers, we should take another glimpse at heaven. After all, the eight blessings are bracketed by the promise that the reward of Jesus' followers would be the kingdom of heaven.

When Jesus talked about heaven His hearers had in mind the promises of the Old Testament. And in that testament one of the books that is most explicit on the topic is Isaiah. So this morning we will take a glimpse at the heavenly reward through the eyes of Isaiah.

One of my favorite heavenly passages in Isaiah is the one that tells us that "The wolf . . . shall dwell with the lamb, and the leopard shall lie down with the kid; and the calf and the young lion and the fatling together; and a little child shall lead them. . . . They shall not hurt nor destroy in all my holy mountain: for the earth shall be full of the knowledge of the Lord, as the waters cover the sea" (Isa. 11:6-9).

A second passage comes from Isaiah 35: "'Your God . . . will come to save you.' Then will the eyes of the blind be opened and the ears of the deaf unstopped. Then will the lame leap like a deer, and the mute tongue shout for joy. Water will gush forth in the wilderness and streams in the desert. . . .

"Only the redeemed will walk there, and the ransomed of the Lord will return. They will enter Zion with singing; everlasting joy will crown their heads. Gladness and joy will overtake them, and sorrow and sighing will flee away" (verses 4-10, NIV).

What promises! What blessings! These are promises that God wanted to bestow on Israel. But because of Israel's rejection of Jesus, they are now promises to the church. They are promises to each of us.

Lord, I want to be there. I look forward to living in the fullness of Your kingdom, a kingdom in which the sickness of the current age has become history.

"WOE IS ME" IN THE FACE OF GOD'S IDEAL

The Lord is my light and my salvation; whom shall I fear? the Lord is the strength of my life. Ps. 27:1.

For the past two months our thoughts have focused on Matthew 5:2-12—the Beatitudes. We noted early in our study that those eight characteristics were to stand at the center of every Christian's life. In fact, we might even say that they define what it means to be a Christian. A Christian *is* a person who is poor in spirit, meek, hungry for God's righteousness, merciful, and so on.

Without *all eight* of those characteristics we are not living the Christian life. God's ideal is for each of us to live the Beatitudes every day through the power of the Holy Spirit. They are the principles of His kingdom here on earth and in the earth to come. They define Christian character.

But you may be thinking, *My life is not all that it should be; I daily fall short of God's ideal.*

You're right! You and I do fall short. Isaiah, in his vision of God, cried out, "Woe is me!" When we come face-to-face with God and His principles, it leaves us "undone" (Isa. 6:5).

The good news is that Jesus knows our shortcomings and provides an answer to our dilemma in the Sermon on the Mount.

First, the recognition of our character weakness stands at the center of the Beatitudes. That recognition is what makes us poor in spirit, leads us to mourn over our shortcomings, helps us shed spiritual arrogance for meekness, and drives us to Jesus as we hunger and thirst after righteousness.

Jesus' second and third provisions for our shortcomings in living the Christian life are found in His great prayer. He counsels us to pray that God will "forgive us our debts" and "deliver us from evil." The first of those injunctions has to do with God's forgiving grace; the second, in part, has to do with God's empowering grace.

Praise God that He makes provision for our weakness. Praise Jesus for ideals that help us see where we fall short and that drive us to Him for forgiveness and power.

A SECOND STEP
IN OUR WALK WITH JESUS

You are the salt of the earth. But if the salt loses its saltiness, how can it be made salty again? It is no longer good for anything, except to be thrown out and trampled upon by men. Matt. 5:13, NIV.

We have come to our first major turning point in our walk with Jesus on the Mount of Blessing. In the Beatitudes of Matthew 5:3-12 Jesus outlines the essential elements of *a Christian's character*. Now in the salt and light metaphors of verses 13 to 16 He discusses *a Christian's influence*.

In actuality, these two sections of the Sermon on the Mount are quite closely related. After all, a Christian's influence depends upon his or her character. Without a Christian character, there can be no Christian influence.

That last sentence may seem too commonplace to most of us to have much meaning. What do we mean when we say that without a Christian character, there can be no Christian influence?

Simply this, that a so-called Christian who is not merciful and meek and pure in heart and so on is not a Christian even though he or she may belong to the church. Such a person will have an influence, but that influence will not be Christian.

And here is a problem for the church. Because such a person calls himself or herself a Christian and may belong to the church, his or her actions are viewed by the larger community as representing what Christianity stands for. But it is a false witness. The sharp business dealings of some and the pride or backbiting of others set forth a false witness to the community. This is not a Christian witness. A person must be a Christian in the Beatitudes sense of the word if he or she is to have a Christian influence.

We should note also that Matthew 5:13 says that Christians *are* salt. If they are Christians, they have no choice. This is Jesus' ninth statement about Christians in His sermon. Thus just as they *are* meek and peacemakers, so they *will be* salt to the world. Because we *are* salt to the world, we need to study the uses of salt carefully.

THE PROBLEM WITH THE WORLD

The Lord saw that the wickedness of man was great in the earth, and that every imagination of the thoughts of his heart was only evil continually. And the Lord was sorry that he had made man on the earth. Gen. 6:5, 6, RSV.

An important point to grasp in Jesus' saying that Christians are the salt of the earth, or world, is that it not only describes the Christian but also infers a description of the world in which the Christian is to function as salt. Jesus sets the salt over against the world; He signifies that Christians are different and distinct from the world. It is only because they are different and distinct that they can be recognized as salt and have the effect of salt.

This chapter has already described the Christian, but it does not describe the world. That description is found throughout the Bible.

The first picture in the Bible of the earth or the world is: "God saw everything that he had made, and behold, it was very good" (Gen. 1:31, RSV). But that goodness did not last. Genesis 3 tells of the entrance of sin and the corruption of the world and human nature.

Genesis 4 picks up that picture of corruption and forwards the history of the world through the Cain and Abel story. By Genesis 6 we find God declaring that the earth and its human inhabitants were indeed corrupt to the core.

Subsequently, the Bible describes the Flood and God's new start with Noah. But the new start also failed. The corruption went on.

The Bible is the story of a sick world and of a God who is seeking to rescue it. It is in that light that we need to read the words of Jesus. G. Campbell Morgan said it nicely when he wrote: "Jesus, looking out over the multitudes of His day, saw the corruption, the disintegration of life at every point, its breakup, its spoilation; and because of His love of the multitudes, He knew the thing that they needed most was the salt in order that the corruption should be arrested."

Christians have a function in the world. They *are* the salt of the earth.

THE NATURE OF SALT

I do not pray that thou shouldest take them out of the world, but that thou shouldest keep them from the evil one. They are not of the world, even as I am not of the world. John 17:15, 16, RSV.

One of the great tensions in daily life is that we as Christians are citizens of two kingdoms at the same time. We are citizens of the kingdom of heaven, but our daily existence takes place in one of the kingdoms of this world. Jesus said it slightly differently when He noted that Christians live *in* the world, but are not *of* the world.

That is, they do not live in isolation from the world. Christians are told that they must be otherworldly in their minds and outlook, but never that they are to retire out of the world or leave the world to itself. That was the error of monasticism. According to that concept, to live the supreme Christian life one should withdraw from society and live a life of contemplation.

Jesus' statement about salt flatly denies that assumption. Christians are to be the salt of the earth. That is, as Dietrich Bonhoeffer puts it, they "must not only think of heaven; they have an earthly task as well."

Salt has many functions. In societies without refrigeration, it is used as a preservative. It is rubbed into meat to prevent decay. Another positive function of salt is flavoring. Many foods taste better when salt is added. But to be effective, salt must be in contact with the food. Salt left a fraction of an inch away from food can neither preserve nor flavor.

Christians function as salt by intermingling with the surrounding culture. Although Christians often don't realize it, their daily lives moderate the people and society around them as they live out the Beatitudes. Their daily lives "flavor" the society through the little kindnesses they show, the humility they demonstrate, and so on. Even proud and hardened people often find it difficult not to respect true Christians, although they may not choose to emulate them.

Lord, help me to be salt today—in my family, in my neighborhood, and in my workplace.

LIVING THE SALT LIFE

Know ye not that a little leaven leaveneth the whole lump? 1 Cor. 5:6.

S alt is like yeast in terms of its ability to permeate the food it comes into contact with. Just as yeast transforms the mass of flour and water in which it is embedded, so does a little salt flavor a large pot of beans. Salt changes things.

So it is with the Christian life. Its influence flavors the attitudes and actions of those it comes in contact with.

Influence, of course, can be for good or bad. Oliver Wendell Holmes is reported to have said, "I might have entered the ministry if certain clergymen I knew had not looked and acted so much like undertakers." And author Robert Louis Stevenson entered into his diary, as if he was recording a unique phenomenon, "I have been to church today, and am not depressed."

The salt of Christian influence will be positive rather than negative. It will be upbuilding and hopeful. A Christian's daily life will leave in its wake a trail and an atmosphere of peacefulness, even in troublous times. It will flavor everything it touches, because by faith it is in contact with the God who cares for His children. The Christian exudes God's characteristics because "the fruit of the Spirit is love, joy, peace, longsuffering, gentleness, goodness, faith, meekness, temperance" (Gal. 5:22, 23). What a flavor for any soup, for any community.

Perhaps the key ingredient in a Christian's influence is outgoing, genuine love. "When love fills the heart," we read in *Thoughts From the Mount of Blessing*, "it will flow out to others, not because of favors received from them, but because love is the principle of action. Love modifies the character, governs the impulses, subdues enmity, and ennobles the affections. This love is as broad as the universe, and is in harmony with that of the angel workers. Cherished in the heart, it sweetens the entire life and sheds its blessing upon all around. *It is this, and this only, that can make us the salt of the earth*" (p. 38; italics supplied).

THE SOCIAL SIDE OF SALT

Moreover, brethren, I declare unto you the gospel [good news] which I preached unto you. . . . For I delivered unto you . . . how that Christ died for our sins according to the scriptures; and that he was buried, and that he rose again the third day according to the scriptures. 1 Cor. 15:1-4.

The good news of the gospel is that Jesus died for our sins; further, His resurrection is a guarantee of our future resurrection. Some would have us believe that the good news is that the Christian church will bring about social reform in human economies and governments. They see the salt function of the church as one in which the church's role is to make pronouncements about the general situation of the world in terms of such things as politics, economics, and international affairs.

The problem with that approach to the analogy of salt is that it is not found in the New Testament. Nowhere do we find Jesus or Paul working for the reform of the Roman government or sending resolutions up to the imperial court to do this or that.

Those who have seen the salt function of Christians as primarily social have based their understanding on the Old Testament prophets. But there is a problem with that approach, since in Israel there was no distinction between church and state. Thus the Old Testament prophets had to address the entire life of the nation.

It is different in the New Testament. The church is not identified with any nation or special-interest group. To the contrary, the primary function is to preach the saving gospel of Jesus to all nations. But once the church begins to intervene in this or that economic or social issue, it has cut off its outreach to those on the other side of the issue.

Here, however, we must be careful not to go from one extreme to the other. While the church must beware of taking sides, individual Christians have a responsibility to vote and make their voice heard in the community as well as witness to the principles of the Bible in their daily lives.

Lord, help us today as both a church and as individuals to best learn how to be the salt of the earth.

SALTLESS SALT

Salt is excellent. But if the salt goes flat, it's useless, good for nothing.
Are you listening to this?
Really listening? Luke 14:34, 35, Message.

S alt is salt. Salt is salty. Without saltiness it is not salt.
How, therefore, can salt lose its saltiness? The plain fact is that it cannot. If it is not salty, it is not salt.

"So what?" you may be asking at this point. "What meaning does this rather esoteric point have for my life?"

It means everything, because Jesus does not say that His followers ought to be salt, or may be salt, or might possibly become salt. No! He categorically says that Christians *are* salt.

Christians have no choice as to whether they will be salt. Jesus declared, "Ye *are* the salt of the earth." The only choice we have as Christians is to reject our God-given function as salt.

And how can we do that? By not being like Jesus, who lived and died for the good of others.

We deny the salt function when we fail to mix with the world, when Christians segregate themselves from that which needs their preserving influence. We deny the salt function when we are less than loving and kind. We deny the salt function when we put our wishes and wants above the needs of others. We deny the salt function when we fail to live the Beatitudes.

When we do these things we have lost our saltiness, because we are not salt. We have become part of the world and are living by its principles. We are no longer salt. We have become part of the problem rather than part of the solution. To deny the salt function is to deny the principles of the kingdom. To deny those principles is to deny the Lord who gave them.

The result? Such will be "cast out." With that statement in Matthew 5:13 we come to the first hint of judgment in the Sermon on the Mount. Jesus will return to that theme throughout the sermon.

The moral of the story is simple. It makes a difference what principles we accept in our lives and how we relate to people in daily life. After all, Christians *are* salt.

YOU ARE LIGHT

Ye are the light of the world. A city that is set on a hill cannot be hid. Matt. 5:14.

"You *are* the light of the world." That is an outstanding statement when you consider whom Jesus was talking to. He was not addressing the religious leaders. He was not encouraging preachers or theologians. He was speaking to common people—those who were entirely unimportant from the perspective of their world.

Such a statement should cause us to stand up and take note. It is a remarkable thing to be a Christian. Jesus did not say that the world's learned philosophers or political strategists were the light of the world, but *you*, Mr. or Mrs. or Miss Average Christian. A remarkable statement, to say the least.

Note once again the "you *are*." Christians are the light of the world by the very fact that they are Christians.

How is that so? you may be thinking. It is so because you are a Christian who knows Jesus. You know that He died for your sins and was raised the third day for your life. That is the message of salvation. It is the message that the world desperately needs to hear and accept.

Paul tells us that "the world by wisdom knew not God, [thus] it pleased God by the foolishness of preaching to save them that believe" (1 Cor. 1:21). The cross of Christ is foolishness to the world at large, but it is *the* heart of the Christian message. It is the crucial element in our salvation.

Every Christian is a light to help others find salvation in Jesus. Every Christian is a missionary to tell others of God's love and of His forgiveness in Jesus.

That means *you*. "*You are* the light of the world." Every day God gives you an opportunity to witness for Him. What a privilege.

Lord, help me today to be Your light in a dark world. Bring someone into my life today who needs a glimpse of Your love. Then give me wisdom to be Your light in an effective manner.

But You Are Not the Real Light

Then spake Jesus again unto them, saying, I am the light of the world: he that followeth me shall not walk in darkness, but shall have the light. John 8:12.

I guess you can afford to be humble after all. You are not the real light of the world. Jesus is. You are light because you are connected to Him, because you follow Him.

You have no light of your own any more than the moon has light without the sun or a light bulb has light without being connected to a power source.

Yes, we can rejoice because God has given us great privileges as Christians, but we must be humble in our rejoicing. We are not the real light, but a reflection or extension of the light in Jesus.

It is therefore of crucial importance that we, moment by moment, remain connected to our source of spiritual power.

An illustration based on a Near Eastern lamp will help us here. Such a lamp consisted of a bowl filled with oil, with a wick sticking out.

The oil was absolutely essential to the functioning of the lamp. Without a supply of oil the lamp was useless and lightless.

So it is with us. We need the infilling of Christ through the Holy Spirit each day. We cannot function as light without daily filling, without a relationship with the Lord of light.

This filling is not something that takes place once for all time, at conversion. No, we need to go to Jesus daily through prayer and a study of His Word. As we receive the daily oil, we have light to pass on.

The wick is the other essential in such lamps. Once a wick gets frayed and begins to smoke it fails to give light efficiently. It needs to be trimmed so that its light can shine brightly again.

So it is in our spiritual life. We need to day by day take stock of ourselves in the light of God's love and the Beatitudes, and "trim" our lives so that they can burn in such a way that they give light rather than smoke.

THE MISSIONARY MANDATE

Go ye therefore, and teach all nations, baptizing them in the name of the Father, and of the Son, and of the Holy Ghost: Teaching them to observe all things whatsoever I have commanded you: and, lo, I am with you alway, even unto the end of the world. Matt. 28:19, 20.

Let's take another look at Jesus' statement in Matthew 5:14 that we as Christians "are the light *of the world.*" When we look at the last three words of that sentence we are even more awed than we are with the first part of the sentence. The common people Jesus was speaking to were not only the light; they were the light "of the world."

Here we find a theme that Matthew will continue to develop throughout his Gospel. Jesus didn't say a light to Palestine or the Roman Empire or a part of the world. No! He said that His followers would be the light of the entire world.

Here we find the missionary mandate that will be picked up and emphasized in the concluding verses of the first Gospel. As Christ's disciples we are to take His teachings to every nation.

That idea is especially remarkable when we realize that Jesus was talking to Jews and that at that time the Jewish nation had become exclusive. It had erected a wall or partition between itself and every other nation.

In spite of that exclusiveness, Jesus told His Jewish hearers (and us) that they were to be the light of the world. Thus, as we read in *Thoughts From the Mount of Blessing*, "Christ tears away the wall of partition, the self-love, the dividing prejudice of nationality, and teaches a love for all the human family. He lifts men from the narrow circle that their selfishness prescribes; He abolishes all territorial lines and artificial distinctions of society. He makes no difference between neighbors and strangers, friends and enemies. He teaches us to look upon every needy soul as our neighbor and the world as our field" (p. 42).

"Ye are the light of the world."

GOD'S NEW ISRAEL

If you are Christ's, then you are Abraham's offspring, heirs according to promise. Gal. 3:29, RSV.

When Jesus placed upon His followers His mission to the world by making them the salt of the earth and the light of the world, He was really giving them the mission that had previously belonged to Israel.

In the Old Testament it was Israel who was God's covenant people, it was Israel who was "a light to the nations" (Isa. 42:6, RSV). Israel was God's precious and holy and chosen nation. God had given Israel a mission to the entire world. Eventually, "all the nations" would "call Jerusalem the throne of the Lord" and "be gathered unto it," not to "walk any more after the imagination of their evil heart" (Jer. 3:17). "All who . . . turned from idolatry to the worship of the true God were to unite themselves with His chosen people. As the numbers of Israel increased they were to enlarge their borders, until their kingdom should embrace the world" *(Christ's Object Lessons*, p. 290).

But Israel did not fulfill God's purpose for it. As a result, Jesus gave its mission to His followers. Perhaps that point is made as clear as anywhere in the parable of the tenants (Matt. 21:33-46).

In that parable a landowner plants a vineyard and lets it out to tenants. When he sends servants to collect his rents they were mistreated. Finally he sends his son, whom they kill. As a result, "he will miserably destroy those wicked men, and will let out his vineyard unto other husbandmen." Then Jesus sums up His lesson: "The kingdom of God shall be taken from you, and given to a nation bringing forth the fruits thereof" (verses 41-43).

That "nation," of course, is the Christian church. It has been called as "an holy nation" and "a peculiar people" to witness for God to all the world. Thus "those who believe [in Jesus] are the descendants of Abraham" and the "Israel of God" (Gal. 3:7; 6:16, NRSV).

It is upon the church that all the blessings of the Old Testament fall. But not only the blessings. The church, you and I, now have the responsibility to fulfill Israel's mission as light to the world.

MISSING CANDLESTICKS

Remember therefore from whence thou are fallen, and repent, and do the first works; or else I will come unto thee quickly, and will remove thy candlestick out of his place, except thou repent. Rev. 2:5.

The first three chapters of Revelation picture Christ as walking in the midst of seven golden candlesticks, which represent His church. For the past two days we have been studying the great truth that we as God's church are to be a light to the world. Thus the candlesticks of the Temple are an apt representation of God's church. It was the candlesticks or lampstands that provided light for the Temple on earth in Old Testament times.

But what happens when candlesticks don't operate as faithfully as they should? They are removed. Thus, as we noted yesterday, Israel was removed from its position as God's covenant people at the first coming of Christ, and His commission to be God's light to the world was given to the Christian church. Since then history has witnessed a succession of Christian bodies that have shed God's light abroad brightly in their youth, but lost their clear biblical witness in their later years. As a result, their candlesticks were removed, so to speak, as reform movements arose in an effort to get back to a clearer vision of God's word in the Bible.

Adventism is one such reform movement. God has a mission for Adventism to preach the message of the three angels of Revelation 14:6-12 "to every nation, and kindred, and tongue, and people" before the great harvest of the earth.

As Seventh-day Adventists we need to pray this morning and every morning that God will help us to be faithful candlesticks to Him, faithful lights to the world, so that our candlestick might not be removed.

What a blessing God has given to us to live His life and share His Word with others. What a privilege to be light rather than darkness, to be a blessing to those around us, even to the ends of the earth.

Lord, please help our candlestick.

THE TASK OF LIGHT

In the midst of a crooked and perverse generation . . . you shine as lights in the world. Phil. 2:15, RSV.

Underlying our study of Christians being "the light of the world" is the understanding that light is different from darkness in the same way that Christians, by definition, are different from their non-Christian neighbors. Thus light is significant because it is different from the medium it finds itself in, just as salt is different from whatever it is to flavor or preserve.

The forcefulness of Jesus' illustrations is built upon those differences. If salt has no saltiness or light has no "lightness," they have no function or use. We as born-again Christians are only light and salt to the earth as we are different from the surrounding culture in the same way that Jesus was different from the world. We have influence in the world because we show up, because we stand out, because we live the Beatitudes, and because our values are radically different from those of our neighbors.

"Well," we might ask, "how is a Christian to show that he or she is indeed 'the light of the world'?" The answer is to look at the functions of light.

Light has many functions. One of them is to expose darkness and the things that belong to darkness. There is a sense in which people are not aware of darkness until a light is switched on. Here we need to imagine the lights of an automobile suddenly piercing the darkness of a country road. The light changes everything for both the driver and those who had been groping down the road in the darkness.

There is a sense in which Jesus performed that function when He came. Matthew tells us that "the people which sat in darkness saw great light" (Matt. 4:16). In the light of Jesus' life, darkness was exposed, things looked different.

How is it with my life? Do I merely blend in with the larger culture, or do I stand out as something special and different? Does my life help people see the "better way" more clearly?

MORE WORK FOR LIGHT

Thy word is a lamp unto my feet, and a light unto my path. Ps. 119:105.

Yesterday we saw that as "the light of the world" the lives of Christians expose darkness by their very principles and lives. But exposing darkness is not the only function of light. There is a very real sense in which light serves as a guide.

When I think of the guiding function of light, I think of the rows of lights that extend along each side of an airport runway. The lights show the pilot exactly where the runway is, where it is safe to land.

A light is a guide that helps us know the direction that we should go. When we follow the light's guidance we are safe. But when we "try to land" in the dark, or drive in the dark, or even walk through a strange woods in the dark, we soon find ourselves in difficulty. We soon discover that we need the guidance of light.

Jesus came into this world to provide that guidance. And even though He has returned to heaven, He has not left us in darkness. He has given us His Word as a lamp to guide our feet through the complexities of life.

Christians become lights to those around them when they share God's Word with others, not only in their daily lives, but through Bible study and other means of sharing the counsel of the Bible.

Light not only has a guiding function; it also has a warning function. I still remember when stoplights came to our community. It was soon after World War II. My nondriving mother, wishing the safety of her 6-year-old on his first solo trip to town after the lights were in, carefully explained to me that red means go and green means stop. Fortunately, my father overheard the instruction and rushed into the room to put the instruction right.

It is important that we as Christians not only recognize the warnings and guidance of God's Word but also put them into practice in our walk with Jesus.

And as we heed the light ourselves, a wonderful thing takes place— we become light for God in a dark world.

LIGHT IS TO BE SEEN

When a lamp is lit, it is not put under the meal-tub, but on the lampstand, where it gives light to everyone in the house. Matt. 5:15, REB.

The Lord wants to do with us the same as normal people do with lights. As one author puts it: "He will not light us, make us disciples, beautify us, and twice tell us that we are something, and then stick us under a basket."

The function of light is to be seen. The children's song says it nicely: we are to let our light shine for Jesus.

Christianity is something that is meant to be seen. There is no such thing as secret discipleship. Either the secrecy destroys the discipleship or the discipleship destroys the secrecy.

True Christianity is visible to everyone. It is not visible only in the church. A Christian whose effects stop at the church door or at the edges of the community of faith is of not much use.

Christianity's visibility must be evident in all the activities of daily life. It is visible in the manner in which I order a meal in a restaurant, in the way I treat those I live with, in the way I relate to those I work with, in the way I use my tongue, in the way I play a game or drive a car, in everything I do (or don't do).

Christianity knows of no days off or places off. It is a visible way of life for all to see. And see it they will. And in the seeing I will either be exposed as a hypocrite (literally, "play actor") or as a follower of Jesus.

Some people become a bit nervous when they think of their responsibility to be the light of the world. They worry about when and where they should be lights, when and where they can witness.

Jesus' answer is not to worry about that. Just be light at all times wherever you are. Just live the Jesus life of the Beatitudes, and people will see the light. The success of the missionary program is not up to us. Our job is to let God shine through us.

BUT NOT EVERYBODY LIKES LIGHT

And this is the condemnation, that light is come into the world, and men loved darkness rather than light, because their deeds were evil. For every one that doeth evil hateth the light, neither cometh to the light, lest his deeds should be reproved. But he that doeth truth cometh to the light, that his deeds may be made manifest, that they are wrought in God. John 3:19-21.

L ight is a great divider. It separates light from darkness. When faced with light, we have two choices—to greet it and accept it or to shut our eyes and turn away from it. We must either accept it and use its benefits or reject it. With light there is no neutral ground.

The same is true of Christianity. Our verse for today tells us that some come to the light of Jesus, while others do all they can to avoid it.

The difference between the two responses resides in human nature. Fallen human nature loves darkness rather than light. It doesn't like to have its actions or its motives exposed. Even many who belong to the church and attend every Sabbath don't like the light.

Why? Why would anyone prefer darkness to light? The Bible gives us the answer when it says that their deeds are evil.

But how do they know they are evil? Because every person has a conscience that impresses him or her with glimmers of right and wrong.

The problem is that we do things we know to be wrong. Why? Because we like to do such things.

The trouble with people is not so much in their intellect as in their nature. That is why the Bible tells us again and again that we need new natures, that we need to be converted, that we need to put God at the center of our life rather than our own pleasures.

In short, we need to come to the light and be transformed by the light. That is what Christianity stands for. Those who are not born again hate the light, but those who are truly right with God not only love the light; they want to share their joy in the light with others.

THE GOSPEL COVER-UP

No one after lighting a lamp puts it in a cellar or under a bushel, but on a stand, that those who enter may see the light. Luke 11:33, RSV.

In today's text Jesus is accurate, but there were good reasons at certain times for putting a lamp under a bushel. Let me explain.

When we think of a first-century Palestinian house, we must move away from thoughts of our well-lit homes that can be flooded with light at the flip of a switch.

By way of contrast, Palestinian homes were quite dark, generally having only one small window of perhaps 18 inches across. And they certainly didn't have electricity or light switches.

The lamp Jesus is speaking of consisted of a small dish filled with oil. A wick floated in the oil. This lamp would be elevated on a stand when the family needed the light. The trick with such lamps was in lighting them. Remember, no one had matches or cigarette lighters.

As a result, no one wanted to quench the burning wick. It took too much energy to get it burning again. But when people went out of the house it could be dangerous to just leave the burning lamp in its stand from where it could fall off and start a fire.

Thus for safety's sake, when people left their home, the lamp would be taken from its stand and put under an earthen vessel where it could burn risk-free until someone returned. But as soon as someone returned, the lamp would go back on its stand. The primary function of the lamp was to be seen and give light.

That last point is the one Jesus is speaking to in Matthew 5:14-16. No one in his or her right mind would merely light a lamp only to put it under an earthen vessel.

Yet some people who claim to be Christians do just that. All such need to be told that there is no danger of burning down the Lord's house. To the contrary, the world needs all the light it can get. Thus we as Christians are to constantly let our lamps burn at their maximum. After all, we are "the light of the world."

"GOOD" WORKS AND "BAD" WORKS

Let your light so shine before men, that they may see your good works, and glorify your Father which is in heaven. Matt. 5:16.

This is an interesting passage because it suggests that Christians are to have "good works." To hear some people talk, good works have no place in the Christian life. No one told that to Jesus. He plainly said that we should not only have good works but also that those works should be evident as light to the community.

Because of this statement it is important to spend a few moments with the concept of works in the New Testament.

The New Testament directly opposes three types of works: (1) works of the flesh (Rom. 8:3-10), which are the outworkings of the sinful nature; (2) works of the law (Rom. 3:28; Gal. 2:16; Eph. 2:9), which are carried out in the hope of gaining salvation; and (3) "dead works" (Heb. 6:1), which are the activities of individuals out of relationship with the living God and hence devoid of grace.

Over against those less-than-sanctified works, the New Testament places works of faith. Paul speaks approvingly of "faith working through love" (Gal. 5:6, RSV). He commends the Thessalonians' "work of faith and labor of love" (1 Thess. 1:3, RSV). And part of his task was to call the Gentiles to "the obedience of faith" (Rom. 1:5; 16:26, RSV). Paul clarifies the distinction between "good" and "bad" works when he writes that "whatever does not proceed from faith is sin" (Rom. 14:23, RSV).

A legal work is one done out of our own resources in an attempt to gain favor or salvation from God. On the other hand, works of faith flow out of a saving relationship with Jesus, are energized by the Holy Spirit, and are shaped and softened by the love of the Father.

A Christian does not work to get saved any more than a tree produces fruit to prove that it is a tree. A tree produces fruit because it is alive.

So it is with the Christian. The actions of a saved person are a response to God's love. Martin Luther makes that point when he writes that "it is impossible for it [faith] not to do good works incessantly."

SHINING FOR GOD

And immediately he received his sight, and followed him, glorifying God:
and all the people, when they saw it, gave praise unto God. Luke 18:43.

The story is told of D. L. Moody's attendance at a convention of
young people who took their faith very seriously. One event at
the convention was an all-night prayer meeting. They met the
great evangelist as they were leaving the next morning.

Moody asked them what they had been doing. They told him and
then added: "Mr. Moody, see how our faces shine?" Moody gently answered, "Moses wist not that his face shone." His point? Goodness that
calls attention to itself is not Christian goodness. Thus, as we find in
Matthew 5:16, our good works are not for our glorification, but to "glorify your Father which is in heaven."

In short, doing good must be done in the right way. The Christian
is not interested in ostentation or display. We are not to live the
Christian life so that people will praise us. We are not to give of our
time or money so that people will think that we are remarkable in our
dedication. Nor must we teach a Sabbath school lesson, preach a sermon, or write a book so that people will look to us.

These may (or may not) be good works for us, but they are Christian
good works only when they are done to glorify our Maker and Sustainer.

One of the most difficult problems we face as Christians is to move beyond the desire for self-glorification and self-centeredness. We were born
with that problem, and it is part of the very root of sin in our natures.

We are to be lights so that people may see God more clearly and
glorify Him more abundantly. That is what Jesus did in His ministry.
His good works, as we saw in our Bible reading for today, led people to
praise and glorify God.

Lord, as we kneel in prayer today, help us to have the spirit of John
the Baptist, who said of Jesus, "He must increase, but I must decrease."
Help me to live for Your glory, dear Father. Help me to shine for You.

THE DIFFERENCE
BETWEEN SALT AND LIGHT

If any of them do not believe the word, they may be won over without words by the behavior of their wives, when they see the purity and reverence of your lives. 1 Peter 3:1, 2, NIV.

Go and stand . . . and speak to the people all the words of . . . Life. Acts 5:20, RSV.

When I first read Matthew 5:13 on Christians being salt and light I felt that Jesus was saying the same thing twice for emphasis. And there is a sense in which that is true. Both teachings concern a Christian's witness in the world. And both salt and light are self-giving. They expend themselves for the good of the substance they come in contact with. Thus they represent the very opposite of every kind of self-centered religiosity. As a result, both are fit illustrations of the Christian virtues represented by the Beatitudes.

But there is a major difference between salt and light, a difference that is crucial to understand for the fullness of our witness for Jesus. Salt works and expends itself in secret. You can't see it operating. It quietly and unobtrusively does its thing—it makes things salty without really being seen or heard.

In the Christian life we find this kind of "salt witnessing." One thinks of the Christian's quiet daily influence among his or her acquaintances, which is exerted just because they are kind, humble, peaceful, happy, and polite. People know that such individuals are Christians because they exude caring and love to their total environment.

Being salt is good, but some people talk as if being salt is all there is to Christian witness. Not so! Jesus told us we are *both* salt and light.

And light has a different sort of witness. Light is seen. It works openly and visibly. And here we think of our responsibility to share the Word of God publicly in Bible study with others. Here we think of every Christian's responsibility to tell others the truth of the Bible.

Christians are both salt and light. Combined, these two forms of witness provide a rounded witness to our community. People not only see we are different, but through our sharing God's Word at the proper time they know why we are different.

THE ULTIMATE CONTRADICTION— A FORMAL CHRISTIAN

Having a form of godliness, but denying the power thereof: from such turn away. 2 Tim. 3:5.

For the past three weeks we have been studying a Christian's influence. According to Jesus, each of us is both salt and light. That is, we witness to the world both in the unconscious quality of our daily lives and through consciously sharing the truth of God's Word.

There is even something to note in the order of the salt and light metaphors. Salt comes before light. Thus Jesus emphasizes what we *are* before what we *say*. A witness who is merely a sayer but not a doer is not a witness of Christ. Giving all the Bible studies and preaching all the sermons in the world will have little positive impact if one is not living the Beatitudes. Silent witness comes before public witness. A Christian is both salt and light.

But what about the merely formal "Christian," the person who has the name of Christian but doesn't have a Christian's qualities? Such people want to appear to be Christians without functioning as Christians. In short, they are salt without flavor and light without light.

There is no such thing.

D. Martin Lloyd-Jones has pointed out that "there is nothing in God's universe that is so utterly useless as a merely formal Christian." The formal Christian is the person who understands enough about Christianity to spoil the world for him or her, but not enough to provide real happiness, peace, or joy.

Such people are indeed to be pitied. As Lloyd-Jones puts it, "They are the most pathetic people in the world."

God wants us to be the genuine thing. He desires us each to be a "real" Christian. Beyond that, He gives us the power we need to be such in our daily lives.

Today He wants to come into my life and give me all the blessings that Jesus came to bestow upon us. Today He desires to fill me with His love, joy, and peace.

Lord, help me today to surrender myself totally to You so that I can be filled completely.

TAKING A THIRD STEP
IN OUR WALK WITH JESUS

Think not that I have come to abolish the law and the prophets; I have come not to abolish them but to fulfil them. Matt. 5:17, RSV.

For nearly three months we have been walking with Jesus on the Mount of Blessing. During our walk we have explored a Christian's character in the Beatitudes of Matthew 5:3-12 and a Christian's influence in Matthew 5:13-16.

We have now come to the longest section of the Sermon on the Mount. Matthew 5:17-48 deals with a Christian's righteousness. In a sense, this is returning to a second look at Christian character, but this time Jesus deliberately treats it in the context of the Old Testament and the Jewish legal code.

Verses 17-20 can be thought of as kind of a general introduction to Jesus' views of a Christian's righteousness. Before He comes to the details, He first sets forth some basic principles. And the principles He sets forth in these four verses are some of the most important in the New Testament.

In essence, Jesus sets forth two general propositions in Matthew 5:17-20. The first is that everything He will teach is completely in harmony with the Old Testament. He will not contradict it in any way. His first proposition is found in verses 17 and 18.

Jesus' second major proposition in Matthew 5:17-20 is that while His teaching is in harmony with the Old Testament, it is quite out of harmony with much of the teachings of the scribes and Pharisees, which were widely accepted by the populace of the day. That second point is found in verses 19 and 20.

The rest of Matthew 5 is a commentary or expansion of verses 17-20. Point by point, across six illustrative topics in verses 21-48, Jesus tells us that He accepts the law of the Old Testament, but rejects the Pharisaic interpretation of it. In the process, Jesus helps us see deeper meanings in the law and its spiritual nature.

A person can never look at law the same way once he or she really understands what Jesus is teaching in the second half of Matthew 5. Buckle up; Jesus is ready to give us the grand tour in understanding the depth and essence of God's law.

THE LAW AND THE PROPHETS

And beginning with Moses and all the prophets, he interpreted to them in all the scriptures the things concerning himself. Luke 24:27, RSV.

When Jesus talks about the law and the prophets, He is talking about the Bible of His day—the Old Testament. The Law was the five books of Moses that run from Genesis to Deuteronomy. And the Prophets were the books of those later Bible writers who taught the law, interpreted it, and applied it to the nation of Israel.

Law is a central concept in the Bible from beginning to end. Thus it behooves us to spend a little time understanding the topic, especially since Jesus says it is important.

The law of Moses was, in actuality, made up of several kinds of laws. The first was the moral law of the 10 commandments, which God etched in stone for all time on Mount Sinai. The moral law sets forth the great principles that undergird every human action and relationship.

The second category of law found in the books of Moses is legislative law. We must never forget that Israel was not only God's church; it was a distinct nation. And like other nations it had to have civil laws.

The third category of law in the books of Moses is the ceremonial law. These laws deal with how God was going to handle the sin problem. They center on the sanctuary, blood sacrifices, and priestly ministry. The ceremonial law is of crucial importance because it foreshadows the significance of Jesus and the nature of His work.

There is a fourth category of law that we should note. But this one is not found in Moses. Rather, it is the oral law, or the interpretation of the Law of Moses by the scribes and Pharisees.

Of particular importance to the rest of Matthew 5 are the moral law and the scribal interpretation of it. Here was the area of conflict between Jesus and the Pharisaic party. It is important to be correct in our understanding of God's law—so important, in fact, that Jesus devotes one of His largest blocks of teaching to it.

JESUS UNDER CRITICISM

And behold, there was a man [on the Sabbath] with a withered hand. . . .
Then he said to the man, "Stretch out your hand." And the man stretched
it out, and it was restored, whole like the other. But the Pharisees went out
and took counsel against him, how to destroy him. Matt. 12:10-14, RSV.

Jesus stood for truth. That was the source of all His problems with
the Jewish leaders. He not only taught truth; He lived it.

The Jewish leaders found fault with Jesus on at least four counts.
First, He rebuked their false understandings of God and the law.
Some people have the idea that a Christian never disagrees with anyone,
that a Christian never criticizes another person's religion or beliefs.
Such an idea certainly doesn't come out of the Gospels. Jesus lovingly
but firmly confronted error wherever it was found. That brought Him
into conflict with the scribes and Pharisees over such issues as the law.

Second, Jesus taught grace, that God freely forgives people who
have rebelled against Him if they repent. The teaching of grace (giving
people what they don't deserve) upsets the Pharisees and legalists of
every generation.

Third, Jesus not only taught grace; He practiced it when He re-
demptively mixed with publicans, prostitutes, and sinners. There is a
"churchy" class of people in every age who look down their spiritual
noses at such mixing.

Fourth, Jesus didn't have the right sort of credentials to be a
"good" minister. He didn't have a Pharisaic education, nor had they
ordained Him.

As a result of all these things, Jesus was suspect from the beginning
among both the common people and the religious leaders. Was He
really orthodox? How could He believe the Old Testament and still
teach and act the way He did?

It was to answer all such questions that Jesus affirms at the very out-
set of His ministry that He firmly believes in the Old Testament and
that He has not rejected the law and the prophets.

Jesus' stance on these issues must be my stance. It is crucial for me
today to teach and live the truth as it is found in the Bible. Help me
today, Lord, to live the Jesus life, to think the Jesus thoughts.

"I Am Come"

In the beginning was the Word, and the Word was with God, and the Word was God. He was in the beginning with God; all things were made through him, and without him was not anything made that was made. In him was life. . . . And the Word became flesh and dwelt among us. John 1:1-14, RSV.

I bet you didn't even see those words!

Which words?

"I am come," in the verse we have been studying the past few days—Matthew 5:17.

Those words are rich in meaning and very important for an understanding of the rest of Matthew 5.

"I am come." Jesus made few statements of more importance.

He never just came. He came from somewhere. That somewhere was from the side of God the Father. He came down to earth from heaven. As John tells us in our reading for today, Jesus had been with God from the beginning. As Paul put it, Jesus "made himself of no reputation" in that He "took upon him the form of a servant, and was made in the likeness of men" (Phil. 2:7).

But the Incarnation was not the beginning for Jesus. Far from it. "In the beginning God created the heaven and the earth" (Gen. 1:1). As part of the Godhead, Jesus was Creator; He was God come to earth.

In the book of Exodus we find Jesus as the "I Am" who calls Moses to the burning bush (Ex. 3:14; John 8:58). And it was Jesus who proclaimed the law on Mount Sinai amid thunder and flame.

"I am come." Meaningful words. Rich words. Especially in the context of Matthew 5:17-48. It is the very Jesus who gave the law on Mount Sinai who will now explain the depths of its deeper meaning on the Mount of Blessing. What a privilege to hear His words. What a blessing to be able to read them so that we can live them.

"I am come." Those words tell us that when we are listening to Jesus we are listening to God. When we worship Jesus we are worshiping God.

Help me, Lord, to devote my life to You in thankfulness that You did come, not only to teach me, but to die in my place.

CHRIST, THE END OF THE LAW

For Christ is the end of the law. Rom. 10:4.

Jesus is the end of the law, but He is not the *end* of the law. After all, He plainly states in Matthew 5:17 that He did not come to abolish the law. But He did come to put an end to the wrong use of law among His followers.

That wrong use of law takes on several aspects. We would have discovered one of them had we quoted more of Romans 10:4 above. The passage reads that "Christ is the end of the law for righteousness to everyone who believes" (NASB). Down through Christian history people have tried to gain salvation through lawkeeping. Paul tells us that belief in Jesus puts an end to that way of thinking and acting.

But Jesus also put an end to other ways of thinking about law. In all sincerity the Jews had multiplied rules and restrictions. They wanted to protect God's law and make sure it was kept perfectly. To that end, they felt they had to define everything. Thus when the Bible said that one should not work on the Sabbath, they had to define work. One definition had to do with carrying a burden.

What was a burden? Scribal law concluded that carrying a burden was carrying "food equal in weight to a dried fig, . . . milk enough for one swallow, . . . ink enough to write two letters of the alphabet," and so on and on.

They spent hours arguing over such things as whether a tailor committed a sin if he went out with a needle stuck in his robe on the Sabbath, or whether a woman might wear a brooch or a false hairpiece on the holy day. They even argued over whether it was permissible on the Sabbath to wear false teeth.

The definitions were endless and covered every aspect of life seven days a week. These people were the original perfectionists. To them, keeping their interpretation of the law was the center of religious experience.

Jesus did not come to do away with the law, but He did come to put an end to all unhealthy approaches and attitudes toward law. Even the law becomes good news in the hands of Jesus.

THE LAW IS GOOD (SOMETIMES)

So the law is holy, and the commandment is holy and just and good. Rom. 7:12, RSV.

The law is good in itself, but it is not good for everybody in every circumstance. It certainly had its downside for the Jews of Christ's time.

How is that?

Perhaps the best way to look at the question is through examining Israel's history. God gave the law to Moses, who passed it on to the Israelites. But the Israelites in their early history didn't pay sufficient attention to God's injunctions to them in the law of Moses. They sacrificed in pagan style, took on the ways of the people of the surrounding cultures, and often just ignored God's counsel.

As a result, God sent prophet after prophet to warn them and to lead them back to faithfulness. But by and large, Israel paid little attention to the prophets.

The result was the Babylonian captivity, with its 70 years of exile.

After the return from captivity a significant core of Jewish religious and political leaders decided that they would not repeat their experience. They would keep the law and would not mix with pagan people and pagan ways.

The result? Israel managed to make the opposite mistake. Under the leadership of such groups as the Pharisees they made the law an end in itself and utilized it as a way to separate themselves from other people. They became fanatical lawkeepers. Religion became a ceaseless round of rites and ceremonies. Law became central to their life. In the process they failed to realize that the law was good only if its spiritual nature was at the center of lawkeeping.

But once again they needed to listen to the prophets. They needed to hear Micah, who wrote that God is not satisfied with mere outward compliance to the sacrificial system. If the law is kept in spirit, we will "do justice," "love kindness," and "walk humbly" with our God (Micah 6:8).

We need balance in our lives. We need to listen to both the law and the prophets. We need to keep the law in the spirit in which God meant it to be kept. Then it is good for everyone everywhere at all times.

FULFILLING THE LAW

I have kept my Father's commandments, and abide in his love. John 15:10.

Jesus' saying that He came not to destroy the law but to fulfill it (Matt. 5:17) has confused a lot of people. In spite of His plain words, they still read it to mean that He did away with God's law. But fulfill does not mean to do away with, but to fill full, to fill it up, to full-fill. Thus the word "fulfill" can be understood in at least three ways: (1) Jesus fully obeyed the requirements of the Old Testament law through His obedient life, (2) He fulfilled the predictive elements of the Old Testament, and (3) He brought out the full meaning of the Jewish Scriptures through His teachings.

There is a sense in which Jesus fulfilled the Old Testament in all three ways. We will examine each.

There is no question about the sinlessness of Jesus' life on earth. At the end of His life He could claim without fear of contradiction that He had kept His Father's commandments. There was no one who could bring a just accusation against Him.

Thus Jesus lived a life of perfect obedience. He obeyed the law down to its minutest detail. He lived it fully and obeyed it perfectly.

As a result, He could become our spotless, "without blemish" sacrifice on the hill called Calvary. He proved false the charge of Satan that no person could keep God's law, and His perfect life made Him our substitute in life as well as in death. In the books of heaven the record of His perfect life stands in place of ours if we have accepted Him by faith. We have a Saviour who lived and died for us.

Jesus not only lived a life of obedience to God's law; He also taught others to love God's law and to keep it. That will become increasingly evident in the rest of Matthew 5.

So there is a sense in which Jesus fulfilled God's law by living it fully, by keeping it perfectly, by helping us see the full meaning of the law by the life He lived and the teachings He provided.

MORE ON FULFILLING THE LAW

And he said unto them, These are the words which I spake unto you, while I was yet with you, that all things must be fulfilled, which were written in the law of Moses, and in the prophets, and in the psalms, concerning me. Luke 24:44.

The second sense in which Jesus fulfilled the law and the prophets is that He fulfilled the Old Testament prophecies concerning the coming Messiah. The Messianic predictions and their fulfillments in Jesus of Nazareth have built faith in Christians from the time of Jesus Himself. Let us look at a few of the Old Testament prophecies that Jesus fulfilled.

Micah tells us the place of His birth: "But thou, Bethlehem Ephratah, though thou be little among the thousands of Judah, yet out of thee shall He come forth unto me that is to be ruler in Israel" (5:2; cf. Matt. 2:6). And numerous Old Testament passages tell us that the Messiah would be from the tribe of Judah through the seed of David. It is no accident that the Gospels often refer to Jesus as the Son of David.

Isaiah tells of the nature of Christ's ministry when he penned of the Messiah: "The Spirit of the Lord God is upon me; because the Lord hath anointed me to preach good tidings unto the meek; he hath sent me to bind up the brokenhearted, to proclaim liberty to the captives, and the opening of the prison to them that are bound" (61:1; cf. Luke 4:18).

The whole Old Testament sacrificial service pointed forward to Jesus as the "Lamb of God" (John 1:36) who would die for the sins of the world.

And Isaiah 53 tells us that Jesus would be "despised and rejected of men" (verse 3), would not fight back when brought as "a lamb to the slaughter" (verse 7), would die for the transgression of His people (verse 8), and would make "his grave with the wicked" (the thieves on the cross) and "with the rich in his death" (verse 9)—the tomb of Joseph of Arimathaea.

We could go on and on with this topic. Jesus fulfilled the Old Testament prophecies. We serve a God who knows the end from the beginning.

THE REAL FILLING UP OF THE LAW

All things that I have heard of my Father I have made known unto you. John 15:15.

While it is true that Jesus filled up or fulfilled the Old Testament by fulfilling its Messianic prophecies and by keeping the Old Testament law perfectly, those meanings are not at the heart of what Jesus is driving at in Matthew 5:17.

The primary meaning of any text is best determined not only by the words of the text, but also through examining its context. And what do we find when we examine the context of Matthew 5:17?

We find Jesus filling out (fulfilling) the *meaning* of the law. That is clear from the rest of Matthew 5. After providing some preliminary remarks in verses 17 through 20, Jesus focuses on several Jewish teachings—the sixth and seventh commandments of the Decalogue and the Jewish practices on divorce, oath taking, retaliation, and neighborly love.

Jesus prefaces each of these six teachings with "Ye have heard that it hath been said." He then goes on to give the contemporary understanding of the issue. Then He says, "But I say unto you . . ." At that point in each case Jesus goes on to explain the depth and breadth of the law or practice and its deeper meaning.

That is how Jesus is filling up or fulfilling the law. He is filling it up with meaning. As Ellen White puts it: "His mission was to 'magnify the law, and make it honorable.' Isaiah 42:21. He was to show the spiritual nature of the law, to present its far-reaching principles, and to make plain its eternal obligation" (*Thoughts From the Mount of Blessing*, p. 49).

In the process, as we shall see in the next few weeks, Jesus gave us some of His most precious teachings. And what He begins in the Sermon on the Mount, He continues throughout His ministry. Jesus shucks off misconceptions of God's teachings that had been added by human beings, and consistently drives at the depth of meaning and purpose undergirding God's rules and regulations. He helps us come to grips with the spirit of the law—the spirit of love, which makes law-keeping and obedience Christian.

Lord, help us today to listen to what the Master has to say.

THE PERMANENCE OF LAW

For verily I say unto you, Till heaven and earth pass, one jot or one tittle shall in no wise pass from the law, till all be fulfilled. Matt. 5:18.

Jesus couldn't have said it stronger. God's law can never be changed to the slightest extent. The demands are permanent.

Just as heaven and earth are signs of permanence in the sense that they are always there, so is God's law permanent. It is not something that He changes from time to time because He might feel the urge to do something different. No, its principles are built into the very fabric of the universe.

I like the way *The Message* renders the first part of our verse: "God's Law is more real and lasting than the stars in the sky and the ground at your feet. Long after stars burn out and earth wears out, God's Law will be alive and working."

Now, that is permanent!

But why this permanence? Doesn't God have a free will? Can't He choose to do what He wants?

Of course He can do as He pleases. But the questions miss the point. The way of God's basic law is the way of health and life. Contrary to the law is death, destruction, and disorder. Take the Ten Commandments, for example. You can't have a healthy society in which people are killing one another and in which no one can be trusted.

God's law can't be changed because it is an outward representation of His character. Its very principles are for our eternal good.

Thus not even the smallest part of God's law, not a "jot or a tittle" (the smallest letter and smallest point in the Hebrew alphabet), will be changed. It is for our good.

And while that is true for the Ten Commandments, it is also true of the entire Old Testament—the law and the prophets. The Old Testament still has validity for Christians.

Even the ceremonial law has meaning for us. Jesus may have filled up the sacrificial type, but the principles of the system are still being worked out in the great heavenly sanctuary.

We can be thankful that our God is a God of continuity and permanence.

THE TEN COMMANDMENTS AREN'T ETERNAL

Owe no man any thing, but to love one another: for he that loveth another hath fulfilled the law. . . . Love is the fulfilling of the law. Rom. 13:8-10.

Now, you may be thinking, *yesterday we noted that God's law is permanent. How then can you say that the Ten Commandments are not eternal?*

Think about it for a moment. Can you imagine God going around to the holy angels and saying, "Now, don't commit adultery with any of your neighbors." I'm not even sure if angels are capable physiologically of committing adultery.

Again, think of God instructing the angels to honor their fathers and mothers. Tell me: Do they have fathers and mothers?

The angels kept God's law without knowing it, because it was written in the very fabric of their hearts (compare Heb. 8:10; 2 Cor. 3:3). Angels didn't have to be told "Thou shalt not kill" or "Thou shalt not steal," because they were positively motivated from the heart to care for others.

As we know them, the Ten Commandments are not eternal. Take the fourth commandment, for example. It plainly states that the Sabbath was given as a memorial of the creation of earth. Even the seven-day cycle of 24 hours points to the creation of our planet and solar system as determinants of the Sabbath law found in the Decalogue.

The Sabbath law in the Decalogue does represent, however, a universal and eternal principle. Jesus brought out that principle when He was questioned on the great commandment. It is the principle of love to God and our fellow beings.

Because of sin God made His eternal law more explicit. He set forth the principle of His love in 10 illustrations or commands that represent crucial ways that we can love God and others. But undergirding them all is the principle of love, the very principle of His character (see 1 John 4:8).

God wants to write His eternal law of love on the very fabric of our hearts. When that is done, it will be natural for us to care about Him and others.

What wonderful places our homes and churches would be if we would let God write more.

WHAT LAW CAN'T DO

No human being will be justified in his sight by works of the law, since through the law comes knowledge of sin. Rom. 3:20, RSV.

There is one all-important thing that God's law can't do. It can't save us. Paul tells us that the function of the law is not justification but telling us where we have gone wrong. As he says in Romans 7:7: "If it had not been for the law, I should not have known sin" (RSV).

James 1:23-25 likens the law to a mirror. Before I go to work in the morning, I go to the mirror to discover what is right and wrong with my face and hair. The mirror tells me that not all is quite ready for public exposure, that there is egg on my face or that my hair is only half combed.

Now the function of the mirror is to point out things that need improvement. With that knowledge I can go to the soap, washcloth, and comb. It will not do to rub the mirror on my face to get the egg off or to run the mirror through my hair to comb it. The purpose of the mirror is to point out needed improvements.

So it is with God's law. When I compare myself with the law, I find that I have problems in my life. But the law cannot correct those problems. It has another function: to tell me I am a sinner. The law points out my problems and needs, but it does not solve them.

Paul is correct when he tells us that God's law is holy, just, and good (Rom. 7:12). But He is just as correct when he writes that "the law is good, *if* . . . one uses it lawfully" (1 Tim. 1:8, RSV).

The astounding truth is that the law can be used properly or improperly. One of the great temptations of human nature is to use God's law unlawfully.

The law is not a ladder to heaven. But it makes us aware of our need for such a ladder. The broken law tells us we are lost sinners. If the broken law was all we had, we would be most miserable. But the law points beyond itself to Jesus and the real solution to our problems.

THE LAW POINTS TO JESUS

The wages of sin is death; but the gift of God is eternal life through Jesus Christ our Lord. Rom. 6:23.

The message of the broken law is not nice. It tells us that we have rebelled against God, or sinned. As a result, we stand under the condemnation of the law. And that condemnation is severe indeed. It is nothing short of the death penalty. "The wages of sin is death."

Now, that is not good news. It is the worst of news.

But that's where the good news comes in. Because our text goes on to say that "the *gift* of God is eternal life through Jesus Christ."

The good news (gospel) is that "*God so loved the world [me], that he gave* his only begotten Son, that whosoever believeth in him should not perish, but have everlasting life" (John 3:16).

The good news of the gospel is the exact opposite of the bad news of the broken law. Salvation is a gift in Jesus. And it should be noted that the word for "gift" in Romans 6:23 has the same root as the word for "grace." Grace is God's gift to us in Jesus. We grab hold of that grace through faith in Jesus when we finally realize our own helplessness in the face of the condemning finger of the broken law.

Thus we might say that the law literally drives us to Jesus. Law and grace do not work in opposition to each other. They work with each other. The broken law tells me I am dirty and in need of cleansing. And that need points me to Jesus. "If we confess our sins, he is faithful and just to forgive us our sins, and to cleanse us from all unrighteousness" (1 John 1:9).

We can praise God today that He loves us so deeply that He made provision for our every need. We can praise God today that through grace He gives those who accept the sacrifice of Jesus the eternal life that they don't in themselves deserve, in place of the eternal death that they have earned as "wages."

THE BIBLE'S MOST DISGUSTING TEACHING

For the life of a creature is in the blood, and I have given it to you to make atonement for yourselves on the altar; it is the blood that makes atonement for one's life. Lev. 17:11, NIV.

It was 1:30 in the afternoon of April 12, 1995. I had just arrived home from church.

After a quick microwaved lunch, I went out to the garage to get Scottie, a vibrant little cockapoo. As usual, his compliant little body responded to my call. Trustingly he looked up at me, hoping, no doubt, that I had a dog biscuit behind my back.

Picking the dog up gently, I took him to the basement, since my strange work for the day was not something I wanted the neighbors to see. Safely secluded, I let the dog lie beside me as I set up my apparatus and knelt in prayer.

Then, placing my right hand on his head, I confessed my sins. Meanwhile, my left hand ran a well-honed knife across Scottie's unsuspecting and trusting throat. It was all over by 1:50.

The experience devastated me. I hadn't killed anything at all for years, let alone with my bare hands. As I knelt in a semistupor, I could feel the dying dog's arteries pulsating out the remaining blood—every pulsation thundering out the message that "the wages of sin is death, the wages of sin is death." Nauseated beyond description, I stumbled over to the washbasin, where I sought to cleanse my sticky hands from the reminder that innocent little Scottie had died for my sins.

Now, before you call the humane society, please realize that the above account is *entirely fictitious*. The story was told so that you could get a "feel" for the Old Testament's sacrificial system.

If the illustration disgusted you, I achieved my purpose—a purpose aimed at highlighting the costliness of sin and its ugly consequences in Christ's life. Remember, He died for my sins. He died in my place. He took the death penalty for me, that I might have His life. That is the mystery of the cross. The focal point of both testaments.

JESUS DIED FOR ME—OLD TESTAMENT

By faith Abel offered to God a more acceptable sacrifice than Cain, through which he received approval as righteous, God bearing witness by accepting his gifts; he died, but through his faith he is still speaking. Heb. 11:4, RSV.

I first read the Cain and Abel story when I was 19 years old. I was incensed at its conclusion. Coming into Christianity at that time through the Adventist gate, I reasoned that a sacrifice of vegetables had to be better than blood. I even thought that Cain's offering was superior to Abel's because it took more human effort (work) to raise fruit and vegetables than it did to sit on a rock while the sheep ate and multiplied their numbers.

That made it all the worse for me when God chose Abel's blood offering and "had no regard" for the good works of Cain. I found myself sympathizing with Cain and sharing his anger at such an injustice (Gen. 4:1-6). I had no idea concerning what God meant when He told Cain that if he did well, he would also be accepted.

That story is senseless outside of a knowledge of substitutionary sacrifice. It wasn't until later that I came across Hebrews 11:4, which tells us that Abel received "approval as righteous" because of his blood sacrifice. By that time also I was coming to grips with the truths that "without the shedding of blood there is no forgiveness of sins" (Heb. 9:22, RSV) and that Christ is "the Lamb of God, who takes away the sin of the world" (John 1:29, RSV).

In my maturer years I could see that Cain knew what I had not known when I first read the Bible. And whereas the substitutionary death of the Saviour is implicit in Abel's sacrifice, it is presented in greater depth and breadth in the sacrificial system set forth by Moses. That system is the primary object lesson of the plan of salvation in the Old Testament.

Substitutionary sacrifice stands at the foundation of all the symbols of salvation from the very beginning of post-Fall scriptural history. But it is only in the death of Jesus that we see the full meaning of the symbols. He literally *filled full* the meaning of the laws of sacrifice.

JESUS DIED FOR ME—NEW TESTAMENT

And he took a cup, and when he had given thanks he gave it to them, saying, "Drink of it, all of you; for this is my blood of the covenant, which is poured out for many for the forgiveness of sins." Matt. 26:27, 28, RSV.

Jesus not only fills out the law and the prophets in the Old Testament. He does the same in the New by dying for each of us on the cross of Calvary. He not only died in place of me, thus absorbing the penalty of the law, but He filled out (fulfilled) the meaning of the ceremonial law of sacrifices.

Sacrifice stands at the very center of the language used by New Testament writers to describe the significance of Christ's death and the meaning of the gospel. The language and imagery of the Jewish system permeates New Testament discussion. Thus John the Baptist calls Jesus "the Lamb of God, who takes away the sin of the world" (John 1:29, RSV); Paul refers to Christ as "our paschal [passover] lamb, [who] has been sacrificed" (1 Cor. 5:7, RSV); and Peter claims that his readers were not ransomed "with perishable things such as silver or gold, but with the precious blood of Christ, like that of a lamb without blemish or spot" (1 Peter 1:18, 19, RSV).

But it is the book of Hebrews, with its extended comparison of Jesus' work with the Jewish sacrificial system, that most clearly sets forth Christ's death as a sacrifice for human sin. "Without the shedding of blood," claims Hebrews, "there is no forgiveness of sins. Thus it was necessary for the copies of the heavenly things to be purified with these rites [the Jewish sacrificial system], but the heavenly things themselves with better sacrifices than these" (9:22, 23, RSV). Jesus "appeared once for all at the end of the age to put away sin by the sacrifice of himself" (verse 26). While "it is impossible that the blood of bulls and goats should take away sins," "Christ . . . offered for all time a single sacrifice for sins" (10:4, 12, RSV).

Over and over we have seen that Jesus fulfilled the law, not only in His life and teaching, but in His death.

I have a Saviour who died in my place.

MORE ON JESUS FULFILLING THE LAW

But if we walk in the light, as he is in the light, we have fellowship one with another, and the blood of Jesus Christ his Son cleanseth us from all sin. 1 John 1:7.

Christ filling out the law and the prophets is one of the most comprehensive ideas in the New Testament. And at the very center of the New Testament and Christian faith is the cross of Christ. Have you ever thought about the shape of the Gospels compared with other biographies? The Gospels are "abnormal" biographies in the sense that they give a disproportionate amount of space to the story of Christ's last few days on earth, His death, and His resurrection.

The Gospels are different from most biographies of great people. A "normal" biography might have several hundred pages on the life and contributions of its subject, but only five to 10 pages on the subject's death. That is because the biographer is primarily concerned with the subject's life.

The Gospels may be unique in the history of world literature in this regard. Their focal point is the death of their hero. John gives nearly half his Gospel over to the topic. Stranger yet, the Gospels' hero did not die a hero's death; His was (to outward appearance) a godforsaken death (Mark 15:34), because, as we learn from the New Testament authors, He was bearing the sins of the world and dying for the sins of all humanity.

That is why the blood of Jesus is so important to the New Testament authors and to us. Every New Testament image of salvation is based upon the shed blood of Christ. Thus we read that "God put forward [Christ] as an expiation by his blood" (Rom. 3:25, RSV), "in him we have redemption through his blood" (Eph. 1:7, RSV), "we are now justified by his blood" (Rom. 5:9, RSV), and God acted "to reconcile to himself all things, . . . making peace by the blood of his cross" (Col. 1:20, RSV).

Thank You, Jesus, for filling out the law in Your life and death. Thank You for absorbing the penalty of death for me that I might have resurrection life in You. Thank You for being the Lamb of God.

THE JUSTICE OF GOD
AND THE CROSS OF CHRIST

"Worthy art thou to take the scroll and to open its seals, for thou wast slain and by thy blood didst ransom men for God from every tribe and tongue and people and nation. . . . Worthy is the Lamb who was slain, to receive power and wealth and wisdom and might and honor and glory and blessing!" Rev. 5:9-12, RSV.

Have you ever noticed that the songs of Revelation are deeply concerned with God's worthiness and justice? Let's look at them. The first round of these worshipful doxologies is found in Revelation 5. In that round the worthiness of Jesus is based on the fact that He died on Calvary for humanity.

The second major round is found at the time when the seven last plagues are poured out. At least three times God's justice and truthfulness are praised. "Just art thou in these thy judgments," the angel proclaims at the pouring out of the third plague. The altar responds with the cry: "Yea, Lord God the Almighty, true and just are thy judgments" (Rev. 16:5, 7, RSV; see also Rev. 15:3, 4).

The third scene takes place at the Second Coming. Chapter 19 opens with "a great multitude in heaven, crying, 'Hallelujah! Salvation and glory and power belong to our God, for his judgments are true and just'" (verses 1, 2, RSV). Later in the chapter, Christ, portrayed as coming on His white horse, "is called Faithful and True, and in righteousness he judges and makes war" (verse 11, RSV).

Why this concern with God's justice? The answer lies in a core issue of the plan of salvation. If the law condemns to death all who have broken it, and all have broken it, how can God save some sinners but not others? And isn't grace (giving some people forgiveness in spite of their sinful lives) about as unfair as one can get?

That is where the cross comes in. Because Jesus died for me and I have accepted that sacrifice by faith, God is free to forgive me. He has maintained His justice in that He upheld the law and its penalty, but He is also able to show mercy to all those who desire it because of the Lamb's sacrifice. The cross stands at the very center of our faith.

FULFILLING THE LAW IN HEAVEN

Now of the things which we have spoken this is the sum: We have such an high priest, who is set on the right hand of the throne of the Majesty in the heavens; a minister of the sanctuary, and of the true tabernacle, which the Lord pitched, and not man. Heb. 8:1, 2.

Jesus not only fulfilled or filled up the law in His perfect life, His teaching ministry, and His death on Calvary, but He also is continuing to do so as He ministers for us in the heavenly sanctuary. Just as the earthly priests offered the blood of goats and rams for the sins of the people, so our great High Priest offers His own blood to cover the sins of His people.

Christ offered Himself "once for all" (Heb. 10:10). But He is not only the offering typified in the sanctuary service, He is also the priest. As Hebrews puts it, "Christ is not entered into the holy places made with hands [the earthly sanctuary], which are the figures of the true [the heavenly sanctuary]; but into heaven itself, now to appear in the presence of God for us" (Heb. 9:24).

Christ is our heavenly Priest, our Advocate. And His is a ministry that will be the most successful of all time. Along this line, the author of Hebrews penned that "he is able also to save them to the uttermost that come unto God by him, seeing he ever liveth to make intercession for them" (Heb. 7:25).

And perhaps the most wonderful thing about Christ's ministry for us in the throne room of God is that we can have, as Hebrews puts it, "full assurance" (6:11; 10:22) in His success as our defense counselor against the accusations of Satan.

We can learn a great deal about the work of Jesus by studying the Old Testament sanctuary system. It is unfortunate that too often we have focused on the physical aspects of the tabernacle. It is the ministry of Jesus in both the forgiveness of sins and the vindication of His followers in the final judgment that is at the center of the system. The service is more than bricks and boards; it is an object lesson of the surety of our salvation.

THE OLD TESTAMENT LAWS TODAY

It is easier for heaven and earth to pass, than one tittle of the law to fail.
Luke 16:17.

That doesn't mean that the Law has lost its force in even the smallest point.
It is as strong and unshakable as heaven and earth. Luke 16:17, TLB.

Well, what about the law? How am I as a Christian to relate to the multitude of laws in the books of Moses?

Let's take a look at those types of law one by one.

The first branch of Moses' law is the legislative law governing the nation of Israel. But Israel is no longer a theocratic nation with God at the head. Jesus pointed out near the end of His ministry that a change would come when He said, "Therefore I say unto you, The kingdom of God shall be taken from you, and given to a nation bringing forth the fruits thereof" (Matt. 21:43). That new nation is the Christian church. Because there is no longer a theocratic nation of Israel, the legislative laws of Moses have been fulfilled.

Second, we noted that the ceremonial law pictures in types the life, death, and heavenly ministry of Jesus. Part of that has been fulfilled and part is still being filled up. A Christian by New Testament definition is one who accepts Jesus as his or her burnt offering, sacrifice, and priest. Thus the ceremonial law still applies for each of us, not in the sense that we continue to make blood sacrifices, but in that we daily apply the sacrifice of Christ to our lives and daily utilize the ministry of Jesus in the sanctuary above.

Third, the moral law reflected in Jesus' great commandments of love and expounded upon in the Ten Commandments is still providing the moral order of the universe. By its very nature God's moral law is unalterable. It is to be written in our hearts so that it will inform every one of our thoughts and actions. Because of the importance of the moral law, Jesus will turn to a major exposition of the Christian's relation to it in Matthew 5:20-48.

TAKING GOD SERIOUSLY

Whosoever therefore shall break one of these least commandments, and shall teach men so, he shall be called the least in the kingdom of heaven: but whosoever shall do and teach them, the same shall be called great in the kingdom of heaven. Matt. 5:19.

Because we believe in grace and forgiveness and love, it is all too easy to think that God is so easygoing that it doesn't matter how we live or what we do. That is not so.

Above all things, God wants our happiness, both now and eternally. And because He wants us to be happy, He takes our needs seriously. We are important to Him.

As a result of that importance, God is doing all He can to guide His people through life. In the process He sets forth principles of life so that we can be healthier in our spiritual, physical, social, and mental aspects.

He gave many such principles to His ancient people in the Old Testament. He gave additional insight into the happy and healthy life in the New Testament, and He has continued to guide His people in modern times through the gifts of His Spirit.

He desires us to take His counsels in the utmost seriousness, even those that may seem "least" or unimportant to us. It will not do for us to explain away this or that instruction in the Bible because it doesn't fit into our agenda.

We are not only to practice God's principles in our daily lives; we are also to teach them to others. That teaching includes our responsibility as parents and family members, our opportunities in the church, and our opportunities in the community and workplace.

We are representatives of the King of the universe. And He wants us to take Him just as seriously as He has taken us and our needs and problems.

Thus as Christians we will be faithful in both the "least" and the great things in God's book. And we will live all of it in the sweet spirit of Jesus. Help us, Father, is our prayer.

PHARISEES ARE GOOD PEOPLE

For I say unto you, That except your righteousness shall exceed the righteousness of the scribes and Pharisees, ye shall in no case enter into the kingdom of heaven. Matt. 5:20.

This is one of the most astounding sayings in Jesus' entire repertoire of ideas. It must have all but knocked His disciples and other hearers off their feet.

How could anyone have more righteousness than the scribes and Pharisees? Such a thought loomed as the largest of impossibilities in the minds of first-century Jews.

The scribes were a class that spent all their time in teaching and expounding God's law. Their entire life was given over to studying God's Word. Talk about dedication—the scribes had a superabundance of it.

In the time of Jesus, the Pharisees were a select class of some 6,000 men. Their lives were totally dedicated to bringing about the coming of the Messiah (the Greek equivalent for Messiah is translated as "Christ") through living perfect lives.

Most Christians need to revise their picture of the Pharisees. They were not merely good men; they were the best of men. Not only were they morally upright; they were desperately in earnest in their search for God and in their veneration and protection of His holy name, law, and Word. Certainly the church and the world would be infinitely better if more of us daily came to God with the central Pharisaic question: "What shall I do to inherit eternal life?" (Luke 10:25; Matt. 19:16, RSV). Here was a people totally dedicated to serving God from the time they arose in the morning to the time they retired at night.

We miss the New Testament picture if we fail to see the goodness of the scribes and the Pharisees.

What the church could do if each of us were as dedicated as they were! But that does not mean that they had everything straight, even though it does suggest a devotion and dedication to God second to none.

Help me, Lord, to learn a positive lesson of dedication from the scribes and Pharisees. Help me to take Your Word seriously.

MORE ON PHARISAIC GOODNESS

"Do not murder, do not commit adultery, do not steal, do not give false testimony, honor your father and mother," and "love your neighbor as yourself."
"All these I have kept," the young man said. "What do I still lack?" Matt. 19:18-20, NIV.

Jesus did not contradict this young Pharisee, who had claimed to keep the commandments from his youth up. Nor did He take issue with the praying Pharisee in Luke 18, who thanked God in prayer that he was "not like other men, extortioners, unjust, adulterers" (verse 11, RSV).

There is a lesson in examining the "good" side of this dedicated group. Let us note their praiseworthy qualities.

First and foremost, they were lovers and protectors of the Bible as the Word of God. Their oral tradition had been established to preserve the true meaning of Scripture.

Second, Pharisees were completely dedicated to God's law. They loved the law with all their heart. R. Travers Herford sums up this aspect of Pharisaism concisely when he states that "the primary concern of the Pharisees was to make the Torah (law) the supreme guide of life, in thought, word, and deed, by study of its contents, obedience to its precepts, and, as the root of all, conscious service of God who had given the Torah."

Their dedication to keeping God's law inspired them to develop thousands of guidelines so that they wouldn't even come close to the appearance of evil. Thus they had some 1,521 oral rules on how to keep the Sabbath. These laws touched every aspect of their lives.

Beyond these qualities, the Pharisees were filled with missionary and evangelistic zeal and they were good "adventists." That is, they awaited the coming of the Messiah with anticipation. Many of them believed that the Messiah (Christ) would come if the Torah (the law) were kept perfectly for one day.

Pharisees are like some of us church members. They believe all the right things and desire to do good.

But here is the tragedy: they fell short of the kingdom. We need to take stock of ourselves that we don't end up like the Pharisees. You see, somehow they weren't good enough.

GOOD BUT NOT GOOD ENOUGH

Woe to you, scribes and Pharisees, hypocrites! for you cleanse the outside of the cup and of the plate, but inside they are full of extortion and rapacity. You blind Pharisee! first cleanse the inside of the cup and of the plate, that the outside also may be clean. Matt. 23:25, 26, RSV.

Pharisees were good people, but they weren't good enough. No one can read the Gospels in even a cursory way without realizing that there was nothing that called forth the wrath of Jesus more than the religion of the scribes and Pharisees.

Why? Why didn't Jesus thunder at the prostitutes and tax collectors? Why didn't He spend more time condemning the worldly priestly class (the Sadducees) or the careless common people? Why the Pharisees, who were to all outward appearances the best of men?

That last point is the problem. Their religion looked good on the outside. They were the shiny people who wore the right kinds of clothes, lived in the better type of neighborhoods, and did the right kinds of things.

Today's churches, including those churches called Adventist, would stampede to get these people onto their membership rolls. Undoubtedly many of them would even become lay or clerical leaders. Their talents would be put to good use.

Yet they had a lack. Their religion was one of show and appearance, but it didn't come from the heart.

Jesus is clear on that point. Unless religion softens the heart and transforms the life from the inside out, it is worthless.

Jesus saved His most "violent" words for these "good" church members because they were hypocrites unconsciously. They did all the right things, but it was their very outward goodness that was their narcotic. Their goodness lulled them into a self-complacent sleep, it left them immune to any sense of their real spiritual shortcomings and needs.

They needed to be awakened to the fact that mere outward goodness is not goodness at all. They needed to see the depth of Christianity.

So do I! Lord, give me eyes to see my true condition and ears to hear Your counsel.

THE WRONG KIND OF RELIGION
MAY BE WORSE THAN NONE AT ALL

Woe to you, Pharisees, and you other religious leaders. Hypocrites! For you won't let others enter the Kingdom of Heaven, and won't go in yourselves. Matt. 23:13, TLB.

The young lady was a sincere seeker after God. And she had found the Seventh-day Adventist Church. How happy she was. How sincere she was. How transparent she was.

She found some things about Adventism to be a bit different from what she had known before, but she had a desperate desire to fit in, to please the established members, and to do God's will.

She had attended about a month when a potluck was announced for the next week. She was overjoyed.

Having picked up somewhere that Adventist potlucks were vegetarian, she went all out to do her best at vegetarian cooking. She was excited to be a part of God's people.

But the meal was a disaster. One of the church matrons noted that the young lady's offering wasn't quite good enough. It contained cheese, and this "good saint" was beyond that sort of thing. She let her feelings on the topic be known.

The result? Our young friend was crushed. In bewilderment she went elsewhere for spiritual nurture.

Variations of that story show up again and again. Stories of harsh deacons, of remarks being made about jewelry or dress, and of the treatment of young people who are a bit different abound in Adventism.

The result: Multitudes have gone elsewhere. And from reading the New Testament, I believe that Jesus would have gone with them.

Ellen White hits this gospel nail on the head when she writes that "a legal religion is insufficient to bring the soul into harmony with God. The hard, rigid orthodoxy of the Pharisee, destitute of contrition, tenderness, or love, was only a stumbling block to sinners" *(Thoughts From the Mount of Blessing,* p. 53).

New Testament religion leads men and women to God through exhibiting the character of Jesus. Jesus was much more accepting than many of us. That very acceptance, of course, offended the scribes and Pharisees, just as it would offend some Adventists.

WHOSE KIND OF RIGHTEOUSNESS?

What doth it profit, my brethren, though a man say he hath faith, and have not works? can faith save him? . . . Faith, if it hath not works, is dead, being alone. James 2:14-17.

One of the key words in Matthew 5:20 is "righteousness." "Except your righteousness shall exceed the righteousness of the scribes and Pharisees, ye shall in no case enter into the kingdom of heaven."

Note that Jesus does not focus here on His own righteousness imputed to us. No, it is "*your* righteousness."

Jesus doesn't beat around the bush when He talks about Christianity affecting our daily lives. He is not talking about saving righteousness based on saving faith. Attention in Matthew 5:20 is focused entirely on human obedience to God's will.

That fact becomes transparently evident when Jesus begins to illustrate His point in verses 21 through 48. Over and over He will tell His hearers exactly how their righteousness must exceed that of the scribes and Pharisees. Each of His six illustrations had to do with things we as Christians do in our daily lives. And Jesus ends up this important passage by saying that we must be as perfect as God in heaven is perfect (verse 48). That is how far our righteousness must exceed that of the scribes and Pharisees.

That is powerful, especially when we realize that Jesus is talking about *our* righteousness rather than His own righteousness imputed to us.

In that way Matthew is similar to James. For both of them, faith produces good works. For both, faith produces a religious life lived in the community that does good for one's fellow men and women. For both of them, faith in God leads to exemplifying the character of God in daily life. For both Matthew and James, worshiping God leads to life-changing results. It leads to *our* righteousness. And that righteousness must exceed that of some of the most zealous religious zealots in history—the Pharisees.

It behooves us to pay very close attention to what Jesus will be telling us about righteousness in the rest of Matthew 5. He has words that the church desperately needs to hear.

DON'T TRY TO BAPTIZE MATTHEW INTO PAUL

If, in fact, Abraham was justified by works, he had something to boast about—but not before God. What does the Scripture say? "Abraham believed God, and it was credited to him as righteousness." Rom. 4:2, 3, NIV.

Many have been troubled regarding Matthew's teaching on righteousness. As a result, in order to escape the seeming works-righteousness of Matthew, they have suggested that Jesus is not here talking about "our" righteousness, but the righteousness of Jesus imputed to us.

Watch out here. Let Matthew's Jesus speak for Himself. He is not talking about Christ's righteousness. He is emphasizing "your righteousness." F. D. Bruner is correct when he notes that even though the intention of those who want to see Christ's righteousness rather than our righteousness as the correct understanding of Matthew 5:20 is praiseworthy, their position is found wanting in exegesis. It doesn't fit the context.

Let Matthew speak for himself, cautions Bruner. Don't be too eager to baptize him into Paul.

You see, Matthew has his own way of teaching the gospel. It is different from Paul's but not less biblical.

Matthew's view of righteousness as expressed in 5:17-48 and in the Beatitudes will eventually drive us to the Father for forgiveness (see Matt. 6:12) and grace (see Matt. 19:16-20:16). Matthew is not short in the Gospel of free grace, but here in 5:20 he is presenting the need for "our" righteousness. He is speaking to our relationship to God's law, our keeping of it in spirit as well as letter.

And Paul comes to the same conclusions, but in a different order. In the early chapters of Romans, for example, Paul tells us of hope in Christ's righteousness. But by Romans 6 through 8 he is into God's sanctifying work in our lives, and by chapters 13 and 14 Paul is also talking about our righteous keeping of the law of love.

Matthew and Paul have one gospel, not two. But as Bruner notes, "Paul, more comprehensively than Matthew, shows us the source of divine righteousness. On the other hand, Matthew, more clearly than Paul, shows us the goal of Christian righteousness."

TRUE HOLINESS

Go and learn what this means, "I desire mercy, and not sacrifice." For I came not to call the righteous, but sinners. Matt. 9:13, RSV.

Jesus leaves us in absolutely no doubt in the Sermon on the Mount. He is interested in our righteousness, concerned with our holiness of life.

And what does that righteousness and holiness consist of? Certainly not the outward formalism of the scribes and Pharisees. That type of religious living is consistently condemned by our Lord. Christian righteousness is much more than tithe paying or Sabbathkeeping.

It reaches down to the heart of the human problem. Jesus in Matthew's Gospel (and in the rest of the New Testament) is seeking to move us beyond religious rituals to real religion, a heartfelt religion that leads us to care for other people as God cares for us.

Let's let Jesus speak on true righteousness in Matthew. It is being merciful and peacemakers in the Beatitudes (5:1-9); it is caring for society's outcasts, such as lepers and nonbelievers in Matthew 8:1-17; it is His repeated admonition to mercy in such passages as Matthew 9:13 and 12:7; it is His summons to love in Matthew 5:43-48 and 22:34-40; it is to become as little ones in Matthew 18:1-5 and 19:14; it is the call to humility in Matthew 5:5 and 23:8-12; and it is the invitation to suffering in Matthew 10:16-39 and 16:24-28.

Holiness is all of those things and much more. It is giving a cup of cold water to the thirsty, it is feeding the hungry, it is loving God with all our heart and mind.

"Your righteousness" or holiness in the mind of Jesus is all-encompassing. It touches every aspect of our life. It is an attitude, it is a way of living, it is a way of being. When Jesus said that our righteousness needs to exceed that of the scribes and the Pharisees, He touched every part of our lives—both inward and outward.

Lord, as we realize more fully what it means to be a Christian, we ask for Your empowering grace in our lives; we ask for sensitivity both to Your will and to the needs of others.

OK, JESUS, WHAT ARE YOU DRIVING AT?

Be not conformed to this world: but be ye transformed by the renewing of your mind, that ye may prove what is that good, and acceptable, and perfect will of God. Rom. 12:2.

Matthew 5 in its first 20 verses has taken us through some pretty heavy seas. First we saw what our character *must* be in the Beatitudes. Now He is telling us that our righteousness must exceed that of the scribes and Pharisees.

What is He driving at? It is really quite simple to explain. He wants us to be the exact opposite of what we are naturally. In the words of John, it can be described as being born again (John 3:5, 7). In the words of Paul in 2 Corinthians 5:17 it is being a new creature. But of all these descriptions I find the one in Romans 12:2 (today's reading) to be the most picturesque.

Paul tells us that we must be "transformed." That word "transformed" is an interesting one. It comes from the Greek word *metamorphoō*. That is the same word from which biologists derive the English word "metamorphosis."

And what is metamorphosis? Webster tells us that it is "a marked or complete change of character, appearance, condition, etc."

Metamorphosis is what happens to a sluglike caterpillar when it becomes a butterfly. To me, that is one of the most graphic illustrations of what happens to a person when he or she meets Jesus.

God finds us in our self-centered, proud, and self-serving ways, and takes us and transforms us. Now, that is a miracle! Perhaps it's the greatest of all miracles.

God wants to take a slug like me and teach me to fly. God wants to take drab crawlers and paint them in beautiful hues and give them wings.

And the good thing is that He can do it. Praise God, He wants to transform me. He wants to make my righteousness exceed even that of the scribes and the Pharisees. He wants to make me into something I am not. He wants to make me into a new creature after the image of Jesus.

EXCEEDING THE EXCEEDINGLY

Sanctify yourselves, therefore, and be ye holy: for I am the Lord your God. And ye shall keep my statutes, and do them: I am the Lord which sanctify you. Lev. 20:7, 8.

If righteousness is one of the key words in Matthew 5:20, a second is "exceed." "Except your righteousness shall exceed the righteousness of the scribes and Pharisees, ye shall in no case enter into the kingdom of heaven," said Jesus.

In this passage Jesus definitely puts His followers on notice that Christianity is not easy. The one aim of the scribes and Pharisees was to satisfy the demands of the law. They sought to be holy, but failed to sense the depth of holiness. They failed to see that true holiness is not merely an outward round of religious obligations, but an inward motive of love to God and other people that constantly finds expression in the life.

To be holy is to live the sanctified life. The word "sanctify" means "to dedicate," "to consecrate," or "to set apart." Thus Moses was told to "sanctify" ("consecrate," RSV) the entire people of Israel to the Lord (Ex. 19:10). Not only were the Israelites sanctified or set apart for holy use, but so were the tabernacle and the instruments used in the sanctuary service (Ex. 30:25-29; 40:9-11; Lev. 8:10-13).

The New Testament word translated as "sanctify" means "to make holy." Thus a saint (one who has been sanctified) is a person who has been set apart for holy use by God.

The New Testament often speaks of sanctification as an accomplished fact. As a result, Paul can write of the Corinthians as "those sanctified in Christ Jesus, called to be saints" (1 Cor. 1:2, RSV).

Being a true Christian means to allow our self to be set aside for holy use. It means living a life for God. It means living the life of God as portrayed by Jesus.

When Jesus used the word "exceed" in the Sermon on the Mount, He spoke in great seriousness. As we will soon see in verses 21-48 of Matthew 5, His view of spirituality is much deeper and broader than that of the Jews. Through the power of His Spirit He wants us to exceed exceedingly.

OUR RIGHTEOUSNESS: A SAVING MATTER

"Let us rejoice and exult and give him the glory, for the marriage of the Lamb has come, and his Bride has made herself ready; it was granted her to be clothed with fine linen, bright and pure"—for the fine linen is the righteous deeds of the saints. Rev. 19:7, 8, RSV.

Some people don't like this type of talk. If so, they don't like the type of talk Jesus used. In Matthew 5:20 He flatly stated that unless a person's righteousness exceeded that of the scribes and Pharisees they would not enter the kingdom of heaven.

Frederick D. Bruner, a Presbyterian theologian, nicely sums up for us Jesus' intent: "We have seen that between verses 17 and 20 the command has moved gradually from the theoretical to the practical. Now finally Jesus leaves us with this supreme warning: If Scripture does not make us righteous, righteous beyond the righteousness of the most serious people in the community of the old people of God—the Bible teachers and the members of the separatist *Pharisaism*—we won't get in the kingdom. The purpose of Scripture, finally, is not so much a right doctrine of it as it is a personal obedience to it. The goal of Scripture is the piety of obedience. The point of the dotted *i*'s and the crossed *t*'s is the behavior of those who read them. The final verse in Jesus' doctrine of Scripture [Matt. 5:20] is completely moral and even salvific. Jesus warns us that if Scripture does not reach its end *in* us—righteousness—it will be the end *of* us. Life or death depends on our response to this Book."

With Matthew 5:20 Jesus has set the stage for what is to follow. In verses 17 through 20 He has not only told us that His teaching is in no way inconsistent with that of the law and the prophets (the Old Testament), but He has also indicated that it is quite different from the teaching of the scribes and Pharisees.

We are now ready to examine both those continuities and those differences as Jesus the lawgiver gives us a personal tour and exposition of the depth and breadth of the meaning of the law.

"I Say"

Ye have heard that it was said by them of old time, Thou shalt not kill; and whosoever shall kill shall be in danger of the judgment: But I say unto you, That whosoever is angry with his brother without a cause shall be in danger of the judgment: and whosoever shall say to his brother, Raca, shall be in danger of the council: but whosoever shall say, Thou fool, shall be in danger of hell fire. Matt. 5:21, 22.

With Matthew 5:21 we have come to the first of six illustrations on how our righteousness must exceed that of the scribes and Pharisees.

Common to each of these illustrations are the words "you have heard it said" and "I say unto you." Those who had done the initial saying were such Jewish leaders as the scribes and Pharisees, who had taken God's Old Testament law and created oral tradition to protect that law and to apply it to the life of the people. Those Jewish leaders were generally sincere in their attempts to make the law meaningful. But their sincerity did not protect them from error.

That is why Jesus comes in with His "but *I say*." Those words are of crucial importance in understanding both Matthew 5:21-48 and the entire Sermon on the Mount.

Note that Jesus does not hesitate to set Himself up as an authority. He is not acting like an ordinary rabbi who would start out "There is a teaching that . . ." or "Rabbi so and so has said that . . ." Jesus was not basing His teaching upon the authority of others. No, He *was the* authority on the law.

Jesus approaches the law not as a mere teacher, but as the lawgiver, the One who knows the height and depth of the law because He is the God who gave the law in the first place.

Jesus Christ was not a mere man, a mere expounder of the law, or just another prophet. He was infinitely more than that, and He is not bashful in claiming His unique authority as Lord of the law. After all, He is God the Son. Though He came in the likeness of sinful flesh, He still speaks with divine authority. Thus His every word is of crucial importance to us.

TWO VIEWS OF THE LAW

Who . . . hath made us able ministers of the new testament; not of the letter, but of the spirit: for the letter killeth, but the spirit giveth life. 2 Cor. 3:6.

The Pharisees were excellent on the letter of the law, but poor in its spirit. They were perfectionists at heart, and all perfectionists need a list of do's and don'ts. Perfectionists need to make the law manageable if they are going to keep it perfectly.

Thus the Pharisees of old, like the pharisees of our day, need to be careful how they define sin. For them sin was an action.

Thus they restricted the biblical prohibitions of such things as murder and adultery to the act alone. A person was not a sinner until he or she had actually committed murder.

Not only did the Pharisaic party restrict the meaning of the commandments to make perfection possible, but they also extended the permissions of the law so that, for example, a man might divorce his wife for the most trivial reason without being considered a lawbreaker.

Jesus reversed the Jewish tendency to restrict the meaning of the law and to extend its permissions. He refused to play their game. He moved beyond the outward letter of the law to its inward spiritual intent. Thus He pointed out that the root problem is not the act but the thought behind the act. As a result, even to lust after another person is sin; even to be angry with another person is wrong.

In this way Jesus shattered the easy perfectionism of the Pharisees. After all, while good religious people may not have committed the very act of murder or adultery, there are none that have never had a wayward thought of anger or desire.

And Jesus not only filled up the spiritual depth of the meaning of the law; He also removed the legalistic permissions that the Pharisees had erected to protect their self-images.

This day Jesus is pointing us to the true meaning of His law. He wants us to live by the spirit of the law and not merely its letter.

THE SECOND TABLE

The whole law is fulfilled in one word, "You shall love your neighbor as yourself." Gal. 5:14, RSV.

One thing that should be noted about Jesus' six illustrations of the true meaning of God's law in Matthew 5:21-48 is that all of them come from the second table of the law. That is, all of them have to do with our love toward other people. Not one of the six focuses primarily on our love to God as set forth in the first table of the law.

Why, we might ask, is that so? Why spend so much time illustrating the second table without expounding on the first?

The answer seems to be that Jesus considered the law to be a unity in the sense that it is impossible to love God without loving one's neighbor. Please remember that in Genesis 3 when Adam and Eve rebelled against God they also started bickering with each other. Thus the entrance of sin meant disrupted relationships both between human beings and God, and between people. When we are not right with God, we are at odds with one another. That is so because when I put myself at the center of my life, I live by the principles of selfishness.

But conversion changes all that. When I get healed by God, the basic principle of my life changes. I am born again with a new heart and a new mind. I no longer live by the principles of selfishness, but by the principle of God's caring love.

That new principle leads me to care for you as a person. You are no longer an object or a thing to me. You are a person for whom Christ died, just like I.

It is impossible for me to be right with God without being right with other people. That is one of the great central truths of the Sermon on the Mount.

How I treat you (and how you treat me) is where the rubber meets the road. Human relationships are where we live out our Christianity in daily life. Human relationships are the acid test as to whether we have really become Christians. Jesus is emphasizing that point in Matthew 5:21-48.

MURDER'S SOURCE

Thou shalt not kill. Ex. 20:13.

I have to admit it. I have never killed anyone. And in all probability I won't murder anyone in my entire life.

That is a comforting thought. It is a thought that makes me feel good. It is a thought that makes me feel right about myself.

But it's better than that. Not only have I never murdered anyone, but no one has ever accused me of such an act.

I guess I am a pretty good guy, a person who at least has part of his act together.

But such self-righteous feelings are destroyed when I begin to read Jesus on the law. He tells me that I can't even be angry. I find that to be problematic. For, you see, I become angry from time to time. I don't like this new theology. I am more comfortable with my own definitions. They make me feel good.

But Jesus' purpose isn't to make me feel good. It is to help me see the nature of sin and my great need of His forgiving and empowering grace.

What did Jesus mean by saying that being angry with another person is included in the true meaning of the sixth commandment?

There are two words for anger in the Greek language. The first is *thumos*, that momentary anger that flares up like a flame in dried straw. It is anger that quickly blazes up and just as quickly dies down. This is not the anger that Jesus is talking about in Matthew 5:21.

Jesus uses the word *orgē*. *Orgē* is anger that is long-lived, it is the anger of the person who nurses his or her wrath against another person, it is an anger that a person cherishes and refuses to let die, it is the anger that seeks revenge.

Such anger, implies Jesus, is the same thing as murder. It is the root sentiment of heart and mind that leads to murder in action. But even if one doesn't carry out the act, a person with *orgē* anger is out of harmony with God and is under judgment.

Help me this day, Lord, to put away my destructive anger. Help me to love others as You have cared for me.

IS ANGER ALWAYS WRONG?

Be ye angry, and sin not: let not the sun go down upon your wrath. Eph. 4:26.

You may be wondering by this time if there is ever a time when a true Christian can get angry. After all, you may be thinking, didn't Jesus get angry with the scribes and Pharisees over in Matthew 23? And didn't He address them by the forbidden term *fools* in verses 17 and 19 of that same chapter? And doesn't God destroy people at the end of time?

You are right. God hates sin. Jesus hates sin. Their loving hearts are burdened as they see the happiness and lives of their earthly children destroyed. They are angry with sin and its results. Beyond that, They will eventually put an end to sin and those who choose to cling to destructive, unloving ways. Because of the Godhead's great love for each person, They are angry at those things that destroy people. God's anger is one of holy indignation.

Christ's followers not only may have but *should* have this same anger toward sin. As I write this page, the rubble of the bombing of the Alfred P. Murrah Federal Building in Oklahoma City is still being sifted for survivors. Who could be sick enough to perpetrate such a crime? I am angry that innocent children and other innocent people were destroyed. It also angers me that millions of people are needlessly starving around the world while other people have more than they can possibly consume. I am angry that young men and women are being led astray by drug dealers and others who prey on the lonely and weak. I am angry at meanness in the church by those who are pushing the letter of the law while transgressing its spirit.

As Christians we are to hate sin but love sinners. Unfortunately, we too often take just the opposite course. As a result, we generally feel anger at those who have slighted us or injured our sinful pride.

Jesus wants us to get it straight. We are to have the right kind of anger, His kind of anger, the kind of anger that hates sin but wants the best for sinners and refuses to harbor personal grudges.

PAUL DISCOVERS THE SPIRIT OF THE LAW

Is the law identical with sin? Of course not! Yet had it not been for the law I should never have become acquainted with sin. For example, I should never have known what it was to covet, if the law had not said, "You shall not covet." Through that commandment sin found its opportunity, and produced in me all kinds of wrong desires. . . . When the commandment came, sin sprang to life and I died. Rom. 7:7-9, REB.

Paul had been a proud man. He was a Pharisee of the Pharisees, one of the most zealous of their sect. If any of them could have kept the law perfectly, it would have been Paul.

And he had done pretty well. He worshiped God supremely, didn't bow down to idols or use God's name in vain, and he was zealous in keeping the multitude of Sabbath rules. Nor did he commit adultery, steal, or bear false witness. All in all, he concluded, he was a pretty nice guy. Paul had good reason for a certain spiritual smugness.

But then he saw the light. He saw the "different" commandment, the one that says "Thou shalt not covet." Suddenly sin took on new shapes. After all, this sin implies a mental attitude rather than a physical act.

It's true that he had avoided the very acts of stealing, adultery, and so on, but here Paul the Pharisee had stumbled onto the deeper meaning of the law. The law also had to do with attitudes.

"Thou shalt not covet" hit Paul like a thunderbolt. He began to see the deeper meaning of the law and was, in the words of Isaiah, "undone." Or as Paul himself would put it: "Sin sprang to life and I died."

Paul could be happy with his accomplishments as long as he was dealing with the letter of the law, but his delusions of behavioral perfection were smashed once and for all when he saw the law's true depth.

The experience of Paul is to be our experience. The depth of the sin problem is revealed in the spirit of the law and we are driven to the cross, where we also die to any hope in ourselves or our accomplishments.

CONTEMPT IS MURDER

Take heed that ye despise not one of these little ones; for I say unto you, That in heaven their angels do always behold the face of my Father which is in heaven. For the Son of man is come to save that which was lost. Matt. 18:10, 11.

In Matthew 5:22 we are told not to say "Raca" to anyone. Now, my guess is that you haven't called anyone Raca this past week, or even for your entire life.

That means you're safe, right? No! Once again we need to look at the deeper meaning implied by Jesus. Raca is one of those words that is difficult to translate, but there is no doubt that it is a word of abuse. The translations into English are many. "Idiot," "worthless one," "I spit on you," "simpleton," "empty-headed," and "whoever insults his brother" are a few of the translations I have come across. The basic idea is that anyone who shows contempt for another is in the wrong.

Matthew 5:22 also claims that "whoever says, 'You fool!' shall be liable to the hell of fire" (RSV). Once again we are dealing with an attitude of abuse, the vilifying of a person.

Who are you to vilify anyone? Who am I to be contemptible of another person for any reason? Those who are so glib in throwing around spiritual insults or so prone to gossip about the shortcomings of others fall under the condemnation of this verse.

All of us have sinned and come short of God's ideals. To put it bluntly, because of sin we all are indeed idiots and worthless ones. But God in His grace has reached down and made us into His children again. He sent Jesus to die in our place. Our worth and our true intelligence is in Him. Outside of Him we are nothing.

And Jesus died not only for me; He died for others. Thus I must treat them with respect.

According to Matthew 5:22, the gossiper or backbiter is a murderer of reputations. Contempt for others is the root of murder. We do well to follow the injunction of Jesus: "He that is without sin among you, let him first cast a stone" (John 8:7).

A TRIP TO GEHENNA

Then shall he say also unto them on the left hand, Depart from me, ye cursed, into everlasting fire, prepared for the devil and his angels. Matt. 25:41.

And where is Gehenna? It is southwest of Jerusalem and known as the Valley of Hinnom.

The Valley of Hinnom has had quite a history. It was the place where King Ahaz introduced Israel to the worship of Molech, to whom little children were sacrificed in the fire (2 Chron. 28:3). King Josiah later stamped out Molech worship and ordered that the valley should forever be an accursed place.

Jeremiah predicted that because of this sin the Lord would make the Valley of Hinnom a "valley of slaughter," where the corpses of the Israelites would be buried till there was no more place for them, and the remaining dead bodies would be food for the fowls of the heavens (Jer. 7:32, 33). By the time of Jesus the Valley of Hinnom had become the place where the refuse of Jerusalem was cast out and destroyed. It was kind of a public incinerator, with a perpetual smoldering fire in it and a pall of thick smoke over it.

In short, the Valley of Hinnom or Gehenna was not a nice place. By New Testament times it had come to be regarded as a place of judgment of the wicked. Thus most English Bibles translate Gehenna in Matthew 5:22 as "hell."

This brings us to an interesting aspect of Jesus' teaching in the Sermon on the Mount. Not only had the scribes and Pharisees reduced the requirements of the law, they had also reduced the penalties associated with breaking the law. The scribes and Pharisees had said that whoever committed the physical act of murder would be in danger of judgment by the civil courts, but Jesus said that those who even despised their neighbor would be in danger of hellfire.

Jesus takes us seriously. And He knows that lives can be destroyed inch by inch by those who gossip about others, those who treat others carelessly, and those who are spiritually arrogant.

Jesus is not playing games with us. He is speaking straight, and His message is that we need to be just as kind and understanding and loving as is God the Father. We too must avoid murder in all its forms.

UNACCEPTABLE OFFERINGS

So if you are offering your gift at the altar, and there remember that your brother has something against you, leave your gift there before the altar and go; first be reconciled to your brother, and then come and offer your gift. Matt. 5:23, 24, RSV.

One of the important contributions of these verses is that they move us beyond the negative to the positive side of religion. In Matthew 5:21, 22, Jesus told us to avoid self-centered anger and treating other people with contempt. But a person can avoid all the negative things and still not be right with God.

Christianity moves beyond the mere avoidance of the negative to accomplishing the positive. If you, my friend, think that you are a Christian because of what you have avoided, you are wrong. Christianity is basically a positive; it is a reaching out to other people—even if they don't deserve it. No one will ever be in heaven because of what he or she avoided. Jesus tells us that we need to put our Christianity into practice in our daily life.

The picture Jesus paints in Matthew 5:23, 24 is quite vivid to His hearers. A man brings his sacrifice to the Temple to be sacrificed for his sin by the priest. The worshiper is standing at the rail, ready to hand his victim over, ready to confess his sins on the head of the sacrifice. But then he remembers that he has an unresolved problem with his neighbor. Jesus makes the worshiper's duty plain. If the sacrifice is to be accepted, he must first go out and make things right with the other person.

This speaks to my heart and yours. It should speak to us in a special way at Communion time. Before we partake we need to make things right with our fellow church members, even volunteering to wash their feet.

It speaks to us when we have gossiped about others or even feel anger because they have mistreated us. It won't do to put an extra $20 in the offering plate as a special sacrifice.

As usual, Jesus gets to the heart of the matter. If you want to be right with God, you need to be right with other people.

MAKE PEACE QUICKLY

Agree with thine adversary quickly, whiles thou art in the way with him; lest at any time the adversary deliver thee to the judge, and the judge deliver thee to the officer, and thou be cast into prison. Verily I say unto thee, Thou shalt by no means come out thence, till thou hast paid the uttermost farthing. Matt. 5:25, 26.

In these verses Jesus again paints a meaningful word picture. It might seem strange that He would picture two adversaries walking to the courtroom together. That would indeed be rare in a modern city, but not so in a rural Palestinian village.

In these verses Jesus gives each of us some excellent advice that if taken to heart could make our lives more pleasant. There are several lessons in these verses.

A first lesson is not to let things fester. I am reminded of my grandfather's missing finger. He wasn't born that way; he became that way. As a young man he had gotten a sliver in his finger. It was painful, but difficult to extract. So he let nature take its course. Unfortunately, the finger became swollen and infected. Some of that was to be expected, but in his case the infection got out of control. The result was one less finger.

Jesus is telling us something like that in regard to human relationships. Many a quarrel that could have been easily healed soon after it began is left to fester and infect the relationship. Bitterness breeds bitterness. It is best to move "quickly" to heal injured relationships, even if we are not at fault. That is good advice in families, in churches, and in the community. Believe it or not, things can get worse.

Of course, Jesus could also be implying that we should make and keep things right with other people because we never know when our own earthly end will come, when it will be too late to make things right.

The call of Jesus is the call to care for others, even those we see as adversaries. That is not always easy, but it is Christian. May God help each of us today to make something right with someone we have wronged or with someone who has wronged us.

DRIVEN BACK TO THE BEATITUDES

Wherefore the law was our schoolmaster to bring us unto Christ, that we might be justified by faith. Gal. 3:24.

We have now walked with Jesus for about 10 days on the path of His first illustration of the depth and breadth of the law. He pointed out things most of us never wanted to know. For example, it's one thing to say that I shouldn't kill, but it is quite another to say that I shouldn't harbor anger or look down my social or spiritual nose at someone else, or, worse yet, that I shouldn't even talk disparagingly about others or gossip about them. Did He really mean that destroying (murdering) a person's reputation comes under the sixth commandment?

This is too much. Who can live up to such a standard?

The truth is that no one can when they realize the depth and breadth of the law. In the face of God's ideal, we are driven back to the first table of the Beatitudes. Afresh we realize our poverty of spirit, our massive shortcomings compared with what we should be. As we agonize and mourn over our shortcomings and our need to be more like Jesus, our pride is transformed into meekness.

As a result, we hunger and thirst after that righteousness that can come only through the forgiving grace of God. The law has driven us back to Christ that we might be justified. While that Galatians passage in its context relates to the experience of Israel in being historically led to Christ by the law, it is also true in our personal experience. In the face of Jesus' exposition of the depth of the law, we are literally driven to the foot of the cross for God's cleansing grace.

And that cleansing grace once again leads us on to the second table of the Beatitudes. We hunger and thirst after God's empowering grace so that we will truly be merciful, pure in heart, and peacemakers.

Christ's great sermon is a unit. It is not an isolated group of sayings without rhyme or reason. The various parts fit together, and they all reflect God's ideals and His plan of salvation.

ADULTERY IS MORE THAN ADULTERY

Ye have heard that it was said by them of old time, Thou shalt not commit adultery: But I say unto you, That whosoever looketh on a woman to lust after her hath committed adultery with her already in his heart. Matt. 5:27, 28.

This is serious.

I remember the first time I came to grips with this passage. I was 19 years old and had been baptized from an agnostic background a few months before.

There I was in a five-and-dime store gawking at a woman while waiting for my wife. Of course, I wasn't just gawking, I was thinking the same sort of thoughts I had thought before I had become a Christian.

Suddenly it hit me like a ton of bricks. The Holy Spirit spoke to my conscience loud and clear. "You can't do that. It is wrong to lust after a woman, to think the kinds of thoughts you are thinking."

I didn't care for the lesson. I had been "innocently" enjoying myself, and then He had to break into my meditations. I felt like telling the Holy Spirit to take a hike.

In actuality, I had come face-to-face with the frontier between temptation and sin. Temptation can become sin at the point that I become conscious of the temptation, when I recognize that my thoughts have wandered into forbidden paths. At that very point I can choose to do one of two things. I can reject the temptation through God's power, or I can choose to dwell on the temptation and cherish it a bit. In other words, I can ask God into my life to help me overcome, or I can tell Him to "scram" for a while so that I can enjoy my private lust.

I have discovered that desire for willful sin leaves me when I am in a state of prayer. It is God's Spirit who comes to my aid in prayer, not only to give me a distaste for my sinful desire but also to enliven Christian love in my soul for another person, myself, and God. Then I do not want to perform actions that hurt or destroy people or relationships.

God wants to help us, even in our thought life, if we will let Him do so.

ANOTHER LOOK AT BIBLE READING

"You are those who justify yourselves in the sight of men, but God knows your hearts; for that which is highly esteemed among men is detestable in the sight of God." Luke 16:15, NASB.

The real trouble with the scribes and Pharisees was that they had never read the Ten Commandments properly. If they had, they would have seen their depth and that they can't be read in isolation from one another. We noted a few days ago that for Paul, the law took on a new depth of meaning when he finally came to understand the tenth commandment, "Thou shalt not covet."

At that point the magnitude of the law hit him square on. Suddenly he came to the realization that the Ten Commandments speak to more than actions, that they also speak to the thoughts that undergird actions. Only when Paul understood the mental nature of "Thou shalt not covet" could he begin to understand the meaning of lust.

The problem with a legalistic reading of the Bible is that it fails to grasp the intent and the extent of the Bible's injunctions and warnings. As a result, the Pharisees of Christ's day felt they were safe if they had avoided the physical act of adultery. They had concluded that as long as they were not actually guilty of the act itself, the seventh commandment had nothing to say to them and they were perfectly innocent as far as it was concerned. As with the sixth commandment, they had taken the letter of the law and reduced it to one particular matter and thereby nullified it.

That kind of reading of Jesus' words in Matthew 5:28 would leave a woman technically free to lust after a man. After all, didn't Jesus speak only of a man lusting after a woman?

In the Sermon on the Mount, Jesus puts an end to all such legalistic reading of mere words. Point by point He drives to the deeper meaning underlying the words. He drives beyond the letter to the spiritual meaning that gives life to the words. He wants us to read with fuller understanding.

THERE IS MORE TO SIN THAN MEETS THE EYE

So when the woman saw that the tree was good for food, and that it was a delight to the eyes, and that the tree was to be desired to make one wise, she took of its fruit and ate; and she also gave some to her husband, and he ate. Gen. 3:6, RSV.

When did Eve sin—when she took the fruit or before she took the fruit?

Stop and think about that question. What is your answer, and what reasons can you give for your answer? What are the implications of those reasons? How do those reasons relate to Matthew 5:27, 28?

Think about the sequence in Genesis 2 and 3. God told Adam and Eve to avoid the tree of knowledge of good and evil (Gen. 2:17), but the evil one suggested to Eve that God couldn't be trusted (Gen. 3:1-5). As a result, Genesis 3:6 tells us that she took the fruit and ate it.

She took. But note: Something happened in Eve's head and heart before she took the fruit. By the time she had taken the fruit, she had already sinned. In essence, she had told God to bug off, that she knew better than He did what was good for her. She had rejected His word and will and replaced it with her wisdom and will. Before reaching for the fruit, she had chosen her own will over the will of God. She had put herself on the throne of her life, at the center of her universe, thus displacing God. In actuality, she had focused her love on her self rather than on God. And that is the core of sin.

Eve committed sin when she loved her self and her desire more than she loved God and His will. She committed sin in her heart. And that sin in her heart led to the taking and eating of the fruit. Sin in the heart leads to sins in terms of actions.

It is that insight that Jesus is building upon in the Sermon on the Mount. Sin is much more than meets the eye. Sin is much more than actions. Just because I have avoided performing the action does not mean that I am right with God.

SIN ALSO HAS DEPTH

We know that the law is spiritual; but I am unspiritual, sold as a slave to sin. I do not understand what I do. For what I want to do I do not do, but what I hate I do. Rom. 7:14, 15, NIV.

The Greek philosopher Plato was not a Christian, but he was a keen observer of human activity. Plato likened a person's innermost self to a character whose task it was to drive two horses. The one horse was gentle and obedient to the reins and word of command, but the second horse was wild, untamed, and full of rebellion. The name of the first horse was reason, while that of the second was passion.

While Plato's labeling of the problem may not have been completely correct from a biblical standpoint, his analysis of the human problem is quite close to that of the apostle Paul, and it is illustrative of the struggle we find within ourselves in daily life.

Even converted Christians still have to deal with the residue of sin in their lives. We may have new hearts and new minds, but the old way of thinking and acting always lies beneath the surface, ready to spring forth and take charge. Thus, as Paul puts it, we need to die daily (1 Cor. 15:31). Or as the Adventist hymnist Frank Belden wrote: "Self is worse than a nine-life cat, and must be killed by the Word *daily*." Progressive sanctification is truly the work of a lifetime.

The root of the human problem is tenacity of the sinful nature. When I joined the church I thought everyone on the inside would always desire to do the right thing. I was sorely disappointed. I found that some *thought* that they always did the right thing; but they were so much like the scribes and Pharisees that I came to wonder if they had yet found the first table of the Beatitudes. Their spiritual arrogance merely made them critical of others.

It is important that we as Christians realize the depth of the sin problem in our lives. Only then will we feel our need of God's bountiful grace for both forgiveness and for the true keeping of His law.

GOD'S POWER
VERSUS THE POWER OF SIN

The heart is deceitful above all things, and desperately wicked: who can know it? Jer. 17:9.

Jesus did not fear to call sin by its right name. Down through the ages, Pharisees and their like have wanted to define sin only as the transgression of the law, only as an action. But Jesus puts an end to such a definition for Christians. Sin is first inward. Then it is outward.

The inward aspect of sin is many things. First, it is a power that enslaves people. That is clear from Romans 6:16, where Paul says that sin's practitioners are actually its slaves. The Revised Standard Version translation of Romans 3:9 catches that idea when it says that people "are under the power of sin." Outward sins are nothing but the symptoms of a disease called sin. Yet it is not the symptoms that matter, but the disease.

Second, sin is subtle. It deludes us and fools us, suggesting the idea to our hearts that we really aren't so bad if we just avoid sinful acts. Many highly respected men and women who would never commit adultery carry on an adulterous or less-than-pure mental life. Many of these are the devotees of soap operas, the divorce columns of the newspapers, or stimulating visual or print forms of eroticism. Many are vicarious adulterers.

Third, sin has a perverting effect on human nature. Thus God's good gift of sex and the other appetites are twisted from their lawful uses. As a result, excellent and precious gifts are put to wrong uses.

Jesus came to free us from the enslaving, subtle, and perverting effect of sin. The gospel of His grace is to give us the power to set us free from the power of sin.

God wants to help me today. He wants to help you today. Today is the day of our salvation. Let's invite Him into our hearts and lives right now so that we might this day have a closer walk with Him. A closer walk with Him will also mean a closer walk with our husband, wife, parents, children, and so on. Getting healed with God means getting healed with His other children. You can't have one without the other.

THE SURGICAL CURE

And if thy right eye offend thee, pluck it out, and cast it from thee: for it is profitable for thee that one of thy members should perish, and not that thy whole body should be cast into hell. Matt. 5:29.

Pluck it out . . . cut it off."

Those are radical words for the world's most serious problem. Am I really supposed to pluck out my eye or cut off my hand if they lead me into sin?

Origen, one of the foremost leaders of the third-century church, thought so. As a result, he combined Matthew 5:29 and Matthew 19:12, with its statement that some men "have made themselves eunuchs for the kingdom of heaven's sake," and emasculated himself.

One quick stroke of the knife can solve all your sin problems. Right?

Wrong! After all, if you pluck out your right eye you still have your left one. And isn't the left just as troublesome as the right? Again, if you merely cut off your right hand, you still have the troublesome left hand.

Maybe the answer to the sin problem is to pluck out both eyes, cut off both hands, amputate both legs, and so on. Then you will have your sin problem solved. Right?

Wrong again! Because you would still have your memory and your imagination. The only solution to these problems would be to blow out your brains.

Is that what Jesus wants us to do? No, but it is the obvious, consistent answer for those who say that Scripture doesn't need to be interpreted. Take this text literally and you are left with no option but surgery.

Jesus' meaning is much more radical, much more gutsy. He wants us to realize the serious nature of our problems. But beyond that, He wants us to surrender our lives and all our bodily parts to Him so that they are no longer instruments of sin. Further, He wants to make those same very troublesome instruments of sin into instruments of righteousness. The hands and eyes of a saved person are to be put into God's service.

LIMPING INTO HEAVEN
VERSUS LEAPING INTO HELL

If your right hand causes your downfall, cut it off and fling it away; it is better for you to lose one part of your body than for the whole of it to go to hell. Matt. 5:30, REB.

It is better to go limping into heaven than leaping into hell.

What is Jesus trying to tell us in Matthew 5:29, 30? We focused yesterday on the inadequacy of the surgical solution, that cutting off one's hand or plucking out one's eye is not a sufficient solution. The sin problem is much deeper than the actions covered by our bodily members. It is rooted, Jesus is telling us, in our hearts and minds.

Today we want to focus on the words that it is "better . . . to lose one part of your body than for the whole of it to go to hell." Jesus repeated that same idea twice in verses 29 and 30 because He was seeking to emphasize something.

The part about the plucking out and the cutting off set the stage for the most important part of His teaching in these verses. The amputation statements get people's attention. No one on that hillside was sleeping after those words.

Once Jesus had their attention, He moved in to make His main point.

And what was that point? That there is nothing more important in our lives than the destiny of our souls. He made a similar point when He said, "If any man . . . hate not his father, and mother, and wife, and children, and brethren, and sisters, yea, and his own life also, he cannot be my disciple" (Luke 14:26).

He means in both passages that anything that comes between us and God is harmful to the soul. Anything that militates against the soul and its salvation is an enemy and must be dealt with. Nothing must be allowed to come between us and our eternal destiny.

Jesus is not saying that these bodily parts or our relatives are wrong to have, but that they need to be put in their proper place on our list of priorities. It is better to limp into heaven than to leap into hell.

TAKING SIN TO THE MORTICIAN

If you live according to the flesh you will die, but if by the Spirit you put to death the deeds of the body you will live. Rom. 8:13, RSV.

I cannot," said one ancient Christian leader, "keep a bird from flying over my head. But I can certainly keep it from nesting in my hair or from biting off my nose."

Jesus is telling us in Matthew 5 that we need to take sin seriously. That means in part that Christians need to stop toying with temptation and sin. If we don't, it will someday kill us. The subtlety of sin makes illicit thoughts and pleasures of the flesh look like the way of life. But, like the proverbial poisonous snake in the grass, the way of sin is the way of death.

The biblical way is not to let sin lure us into destruction, but to put it to death, to take it to the mortician. According to our text today, God gives us His Holy Spirit to help us in this warfare. We are not left to our own strength. Rather, we are to "put to death the deeds of the body" through the Spirit. We need to implore the Spirit's power at each step of the way.

But how can the Spirit aid us? For one thing, we need His help so that we can avoid feeding the flesh (our sinful nature). "Put on the Lord Jesus Christ," commands Paul, "and make no provision for the flesh, to gratify its desires" (Rom. 13:14, RSV). There is a fire within each of us. It is foolish to bring that fire within reach of more fuel. We need to stay away from those situations, programs, books, and people that cause the flame of sin to gain strength in us. We need to "cut off" and "pluck out" certain things from our lives.

But we need to watch out here. It is easy to become overconfident in our abilities. We need to be in prayer throughout the day so that we don't seek to fight the evil one in our own strength. To do so is to guarantee our defeat. It is only through God's power that we can mortify sin in our lives.

HOW NOT TO HANDLE
THE SIN PROBLEM

If any other man thinks he has reason for confidence in the flesh, I have more: circumcised on the eighth day, of the people of Israel, of the tribe of Benjamin, a Hebrew born of Hebrews; as to the law a Pharisee, as to zeal a persecutor of the church, as to righteousness under the law blameless. But whatever gain I had, I counted as loss for the sake of Christ. Indeed I count everything as loss because of the surpassing worth of knowing Christ Jesus my Lord. Phil. 3:4-8, RSV.

Some people, like Paul before his conversion, see human effort as the road to salvation. One thing that can be said about the Pharisees of Paul's day and of every other generation is that they are desperately in earnest in seeking to clean up their sin problem so that they can be right with God.

Take Martin Luther (1483-1546), for instance. Before he discovered justification by faith in the book of Romans, as an Augustinian monk he spent entire nights afflicting his body in penance. He sought to dredge up every sin he had ever been tempted to commit. But there was no end to the process. No sooner did he think he had completed his task than he had to repent of the temptation to be proud of his accomplishment. Luther incessantly sought peace of heart but never achieved it through his asceticism.

A similar case is Anthony (c. A.D. 251-356), who fasted, did without sleep, and tortured his body. For about 20 years he lived in the desert in "nonstop battle with the devil." Yet at the end of his vigil, Anthony was no closer to victory than at the beginning.

Paul warned us against the fruitlessness of such attempts to arrive at holiness. Paul the austere, acetic Pharisee finally found victory and peace in accepting Jesus' sacrifice at Calvary. It is little wonder that Paul counted all he had previously cherished as worthless when he found Christ as his personal Saviour. Paul had at last found what Luther, Anthony, and all of us are looking for. Jesus says to each of us, "Come unto me, all ye that labour and are heavy laden, and I will give you rest. . . . My yoke is easy, and my burden is light" (Matt. 11:28-30).

THE BETTER WAY

There is joy in the presence of the angels of God over one sinner that repenteth. Luke 15:10.

Human pride whispers in our ear that we are capable of solving our own problems if we just try hard enough. I remember when I became an Adventist at the age of 19. I looked around the church and came to one conclusion: What a mess!

I believed I knew the problem. You Adventists and other Christians just hadn't tried hard enough. If you just put forth more effort, you could overcome and even be perfect. It was at that point in my life that I vowed to be the first perfect Christian since Jesus. There was no doubt in my mind as to success. Like young Martin Luther and the medieval monks, I set out to conquer the dragon of sin through my own behavior and effort. And try I did, with all my heart.

But less than a decade later I gave up in total failure. There followed years of discouragement and apostasy from what I knew to be true.

Only later did I meet Jesus of the cross. I had been an Adventist, but I didn't know Him. Thus I had to repent of my own self-sufficiency; I had to repent of seeking salvation by the route of the Pharisees.

At that time I realized that the only way to victory over sin was in surrendering my will to God and accepting His will and way into my life. That way is the way of the cross.

The cross is God's answer to the sin problem. If humans could overcome sin through their own strength, there would have been no reason for Jesus to come; there would have been no reason for His death on the cross.

Those who don't recognize the depth and magnitude of the sin problem still try to save themselves through effort. But as with Paul, Martin Luther, and a multitude of others, they will sooner or later be brought face-to-face with their failure. Only then will they be able to truly repent (turn from their self-sufficiency) and turn to God in surrender.

THE GOSPEL SOLUTION

For I am not ashamed of the gospel of Christ: for it is the power of God unto salvation to every one that believeth; to the Jew first, and also to the Greek. For therein is the righteousness of God revealed from faith to faith: as it is written, The just shall live by faith. Rom. 1:16, 17.

There was a tremendous flash of light on the horizon. I didn't understand its significance at first. But then I saw large amounts of dirt blown into the air, and in a few moments I could hear and feel the force of the explosion as sound followed light and reached me at a distance of some 15 or 20 miles from the blast. Only then did I realize that I had witnessed a powerful charge of dynamite go off. As I continued to look through the clear desert air I could see that the detonation had changed the face of a mountain.

God wants to use dynamite to change our lives. A few days ago we examined the surgical cure to the sin problem as it is described in Matthew 5:29, 30. We also noted its weakness. God's solution is much more radical than surgery—it is supernatural power.

Our text for today tells us that the gospel (good news) "is the power of God unto salvation to every one that believeth." That word "power" fascinates me because in the Greek it has the same root word as does dynamite.

Paul is telling us that the gospel works like dynamite in our lives when we let God in, when we give Him permission to reshape our lives into the likeness of Jesus.

God doesn't come in and merely lop off this or that problem. No, He is interested in getting to the root of the problem, blasting it out, and then recreating our lives into something ever more beautiful.

That is truly good news. The truth is that God's solution to the sin problem not only offers forgiveness, it also offers the possibility of new life in Him.

Have you let the dynamite of God into your life? Or are you afraid of the changes He might make if you gave His power free rein?

THE NEW LIFE

Therefore if any man be in Christ, he is a new creature: old things are passed away; behold, all things are become new. 2 Cor. 5:17.

During the past few days we have discussed both the depth of sin and the greatness of God's plan for dealing with sin. God's promises are much greater and much more thorough than most of us realize.

The Bible describes becoming a Christian as a death and a new birth. Being saved in Christ is not a halfway experience. It is a total experience that affects every part of my life, including the way that I think about the opposite sex and even how I might dress to attract the wrong kind of thinking. Too often when we read Matthew 5:29, 30 we think of those having adulterous thoughts. It seems to me that the principle undergirding the text also has something to say to the way we dress, talk, and act, since we have a responsibility for others.

As a result, if I am acting as a Christian, my talk will not be suggestive, nor will my dress give the wrong type of message. When God says all things in our lives can become new, He means it.

But please note once again, we don't make ourselves into new creatures. It is the Creator God at work in our lives. Becoming a Christian means a total transformation of our hearts and minds, so that those things we once hated we now love and those things we once loved we now hate.

Yes, that even affects the way we view sex. Many of us were raised with selfish ideas of sex. It was the law of the street (jungle)—get what you can and let the chips fall where they may. For some it was more subtle, but too often still selfish.

Becoming a Christian changes all that. Suddenly we realize that sex is not so much an act as a relationship—the closest and most caring and unselfish of all human relationships. Sex is God's gift to men and women. Within the marriage relationship it is one of God's greatest gifts.

May God help us think Christianly about sex. May He help us grow into true Christian lovers.

A HIGH VIEW OF MARRIAGE

It has been said, "Anyone who divorces his wife must give her a certificate of divorce." But I tell you that anyone who divorces his wife, except for marital unfaithfulness, causes her to become an adulteress, and anyone who marries the divorced woman commits adultery. Matt. 5:31, 32, NIV.

If one thing is crystal clear from Genesis to Revelation, it is the sacredness of marriage. God not only made our first parents male and female (Gen. 1:27), He also blessed marriage and said that the two "will become one flesh" (Matt. 19:5, NIV; Gen. 2:24). Jesus upheld the sacredness of marriage in both Matthew 5 and in the related Matthew 19:1-9.

Michael Green notes that Jesus made several important points about marriage in these two passages. First, marriage was designed by God. It is a God-given ordinance, rather than a mere social contract.

Second, marriage is an ordinance between the sexes. God "made them male and female." God's intention was not a unisex world. As Green puts it: "There is a God-ordained difference and complementarity between the sexes. That is so obvious that it only needs to be stated in this late twentieth century when homosexuality has come to be seen as an equally valid alternative to marriage."

Third, marriage is intended to be permanent. It was never intended that the marriage relationship be broken. Any deviation from the perpetuity of marriage is a declension from the ideal.

Fourth, marriage is exclusive. The two—not three, four, or five—are to become one flesh. One man and one woman are to be joined together. That ideal rules out the convenient affairs of so many modern people and the polygamy of the ancients. Apparently God's allowance for polygamy in the Old Testament was a less-than-ideal concession to entrenched custom and human weakness. Beyond that, it provided security for females in cultures where they had no rights and there were not enough males to go around.

Fifth, marriage creates a nuclear family unit. It includes both leaving one's parents and uniting with a spouse. Thus marriage becomes the strongest and most important of all human relationships.

Thank You, Lord, for the gift of marriage. Help us to cherish it as we should.

DIVORCE IS A SERIOUS MATTER

"Why then," they asked, "did Moses command that a man give his wife a certificate of divorce and send her away?"

Jesus replied, "Moses permitted you to divorce your wives because your hearts were hard. But it was not this way from the beginning. I tell you that anyone who divorces his wife, except for marital unfaithfulness, and marries another woman commits adultery." Matt. 19:7-9, NIV.

Jesus' words leave no doubt about divorce being an act that falls short of God's ideal. Thus Jesus agrees with the Old Testament, where God said, "'I hate divorce'" (Mal. 2:16, NIV). Every Christian ought to hate it. Divorce signifies a failure to meet God's ideal for two people.

Yet divorces do take place in a less-than-perfect world, as do remarriages. The stigma of failure and the frightful reality of broken families weigh heavily upon the minds of many. The family is the basic building block of both society and the church. We have a right to feel sad and even upset with the high divorce rate in the church.

What is to be done? Everything we can do, both individually and as a church, to keep families together. We certainly need to be supportive of families that are experiencing rocky times—and most do at some point or another. Many of us need to lend a caring heart and a listening ear to those struggling to keep their marriages together.

But what of husbands and wives who have failed? Are they hopelessly lost, especially if they marry someone else? Not if we can believe the New Testament.

Like gossipers and those who are proud of their spirituality, those who suffer from broken marriages are driven back to the Beatitudes of poverty of spirit, mourning, humility, and hungering after righteousness. Such will be filled.

In fact, divorced people are perhaps more likely to be driven back to the Beatitudes and the cross than gossipers and the spiritually proud, because the shortcomings and sins of the divorced are more open and less apt to be covered with piety than those other groups, who may feel no need. But all need cleansing.

Let the one without sin throw the first stone.

Go and sin no more.

THE IMPORTANCE OF OUR SPEECH

Again you have heard that it was said to the men of old, "You shall not swear falsely, but shall perform to the Lord what you have sworn." Matt. 5:33, RSV.

For the past few verses in Matthew 5, Jesus has been expounding upon the depth and breadth of the Ten Commandments. In 5:21-26 He focused on the sixth commandment ("Thou shalt not kill") and in 5:27-32 He discussed the implications of the seventh command ("Thou shalt not commit adultery"). Now in verses 33-37 Jesus will focus on the ninth command ("Thou shalt not bear false witness") and the third ("Thou shalt not take the name of the Lord thy God in vain"). We are getting an exposition on aspects of the meaning of the law from the Lawgiver Himself.

At first glance, Jesus' command against oaths seems to be the least important and least relevant of all His commands. After all, how can the taking of an oath compare with taking life or being unfaithful in marriage?

But think again! Our speech stands at the center of all we do as humans. It stands at the base of business, family relations, government, and international relations. When speech is not honest, all else begins to break down. When a husband can't trust his wife, when a mother can't trust her children, how can a family function efficiently?

And what about the larger world? When business partners lie to each other, their business is in trouble. Likewise, clients must be able to trust professionals to tell the truth.

Of course, one of the great problems of our world is that truth telling is too rare a virtue. And the effects of that scarcity are all too evident in broken families, the necessity for an abundance of courts of law, and international distrust. We live in a world of sin, and at the root of much of that sin is the fruitage of dishonesty. The father of lies has been quite successful.

But as Christians we want to be part of the solution rather than part of the problem. Help us this day, our Father, to recommit ourselves to the importance of true speech.

JESUS VERSUS THE
OLD TESTAMENT ON OATH TAKING

But I say unto you, Swear not at all; neither by heaven; for it is God's throne: Nor by the earth; for it is his footstool: neither by Jerusalem; for it is the city of the great King. Neither shalt thou swear by thy head, because thou canst not make one hair white or black. Matt. 5:34-36.

S wear not at all."

That's what Jesus said.

But how does it line up with the Old Testament? Not altogether clearly, at first glance. In fact, Jesus seems to contradict Moses. "You shall fear the Lord your God; you shall serve him, and *swear* by his name," we read in Deuteronomy 6:13 (RSV). Again, we read in Psalm 50:14, "Offer to God a sacrifice of thanksgiving, and pay your vows to the Most High" (RSV). The psalmist had obviously sworn vows to God.

How can we resolve these apparent contradictions between Jesus and the Old Testament? One lead toward an explanation is found in Leviticus 19:12: "And ye shall not swear by my name falsely, neither shalt thou profane the name of thy God: I am the Lord."

From the beginning of Israel's nationhood, it was faced with a dual problem. On the one hand, God's positive command through Moses to swear by His name was undoubtedly intended to speak to the temptation to be dishonest. On the other hand, as we noted yesterday, a trusting social life is impossible without consistent truth telling. Thus the command to swear by God's name was intended to bridle the tendency to be less than truthful, especially in solemn matters. The command, like the permission for divorce in Matthew 19:8, was given because of the hardness of human hearts.

But sin perverts everything. As a result, when some people discovered that they could get their way if they swore falsely by using God's name, they began to do so as a tool of manipulation. Thus the Levitical condemnation of the practice.

By Jesus' time the issue had become quite subtle, as we shall see tomorrow. As a result, He calls even the Old Testament permission into question as He explores the meaning of God's law.

We can learn much from His teaching here. Especially if we put His positive ideal into practice.

PHARISAIC SWEARING

And ye shall not swear by my name falsely, neither shall thou profane the name of thy God: I am the Lord. Lev. 19:12.

The scribes and Pharisees were good Bible students. In fact, they were excellent Bible students. They knew all the jots and tittles of the law and they were committed to not *outwardly* breaking it. Of course, they wouldn't have thought of it that way. But since they had no insight into the inner meaning of the law, their legalistic interpretation of the law's letter left them with only an outward understanding. It was to that lack of depth in the understanding of sin and the law that Jesus is speaking in Matthew 5.

Now the Jews knew the letter of the law on swearing. They knew that they were not to swear falsely using God's name. But they knew that they could use God's name in an oath. Those were the legal rules. Those rules said nothing about swearing falsely by anything else. Aha! They had discovered a loophole.

Such understandings led the scribes and Pharisees to divide oaths into two classes, those that were absolutely binding and those that were not. Any oath containing the name of God was absolutely binding; any oath evading the name of God was not held to be binding. Such reasoning was the foundation for an evasive practice of oath taking that perverted the very spirit of truth telling.

By Jesus' day the scribes and Pharisees held that taking an oath by the Temple was not binding, but swearing by the gold of the Temple was binding. Likewise, an oath by the altar need not be kept, but swearing by the gift on the altar was absolutely binding (see Matt. 23:16-22). By such machinations and technicalities they could evade honesty and yet be "religious."

It is little wonder that Jesus attacked such practices in both Matthew 5 and Matthew 23. Since God is Creator of all, there is nothing that is not sacred, whether it be the Temple or the hairs of our head. All belong to God. All are connected to His name.

As Christians we must be transparently honest. We must avoid all subtle and not-so-subtle ways of evading the truth, because we serve the God of truth.

MORE ON PHARISAIC SWEARING

Whosoever committeth sin transgresseth also the law: for sin is the transgression of the law. 1 John 3:4.

"S in is the transgression of the law." But what is the law?

The scribes and Pharisees in Matthew 5 would tell us that the law means the outward words of the law and that sin is performing acts or behaviors that break that law.

That is the very interpretation that Jesus is preaching against in Matthew 5. For Jesus (see Matt. 22:35-40) and Paul (see Rom. 13:8, 10; Gal. 5:14) the core of the law is not the quite specific formulation of the Ten Commandments but the moral imperative to love God and our neighbor.

That means that everything that is unloving is sin. And that means that evading the truth by means of an oath is sin. The long arm of God's law of love reaches much further than ancient or modern legalists can ever understand. It covers our entire lives.

But the pharisaic mind is happy as long as it can persuade itself that it is keeping the letter of the law. For example, as long as it is not guilty of physical adultery or actual divorce or physical murder, it believes that it is on the right path.

The pharisaic mind so construes the meaning of the law and so defines it in a legal form that it feels free to do many things that are utterly contradictory to the spirit of the law of love, yet remain without guilt.

The pharisaic mind takes the stand that "to perform a forbidden act is sin, and as long as I am not performing the specified act, all is well." Thus some people frown at others who may wear a wedding ring or some piece of costume jewelry, while they feel perfectly righteous living in an ostentatious home or driving an elite automobile. They have defined being "worldly" in such a way that they are left content in their self-righteousness. The pharisaic mind trivializes sin and contains it within safe bounds.

Jesus utterly smashes all such attempts. Such people miss the point of what Christianity is about.

READ THE ENTIRE WORD

Simply let your "Yes" be "Yes," and your "No," "No"; anything beyond this comes from the evil one. Matt. 5:37, NIV.

How should we read Jesus' commands about swearing oaths? Should we read the text literally for what it at first seems to say? Or does the saying need to be interpreted in the light of the rest of the New Testament?

This is an important question for two reasons. First, many of us will at some time or another be asked to swear a truth-telling oath in a court of law, and many of us have said wedding vows. Thus we are dealing with something quite practical for our daily life.

The second implication is also quite practical. It has to do with how we read Scripture. The lesson stemming from Matthew 5:33-37, just as the lesson about plucking out eyes in 5:29, is that the most literal reading is not in line with Jesus' intent.

The most literal meaning of Jesus' teaching regarding oaths is that one should never swear an oath. Several religious groups, including the Quakers, have adopted that position.

But that literal reading is not supported by the rest of the New Testament. For one thing, Jesus at His trial "did not refuse to testify under oath" (see Matt. 26:63, 64). Ellen White goes on to add that "had Christ in the Sermon on the Mount condemned the judicial oath, He would at His trial have reproved the high priest and thus, for the benefit of His followers, have enforced His own teaching" (*Thoughts From the Mount of Blessing*, p. 67).

Not only did Jesus not object to a governmental oath, but we find the apostles taking oaths (see, for example, Rom. 9:1 and 2 Cor. 1:23). And in Hebrews 6:13 we find God swearing by Himself, "since He had no one greater by whom to swear" (RSV).

Christian life is more complex than just grabbing a proof text and running with it as if it were all that God had to say on a topic. We need to have a balanced view of all the Bible's teaching on a point if we are really to understand God's will.

Lord, help us to become better students of Your Word, more accurate interpreters of Your will.

OATHS IN A SINFUL WORLD

For when God made a promise to Abraham, since he had no one greater by whom to swear, he swore by himself, saying, "Surely I will bless you and multiply you." Heb. 6:13, 14, RSV.

Yesterday we noted that both Paul and Jesus submitted to or used oaths. Thus neither seems to have taken Jesus' words in Matthew 5:33-37 as a blanket prohibition against all oaths. And in today's reading we see that even God has used oaths in a sinful world.

Those last two words capture the reason for certain types of oaths. We live in a sinful world. As Matthew 5:37 puts it, the very need for any oaths "comes from evil" (RSV). For example, whenever oaths are used, as in Jesus' trial, the source of the usage is the evil condition of a world in and to which oaths seem a necessity if citizens are to be impressed with the special seriousness of their word in such places as law courts.

As citizens, we are obliged to sign many legal documents under oath. The source of these oaths and the reason they are necessary is the evil condition of the world, as Jesus noted in Matthew 5:37. Christians take oaths simply because an evil world requires it, but it is not their general mode of expression.

Ellen White helps us see the logic here when she writes that "there are very many who do not fear to deceive their fellow men, but they have been taught, and have been impressed by the Spirit of God, that it is a fearful thing to lie to their Maker. When put under oath they are made to feel that they are not testifying merely before men, but before God; that if they bear false witness, it is to Him who reads the heart and who knows the exact truth. The knowledge of the fearful judgments that have followed this sin has a restraining influence upon them" (*Thoughts From the Mount of Blessing*, p. 67).

But such devices should not be necessary for Christians. The Christian realizes that God sees all, whether he or she is under oath or not. For the Christian, oath taking is a necessary admission that oaths have a place, albeit restricted, in a world in which people need less than ideal motivations.

THE CHRISTIAN YES

But above all things, my brethren, swear not, neither by heaven, neither by the earth, neither by any other oath: but let your yea be yea; and your nay, nay; lest ye fall into condemnation. James 5:12.

In our passage for today, James is quoting Jesus' sentiment in Matthew 5:37. True Christians shouldn't need to swear by this or that. They should have a well-established reputation for truth telling. They shouldn't use those types of legalistic sentences that trick people by their subtle use of words and that leave people with the idea that they are saying one thing when in actuality they mean the opposite. A Christian's speech ought to be open, honest, and transparent. We ought to be able to trust Christians because they are Christians.

Jesus in Matthew 5:33-37 rejects all split-level approaches to truth. That is, He rejects the idea that some agreements must be kept because they have been sworn in such and such a way, while other agreements put their makers under less obligation because they are not connected to a proper oath.

Jesus is fighting for the integrity of all speech, sworn or unsworn. A community in which words cannot be trusted is not stable.

As Christians, we realize that all of our words and all of our agreements are given in the presence of God. Christian speech and action is sacred. After all, Christian speech is from a person who has been set apart for holy use (that is, sanctified) by the living God. Christian speech is given by one who has been born again. The purity of our speech, the integrity of our promises, the transparent honesty of who we are is a witness that we are Christians in deed and not just Christians in name.

Thus a Christian business deal is the most honest of all business transactions. It is a witness to the community that we are Christians.

When Jesus said let your yes be yes and your no be no, He was asserting that each of us should be trustworthy and honest in all that we say and do.

EVEN HIS SCALES WERE CONVERTED

Therefore each of you must put off falsehood and speak truthfully to his neighbor, for we are all members of one body. Eph. 4:25, NIV.

The story is told of a missionary in Poland many years ago who went to buy a goose for dinner. He noted that the shop was surprisingly clean and the chickens and geese were fat and healthy looking.

When the missionary asked the shopkeeper about his salvation, his eyes lit up and his face shone with joy as he answered: "Yes, I am a believer. Several years ago I learned to know Jesus Christ as my Saviour."

"But how do you know you are saved?" asked the missionary.

"Because," he replied, "my life has been changed completely. Now when I sell geese I give the correct weight and do not put my finger on the scales. Everything is right now. Even my scales are converted."

That story reminds me of the counsel God gave through Moses in Deuteronomy 25: "Do not have two different weights in your bag—one heavy, one light. Do not have two different measures in your house—one large, one small. You must have accurate and honest weights and measures. . . . For the Lord your God detests anyone who does these things, anyone who deals dishonestly" (verses 13-16, NIV).

Christianity makes a difference in our lives. As Christians for whom the truth is the truth, our yes really means yes and our no really means no. We do not have a split-level morality that has honest and dishonest weights and measures, honest talk and action and not-so-honest talk and action.

Jesus' reflections on oath taking extend far beyond the actual practice of using oaths. It includes all our speech. It includes not using the name of God carelessly or in vain. It includes, like Jesus' other discussions of the law in Matthew 5, depths and heights to the law of not bearing false witness that we may not have thought through carefully.

Of course, it is one thing to understand the implications of His words. It is quite another to put them into practice. *Today* is the best day to begin to make our practice more consistently Christian.

THE LAW OF RETALIATION

Ye have heard that it hath been said, An eye for an eye, and a tooth for a tooth. Matt. 5:38.

Here we have a reference to the ancient code of *lex talionis*, the law of retaliation. We find it in the earliest human law codes. Thus it was in the Code of Hammurabi, who reigned in Babylon before the time of Moses, but in a less just form than in the Old Testament.

The basic law of *lex talionis* is found in at least three places in the Old Testament. "Your eye shall not pity," we read in Deuteronomy 19:21; "it shall be life for life, eye for eye, tooth for tooth, hand for hand, foot for foot" (RSV). Again, in Leviticus 24:19, 20 we read: "When a man causes a disfigurement in his neighbor, as he has done it shall be done to him, fracture for fracture, eye for eye, tooth for tooth; as he has disfigured a man, he shall be disfigured" (RSV; see also Ex. 21:23-25).

For obvious reasons, these laws are often quoted by critics as the most savage of the Old Testament. But before we get too critical, we need to see their intent.

First, it is important to realize that the aim of those Old Testament laws was not legalized savagery but mercy. Just think for a moment about human passion and retribution. My human tendency, if you do something injurious to me, is to do something at least that mean to you—more mean, if I can get by with it. Thus unregulated retaliation escalates as one side pays the other back in increasingly brutal fashion. A blood feud between two warring families is a possible outcome.

The Old Testament legislation was given to put *limits* on retaliation. Thus one can not insist on more punishment than the crime merits.

Second, the law was not to be enforced by individuals, but by governments in an attempt to keep civil order. It was the judge who set the terms of punishment. In actuality, the later Jews generally substituted monetary funds for literal *lex talionis*.

Even what appears to be the harsh side of the Old Testament needs to be seen in the full light of a merciful God.

PAY ATTENTION TO BOTH SIDES OF AN ISSUE

Do not say, "I will do to him as he has done to me; I will pay the man back for what he has done." Prov. 24:29, RSV.

It is always dangerous to pick out a verse here or there and say that it is what the Bible teaches on the topic. It is important to get the complete picture.

Yesterday we looked at some verses in which *lex talionis* or "an eye for an eye" was taught. We saw that what first appears to be a very harsh law was in fact a piece of merciful legislation in the sense that it set limits on the extent of vengeance.

But God's merciful ideal is much broader than that in the Old Testament. That may have been the *legal* limit of vengeance, but God's true ideal for His people was one of grace. Thus, as we see in our Scripture reading for today, individuals are counseled *not* to pay people back for what they have done to us, not to retaliate in *lex talionis* fashion. And in Leviticus 19:18 we read: "You shall not take vengeance or bear any grudge against the sons of your own people, but you shall love your neighbor as yourself" (RSV). Again: "If your enemy is hungry, give him bread to eat" (Prov. 25:21, RSV).

So then, even in the Old Testament God's ideal for His people as individuals was mercy rather than strict justice. Grace is a feature of both testaments. God gives it to us. Our job is to pass it on.

Unimaginable harm has come to God's people by those amongst them who collect the strongest statements from the Bible (or writings of Ellen White) and push them on everyone without taking contextual or balancing factors into consideration.

Ellen White warns against those who "select from the testimonies the strongest expressions" and "make them of force in every case" in spite of their context. "Let not individuals gather up the very strongest statements, given for individuals and families, and drive these things because they want to use the whip and to have something to drive" *(Selected Messages,* book 3, pp. 285-287).

That counsel is good for using the Bible also. Get all the facts on a topic.

READING THE BIBLE CAREFULLY: THE ROLE OF CIVIL GOVERNMENT •

But I say unto you, That ye resist not evil: but whosoever shall smite thee on thy right cheek, turn to him the other also. Matt. 5:39.

R esist not evil." Now, there is a revolutionary statement. It is also one of the most controverted in the New Testament.

Some have taken this statement to apply to governments. Thus "resist not evil" implies that it is wrong to have police forces or armies.

"Resist not evil." Does that phrase mean that it is wrong to resist such people as Hitler or Stalin or private criminals? Are we just to let ruthless people do what they want? Some believe just that. But is that what the Bible is teaching?

For the answer to those questions we need to examine the context of Matthew 5:39. To whom is Jesus speaking? Whom is He commanding not to resist evil?

The answer is that He is speaking to individual Christians who are living the life of the Beatitudes and are thus meek and peacemakers. He is speaking to converted people who by definition are not like the world and what Paul calls the "natural man." Jesus is speaking to those individuals whose righteousness must exceed that of the scribes and Pharisees.

He is not speaking to national governments or to individuals who are unconverted and not living the life of the Beatitudes. For such people the command to resist evil would be foolishness. Living the Christian life is a matter of the spirit.

Governments in their legal and police function are still under *lex talionis*. That is made clear in Romans 13, where we are told that governments do not bear the sword in vain. They are to "execute . . . wrath on the wrongdoer" (verse 4, RSV). Armies and police and courts of law are still needed in a world of sin. And, according to Romans 13, God uses government to maintain order and resist evil.

But that is not the role of individual Christians. We are not to take the law into our own hands. We are not to live a life of retaliation. We are to live the life of the Beatitudes; we are to be peacemakers and to love our enemies.

TURNING THE OTHER CHEEK

Finally, all of you, have unity of spirit, sympathy, love of the brethren, a tender heart and a humble mind. Do not return evil for evil or reviling for reviling, but on the contrary bless, for to this you have been called, that you may obtain a blessing. 1 Peter 3:8, 9, RSV.

Turning the other cheek. Not so easy when you've just been hit on the right one. A slap on the face was the ultimate personal insult for a Jew. And now Jesus is telling us to turn the other one. Impossible!

Is Jesus telling me that if a drunk person or a violent lunatic comes along and strikes me on one cheek, I am immediately to offer him the other? Such an instruction would make our Lord's teaching seem ridiculous.

Then what is He advocating? Once again we need to consider the context and whom Jesus was speaking to.

In part, He was speaking to the ways of the scribes and Pharisees. In rabbinic tradition each person was permitted to retaliate up to the letter of the law of an eye for an eye. Each person was permitted to become, in effect, judge, jury, and executioner. God's law was used to justify retaliation by a one-sided reading of the Old Testament. Thus Jesus is speaking to their legalistic justification of themselves.

But Jesus is also speaking to His followers, whose righteousness is to exceed that of the Jewish religious leaders. His point in Matthew 5:39 has more to say on what we are not to do than what we are to do. Turning the other cheek symbolizes the nonavenging, humble, and gentle spirit that is to characterize citizens of the kingdom.

In the three illustrations in Matthew 5:39-41, Jesus, in essence, is telling us that we are to die to self. He wants to change both our hearts and our outward expressions. The moment I am hit, I want to retaliate. That's what Jesus is concerned about. He tells us we are to get rid of that spirit. We are to die to self and to our pride. We need to learn to be like Jesus, who sustained personal insult without retaliating. We are to leave vengeance up to God.

That takes grace.

DYING TO SELF

And if someone wants to sue you and take your tunic, let him have your cloak as well. Matt. 5:40, NIV.

This is not an easy saying. Like the turning of the cheek in verse 39, this saying about the cloak hits us at the center of our self-defensiveness.

In order to understand what Jesus is telling us in Matthew 5:40, we need to look a bit more at His words. The tunic was a sacklike inner garment made of cotton or linen. All but the poorest person would have a change of tunics. The cloak, on the other hand, was the warm, blanket-like outer garment that a person wore as a robe by day and used as a blanket at night. The average person would have only one cloak.

Jewish law held that a person's tunic might be taken as a pledge, but not a person's cloak, unless it was returned by sundown (see Ex. 22:26, 27). The point is that by law a person's cloak could not be permanently taken.

Well, then, you may be asking, What is Jesus saying to us? He is giving some counsel we don't want to hear. He is telling us that a concern for our rights is not to be at the center of our Christian walk. Once again Jesus is telling us that we need to die to our own selves. As William Barclay puts it: "The Christian thinks not of his rights, but of his duties; not of his privileges, but of his responsibilities. The Christian is a man who has forgotten that he has any rights at all; and the man who will fight to the death for his legal rights, inside or outside the church, is far from the Christian way."

Jesus' teaching about the cloak does not mean that a Christian will not work for the rights of others or for the integrity of law and order. But it does mean that he or she has died to self. That was the lesson in the preceding verse also. There, however, it had to do with our person; here it has to do with our possessions. Jesus really does expect us to be like Him.

THE SECOND MILE

And if any one forces you to go one mile, go with him two miles. Matt. 5:41, RSV.

The word picture in our verse for today is a strange one for us, but one quite understandable to Jesus' hearers. Roman law gave a soldier the right to enlist a civilian to carry his pack for a Roman mile. Palestine was an occupied country, and at any moment a Jew might feel the touch of the flat of a Roman spear on his shoulder and know that he was compelled to serve the Romans. That is what happened to Simon of Cyrene when he was compelled to carry the cross of Jesus.

The law was designed to relieve the soldier, but it was seen as especially despicable because the oppressed were made to carry the equipment of their oppressors. This task was one that raised the temper of many Jews to white-hot.

Now, here is the radicalness of Jesus coming through again. Not only were His followers to carry the burden for the required distance, but they were to offer to go a second mile without resentment. Jesus is telling His followers that they are never to be grouchy minimalists. They are to do their duty with a smile, even if they are not being treated with the dignity that they feel they deserve. Christians are never to be inefficient workers, resentful servants, or ungracious helpers. To the contrary, Christians undertake every task as cheerful maximalists. They don't even cheat on their taxes when they feel the broadsword of the government.

All three of the illustrations we have been studying in Matthew 5:39-41 have hit on the same point. The illustrations of turning the other cheek, giving the cloak also, and going the second mile each implies the crucifixion of the self, a point at the very center of Jesus' teaching. It is the protection of self and its rights that leads us to take up God's role and retaliate against real or supposed wrongs. Jesus has illustrated that in terms of our persons, our possessions, and our labor. We as Christians are to surrender our self-protectiveness and our self-sensitiveness. If we really did so, the church would be a delightful place to be.

SHOULD I GIVE TO EVERY BEGGAR?

Give to him who begs from you, and do not refuse him who would borrow from you. Matt. 5:42, RSV.

Does this mean that as a Christian I must give to every drunkard who begs money from me? Does it mean that Christian bankers must never refuse a loan, even to a fraud?

Like Jesus' teachings about the other cheek, the cloak also, and the second mile, this teaching, if interpreted in a literal and mechanical manner, can be made to look ridiculous.

Our Lord is not encouraging us to abet frauds and drunkards. But we all have to face such people, so we ought to take a closer look at Jesus' meaning and what it means to help someone.

I remember my days as associate pastor in the San Francisco Central church. It seemed that more than our share of beggars came by our church for a handout. Most of them never asked for money for beer or wine. They usually told us that they had a wife and three kids and needed groceries to sustain them.

The senior pastor and I wanted to be faithful to Jesus' teaching, but we also wanted to really help these people. We didn't believe we were helping them if we gave them money that they would buy beer with.

Our solution was to make an agreement with the local grocer whereby we would write "milk, bread, and fruit" on our calling card and sign our name to it. Upon receiving our card from a needy person, the grocer would make up a bag of food for him or her and send us the bill.

The interesting thing is that most of the cards never reached the store, because the people didn't want food. But this strategy helped us be faithful to Jesus' instruction and at the same time seek to truly provide help.

Jesus wants us to help those in true need. It is important that we give them the benefit of the doubt so that we do not shut doors on the truly needy. But here is a case where we need to be harmless as doves and smart as serpents.

Giving, meanwhile, opens up our hearts and helps us be generous in place of being selfish. In the process we are being transformed into the image of Jesus.

THE SPIRIT OF IT ALL

I am crucified with Christ: nevertheless I live; yet not I, but Christ liveth in me: and the life which I now live in the flesh I live by the faith of the Son of God, who loved me, and gave himself for me. Gal. 2:20.

For the past few days we have been studying the problem of retaliation, the problem of the human desire to hurt those who have hurt us. After all, we think they deserve it!

And they probably do deserve it in most cases. But think it through for a moment. What if God gave us what we deserve for having hurt Him and His other children? Let's face it, if God gave us what we deserve, we would be just so many grease spots polluting the landscape.

God doesn't give us what we deserve. He gives us what we need.

And what do we need? Understanding, forgiveness, love . . . That is exactly what those who have hurt us need also. The Christian is to act like God to them—he or she is to give people what they need rather than what they deserve.

But, you may be thinking, that is not normal. Right! God wants us to live abnormal lives in terms of the standards of this world. He wants us to act like Him rather than like the devil.

Now, that's radical. Right on! It is about as radical as one can get. It means being crucified to the old ways of self-protection, pride, and retaliation, and being born again into the likeness of Jesus, who so loved the world that He died for it—for me, for you, once for all.

Religion is serious. It is not a game played by people who are too old to sin vigorously. To the contrary, Christianity represents a change of heart, rather than a change in biology. It means letting Jesus live out His life in us.

The call is not to argue over whether we are to really turn the other cheek or walk the second mile, but to always be in an attitude of service and humility.

That takes God's grace—transforming grace, empowering grace.

SOME GOOD REASONS TO KILL YOURSELF

And being found in human form he humbled himself and became obedient unto death, even death on a cross. Phil. 2:8, RSV.

J esus was God. Yet He came to this earth as a human being. That is the wonder of the universe. It is somewhat like you becoming an ant, except that, from what we know of the size and complexity of the universe, we must be infinitely closer to ants than God is to us. The point is that Jesus humbled Himself to become like us, and He humbled Himself even more to die for us, especially to die the criminal's death of crucifixion.

The central intent of the passages dealing with the second mile and the turning of the other cheek, as we noted yesterday, is not the exact way we are to live day by day, but the attitude or spirit in which we are to live. We are to live the crucified life.

Why must we do that? Because our uncrucified self is a major cause of our personal problems. Think about it. Why do I want to retaliate? Because someone has injured my pride, beat me to some financial reward, and so on. As a result, my self-defense or selfishness rises immediately and I am on the warpath.

What makes the Sermon on the Mount so difficult is that it says plainly that we must let God kill those attitudes and reactions.

As Christians we have come to realize that self is the primary cause for unhappiness. Protecting our self, coveting for our self, and worrying about the dignity of our self consume us. Such things not only destroy our peace; they also lead us to destroy the peace of others, and vice versa. And what is true on the individual level is true also on the international level. As I write this piece, the war in what used to be Yugoslavia is heating up again because one side feels impelled to regain land and the other side to protect its gains.

Thus the history of the world goes on and on. But Jesus wants to end that history—first in our hearts and at last in a cosmic sense at the Second Advent.

BEING HOLY LIKE GOD

Therefore, prepare your minds for action; be self-controlled; set your hope fully on the grace to be given you when Jesus Christ is revealed. As obedient children, do not conform to the evil desires you had when you lived in ignorance. But just as he who called you is holy, so be holy in all you do; for it is written: "Be holy, because I am holy." 1 Peter 1:13-16, NIV.

Being holy is a Bible command. But what does it mean to be holy? Some see the focal point of holiness in how they keep the Sabbath. Others see holiness as being faithful in diet or the paying of tithes and offerings, or all of those things plus more. But that more is defined in terms of outward actions. Such definitions re-create the very problem that Jesus was speaking against: the problem of the insufficient holiness of the scribes and Pharisees.

They were good at all these things. In fact, they prided themselves that their behavior was far superior to that of other people. Thus their behavior became part of the problem, even though they were outwardly doing all to please God.

But how can that be? How could they fail in being holy if they were scrupulous in keeping the Sabbath, exacting in tithing, and careful in diet?

Their problem was that their motivation for holiness was rooted in the wrong thing. It was rooted in their love for their own selves, rather than in their love for God and other people.

True holiness is not primarily rooted in actions, but in attitudes. True holiness ultimately means that I have been delivered from self-centered living. It means that my life is centered with God in Christ. It means that the center of my life is no longer in what people think of me or what they can do for me, but in what I can do for others.

True holiness is the greatest need of our world. It is my greatest need today. It stands at the center of what the kingdom of God is all about. God wants me to be holy as He is holy.

JESUS RAISES THE ANTE

You have heard that it was said, "You shall love your neighbor and hate your enemy." But I say to you, Love your enemies and pray for those who persecute you. Matt. 5:43, 44, RSV.

Just how much does our righteousness need to exceed that of the scribes and the Pharisees (see Matt. 5:20)? That is the question.

From Matthew 5:21 Jesus has been illustrating that "exceeding" righteousness. And it has been exceeding in the extreme. He has told us that we can't have hateful thoughts, lustful desires, or easy divorces, and that our thoughts and speech must be pure. He has defined sin in such a way as to make it more than behavior. Sin also includes thoughts and motivations.

And then in verses 38-42 Jesus appears to have topped it off by telling us we can't even retaliate toward those who do us wrong. But now in verses 43, 44 He even goes further than that. It is one thing for me not to hit you back when you hit me, but it is quite another for me to love you when you do me wrong, to pray for you when you misuse me and persecute me.

Jesus has upped the ante to the highest possible amount. How can anyone do such things? It's not normal.

That's right. Loving one's enemies isn't normal, but it is Christian, and in the next few verses Jesus will tell us why it is Christian.

The paragraph that tells us to love our enemies is integrally related to the one that went before, commanding us not to retaliate. The first paragraph (verses 38-42) put the principle in negative terms, telling us what we can't do; whereas the present paragraph (verses 43-48) puts it in positive terms, telling us what we must do.

Here in verses 43 through 48 we arrive at the apex of what it means to be a Christian. We are to love our enemies; we are to pray for those who persecute us.

Have you tried to do those things? Do you, through God's empowering grace, practice them in your daily life?

THE MEANING OF LOVE

For God so loved the world, that he gave his only begotten Son, that whosoever believeth in him should not perish, but have everlasting life. John 3:16.

Love is defined by different people in different ways, some of them very unloving.

The Greek language is rich in words for love. It uses four different words. The first is *storgē*, which is family love—it is the love that a parent has for a child.

The second Greek word for love is *erōs*, from which we get our word erotic. This is the love of a man for a woman, and vice versa. It includes sexual love.

The third word is *philia*. We recognize this word in Philadelphia, the city of brotherly love. *Philia* represents an affectionate love, a love that people feel toward their best friends.

The fourth and most important of the Greek words for love is *agapē*. *Agapē* stands for unconquerable benevolence, an invincible goodwill. When we care for a person with *agapē*, we love that person no matter what that person has done to us, no matter how deeply they have hurt us. We want the best for them in spite of the way they may be treating us. *Agapē* is totally unconditional. Jesus uses *agapē* in Matthew 5:44. That is the type of love we are to shower upon our enemies.

At this point it should be realized that *agapē* love is not a feeling, but a deep principle. It is a principle of the heart and mind. It is a determination to love people in spite of their actions and in spite of our human feelings. It represents a determination of the mind. *Agapē* is the power to love even those whom we do not like and who do not like us. It is a part of the fruit of conversion.

Jesus commanded us to love our enemies. He did not tell us we have to like them. We cannot like everybody, but we are commanded to love every person. That command is the most far-reaching in the Bible; it is the most impossible.

Today, O Lord, help me to do the impossible. I pray for a special outpouring of Your grace.

THE MEANING OF "FATHER"

Love your enemies and pray for those who persecute you, so that you may be sons of your Father who is in heaven; for he makes his sun rise on the evil and the good, and sends rain on the just and on the unjust. Matt. 5:44, 45, RSV.

One of the key words in verse 45 is "Father." This image is central to the Sermon on the Mount. "Father" to most people connotes warm feelings of protection and caring. When the Bible uses "Father" in relation to God it does so in terms of loving-kindness. "Our Father" is one in whom we can trust. The Father provides for us. That is part of what Jesus means when He calls God our Father.

That conception of God is special to the Bible. The non-Christian religions have tended to see the Supreme Being as an object of fear rather than of love. They have often set Him forth as an angry God who needs to be appeased by offerings. But the Bible presents God as a loving Father who so loved the world that He gave His only-begotten Son. Jesus' picture of God is revolutionary, but it is also comforting.

God becomes our Father when we become Christians, when we are born again of the water and the Spirit into the family of God. John writes that "as many as received him [Jesus], to them gave he power to become the sons of God, even to them that believe in his name: which were born, not of blood, nor of the will of the flesh, nor of the will of man, but of God" (John 1:12, 13).

God is Father to the Christian. To others He is God the Creator or God the Lawgiver. That does not mean that God doesn't love non-Christians, only that He is not their Father in the way He is "our Father."

That, of course, makes us His children. As a result, we live by a different set of principles (the Beatitudes) from those who belong to another family. "Our Father" is one of the richest images in the New Testament. It is a genuinely Christian image.

THE MEANING OF NEIGHBOR

You shall not hate your brother in your heart, but you shall reason with your neighbor, lest you bear sin because of him. You shall not take vengeance or bear any grudge against the sons of your own people, but you shall love your neighbor as yourself: I am the Lord. Lev. 19:17, 18, RSV.

Neighbor for the Jews of Christ's day meant their "own people." Neighbor meant other Jews. That definition is not difficult to understand if we think of their history. They had gone into captivity because they had worshiped the gods of their Canaanite neighbors. As a result, after their return in the days of Ezra and Nehemiah they decided to stay away from all possible contamination, to avoid non-Jews. They were bound and determined to stay pure. The Pharisaic party had become the leaders of Jewish separation. Other nations were enemies and not to be associated with.

It is in this context that the parable of the good Samaritan takes on special meaning. That parable is Jesus' most precise definition of who our neighbors are. Jesus is particularly responding to the question "Who is my neighbour?" (Luke 10:29). His reply shattered the Pharisaic categories.

It is significant that Jesus answered the question by illustrating the good deed of a Samaritan. The Jews despised the Samaritans because they were seen as apostates from the true religion—they were a mixture of the true religion and the false.

In His parable Jesus tells of a Jew who was attacked by thieves on the road to Jericho. Several Jews passed by but did not help their fellow countryman. But the Samaritan, the enemy, crossed the road to care for that Jew in every possible way. The Jew would not have done the same if the Samaritan was in trouble. Thus the parable illustrates enemy love. It illustrates *true* neighbor love.

Who is my neighbor? Any person who is down because of sin or illness or any other difficulty. A Christian's neighbor is everybody.

Thus Jesus continues to expand our understanding of the meaning and depth of the law. There is no end or limits to the obligation of loving.

THE MEANING OF BEING LIKE GOD

The eyes of all wait upon thee; and thou givest them their meat in due season. Thou openest thine hand, and satisfiest the desire of every living thing. Ps. 145:15, 16.

Being like God! There is a thought that ought to frighten and perplex us. Jesus has flatly told us in Matthew 5:45 that we are to demonstrate that we are the children of the Father in our daily lives. But how? How can we be like God? Is He asking the impossible from us?

Once again we need to be reminded that it is the context of any Bible passage that helps us understand what is being said. And the context to Matthew 5:45 is loud and clear.

Being like God is loving our enemies. Being like God is praying for those who persecute us.

Now, watch out here. It is easy to read these statements in the abstract. It is not so difficult to love enemies in general. It is not humanly impossible to love nebulous persecutors who are extensions of our thought processes.

But put a face on that persecutor and we will have to struggle mightily. I am reminded of Harry Orchard, a hit man hired to kill the governor of Idaho in the early years of the twentieth century.

Orchard carried out his mission with cool efficiency. But he was caught and sent to prison.

How would you feel if you were the late governor's wife? Now you would have an enemy with a face. Now is the challenge.

It so happens that the governor's wife was a Seventh-day Adventist. What would you do in her situation? Take a moment to think through that question. Discuss it with those who may be in your devotional group.

The governor's wife knew what she must do. She must love her enemy. That meant visiting Orchard in his cell, praying with him, forgiving him, doing good to him.

The result was the conversion of Harry Orchard. He became a Seventh-day Adventist Christian and a model prisoner. Such is the power of love. Expressing such love is being like the Father.

MORE ON THE
MEANING OF BEING LIKE GOD

While we were yet helpless, at the right time Christ died for the ungodly. Why, one will hardly die for a righteous man—though perhaps for a good man one will dare even to die. But God shows his love for us in that when we were yet sinners Christ died for us. . . . While we were enemies we were reconciled to God by the death of his Son. Rom. 5:6-10, RSV.

Would you send your young and innocent son into a nest of killers and robbers? Would you send your son so that he could tell them that you are really a nice guy? Would you do so even if you knew they would scoff at him, reject him, and eventually kill him, even as he was trying to help them?

Fortunately, we do not have to make that choice. But God did. He so loved the world that He gave His only Son to come and die for us so that we might have life eternal. That is the kind of God we serve. That is the kind of love He has. As today's Scripture reading puts it, Jesus died for us while we were still His enemies. Jesus meant it when He said that if we want to be like our Father in heaven we will need to love and want the best for even our enemies.

God not only demonstrated what it means to love an enemy (Matt. 5:44) when He sent Jesus to die for us; He demonstrates His love for His enemies daily when "he makes his sun rise on the evil and on the good, and sends rain on the just and on the unjust" (verse 45, RSV). God's love and care is a constant that is continually with us.

Unrenewed human nature wouldn't do it God's way. It would think the matter of allegiance through and come to the conclusion that the evil people didn't deserve rain and sunshine. And that conclusion would be correct.

But the wonder of it all is that God doesn't give us what we deserve. He gives us what we need.

As Christians we are called to be lovers. We are called to imitate the Father who loves even His enemies.

STILL MORE ON
THE MEANING OF BEING LIKE GOD

I have given you an example, that ye should do as I have done to you. John 13:15.

How do people really know if they are like their Father in heaven? It is not through church membership. Being a church member means belonging to a church; it means having your name written in a record book somewhere; it means that you have outwardly subscribed to a body of doctrines held by that church. But it may have very little to do with being like the Father. In fact, many who are church members and even church leaders tend to act more like the devil than like the Father.

Church membership is important because the church ideally provides a fellowship of believers who encourage and strengthen one another in their Christian walk. The church (in spite of all of its shortcomings) also has preserved the Christian message across the ages. But the church is not God any more than church membership means that a person is a Christian.

Being a Christian means being like the Father, who loves even His enemies. It means following the example of Jesus. Jesus zeroed in on what it means to be a Christian and what it means to be like the Father when He said that "all men will know that you are my disciples, if you have love for one another" (John 13:35, RSV). The crucial element is that we love others as God has loved us.

Ellen White helps us understand this point when she writes that "it is not earthly rank, nor birth, nor nationality, nor religious privilege, which proves that we are members of the family of God; it is love, a love that embraces all humanity." She goes on to note that even sinners will respond to kindness, but that "it is only the Spirit of God that gives love for hatred. To be kind to the unthankful and to the evil, to do good hoping for nothing again, is the insignia of the royalty of heaven, the sure token by which the children of the Highest reveal their high estate" (*Thoughts From the Mount of Blessing*, p. 75).

Jesus' command to me is that I must be like my Father.

GOODBYE TO THE GOD OF THE DEISTS

In many and various ways God spoke of old to our fathers by the prophets; but in these last days he has spoken to us by a Son, whom he appointed the heir of all things, through whom also he created the world. He reflects the glory of God and bears the very stamp of his nature, upholding the universe by his word of power. Heb. 1:1-3, RSV.

The eighteenth century witnessed the rise of a breakaway from Christianity called deism. Deism was a religion based on human reason rather than divine revelation. It was greatly stimulated by the rise of modern science.

Such discoveries as the law of gravitation by Sir Isaac Newton set the stage for deists. They began to see the universe as a grand machine that ran all by itself according to the laws of nature. Of course, they still needed a God to create the machine and specify the laws that run it, but it seemed obvious to the deists that once in motion the cosmic machine could run quite well without God's interference.

Thus their God didn't interfere with the earth or its inhabitants. After Creation He went on vacation, so to speak, and left humanity to itself. As a result, they discounted miracles, supernatural revelation, and all other breakthroughs of the divine into human affairs.

The Sermon on the Mount takes a mighty stand against all such theories. Not only was Jesus a divine breakthrough from heaven to earth in the Incarnation, but that very God, according to Hebrews 1, is the Creator God and the upholder and sustainer of day-to-day existence.

Ellen White emphasizes the teachings of Hebrews 1 and Matthew 5:45 when she writes that "it is not because of inherent power that year by year the earth produces her bounties. . . . It is through [God's] power that summer and winter, seedtime and harvest, day and night follow each other. . . . It is by His word that vegetation flourishes. . . . Every good thing we have, each ray of sunshine and shower of rain, every morsel of food, every moment of life, is a gift of love" *(Thoughts From the Mount of Blessing,* pp. 74, 75).

Thank God that He "maketh his sun to rise" and that He "sendeth rain."

THE "MORE THAN" TYPE OF RIGHTEOUSNESS

For if ye love them which love you, what reward have ye? do not even the publicans the same? And if ye salute your brethren only, what do ye more than others? do not even the publicans so? Matt. 5:46, 47.

The flow of the argument in Matthew 5 takes an unexpected turn in verses 46 and 47. Up to this point Jesus had been arguing that our righteousness must exceed that of the scribes and Pharisees. He has provided us with six illustrations of how they failed to truly understand the law. Six times He has contrasted their interpretation of the law with His.

But now, right at the climax of His argument, Jesus twice brings up the publicans. Why? Why mention these people when they are at the social and religious extreme of the scribes and Pharisees? If the Pharisees prided themselves in their separation from all Gentiles (including the Romans), the unjust tax collectors (publicans) were collaborators with the enemy. If the Pharisees were scrupulous in their observance of religious duties, the publicans did their own thing. They could care less about the fine points of religion. They were out to have a good time.

Therefore, we are forced to ask again, why did Jesus illustrate His point by bringing up the publicans when He could have more naturally said that even the Pharisees love those who love them, and that you must exceed their righteousness?

The answer seems to be that Jesus was highlighting the fact that legalistic religion and no religion both live by the same principles—the principles of this world. In short, the real righteousness of the scribes and Pharisees didn't even exceed that of the publicans.

Both religious legalists and libertarians reward those who like them, greet them, and invite them over to dinner. But the righteousness of God's followers is radical from that of the world. Like God, His followers must learn even to bless their enemies, love their enemies, desire the very best for their enemies.

That is the essence of radical religion. That is the essence of true Christianity and the righteousness that must exceed that of the scribes and Pharisees.

NORMAL VERSUS UNNORMAL PEOPLE

For I delight in the law of God after the inward man. Rom. 7:22.

C hristians are not normal!

At least they are not normal as the world defines normal. Again and again in our study of the Sermon on the Mount this year we have seen that Christianity is not the adding on of a belief in Jesus and a few good habits to one's old self. To the contrary, the old life has been crucified in Christ and resurrected to a new way of thinking and acting. Even so-called good lives must die to pride and prejudice. Christianity is a transformed life, a new creation, a born-from-above experience. Anything less than that is not Christianity.

Thus, we might ask again, what is it that undergirds the "more than" of Matthew 5:47? D. Martin Lloyd-Jones, in his excellent study of the Sermon on the Mount, provides a few pointers here.

First, the converted Christian does not think the same as normal worldlings. The natural person may give a grudging obedience, but the Christian delights "in the law of God" in his or her heart. The Christian is the one who has imbibed the spirit of the law of love, not merely its letter.

Those with only the letter still fall short of what it means to be a Christian. Thus a second distinction between "normal" people and Christians is that the natural person always thinks of sin in terms of action, things that are done or not done. By way of contrast, the Christian is interested in the heart. That has been Christ's main point since Matthew 5:20. Both sin and the "more than" type of righteousness are rooted in the Christian's innermost being.

But that righteousness flows out in daily living of the law of love that far exceeds that of both Pharisees and publicans. That is a third distinction between even "normal religion" and genuine Christianity.

A fourth difference between the two groups is the Christian's attitude to self. Whereas the life of the secular person or the legalistic religionist is tinctured with pride, a real Christian has the poverty of spirit and hunger after true righteousness that is at the heart of the Beatitudes.

Christians really are "more than" normal, natural people.

"THEREFORE"

Be ye therefore perfect, even as your Father which is in heaven is perfect. Matt. 5:48.

Therefore" is a key word in verse 48. "Therefore" implies a conclusion to what has gone before.

Verse 48, with its call for Godlike perfection, needs to be linked to verse 20, which calls for greater righteousness than the scribes and Pharisees. Those two texts bracket Jesus' six examples regarding the depth of the law. They present God's ideal before and after those illustrations.

Thus there is a sense in which being perfect like the Father is equated with keeping the spirit of the law, as opposed to the legalistic letter. There is a sense in which each of the six sections in verses 21-48 calls for perfection, each makes an absolute demand that cannot be surpassed. For example, what more can be done about lust than driving it out of the heart (verses 17-30)? And who else is left to love after one has loved the enemy (verses 43-48)?

But while the "therefore" of verse 48 refers in one sense to all Jesus' teachings between verses 21 and 47, it belongs to verses 42 through 47 in an even more specific way. That is demonstrated by a comparison of verse 45 with verse 48. These are the only two verses in the entire passage that call for Christians to be like their Father in heaven. Verses 43 to 47 make explicit the essence of that likeness.

Jesus is not dealing with abstractions here. Being like the Father means loving one's enemies, just as God loves His enemies. After all, doesn't He provide sunshine and rain for evil people, just as He does for good? Anybody, even tax collectors, can love his or her friends. God demands of His children supernatural love for *all* people. Just as the Father so loved the world that He gave His Son to die for people who were ungodly and His enemies, so are Christians to love even those who despitefully use them. That is the ultimate in God-likeness in Godliness.

As a result, "therefore" is one of the most important words in Matthew 5:48. Without that word we cannot see clearly what Jesus is referring to when He tells us to be perfect.

PERFECTION IS A PROCESS

And he said, "The kingdom of God is as if a man should scatter seed upon the ground, and should sleep and rise night and day, and the seed should sprout and grow, he knows not how. The earth produces of itself, first the blade, then the ear, then the full grain in the ear. But when the grain is ripe, at once he puts in the sickle, because the harvest has come." Mark 4:26-29, RSV.

As I write these lines it is springtime in Michigan. The farmers are just now readying their powerful tractors for seed planting. Before long the corn will be up. Then will come the incredibly rapid growth as Michigan's long northern days share their sunlight with the developing plants. But before long the state's relatively short growing season will be over and the combines will be in the field harvesting the crop.

I love to see things grow. I like gardening—especially vegetable gardening. It is a pleasure to go out in the early morning or at dusk and examine the growing plants. Over the years there is one thing that has struck me. That is that a perfect piece of fruit at harvesttime has been through a process that shows its perfection at each stage of its development. A perfectly shaped ripe tomato, for example, had a perfection at each stage of its development, even though it was not mature until its final stage.

Becoming like God is like that for the developing Christian. Perfection is more like a line than a point. Perfection is a process that begins to take place in the newborn Christian and continues throughout the ceaseless ages of eternity. A Christian becomes more and more like God without ever equaling exactly what God is. Thus Paul can say that a person can be perfect but not yet perfect (see Phil. 3:15, 12).

Ellen White presents us with a similar idea when she compares the development of Christian life to plant growth: "At every stage of development our life may be perfect; yet if God's purpose for us is fulfilled, there will be continual advancement" *(Christ's Object Lessons, p. 65).*

THE MEANING OF PERFECTION

Beloved, let us love one another: for love is of God; and every one that loveth is born of God, and knoweth God. He that loveth not knoweth not God; for God is love. 1 John 4:7, 8.

The word for "perfection" in Matthew 5:48 is from the Greek word *teleios*. That word has nothing to do with concepts of absolute perfection or absolute sinlessness. To the contrary, *teleios* means "maturity" and is translated as such in most instances in modern Bible translations.

In the biblical use of the concept, people are *teleios* (perfect) when they are full-grown or have reached full stature. Thus a student who has a mature knowledge of mathematics is *teleios* (mature or perfect) as opposed to a learner who is just beginning.

The idea underlying this biblical word and those words closely related to it is that things have an end, a purpose, an aim, or a goal. That concept has found its way into English through our word teleology. A thing is *teleios* if it realizes the purpose for which it was made or planned.

We must therefore ask for what purpose or end human beings were created. The Bible leaves us no doubt on that point. "Let us make man in our image, after our likeness" (Gen. 1:26, RSV). Humans are to be like God. Thus it is only natural for Jesus to claim in Matthew 5:48 that the Christian should become *teleios* (perfect or mature) in love like the Father in heaven. After all, "God is love" (1 John 4:8). Christians are to act in love like God rather than to act like the devil.

Thus, according to the New Testament, the "perfect" Christian is the mature, whole, complete Christian. The same holds true of the Old Testament, where the words translated as "perfect" generally mean "complete," "upright," or "blameless" in a spiritual sense.

You may be wondering where the interpretation of perfection as absolute, total, flawless sinlessness came in. It came in with the same apostasy of the medieval church that accepted other Greek philosophical ideas, such as the consciousness of the soul in death. It is that misinterpretation of the Middle Ages that literally drove men and women into monastic attempts at perfection.

God's way is a better way.

THE CHARACTER OF CHARACTER PERFECTION

But love ye your enemies, and do good, and lend, hoping for nothing again; and your reward shall be great, and ye shall be the children of the Highest: for he is kind unto the unthankful and to the evil. Be ye therefore merciful, as your Father also is merciful. Luke 6:35, 36.

Seventh-day Adventists have been concerned with character perfection for good reasons. Not only does Jesus command it in Matthew 5:48, but Ellen White has a fair amount to say on the topic.

One of Mrs. White's most noted statements on the subject is found in *Christ's Object Lessons*, page 69, where we read that "Christ is waiting with longing desire for the manifestation of Himself in His church. When the character of Christ shall be perfectly reproduced in His people, then He will come to claim them as His own."

Unfortunately, many come to that passage with a definition of perfection that is more closely related to that of the Pharisees, Greek philosophy, and the teaching of the medieval church than to the Bible definition of perfection. As a result, they think of character as primarily a list of behaviors and immediately set out to collect Ellen White quotations to buttress their new theology.

It would be better to read the context of the *Christ's Object Lessons* statement on pages 67 and 68. Ellen White is quite clear that "Christ is seeking to reproduce Himself in the hearts of men." As a result, "as you receive the Spirit of Christ—the Spirit of unselfish love and labor for others—you will grow and bring forth fruit. . . . Your faith will increase, your convictions deepen, *your love be made perfect. More and more* you will reflect the likeness of Christ" (italics supplied).

Like Jesus in Matthew 5, Ellen White's definition of character perfection centers on developing the loving character of our God. That insight is deepened when we compare Luke's version of the Sermon on the Mount. After providing essentially the same discussion as Matthew 5:43-47, Luke has Jesus concluding: "Be ye therefore *merciful*, as your Father also is merciful" (Luke 6:36). Thus the Gospel writers equated the perfect or mature Christian with the merciful Christian. That equation stands at the heart of character perfection.

ANOTHER TRIP TO THE BEATITUDES

Hide thy face from my sins, and blot out all mine iniquities. Create in me a clean heart, O God, and renew a right spirit within me. Cast me not away from thy presence; and take not thy holy spirit from me. Restore unto me the joy of thy salvation; and uphold me with thy free spirit. Then will I teach transgressors thy ways; and sinners shall be converted unto thee. Ps. 51:9-13.

Between verses 20 and 48 of Matthew 5, Jesus has been telling us not only that our righteousness must exceed that of the scribes and Pharisees, but that the implications of the law for daily living are much deeper and broader than any Pharisee even dreamed.

As long as they kept to their narrow little definition of sin as an outward action they were safe in relating to their restricted understanding of perfection.

But Jesus has exploded their smugness again and again in Matthew 5. Not only is murder a sin; so is evil thinking and evil talking. Not only is adultery a sin; so is evil imagining. And to top it all off, we as Christians can't even retaliate. To the contrary, we are commanded to love our enemies and thus be as perfect as God.

Who is sufficient for such things? None of us! We all fall short. I am a person of fairly strong willpower, and I have discovered I can stop doing this or that (say, stop eating peanut butter) under my own steam. But my self-complacency and self-sufficiency are totally shattered by Jesus' teachings in Matthew 5. There is no way I can love all my enemies all the time, except through the power of God's grace.

Thus Matthew 5:21-48, and especially verse 48, drive me again and again back to the Beatitudes as I realize my poverty of spirit, my lack of purity, and my shortfall in being merciful. Like David of old, when I see my life in the light of what I should be, I hunger and thirst after God's righteousness.

I thank God daily that He is merciful and forgiving and loving, even to those who slip and fall, or even rebel.

Help me, Lord, to be more like You!

TAKING A FOURTH STEP
IN OUR WALK WITH JESUS

Beware of practicing your piety before men in order to be seen by them; for then you will have no reward from your Father who is in heaven. Matt. 6:1, RSV.

With Matthew 6:1 we have come to another of the great transition verses of the Sermon on the Mount. For the past six months we have examined Matthew 5. That chapter presented us with three great building blocks in the formation of a Christian's life. The first was the Beatitudes (Matt. 5:3-12), representing what every Christian's character must be. The second was a Christian's witness, in verses 13 through 16. Then came the extremely rich teachings of 5:17-48, in which Jesus expounded on a Christian's righteousness.

There is a sense in which Matthew 6 carries on Jesus' discussion of a Christian's righteousness. But whereas Matthew 5:17-48 dealt with moral righteousness, the first half of chapter 6 presents what might be called "religious" righteousness.

The first part of the chapter deals with three areas of personal piety—almsgiving, prayer, and fasting. Because these were common acts of Jewish piety, Jesus uses these areas to illustrate principles that can be applied to all acts of religious piety. In other words, these three are samples of piety rather than an exhaustive listing of Christian practice.

Note that Jesus does not command these activities. He merely says, "When you give alms . . ." "When you pray . . ." He expects these acts to be practiced by citizens of the kingdom of heaven. That fact is interesting in itself, since one of His three illustrations—fasting—has fallen into disuse by evangelical Christians and is even viewed by some as a perversion of the Middle Ages.

Praying, fasting, and giving. What do they have in common? They are all illustrations of acts of piety; they are all acts of devotion that Christians practice in their relationship to the God of heaven. That is why Matthew 6:1-18 should be thought of as "a Christian's piety."

Help us today, our Father, as we seek to practice the great acts of devotion that are an integral part of Christian living.

IS JESUS CONTRADICTING HIMSELF?

By this my Father is glorified, that you bear much fruit, and so prove to be my disciples. John 15:8, RSV.

Jesus confuses me. In Matthew 5:16 He told me to let my light shine so that others would see my good works and glorify the Father. Now in Matthew 6:1 He tells me to beware of practicing my piety before other people, to be seen by them.

I'm confused! Isn't giving to the poor a good work? How am I to keep my light hidden and let my light shine at the same time?

While on the surface these two verses seem to contradict each other, in actuality they are complementary teachings. The topic in Matthew 5:16 is public witness, while prayer, almsgiving, and fasting are personal devotions.

But more important, the goal of Matthew 5:16 is the glory of God, whereas the false practices of piety in chapter 6 aim at glorifying their practitioners. In that light they are condemned, since all worship and every act in a Christian's life should be directed at honoring God.

Christians are to live in such a way that people looking at them will glorify God. A Christian performs no act of worship to be seen or admired by other people. Frederick Dale Bruner states the fine balance between Matthew 5:16 and 6:1 nicely when he writes: "It is right to do good works in such a way that when people see them they think of God; it is wrong to do good works in such a way that when people see them they think of us."

That is not an easy thing to carry out. We are all tempted to be in love with our selves in unhealthy ways. Because of Jesus' plain words, we know we need to be careful about our "spiritual bragging." And so we announce before the church that God has done some great thing for somebody through our witness the past week, making sure that God's "humble" agent (our self) features prominently. The rest of us quickly see through the ploy and say to ourselves, "I thank God I am not like that." And with that one stroke we fall into the same pharisaical pit. It takes an act of grace to really give God the glory.

REPETITION: A LAW OF LEARNING

Thus, when you give alms, sound no trumpet before you, as the hypocrites do in the synagogues and in the streets, that they may be praised by men. Truly, I say to you, they have received their reward. Matt. 6:2, RSV.

Three times in chapter 6 Jesus uses the same pattern to get His point across. He knew that human minds weakened by sin need to hear things more than once if they are to grasp a lesson. And Jesus is the teacher par excellence.

Note His style. First, He lays out the general principle in verse 1: Don't practice pious acts to be seen of other people. Such people will receive no reward beyond their present ego trip. Next He moves on to illustrate that major lesson in regard to almsgiving (verses 2-4), praying (verses 5, 6), and fasting (verses 16-18).

All three of those illustrations repeat the same pattern. First comes a description of the false way of piety, which focuses on public display of the "worshiper's holiness." Because of their insincere motivation (worshiping or calling attention to themselves while claiming to worship and call attention to God), Jesus calls them "hypocrites" in all three illustrations.

The word "hypocrite" in the Greek meant an actor on the stage. Now, there is a positive aspect of being an actor. After all, a noble person can play the part of another with feeling and accuracy. But it is the negative meaning of the word that is picked up by Jesus. In the negative sense, the stage is a sham world and the actors are deceivers. In those days actors wore masks on their faces; the masks held hidden megaphones so that the actors could be heard. So a hypocrite is one who wears a false face. He or she is pretending to honor God, while really honoring self. Such people already have their reward.

The second half of each illustration suggests a proper way to fulfill the obligation. In each case the central idea is that motivation for devotion should be grounded in a person's relationship with the Father rather than in a desire to look good. All three illustrations close with a statement that the faithful will be rewarded by God.

THE QUESTION OF REWARDS

For what will it profit a man, if he gains the whole world and forfeits his life? Or what shall a man give in return for his life? For the Son of man is to come with his angels in the glory of his Father, and then he will repay every man for what he has done. Matt. 16:26, 27, RSV.

The story is told of a man walking down a road with a bucket of water in one hand and a bucket of fire in the other. When asked what he was going to do with his buckets, he replied that he was going to burn up heaven with the bucket of fire and drown hell with the bucket of water. His interest was in neither. He claimed his reason for being a Christian was deeper than rewards. He preached goodness for goodness' sake alone. He inferred that the whole idea of rewards was less than Christian.

Many people have found the idea of rewards for personal piety to be distasteful. Yet the passage running from Matthew 6:1 to 18 states repeatedly that those who are faithful in secret will be rewarded. Apparently Jesus never found the topic to be nearly as distasteful as some of His followers.

One reason some people seem to be against the idea of rewards for personal piety is that at first it appears to express the idea of salvation by merit. But such reasoning fails to take into consideration that the Sermon on the Mount is addressed to those already saved. Again and again in these chapters Jesus speaks to those who address God as "Father." They already belong to the family of God.

Thus their acts of devotion are not meritorious acts to get into the kingdom, but responses of love and adoration because they are already on the inside.

Jesus had no problem with the idea of either heaven or hell. He held both of these up repeatedly as the respective conclusions of the choices people make throughout life. The most important choice that any of us will ever make is the decision as to who will be the Lord of our life. It is quite proper to look forward to our blessed reward.

THE CHRISTIAN'S REWARD

But as it is written: Eye hath not seen, nor ear heard, neither have entered into the heart of man, the things which God hath prepared for them that love him. 1 Cor. 2:9.

A small boy sat quietly in a Western train. It was a hot, dusty day, one very uncomfortable for travelers, and that particular day's travel was one of the most uninteresting of the whole trip. But the little fellow sat patiently watching the fields and fences hurrying by, until a motherly older lady leaned forward and asked sympathetically, "Aren't you tired of the long ride, dear, and the dust and the heat?"

The youngster looked up brightly and replied with a smile, "Yes, ma'am, a little. But I don't mind it much because my father is going to meet me when I get to the end of it."

That is a beautiful thought. No matter how monotonous life gets, no matter how discouraging or even painful, we as Christians have something to look forward to at the end of our earthly journey. Our Father is waiting for us. That is our incentive. That promise keeps us going. Our Maker will meet us, and His reward will be with Him. But while Christians look forward to their end-time rewards, they should not overlook the day-by-day rewards of a Christian life. First, we have an assurance that we are doing the right thing. That provides Christians with an unequaled peace of mind.

Second, we presently have the reward of helping other people. That is a satisfaction that is worth more than silver or gold. As Christians we need to consciously make room for more of the blessings that come from helping people.

A third present reward for faithful work for the Lord is still more work. That is one of the great lessons of the parable of the talents. Those who had done much will have the privilege of wider service as they become more and more like their Master.

Our Father, as we think of our Christian reward in both the here and the hereafter, we ask for a renewed portion of Your grace that we might continue to be recipients of Your blessings.

HONOR FROM WHOM?

I receive not honour from men. . . . How can ye believe, which receive honour one of another, and seek not the honour that cometh from God only? John 5:41-44.

One of life's crucial choices is whom we want to honor us, God or other people? Whose favor do we curry? Whose applause do we seek? What are we willing to do to receive that favor or hear that applause?

These are rather frightful questions, because they come close to the center of who we are and how we live our daily lives.

We all know the right answer to these questions. We should be like Jesus, who cared not a fig for the applause of humans, but only for the approbation of the Father.

The problem is that we are not Jesus. All too often we are looking over our shoulder to see what other people think of us. As Christians we know that we shouldn't be after the kind of worldly applause we might get in Hollywood, or the kudos we might receive as president of General Motors. Of course, we recognize that it is not the success that is wrong, but the attracting of attention to ourselves as the supposed engineers of that success.

We as Christians can generally see beyond that kind of worldly pride. That's most often not our problem. But we have a spiritual equivalent to it. We struggle with spiritual and churchly pride.

Look what a great evangelist I am! Look what a tremendous sermon I preached! I give more to the church than anyone else! Why can't you just be humble like me?

The moral: There is no end to the ways we can seek honor from other people or even our selves. That is the problem the Pharisees struggled with. And Jesus wants our righteousness even in these areas of our lives to exceed that of the scribes and Pharisees. But if it does, please don't brag about it or point it out. My guess is that if we ever get to where we should be in our Christian lives, we will not even know that we have arrived, because God will be everything and we will recognize that without Him we are nothing.

YOU CAN FOOL SOME OF THE PEOPLE SOME OF THE TIME, BUT . . .

Nothing in all creation is hidden from God's sight. Everything is uncovered and laid bare before the eyes of him to whom we must give account. Heb. 4:13, NIV.

It was a terrible cake. In fact, it was the worst cake I had ever tasted. But what to do about it? That was the problem. After all, it had been specially baked for my birthday by my new bride. I couldn't hurt her feelings, but I most certainly couldn't *eat* it.

Fortunately, the day after my birthday she went off to her sister's home for a few days, leaving the rest of the cake with me. But those days were now gone. In a few guilt-ridden hours she would return and I would be caught.

Maybe, I mused, I could toss it into the tall weeds of the empty lot across the street. But with my luck she would hike through that lot and come home with cake on her shoes. That wouldn't do. Neither would the garbage can. A few telltale crumbs stuck to the bottom might be my undoing.

Finally it hit me! Why hadn't I thought of it before?

I picked up the cake and tiptoed into the bathroom. With the door shut, I quickly broke it into small pieces, dropped them in, pulled the handle, and witnessed a potential family disaster rush into oblivion.

Free at last! How great the feeling! My young bride was delighted that I had "enjoyed" the cake.

The lesson is simple: You can fool some of the people some of the time.

Of course, what works with people doesn't work with God. He sees not only the action but also the motive behind the action.

He wants to take my life, my heart, today and purify it. He wants to go deeper than the things I do, He wants to change why I do things—even Christian things. He wants me to worship Him for no other reason than that He is the Lord of my life.

Lord, today please help me with my inner struggles. Help me not only to do the right things, but to do them for the right reasons.

GIVING AS JESUS GAVE

But when you give to the needy, do not let your left hand know what your right hand is doing, so that your giving may be in secret. Then your Father, who sees what is done in secret, will reward you. Matt. 6:3, 4, NIV.

It was really quite disgusting.

The church was midway in a building program, and the pastor was calling for a public offering from the front. "Who will give $2,000?" he cried out with enthusiasm. "Will those willing to give $2,000 please stand?" One brother did, and every eye turned to see who had made the big offering. There he stood, smiling ear to ear and holding his checkbook high over his head.

And there I sat as a somewhat regular attendee of an Adventist congregation that I refused to join. As a non-Christian visitor I was appalled. I hadn't read through my New Testament very far by that time, but I had gotten as far as Matthew 6.

Why, I asked myself, does a church that claims to have the truth stoop to such unbiblical methods of raising money? Does the church need to manipulate the obvious vanity of a showy brother like the one who was standing in order to raise money? Why was he giving? Why was the pastor using such methods?

I wish I could say that that was the last time I have seen that technique used. Unfortunately, vanity may be easier to appeal to than dedication. But without dedication the gift is less than worthless.

The good thing is that we don't have to respond to such tactics. And if we are following Jesus, we won't use them or respond to them. Jesus said we should let our giving be done privately—let it be unto God.

In saying this, He was not hitting at the edge of the sin problem, but at its center. God wants us to give to Him from our hearts. In fact, He wants all of our Christian actions to grow out of a heart that loves Him supremely.

Giving is acting like God, who gave His Son. He wants us to become like His giving self, but He wants us to do so for the right reason.

THE TWICE-BLESSED ACT

The poor shall never cease out of the land: therefore I command thee, saying, Thou shalt open thine hand wide unto thy brother, to thy poor, and to thy needy, in thy land. Deut. 15:11.

The work of beneficence," we read in *Thoughts From the Mount of Blessing*, "is twice blessed. While he that gives to the needy blesses others, he himself is blessed in a still greater degree. The grace of Christ in the soul is developing traits of character that are the opposite of selfishness—traits that will refine, ennoble, and enrich the life. Acts of kindness performed in secret will bind hearts together, and will draw them closer to the heart of Him from whom every generous impulse springs. The little attentions, the small acts of love and self-sacrifice, that flow out from the life as quietly as the fragrance from a flower—these constitute no small share of the blessings and happiness of life. And it will be found at last that the denial of self for the good and happiness of others, however humble and uncommended here, is recognized in heaven as the token of our union with Him, the King of glory, who was rich, yet for our sake became poor" (pp. 82, 83).

The twice-blessed act. A delightful thought. In silently helping others we are helping ourselves. We are developing our characters. We are becoming more like the God who has given so much to us. And in the process, we are helping someone who truly needs help.

The ministry of silent giving works upon our own lives. It is part of the process by which God takes selfish people and transforms them into His image.

But it is not a natural process. Far from it. The natural thing is for us to keep what is ours and build bigger and bigger homes and buy finer and finer cars. Or if we do give, we feel we should at least get a building or a room named after us as a remembrance of our generosity.

Giving in secret is quite a different thing. But, says Jesus, it brings its own unequaled reward.

Help me, Lord, to be like You rather than like me.

THE CHEERFUL GIVER

He which soweth sparingly shall reap also sparingly; and he which giveth bountifully shall reap also bountifully. Every man according as he purposeth in his heart, so let him give; not grudgingly, or of necessity: for God loveth a cheerful giver. 2 Cor. 9:6, 7.

I t's a law of nature. If you don't plant seeds, you can't harvest a crop. If you plant only a few seeds, you can at least harvest a small crop. If you plant much, you can hope to harvest much.

Paul is telling us that the same law holds true in the spiritual realm. Those who are stingy toward God and others can expect few blessings in terms of others being generous toward them. Generosity is catching, and we influence those around us, including our children. If they see that we are tight-fisted, they will tend to grow up to be tight-fisted and stingy. What and how we sow has its effects as our influence ripples across space and time.

God doesn't merely want us to give and to give secretly (as we have noted during the past few days), but He wants us to give cheerfully.

One of my favorite Bible stories about cheerful giving is the story of the widow who put two mites into the Temple treasury. The cash value of her offering was extremely small, yet Jesus "called unto him his disciples, and saith unto them, Verily I say unto you, That this poor widow hath cast more in, than all they which have cast [large amounts] into the treasury. For all they did cast in of their abundance; but she of her want did cast in all that she had, even all her living" (Mark 12:43, 44).

Her offering was recognized in heaven because her heart was in it. She was a cheerful giver. That is what God wants from each of us. He wants us to give from our hearts. More important than the amount is the spirit in which we give our offerings.

The very purpose of giving is to make us more like God the Father and Jesus the Son, who gave of themselves that we might be blessed both here and hereafter. God desires me to be a cheerful giver.

SIN FOLLOWED ME TO CHURCH

And when thou prayest, thou shalt not be as the hypocrites are: for they love to pray standing in the synagogues and in the corners of the streets, that they may be seen of men. Verily I say unto you, They have their reward. Matt. 6:5.

The most frightful thing about this text is its implications for the extent and omnipresence of sin.

When we think of sin, we generally think of something that happens in the dark, in an out-of-the-way place, in secrecy. When we think of sinners we think of heroin addicts and drug dealers, thieves, or adulterers.

But in Matthew 6:1-18 we find sin following us right into church. We find it in our devotions to God. We find it in our giving, in our praying, in our fasting.

Now you may be asking, "If we can't escape from the effects of sin in prayer, where can we escape?" The painful answer is: Nowhere. Sin taints everything we do. The problem with the scribes and the Pharisees is that they failed to see the depth and extent of sin. As a result, it caught them even in their acts of devotion. That is why Jesus spends so much time on this topic. In their drive for perfection before God, they fell once again into Satan's pit.

In the Sermon on the Mount, Jesus is telling His hearers that the Pharisees didn't really understand sin. They thought it was an action that needed to be avoided. But again and again He pounds home the frightful truth that sin is a disposition that infects our entire life. It is a prideful self-worship that follows us everywhere we go. Even when we claim to be worshiping God, we are too often actively worshiping ourselves.

That is what Jesus is telling us in these forceful teachings on prayer, fasting, and giving. He is telling us that there is "sinful sin" and "religious sin."

The good news is that He wants to cleanse us from all unrighteousness. But first He knows that we need to see the depth of sin so that we can go to Him on our knees for in-depth cleansing.

SAVED FROM EVEN "VEGETARIAN SINS"

Jesus declared, "I tell you the truth, no one can see the kingdom of God unless he is born again. . . . I tell you the truth, no one can enter the kingdom of God unless he is born of water and the Spirit." John 3:3-5, NIV.

The more delusive and deceptive sort of sins are what might be called "vegetarian" sins.

What, we might ask, are "vegetarian" sins?

They are the kinds of sins Jesus illustrates in Matthew 6:1-18—sins that are essentially tied to religious practices, such as praying and helping the poor. I have termed them vegetarian because they look so good, so wholesome.

But therein is their power to capture us unawares. Such sin is deceptive because it looks and feels so religious. And it may be truly religious, or it may be just another way of making us feel good about ourselves, except this time it is not how wicked I am that provides the pleasure, but how righteous. The deceptive power of vegetarian sins lies in the very fact that they make us feel clean when we are still filled with the rotten core of sin—prideful self-sufficiency.

Jesus wants to save us even from our self-sufficiency, even from our spiritual pride, even from feeling good about our prayer life.

And how does He propose to do this? The same way He does for prostitution and drug dealing. He wants our prideful spirit to fall at the foot of the cross and be crucified. He wants us even to be crucified to wrong attitudes in worship and to the attitude that we are superior to other people in other churches or in no church at all.

But beyond crucifixion of our prideful self-righteousness, Jesus wants to engineer our rebirth through life in the Spirit. He wants us to be born again with a new attitude. He wants us to be born from above. He wants to save us even from vegetarian sins. And the good news is that He is able. That is, He is able to do so if we will humbly cry out to Him this day and every day for His help.

PRAYER WAS IMPORTANT
TO THE PHARISEES

Hear, O Israel: The Lord our God is one Lord: And thou shalt love the Lord thy God with all thine heart, and with all thy soul, and with all thy might. And these words, which I command thee this day, shall be in thine heart. Deut. 6:4-6.

Today's Scripture passage is important to both Christians and Jews. Christians recognize it because when Jesus was asked concerning the greatest commandment of the law, He set forth Deuteronomy 6:5, with its love to God.

But that passage was important to the Jews before Jesus was born. It was important because it was part of the Shema. The Shema consisted of three short passages of Scripture—Deuteronomy 6:4-9; 11:13-21; and Numbers 15:37-41—that had to be recited in prayer fashion by every Jew every morning and every evening.

The Shema wasn't the only prayer the Jews had to recite every day. They also had to recite what became known as The Eighteen, which consisted of 18 prayers. The Eighteen had to be recited three times a day—once in the morning, once in the afternoon, and once in the evening.

The Jews were a people of prayer. They took their praying seriously. Not only did they have the daily Shema and The Eighteen, but they had prayers for nearly every event in their lives. Thus they had prayers before and after every meal; and there were prayers connected with such things as light, fire, lightning; on seeing the new moon, comets, rain, storms; at seeing the sea, lakes, rivers; on receiving good news; on using new furniture; on entering or leaving a city, and so on. Everything had its prayer.

As Christians we have something to learn here. We need to also see the sacredness of everything that exists or that happens in our lives. We need to have a sense of God's presence constantly. We ought also to live lives inundated with prayer.

But we also must be aware of the dangers that the Jews fell into. Satan can pervert even prayer. But Jesus can do one better. He can resurrect prayer and sanctify it in our daily lives.

RELIGION IS
A GOOD THING—SOMETIMES

They do all their deeds to be seen by men; for they make their phylacteries broad and their fringes long, and they love the place of honor at feasts and the best seats in the synagogues, and salutations in the market places, and being called rabbi by men. . . . [But] whoever exalts himself will be humbled, and whoever humbles himself will be exalted. Matt. 23:5-12, RSV.

Religion is a good thing—sometimes. I say "sometimes" because even religion can be perverted.

Yesterday we saw that the Pharisees were high on prayer. They not only had the twice-daily Shema and the thrice-daily Eighteen, but they also had special prayers for just about every occasion. That was good. What was bad was that some of them at times used occasions for prayer as times for display and dramatics. That took place in at least two different ways.

The first avenue of perversion had to do with location. Since certain prayers had to be said at specific times during the day, it was all too easy for some Jews to plan to be at a public spot when the time arrived for prayer. Thus they could "just happen" to be at a busy street corner or in a crowded village square when the time came. The result—all the world could see the devotion of the one praying. It was easy, for example, to be at the top step of the entrance to the synagogue when the time came. At that location a lengthy and demonstratively fervent prayer could be offered in such a way that many could appreciate the piety involved.

A second avenue open to perversion was the manner in which prayer was offered. The Jewish system of prayer made ostentation very easy. The Jew prayed standing, with hands outstretched, palms upward, and head bowed. Passersby couldn't help but notice that such a person was praying.

The wisest of the Jewish rabbis fully condemned such dramatics. So did Jesus.

Jesus knew that prayer was talking to God, that it was a spiritual experience. He wants us to pray from the heart and receive God's extended blessing.

DIFFERENT WAYS OF PRAYING

The tax collector, standing far off, would not even lift up his eyes to heaven, but beat his breast, saying, "God, be merciful to me a sinner!" I tell you, this man went down to his house justified rather than the other; for every one who exalts himself will be humbled, but he who humbles himself will be exalted. Luke 18:13, 14, RSV.

Perhaps the very best illustration that Jesus has given concerning correct and incorrect attitudes in prayer is the parable of the Pharisee and the publican, found in Luke 18:9-14.

The Pharisee in this case was one of the shallower ones, one of the type that Jesus was so hard on in Matthew 6 and Matthew 23. Jesus gives a brief but telling profile of this religionist. We are told that he trusted in his abilities and his righteous achievements, and that he despised others who had not reached his "exalted" spiritual state. He prayed, emphasizing the fact that he was not a sinner like others, including a tax collector who happened to be praying nearby. The Pharisee went on to list his religious devotions. He was faithful in paying tithe and fasted twice a week. All in all, he was quite satisfied with himself.

By way of contrast, Jesus pictures the tax collector as humble in prayer and pleading with God to be merciful to him because of his many faults.

What Jesus has to say about these prayers is of great interest. The Pharisee, said Jesus, was not praying to God, but praying *"with himself."* He was giving himself a testimonial and calling it prayer. One is reminded of Rabbi Simeon ben Jochai, who claimed: "If there are only two righteous men in the world, I and my son are these two; if there is only one, I am he."

The publican, on the other hand, was praying to God. Not only that, but he was heard by God. He went away justified and forgiven, whereas the Pharisee remained in his sinful pride, lost without being aware of it.

How do I pray? is the question that I am left with after reading this parable. How should I pray? How can I improve my prayer life today?

PREACHING AND PRACTICING

Then said Jesus to the crowds and to his disciples, "The scribes and the Pharisees sit on Moses' seat; so practice and observe what they tell you, but not what they do; for they preach, but do not practice." Matt. 23:1-3, RSV.

It's easier to preach than to practice. Every parent knows that; every husband and wife, every pastor, every employer. But practicing is the bottom line. Practicing is what it's all about. But still, I would rather preach.

And so would the Pharisees. Many of their ideas were quite helpful and true, but they failed to live the spirit of their religion. They kept laws and performed religious devotions outwardly, but too often they lacked inward depth.

That was their problem with prayer in Matthew 6:5. They prayed not just because they wanted to talk to God, but also because they wanted others to think of them as men of prayer.

The important point for us today is that we sometimes act from the same motivation as the Pharisees of old. We sometimes also pray for outward effect. We too are at times tempted to have a reputation as a person of deep prayer, or a person who is "spiritual." Jesus, in the Sermon on the Mount, says that the source of that ambition is not God. In prayer, our interest should not be in ourselves or our reputations, but in the One whom we are praying to. We may not pray ostentatiously on street corners or sound a trumpet so all will know we are praying, but sometimes we let others know that we are tired (or refreshed, as the case may be) because we got up at 3:00 a.m. to wrestle with God in prayer. That tactic is subtle but not secret.

Others fall into the pharisaic prayer pit in their public prayers on Sabbath morning. They love others to comment on their "beautiful" prayer. All that really counts in public or private is heartfelt prayer. It is more important for prayers to be moving than beautiful. It is absolutely crucial that their focal point be God.

Lord, today, as with Your disciples, our hearts cry out, "Teach us to pray."

PRAY TO GOD

But thou, when thou prayest, enter into thy closet, and when thou hast shut thy door, pray to thy Father which is in secret; and thy Father which seeth in secret shall reward thee openly. Matt. 6:6.

It may seem strange that I have titled today's reading "Pray to God." But that's what Jesus told us to do in Matthew 6:6: You are to "pray to thy Father."

But, you ask, who else could we pray to? I suppose there are lots of answers to that question. Jesus provided one in Luke 18:11 in His story of the Pharisee and the publican. He said that the Pharisee was praying "with himself" rather than to God. Just because we are spending time in prayer does not mean that we are praying to God.

There are several points that we ought to consider in praying to God. The first is what might be thought of as the process of exclusion. We must exclude certain things when we pray to the Father. We need to exclude the multitude of daily thoughts and cares that block us from God. We need to focus on communicating with Him, just as we give full attention to any person we care about and respect. In private prayer we need, so to speak, to enter into a closet with Him, so that it is only the two of us there communicating. We need to seek God and praise God with all our hearts, minds, and souls. That closet may be a real one or it may be in a crowded streetcar. We can pray to God secretly and exclusively anywhere.

A second point that we need to consider as we think about praying to God is that when we pray, we enter His very presence. We are in the audience chamber of the Infinite. And the Father, being the Father, is concerned for us just as we have concern for our children. He listens!

Third, when we pray to God, we can have confidence. We can come boldly before the throne of Grace because of what Jesus did for us on Calvary and is doing for us in heaven.

That is good news. Why not pray to God more often?

HAVE A PLACE OF SECRET PRAYER

He went up on the mountain by himself to pray. When evening came, he was there alone. Matt. 14:23, RSV.

J esus was a man of prayer. The New Testament frequently points out that He went apart to pray or that He spent all night in prayer.

There were times He prayed in public, as in John 17. He did not downplay the role of public prayer, but He also believed in and practiced private prayer. He needed special times to spend alone with the Father.

We have the same need. We need to come apart from the cares of life and be with God. Going to church, prayer meeting, and Sabbath school is good, but every individual Christian needs special time in the audience chamber of the King. We need it to praise His name, to thank Him for His goodness, to confess our sins, to ask for strength, to intercede for others, and just to visit with One who cares.

In short, each of us needs to set apart sacred time each day for prayer in our "secret" place. We need to take our devotional life seriously. We need to nourish our spiritual selves just as we nourish our physical, social, and mental selves. And that nourishment takes time. Proper nourishment is not the work of a brief minute.

Many have found that the best time for their secret period with the Father is first thing in the morning. They have found that when their devotional time is put off till later, the flow of pressing duties makes it impossible or erratic.

During our time apart with God we need not only to speak to Him in prayer, but to listen to Him through His words in the Bible. This listening should be deeper than merely reading the morning devotional book or even reading a few pages from Ellen White or the Sabbath school lesson. We need to follow Ellen White's advice and become a people of the Bible.

I have spent a day on this topic because more and more Seventh-day Adventist Christians are being caught up in the affairs of this world. That has resulted in less emphasis on personal devotion.

Today is the day to turn that drift around.

QUALITY, NOT QUANTITY

But when ye pray, use not vain repetitions, as the heathen do: for they think that they shall be heard for their much speaking. Matt. 6:7.

It is a wonderful thing to pray several times a day and to even have set times for private prayer. Daniel in Babylon prayed three times a day, facing Jerusalem. And Christians of our day say grace before meals and offer a prayer on rising in the morning and on going to bed in the evening.

Yet there is a danger in all this. It is easy for prayer to become formalized rather than heartfelt. It becomes something you do on certain occasions or at certain times. As a result, it is easy to mumble through one's prayer in a meaningless manner. In my own life there have been times when table grace or bedtime prayers have become so routine that I couldn't remember if I had prayed.

Some prayer that must have been. Routine prayer has its dangers.

In our text for today Jesus talks about "vain repetition" in prayer, or, as the Revised Standard Version has it, some feel "they will be heard for their many words."

That has been true in all cultures. Thus in 1 Kings 18:26 we read that the prophets of Baal cried out, "O Baal, hear us," for half a day. And in Acts 19:34 we read how the Ephesian mob shouted "Great is Diana of the Ephesians" for two hours. And there are some Christians who repetitiously say their prayers through the use of a rosary, while Hindus use prayer wheels to the same effect. In Protestant history it has often been thought that the length of a prayer is an indication of devotion.

Jesus tells us that all such ideas are wrongheaded. God wants us to pray to Him in the same way we would have meaningful conversations with our best friends. We don't judge our success by the quantity of our verbiage in such situations, nor do we put our request in repetitive style. No, we know they are listening and care about us. As a result, we pour out our hearts to them.

THE IDEAL PARENT

Your Father knoweth what things ye have need of, before ye ask him.
Matt. 6:8.

I left a few words off the beginning of our text for today. It really starts out, "Be not ye therefore like unto them."

Like unto whom? Like unto those in verse 7 who thought that God would hear them for their much speaking.

Don't be like them. Why? Because "your Father knoweth what things ye have need of, before ye ask him."

In this verse the word "Father" really comes into its own. Some of us reading this passage are fathers. Others are mothers. None of us (if we are normal) make our children beg for those things that they need in life. In fact, we discourage them from begging and whining to get their way. We don't want to reinforce that type of manipulative activity.

Beyond that, we are pretty smart as far as the needs of our children are concerned. We often know their hopes, fears, and desires. Not only were we once children, but we have raised these special children from infancy. We generally know what they need.

But we like them to ask, anyway. It is a sign of recognition that we are their caring and protective parents. Beyond that, it is their indication that they respect us. It is important for them to say "Please" and "Thank you." Their asking and thanking is a reminder to them that we love them. Of course, we don't give them everything they ask for. Not everything they desire would be good for them.

Our relationship to God is much like the healthy relationship of a parent to a child, except that God *really* knows everything that we desire and everything that would be good for us.

He doesn't want us to be beggars, but He does want us to come to Him respectfully with our requests. It is our Father's delight to fill our needs in the most healthful and helpful manner.

That God is our Father is one of the most important teachings of the New Testament. Today we need to see Him as a loving Father rather than a vengeful judge. He is the God who cares enough to answer our prayers.

ASKING IS SIGNIFICANT

But he was angry and refused to go in. His father came out and entreated him, but he answered his father, "Lo, these many years I have served you, . . . yet you never gave me a kid, that I might make merry with my friends." And he said to him, "Son, you are always with me, and all that is mine is yours." Luke 15:28, 29, 31, RSV.

What a tragedy!

The older son in this parable had been at home all his life, yet he did not share in the father's blessings.

Why? Because he never asked. He worked hard at keeping the law (verse 29) and at avoiding certain sins (verse 30), but he failed to understand the graciousness of the father; that the father was more than eager to pour out his blessing on each of his children.

What a tragedy, to live in the father's home as a servant rather than as a child. We need to remember the words of the father to his son: "All that is mine is yours."

God wants to bless us. Why are we so backward in asking? Why is it that we are not found more often in prayer? "All that is mine is yours" is God's message to us.

One of the great lessons of the Sermon on the Mount is that God is our Father. Over and over that lesson is driven home. Today we need to take it to heart and go to God in prayer to claim our birthright as children of the King.

God wants us to "hunger and thirst" for His gifts; He wants us to "pray without ceasing." He is our Father and He delights to bless His children. He is much more ready to give than we are to receive.

Today is the day that we can begin to grow in the prayer of faith. Let us come to our Father seeking His blessing on our lives and on the lives of those close to us. Remember, we are dealing with One with a heart infinitely more loving than the best of human parents. He wants us to come to Him in faith. He wants us to come to Him as human children come to their parents with their requests.

PRAYER IS IMPORTANT TO CHRISTIANS

After this manner therefore pray ye: Our Father which art in heaven, Hallowed be thy name. Matt. 6:9.

Between Matthew 6:9 and 6:13 we have one of our Lord's most important teachings. We find the Lord's Prayer here and in Luke 11:1-4. In Luke, the disciples had come to Jesus with a request that He teach them how to pray. After all, they reminded Him, John the Baptist had taught his disciples to pray.

That is a significant interchange. It suggests not only the importance of prayer but that prayer can be taught. And Jesus accepts that presupposition when He proceeds to teach them to pray.

Prayer is not just a "bunch of words" that we mumble in a mindless or passionate sort of way. No, prayer is something with order and structure.

We will examine that thought more tomorrow. Today we want to think about the importance of prayer in our individual lives.

The topic of prayer brings us face-to-face with one of the most vital and challenging subjects related to Christian living. One author has noted that "prayer is beyond question the highest activity of the human soul. Man is at his greatest and highest when, upon his knees, he comes face-to-face with God."

The same author goes on to note that nothing we do in the Christian life is easier and more natural than prayer. Most other aspects of Christian living have counterparts among non-Christians. Even people who have never met Jesus may have self-discipline and a spirit of philanthropy. But that is not so with heartfelt prayer.

How is it between you and God? Do you like talking to Him as you would to a friend, or are you uncomfortable with Him? Do you have anything to say to Him? Now there is an important question. Some people have a great deal to say to Him when praying in public, but very little in private. There is a sense in which prayer is a test of our spiritual lives. It is there that we discover if we are really in love with God.

Lord, realizing the significance of prayer, we, along with the disciples, ask You to teach us to pray.

PRAYING WITH UNDERSTANDING

I will pray with the spirit, and I will pray with the understanding also.
1 Cor. 14:15.

It comes as a shock to some people that something as spiritual as prayer could have any system or structure to it. But that very point is one of the most important in the Lord's Prayer.

When the disciples asked Him to pray, Jesus set forth a masterpiece of human communication. Prayer has a pattern to it. That is clear from Jesus' introductory words: "After this manner therefore pray ye" (Matt. 6:9). And then He provides a sample prayer that has all the essential elements of prayer.

While it is not wrong to recite the Lord's Prayer *if* it is done with meaning and thought, it is better to see the Lord's Prayer as a pattern prayer that provides us with an outline of the essential elements that should be in both private and public prayer.

As such, Jesus' outline prayer is much like the outline used by many preachers and other public speakers. Each part of the outline provides a heading of things that need to be remembered in the prayer. Each point is expanded and filled out during the prayer itself.

Perhaps the comprehensiveness of the Lord's Prayer is its most outstanding characteristic. It covers all the elements of both our relationship with God and other people, as well as our personal needs.

Even the order of the petitions in the Lord's Prayer is of crucial importance for our prayers. The first three petitions have to do with God and His glory, whereas the second three petitions have to do with our human needs and necessities. Thus God must be given first and supreme place; then and only then should we turn to ourselves and our needs and desires. It is only when God is given His proper place that other things fall into place.

We thank You today, Lord, for taking the time to teach us to pray, for taking our needs seriously. We want to learn from You, even in our prayer life.

CHOOSING A FATHER IS IMPORTANT

He is not ashamed to call them brethren. Heb. 2:11.

Not all human beings have the same father. Jesus told the Jewish leaders of His day: "Ye are of your father the devil, and the lusts of your father ye will do. He was a murderer from the beginning, and abode not in the truth, because there is no truth in him. When he speaketh a lie, he speaketh of his own: for he is a liar and the father of it" (John 8:44).

According to the Bible, all human beings are born into the family of the devil. People are born with egocentricity and self-sufficiency and pride; they need to be converted and transformed. That is why Jesus said that we need to be born again of both the water and the Spirit.

Joining the family of God is a conscious choice. The Bible teaches baptism as a symbol of death and resurrection to those who make that choice. When we join God's family, we die to old ways of thinking and acting and accept the principles of the kingdom of heaven.

Who is it that can truly pray the Lord's Prayer? Only those who can say with all sincerity, "Our Father." But who can really pray that? Only those who are committed to Jesus, only those who have been born from above, only those who are living the "unnatural" life of the Beatitudes. Only heart Christians can truly pray the Lord's Prayer.

Part of the joy of becoming a Christian is that we change fathers, we change gods. We give up our old father, the devil, for the Father of Jesus. Because of that, the book of Hebrews tells us, Jesus calls us brothers and sisters. We have become a part of the great family of God. We have given up our natural father for adoption by our heavenly Father.

"Our Father" is a beautiful phrase. It signifies God's closeness to us. It represents the personal side of God, the soft side. As a father and mother love each of their children, so God loves us. It is a wonderful privilege to be able to call God "our Father."

THE DISTANT SIDE OF GOD

O Lord, the great and terrible God, who keepest covenant and steadfast love with those who love him and keep his commandments. Dan. 9:4, RSV.

Yesterday we noted that the "close side" of God, His "soft side," is represented by the phrase "our Father." But God not only has a near side, He also has a "distant side," which is represented in the Lord's Prayer by the words "in heaven."

One of the great tensions of the Christian faith is that God is both near and far, He is both immanent and transcendent, He is both "our Father" and the ruler of the universe.

It is important to keep both sides in balance as we read Scripture and seek to apply it to our daily lives. Those who emphasize only God's soft side make Him out to be something like an infinite Santa Claus or a toothless grandmother. Yet those who emphasize only His distant side make Him into an iron-fisted judge who is devoid of all grace and softness.

The paradox of God is that He has more than one side. He is close and loving, but like any good parent, He must be firm. The two-sidedness of God is reflected in Daniel's prayer in our text for today. He is truly "great and terrible" to those who cling to that sin which is destroying human lives, the environment, world peace, and thus their own selves. If God is truly love, He will someday have to bring such destruction to a halt. For those who disregard His principles, God can be and will be "great and terrible."

But, as Daniel notes, God also keeps His covenant of "steadfast love" with those who have accepted His principles and joined His family. It should be noted that He wants all humans to join His family and experience His love. But He won't force them. Love can't be forced out of anyone and still be love.

The wonderful truth is that God is both "our Father" and the great God of the universe. That greatness holds no threat for those who love Him. As Christians we can rejoice in both God's nearness and His farness.

THE SHAPE OF PRAYER

One of his disciples said to him, "Lord, teach us to pray." . . . And he said to them, "When you pray say: "Father, hallowed be thy name." Luke 11:1, 2, RSV.

The Lord's Prayer represents Jesus' ideal prayer. It was given because the disciples asked Jesus to teach them to pray. Thus we can learn much from this great prayer, so broad in its scope, yet so brief in its expression.

The prayer as we have it in Matthew 6:9-13 is made up of seven petitions.

- "Hallowed be thy name."
- "Thy kingdom come."
- "Thy will be done on earth."
- "Give us this day our daily bread."
- "Forgive us our debts."
- "Lead us not into temptation."
- "Deliver us from evil."

Take a minute to examine the prayer. What word do you find in each of the first three petitions but not in the last four? Likewise, what word do you find in the last four that is absent from the first three?

The answers to those questions are "Thy" and "us," respectively. Those little pronouns tell us a great deal about the shape of prayer. Prayer has an order, and you will find that order all through the Bible.

True prayer always begins with God and adoration of Him. First come the "Thy" (You) petitions, then come the "us" petitions. There is a lesson here. We must never start prayer with concerns about ourselves.

Only after addressing God and His concerns does the prayer move into petitions regarding human need. Jesus has put the focus of prayer back on God, where it should be, since He is the source of all that is.

We find it all too easy to let our prayers drift quickly away from God and the broader concerns of the kingdom and into the "gimme" mode that centers on human beings and their wants and needs. Note that roughly one half of the prayer is devoted to the God-related petitions.

And lest any of us, looking at this prayer, come to believe that all prayer must be brief, we need to remember that Jesus spent entire nights in prayer.

THE MEANING OF THE NAME

Some trust in chariots, and some in horses: but we will remember the name of the Lord our God. Ps. 20:7.

In biblical times a person's name stood for much more than it does in modern cultures. The name stood for a person's whole character. The first petition in the Lord's Prayer says God's name should be hallowed. What is His name? What is His character?

God's names in the Bible are many. Among the most common is *El*, or *Elohim*, which emphasizes His "strength" or His "power." A second common name for God is Yahweh (or Jehovah), which means "the self-existent one."

Those names help us begin to see the character of God, but the Bible record gives us several more. D. Martyn Lloyd-Jones lists several for us: "'the Lord will provide' *(Jehovah-jireh)*, 'the Lord that leadeth' *(Jehovah-rapha)*, 'the Lord our Banner' *(Jehovah-nissi)*, 'the Lord our peace' *(Jehovah-Shalom)*, 'the Lord our Shepherd' *(Jehovah-ra-ah)*, 'the Lord our Righteousness' *(Jehovah-tsidkenu)*, and . . . 'the Lord is present' *(Jehovah-shammah)*."

All of those names for God are found in the Old Testament. The name of God stands for the nature and character and personality of God as they have been revealed to humanity. Because God is who He is we can rest assured in our faith. Thus the psalmist can write: "They that know thy name will put their trust in thee: for thou, Lord, hast not forsaken them that seek thee" (Ps. 9:10). We find a similar thought of the faithful care of God in our Bible verse for today: "Some trust in chariots, and some in horses: but we will remember the name of the Lord our God" (Ps. 20:7).

The life of Jesus provides us with new meanings for God's name. In John 17:6 Jesus said: "I have manifested thy name unto the men which thou gavest me." Jesus came to help us understand more fully the name of God and its meaning. He came to help us see God's character.

"The name" of God is rich in meaning for each of us. It is a name that we can put faith in. But it is also a name that must be respected.

TREATING "THE NAME" CARELESSLY

Thou shalt not take the name of the Lord thy God in vain; for the Lord will not hold him guiltless that taketh his name in vain. Ex. 20:7.

I still remember my shock. I was living on a merchant training ship out in San Francisco Bay but was home on leave for the weekend.

I could hardly wait to get to a phone so that I could call a young woman I had met on my last leave. I knew she was a Christian, so I had had enough sense to clean up my language for the sake of appearance. That cleaning up severely limited my usual vocabulary, but it seemed worth the effort.

That is why I was shocked. After all the trouble I was going through for her, she still wasn't satisfied. She claimed in no uncertain terms that if I wanted to take her out again I would have to stop using the Lord's name in vain.

I was truly caught off guard. "What do you mean?" I asked in all sincerity. I had never heard the expression before.

She was quick to answer that it was wrong to use such words as "God" and "Jesus Christ" in careless ways that often bordered on profanity. Thus I got my first lesson on the importance of "the name" of God.

It was an important lesson and one that has meant very much to me over the years. God's name is a beautiful name. God is a wonderful God. Why would anyone want to use His name carelessly or profanely?

The way we use God's name signifies the way we think about God. If I were the devil I would get people to use the divine name carelessly. That would be the first step in my getting them to think of God carelessly and eventually live carelessly and treat others carelessly.

In the long run, the way I relate to God's name is the way I will relate to God. But what a precious name. It represents my salvation, my hope, my everything. I want to praise God's name for what He has done for each of us.

HALLOWING THE NAME

O magnify the Lord with me, and let us exalt his name together. Ps. 34:3.

What does it mean to "hallow" the name of God? One way to get at the meaning is to see how the word is translated in different Bible versions. *The Twentieth Century New Testament* has it as "may thy name be held holy." Moffatt's translation has "thy name be revered." And in the Phillips translation the phrase is "may your name be honoured." To hallow God's name is to reverence it, to treat it with respect, to honor it. It is to treat it as something holy as opposed to something ordinary or common.

The meaning becomes even clearer when we see how the word is used. We find the same word used in the Sabbath command in the Greek translation of Exodus 20:8. The command is to remember the Sabbath day to keep it *holy*. The Sabbath is different from other days; it is to be kept differently from other days. It is to be hallowed. Another Old Testament example comes from the instruction to *consecrate* the priests. Priests were to be different from other men because they were set apart for holy use.

So it is to be with God's name. Christians are to hallow God's name because of who He is. Ellen White suggests that "to hallow the name of the Lord requires that the words in which we speak of the Supreme Being be uttered in reverence. 'Holy and reverend is his name,' Psalm 111:9. We are never in any manner to treat lightly the titles or appellations of the Deity. In prayer we enter the audience chamber of the Most High; and we should come before Him with holy awe. The angels veil their faces in His presence. . . . How much more should we, finite, sinful beings, come in a reverent manner before the Lord, our Maker!" (*Thoughts From the Mount of Blessing*, p. 106).

But hallowing God's name is not only for the prayer room. It is for all our language all day long. Beyond that, hallowing the name comes into our every action because we are the representatives of God on earth. In every act of life we are to make manifest His character because we carry His name.

"FEARING GOD"

The fear of the Lord is the beginning of wisdom: a good understanding have all they that do his commandments: his praise endureth for ever. Ps. 111:10.

What does it mean that we should "fear" God?

I remember my first year of teaching at Andrews University. I had a delightful non-Christian young woman in class who was just coming out of a prolonged hippie experience. One of the requirements for her teaching certificate was a course in the philosophy of education. At Andrews that philosophy is set in the context of the biblical worldview, and for the first time this student had an opportunity to examine the Bible.

She hadn't read too far before she came across the idea of fearing God. The very next morning she was pressing me on the meaning of fearing God.

I was happy to tell her that fearing God did not mean being afraid of Him, but of holding Him in reverential awe because of who He is. It means a deep respect for God. That is the kind of fear that is the beginning of wisdom; that is the kind of fear that is related to hallowing His name. Of course, according to the Bible, those who despise God will eventually have fear of the less desirable type.

We can learn something here from the ancient Jews. They never used God's name in familiar ways. In fact, the name of God was so sacred that they would not even pronounce it, lest they treat it lightly or irreverently. They held God's name in sacred awe.

And whereas they recognized God as their Father, in their prayers they never used the concept of "Father" alone. Rather, they tied the concept of Father with the ideas of King and Lord. That practice is helpful to those of us who may be too prone to sentimentalize God as loving Father. He is that, but He is also King and Lord of all the earth. We as Christians need to keep that balance. Our sentimentality must never overcome our reverence for God. "The fear of the Lord is the beginning of wisdom."

REVERENCING GOD

And he said, Draw not nigh hither: put off thy shoes from off thy feet, for the place whereon thou standest is holy ground. Ex. 3:5.

Y ou must have a small God," said a Muslim to an American tourist. "Oh, no," the American quickly replied. "We have a great and mighty God, at whose word of command the universe and all that is therein came into existence!"

"Still, I believe you Americans have a small God, for when you pray to Him you do it so indifferently and irreverently. When we Muslims pray, we fall prone on our faces in acknowledgment of the mightiness of God."

Reverence. It's something we don't think much about unless someone is being irreverent to us personally or treating us disrespectfully. But how sensitive are we toward our own reverence to God?

A few years ago I had an opportunity to speak in a small Seventh-day Adventist church in Puerto Rico. It was a church of the common people. I will never forget how astounded I was as the people came into the church. Before sitting down, they knelt individually in prayer. They had entered God's house, they were on holy ground, they had come into the presence of the Almighty, and they were open in acknowledging that fact.

While we may not choose to take off our shoes upon entering church, or fall prone or even bow in prayer, we need to recognize constantly by our words and actions that we have entered into God's presence in a special way.

But it is not just in church that reverence is important. All through the day I need to realize the holiness of my God in all I do and say. Thus I am careful about how I treat my Bible, how I use God's name, how I joke, and so on. Reverence extends even beyond the Creator to what He has created. My respect for God leads me to treat other people respectfully; it helps me appreciate a sunset.

Thank You, God, for being who You are. Thank You for being not only Someone I can worship in church but Someone who has made every aspect of life a wonder.

KINGDOMS IN CONFLICT

Thy kingdom come. Matt. 6:10.

Just as in the rest of the Sermon on the Mount, there is a logical order in the Lord's Prayer. The petitions follow one another in a necessary order.

For example, the prayer begins by asking that God's name be hallowed among men. But the moment that that petition is uttered we are reminded of the fact that God's name and person are not thus generally hallowed.

Why, we ask, is this so? Why is God not honored as He should be?

The answer is both simple and complex. The simple answer is that it is sin that has brought about this state of affairs. The answer becomes more complex when we note that there is another kingdom set up on this earth that is in conflict with God's kingdom.

That kingdom is the kingdom of darkness, the kingdom of Satan. The Bible doesn't beat around the bush in talking about Satan's kingdom. The Gospel of John calls Satan "the prince of this world" (John 12:31), while Paul calls him "the prince of the power of the air" (Eph. 2:2). Again, Paul writes to the Ephesians that Christians need to put on the whole armor of God because "we are not contending against flesh and blood, but against the principalities, against the powers, against the world rulers of this present darkness, against the spiritual hosts of wickedness in the heavenly places" (6:11, 12, RSV).

By way of contrast, Jesus is called "the prince of the kings of the earth" (Rev. 1:5). And His preaching certainly centered around the victory of His kingdom over the kingdom of darkness. In fact, Jesus came to make way for the ultimate victory of God's kingdom in the cosmic conflict of the universe.

"Thy kingdom come" stands at the center of the great controversy between Christ and Satan. And each human being (you and I) is a soldier in one or the other of the two kingdoms. We are either actively on the side of King Jesus or we are on Satan's side.

How is it with me today? Whose kingdom am I furthering? How do I know?

A KINGDOM ON THE MARCH

And the kingdom and dominion, and the greatness of the kingdom under the whole heaven, shall be given to the people of the saints of the most High, whose kingdom is an everlasting kingdom, and all dominions shall serve and obey him. Dan. 7:27.

Kingdom talk can become rather confusing—even from the lips of Jesus. The reason for that is that He spoke of the kingdom at times as being in the past, at times as being in the present, and at times as being in the future.

Jesus implied that the kingdom was a past reality when He suggested that Abraham, Isaac, Jacob, and the prophets had made it into the kingdom in their lifetime (Luke 13:28). Jesus spoke of the kingdom being in the present when He noted that "the kingdom of God is within you" (Luke 17:21). And Jesus repeatedly taught that the kingdom of God was future when He mentioned the Second Coming and even when He, as here, commands the disciples to pray for the coming of the kingdom.

How, we ask, can the kingdom be past, present, and future? How can the kingdom be at one and the same time something which existed, which exists, and for which it is our duty to pray?

The answer lies in the fact that the coming of the kingdom is progressive. The struggle between the Prince of God (Christ) and the prince of this world (Satan) began in heaven (Rev. 12:7, 8) and was continued throughout the Old Testament. Even then, some were on the Lord's side while others were opposed to God. But with the coming of Jesus, the battle for the hearts of people and the rulership of God went into high gear. With Jesus the kingdom of grace had arrived in power. The kingdom of grace will extend until the Second Coming, when Jesus returns to reestablish God's physical rulership over the earth.

But even though the arrival of the kingdom can be thought of as progressive, it is not evolutionary. The Second Coming will bring a radical discontinuity to all past history. It will be God breaking into history to claim the earth as His kingdom in an unmistakable manner. Christians hope and pray for that event as for no other.

THE CHRISTIAN HOPE

And then shall appear the sign of the Son of man in heaven: and then shall all the tribes of the earth mourn, and they shall see the Son of man coming in the clouds of heaven with power and great glory. And he shall send his angels with a great sound of a trumpet, and they shall gather together his elect from the four winds, from one end of heaven to the other. Matt. 24:30, 31.

The great event of the ages is the second coming of Jesus. We ought to pray for that event more fervently, work toward it more diligently, think about it more frequently.

One of the best descriptions of the Advent is found in *The Great Controversy*. Today we will sample some of that description.

"No human pen can portray the scene; no mortal mind is adequate to conceive its splendor. . . .

"The King of kings descends upon the cloud, wrapped in flaming fire. The heavens are rolled together as a scroll, the earth trembles before Him, and every mountain and island is moved out of its place. . . .

"Amid the reeling of the earth, the flash of lightning, and the roar of thunder, the voice of the Son of God calls forth the sleeping saints. He looks upon the graves of the righteous, then, raising His hands to heaven, He cries: 'Awake, awake, awake, ye that sleep in the dust, and arise!' Throughout the length and breadth of the earth the dead shall hear that voice, and they that hear shall live. . . . From the prison house of death they come, clothed with immortal glory. . . . And the living righteous and the risen saints unite their voices in a long, glad shout of victory. . . .

"He will change our vile bodies and fashion them like unto His glorious body. . . . The last lingering traces of the curse of sin will be removed. . . .

"The living righteous are changed 'in a moment.' . . . They are made immortal and with the risen saints are caught up to meet their Lord in the air. . . . Little children are borne by holy angels to their mothers' arms. Friends long separated by death are united, nevermore to part, and with songs of gladness ascend together to the City of God" (pp. 641-645).

WORKING AS WELL AS PRAYING

And this gospel of the kingdom shall be preached in all the world for a witness unto all nations; and then shall the end come. Matt. 24:14.

Jesus tells us in the Sermon on the Mount to pray for the coming of the kingdom. But in other places He tells us that we must do more than pray. Christians are to be active in preparing the way for the kingdom. That is what such parables as the one about the talents are all about.

Now, it is true that the kingdom of God finds rootage in the converted human heart. But it is also true that what is in the heart flows out into the life. That is true in both Satan's kingdom and in God's.

As a result, Christians will do more than just pray for the kingdom. They will actively work in the power of the Holy Spirit to spread the kingdom here on earth and to prepare the way for the coming of the fullness of the kingdom in the clouds of heaven.

There is a sense in which the kingdom is spread through every act of human kindness, through every sharing of the love of God. When we live Christian principles, we are pushing out the frontiers of the kingdom and pushing back the borders of the kingdom of darkness.

The preparation for the coming of the kingdom also takes place through preaching, as we read in Matthew 24:14. After quoting that verse, Ellen White says that "His kingdom will not come until the good tidings of His grace have been carried to all the earth. Hence, as we give ourselves to God, and win other souls to Him, we hasten the coming of His kingdom. Only those who devote themselves to His service, saying 'Here am I; send me' (Isaiah 6:8), to open blind eyes, to turn men 'from darkness to light and from the power of Satan unto God, that they may receive forgiveness of sins and inheritance among them which are sanctified' (Acts 26:18)—they alone pray in sincerity, 'Thy kingdom come'" (*Thoughts From the Mount of Blessing*, pp. 108, 109).

Kingdoms do not come about by accident. God wants to use me today as an agent in the spreading of His kingdom.

DOING THE WILL

Thy will be done in earth, as it is in heaven. Matt. 6:10.

What is the will of God that is to be done? In the context of the Sermon on the Mount, it is undoubtedly "doing" or following the injunctions of the sermon itself. Thus "Thy will be done" means "Thy Sermon on the Mount be done." And the will of the Sermon on the Mount thus far in Matthew 5 and 6 is for Christians to (1) live the Beatitudes (5:2-12—e.g., being poor in spirit, meek, merciful, peacemakers, and so on); (2) be witnesses for God as salt and light, in both our daily lives and in our conscious evangelistic outreach (verses 13-16); (3) live the full depth and breadth of the law, even going so far as to be like the Father in having mature (or perfect) love for our enemies (verses 17-48); and (4) be utterly sincere in our acts of devotion as we single-mindedly serve and relate to God as "Father" (6:1-10).

Doing God's will is to follow the teachings of Jesus—all of them. Those who can pray "Thy kingdom come" must certainly want to live the life of the kingdom here on earth. Thus the second petition in Matthew 6:10 flows directly from the first. Doing God's will is the primary occupation of the citizens of the kingdom, both in their present existence and in the kingdom yet to come.

Doing God's will "in earth, as it is [done] in heaven" helps us realize the cosmic nature of the Lord's Prayer. We are praying big when we pray the Lord's Prayer. The issues at stake transcend earthly existence. They represent principles of eternal and universal importance. "As in heaven" teaches us that God has an active enterprise going on with angels in that spiritual realm that lies beyond the bounds of our sin-crippled planet.

Even in our restricted lives we come into contact with galactic principles—the very principles that stand at the foundation of the health of God's universe.

As Christians we are committed to carrying out God's will in every aspect of our lives—in school, in our families, in our work, in our recreation, in everything.

Lord, continue to teach us Your will, that we might be faithful to the words of Your prayer.

A Surprise in the Shape of Prayer

Give us this day our daily bread. Matt. 6:11.

We noted some days ago that the first table of the Lord's Prayer contained those petitions directed specifically at God and His name. Those were the "Thy" petitions of Matthew 6:9, 10.

But with verse 11 we come to a radical shift. The focus moves away from God and onto us, as reflected in such pronouns as "we," "our," and "us." Thus with verse 11 we have arrived at the second table of the Lord's Prayer, those petitions that center around human needs. First comes God, then comes humanity. Both are important, but in their proper order. Without God, we would not be. Without God, we could have no needs or fulfillment of those needs. That truth is reflected in both the Ten Commandments and in the Lord's Prayer. The primacy of God is a truth that needs ever to be kept before our eyes and hearts.

So it is something of a shock and surprise to see how the second table of the prayer begins. One would suppose that it would begin with those human needs that are closest to God; our spiritual needs. But that is not so. Jesus begins the second table with our bodily needs. "Give us this day our daily bread."

There is a lesson in that for us. When Jesus considered our needs, He began in the right place. He began with the physical. Without physical health we would not have continued existence—we would not have spiritual needs. That order often appears in Jesus' ministry. First He healed the people, then He preached to them. First He took care of their physical needs, and only then could He minister in fullness to their spiritual inadequacies.

That is the picture we find in the surprise order of the second table. First we need our daily bread. When that need is satisfied, we become aware of our guilt and our spiritual need for forgiveness.

Our Lord understands us. First we pray for bread, then we ask for forgiveness.

A LESSON IN THE "DAILY"

Then said the Lord unto Moses, Behold, I will rain bread from heaven for you; and the people shall go out and gather a certain rate every day, that I may prove them, whether they will walk in my law, or no. Ex. 16:4.

There seems to be little doubt that Jesus had the manna in the wilderness in mind when He told us to pray for our daily bread. As you will recall, the children of Israel were hungering in the wilderness, and God sent them manna—the food from heaven. But there was one important condition. They must gather only enough for one day. When they gathered too much, it rotted before it could be used. They had to be satisfied with enough for one day.

But there was a major exception to that rule. On Friday they needed to gather enough for two days, because there would be no gathering of manna on Sabbath. Thus the Israelites received a double lesson from the almost-daily manna. First, their daily dependence upon God for all their needs. And second, the specialness of the Sabbath, the day given to them as a reminder that He was the one who created bread (and everything else).

The word used for "daily" in Matthew 6:11 *(epiousios)* has provided translators with no end of problems because until recently this was the only occurrence of the word in all of Greek literature. But some years ago a papyrus fragment turned up with this word used in a shopping list. Against one item on the list was *epiousios*. It was a note to remind the shopper to buy supplies of a certain food for the coming day.

Thus the fourth petition of the Lord's Prayer very simply asks us to pray that God will give us the things we need to eat for the coming day. It is a prayer to help us be able to get what is needful on our shopping list for the coming day so that we and our families might be full.

We have a wonderful God. The One whose hand guides the countless stars is concerned even with my daily bodily needs. What a God!

DIFFERENT KINDS OF DAILY BREAD

I am the living bread which came down from heaven: if any man eat of this bread, he shall live for ever. John 6:51.

While the primary meaning of Matthew 6:11 seems to be physical "daily bread," it is not incorrect to expand the concept to the spiritual realm. Thus Ellen White can say that "The prayer for daily bread includes not only food to sustain the body, but that spiritual bread which will nourish the soul unto life everlasting. Jesus bids us 'Labor not for the meat ["food" in NIV] which perisheth, but for that meat [food] which endureth unto everlasting life.' John 6:27. He says, 'I am the living bread which came down from heaven: if any man eat of this bread, he shall live forever.' Verse 51. Our Saviour is the bread of life, and it is by beholding His love, by receiving it into the soul, that we feed upon the bread which came down from heaven" *(Thoughts From the Mount of Blessing, p. 112).*

It is with this understanding that we sing,

> Break Thou the bread of life,
> Dear Lord, to me,
> As Thou didst break the loaves
> Beside the sea.
> Beyond the sacred page
> I seek Thee, Lord;
> My spirit pants for Thee,
> O living Word.

Like physical life, our spiritual being is not self-sustaining. Both need constant replenishing through the ingestion of the proper physical and spiritual nutrients. One is reminded of the prophets Ezekiel and John, who took the little book of God's words and ate it up.

On a daily basis we need to "eat" the Word of life. We need to see the beauty of His love, we need to imbibe His ways, we need strength to live His life.

Thus, when we pray for our daily bread we are realizing our constant and continuous dependence upon God for everything we are in the physical, mental, and spiritual realms.

We need to daily hunger and thirst after righteousness. We need to daily partake of His bread.

THE BREADTH OF DAILY NEEDS

Give me neither poverty nor riches; feed me with the food that is needful for me, lest I be full, and deny thee, and say, "Who is the Lord?" or lest I be poor, and steal, and profane the name of my God. Prov. 30:8, 9, RSV.

I had never really seen this text until today as I write these words. I had read it, of course, but its meaning had never jumped out at me. I had never understood it with the eyes of my heart.

It is a beautiful text that contradicts much of what church members teach their children. We generally teach people to pray for wealth as a sign of God's blessing. We pray for our children and ourselves that we will be blessed materially.

But have we counted the costs in such a teaching? Have we been just as avid and sincere in warning them against the dangers of prosperity? God wants us to keep in mind our daily need of Him. He wants us to keep in mind our own mortality and weakness. It tends to keep us on the straight and narrow when we are forced daily to remember that we are beholden to Him for daily bread.

We need to remember that we are praying for daily bread, not daily cake, even though cake may come our way from time to time. Jesus promised us that our necessities would be cared for. He is not talking about luxuries.

But daily bread means much more than mere food. It implies an entire realm of things that make bread available on a regular basis. Thus bread costs money, money requires stable work, and stable work requires good government, good business, and good labor. As a result, notes F. D. Bruner, "when we pray for daily bread we are praying at the same time for money, jobs, government, business, labor, good crops, good weather, roads, justice, and for everything economic, political, and social."

Dear Father, today we want to thank You for the multiplicity of blessings that make daily bread a reality. We want to thank You that You are not only Creator but also Sustainer. Lord, every time we see bread we see You.

DAILY BREAD LESSONS

Blessed are all they that put their trust in him. Ps. 2:12.

Behold, God is my salvation; I will trust, and not be afraid. Isa. 12:2.

Perhaps the central lesson in the daily bread petition is our absolute and utter dependence upon God, even among those who would never acknowledge such a dependence.

Think about it. Without God there is no bread—daily or otherwise. Without God there is no bread, period. We are absolutely in the hand of God. D. Martyn Lloyd-Jones is right when he claims that "the supreme folly of the twentieth century is the folly of thinking that because we have acquired a certain amount of knowledge of the laws of God, we are independent of Him."

The truth is that we cannot live for a day without Him. Without His sun and His rain and its influence, we would have no daily bread. And think of seeds. While humans plant them and are absolutely helpless without them, they can't manufacture them. Scientists can analyze seeds and identify their constituent elements, but no synthetic seeds grow. All living things come from God. Our food is a direct gift. By implication, the fourth petition of the Lord's Prayer gives God His proper place.

Furthermore, that recognition of dependence is a daily business. It is as if a wealthy father put an immense bank deposit for his child in an account in the child's name. But the child can withdraw only so much each day, and that by writing a check. Thus the child is constantly reminded of the source of his or her wealth. Our prayers function as the checks by which we make our requests for the riches of God and by which we express our thankfulness for His daily bounty.

God, in His wisdom, does not dump a life's supply of food and wealth on each of us at birth or at our twenty-first birthday. In our sinfulness we would not only squander our fortune; we would forget the Giver. God's daily blessings and the need for them keep us in remembrance of the Father.

MORE DAILY-BREAD LESSONS

Come, O blessed of my Father, inherit the kingdom prepared for you from the foundation of the world; for I was hungry and you gave me food, I was thirsty and you gave me drink, I was a stranger and you welcomed me, I was naked and you clothed me, I was sick and you visited me, I was in prison and you came to me. Matt. 25:34-36, RSV.

Today we want to focus on the word "our" in the petition for daily bread. Jesus does not teach us to pray "Give *me my* daily bread," but "Give *us our* daily bread."

There is a social side to our daily walk with God. We need to pray for the daily bread of others as well as our own. Millions of people starve to death every year, while others die from diseases related to eating too much. The problem is not one of a shortage of food, but rather the distribution of that food.

Most of us reading this book do not have to pray very earnestly for our daily bread. Most of us spend most of our prayer thanking God for an abundant supply of food. At the same time, few of us can pray this prayer without guilt for being able to enjoy bread abundantly while such a large portion of the world lives in starvation conditions. Thus the fourth petition is in one sense a prayer for social justice. Beyond that, it may be significant that this petition precedes the one for forgiveness.

Another lesson from the prayer for daily bread is the highlighting of human activity in connection with answered prayer. As Luther put it, we are not asking carelessly and, at the last minute, expecting God to drop a goose into our mouth.

God may provide the conditions for growing daily bread, but humans need to do their part. One is reminded of the story of the man who admired another's fruitful farm. "It's wonderful what God can do with a bit of ground like this," remarked the visitor.

"Yes," said the farmer, "but you should have seen this ground when God had it to Himself."

Faithfulness in work is a part of the prayer for daily bread.

SIN IS COMPREHENSIVE

And forgive us our debts, as we forgive our debtors. Matt. 6:12.

Before people can pray this prayer they must realize the need to pray it. They need to come to the frank admission that they are sinners. "Forgive us our debts." In order to pray this prayer we must first admit that we are not all that we should be.

Many church members fall short here. They think of sin in terms of being a drunkard, a murderer, an adulterer, or a person with a foul mouth. Yet sin is much broader than that. The five New Testament words for sin show that it infects and affects every aspect of our lives.

First is the word *harmartia*, which literally means to miss the mark. Sin as *harmartia* is the failure to be what we might have been. William Barclay illustrates this point as three stages in our lives. First, there is a time when people say, "He will do something." Later they may say, "He could do something, if he would." And finally people say, "He could have done something."

Sin as *harmartia* is pervasive. It is not being everything we could have been. And who couldn't be a better husband, wife, worker, son, daughter, and so on.

Second is the word *parabasis*, which infers stepping across a line between right and wrong. Once again, sin as *parabasis* is pervasive in our lives. Do we never step across the line into an unkind action or a discourteous word or thought?

Third, sin is *paraptoma*, which infers a slipping, as when a person slips on an icy road. This kind of sin might be illustrated by a slip of the temper or passions.

Fourth, sin is *anomia*, or lawlessness. This is the sin of the person who knows right but does wrong. This is what most of us think of as sin.

Last, sin is *opheilema*, which is the word used in Matthew 6:12. *Opheilema* means debt, a failure to pay our due. And no person can claim to have paid all his debts to God.

Sin is much broader and deeper than many Christians have imagined. All of us need to pray the sentiments of the Lord's Prayer daily.

AUDACIOUS DEBTORS

David pronounces a blessing upon the man to whom God reckons righteousness apart from works: "Blessed are those whose iniquities are forgiven, and whose sins are covered; blessed is the man against whom the Lord will not reckon his sin." Rom. 4:6-8, RSV.

In rabbinic thought every sin created a debt before God, while every righteous deed contributed to the believer's accumulation of assets before God. Whereas the accumulation of good deeds formed a kind of bridge to God; the accumulation of moral debts separated people from Him.

Thus the concept of moral debts was quite familiar to the Jews. Jesus takes the well-known concept of moral debt and the ideas connected to it and tells us that we should go to the Father and ask Him to wipe out our debts.

Think of it! The very idea is quite shameless. It is audacious for a debtor to approach a creditor and ask him to forgive a debt. Yet Jesus teaches us to approach God in that "shameless" way.

Beyond that, the New Testament teaches, through its various authors, that God is more than willing to cancel our debt because of His love and because we have accepted His love in the sacrifice of Jesus. God is a debt canceler for those who seek His forgiveness. That is a miracle of grace. God does not give us what we deserve. He gives us what we need.

It is of interest to note at this point that Luke's version of the Lord's Prayer uses the word sin (Luke 11:4) instead of debt, as we find in Matthew. Sins, of course, represent acts of commission, whereas debts include acts of omission. Thus God's forgiveness includes all our sins. Both those things that we consciously do against God and other people and those things that we should have done for them are all included in the two versions of the Lord's Prayer.

In short, all of our sins may be brought to the foot of the cross. Thank You, Lord, that we can come boldly to You and that You will always grant the faithful petition for forgiveness.

GOODBYE TO CHEAP GRACE

Forgive us our sins, for we ourselves forgive every one who is indebted to us.
Luke 11:4, RSV.

Perhaps the most important word in Matthew's version of the Lord's Prayer is the word "as." We are asking God to forgive us "as" we forgive others. Luke uses the word "for," but the idea underlying both is similar. Human and divine forgiveness are connected. We are to forgive *as* we are forgiven.

Now, that doesn't come easy to most of us. Most of us like receiving forgiveness, but we don't go too far out of our way to look for opportunities to pass it on.

Here Jesus is speaking to Christians. And Christians are people who have experienced the greatness of God's mercies. In fact, Christians are so grateful that they desire to pass on those mercies.

Such an attitude does not come naturally. We are born with a desire to retaliate and pay people back for what they have done to us. We are born with a heart that does not easily forgive.

That brings us to an important point in Matthew 6:12. Christians are transformed people. They not only sit around taking in God's grace; they have become dispensers of that grace. Christians are people who have come to realize that you cannot love God without loving other people, His children.

Cheap grace implies that people get from God and then go about life as they did in times past. But Jesus put an end to cheap grace. The grace of God through Jesus not only forgives our debts; it also changes our lives in the new birth. Jesus doesn't say "Take My forgiveness and go on living as usual." No, He says, "Now that you are forgiven, you will act like Me. You will fulfill the beatitude to be merciful [Matt. 5:7]. You will seek to be perfect as the Father in heaven is perfect because you will love—and forgive—even your enemies [verses 43-48]."

Salvation is a seamless web. You cannot be forgiven or justified without at the same time being sanctified and transformed. Christians will forgive *as* God forgives; they will forgive in the same way.

KEYS TO BEING FORGIVING

Which of these three do you think was a neighbor to the man who fell into the hands of robbers?"
The expert in the law replied, "The one who had mercy on him."
Jesus told him, "Go and do likewise." Luke 10:36, 37, NIV.

I will *never* forgive that woman for what she did to me." "I will *never* forget that cruel act by my pastor."

Have you ever harbored such thoughts? Have you ever had such intense feelings toward another who has genuinely wronged you or someone you care about?

Most of us have. Most of us have struggled to forgive and forget. Most of us have strained to comprehend the fact that we are to be like Jesus, who could pray "Forgive them, for they don't know what they are doing" as they nailed Him to the cross.

Yet God says that we are to be like Him. We are to become forgivers just as God is a forgiver.

But how, we might ask? That brings us to the keys of forgiveness. There are certain things that will help us learn to be forgiving.

First is understanding. There are often good reasons as to why people do things. When we take the time to discover their reasons, it often makes it easier to forgive them.

Second, most of us need to learn to forget. Too many people keep their ugly, unforgiving spirits alive by nursing feelings of resentment and anger. Most of us need the cleansing power of Jesus to flush out our memories. We have a choice. We can hold on to the negative, or we can let Him fill us with new, clean thoughts.

Third is love. God's *agapē* love, we have noted again and again in our study of the Sermon on the Mount, is that unconquerable goodwill toward others that wants only the best for them, no matter how they treat us. True forgiveness is rooted in that love.

Fourth, true forgivers need a daily picture of the cross. We need to see that Jesus died for us. As a result, we realize that we need to be merciful and forgiving, just as our Saviour is forgiving.

THE USES OF TEMPTATION

And lead us not into temptation, but deliver us from evil: For thine is the kingdom, and the power, and the glory, for ever. Amen. Matt. 6:13.

One day Bob was given definite instructions by his mother not to go swimming in the nearby pond. Shortly afterward he had to pass the pond on the way to the store. He decided to take along his bathing suit just in case he was tempted.

That's how it is too often with most of us. We generally lead ourselves into temptation.

But we are not alone. Not only do we have to contend with our personal weaknesses, but the Bible tells us that Satan is actively working to create situations in which we are set up to fall. We must never forget that we live out our daily lives in the midst of a great controversy between good and evil, between Christ and Satan.

God, the Bible tells us, tempts no one (James 1:13). On the other hand, He uses temptations to develop our characters. Thus we read in James 1:2, 3 that we are to "count it all joy when" we "fall in divers temptations; knowing . . . that the trying of . . . faith worketh patience."

There is something wonderful about our God, about a Being who can take essentially evil experiences and turn them into good results. There is nothing that God can't use to work for good.

While it is true that God uses the trials of daily life to develop our characters and our faith, it is also true that He utilizes our effort in the process. We need to be like the farm boy who said, "When I pass a watermelon patch, I can't keep my mouth from watering, but I *can run*."

We need to "run" more often past those places in our lives where we know we have weaknesses. We need to pray each day that God will not only help us to realize our specific weaknesses, but that He will give us a determination to overcome through the power of the Spirit. He is not short on power. But too often we are short on determination and on asking for that power.

THE ROAD FROM
THE PAST TO THE FUTURE

The Lord is my shepherd, I shall not want; he makes me lie down in green pastures. He leads me beside still waters; he restores my soul. He leads me in paths of righteousness for his name's sake. Ps. 23:1-3, RSV.

God is leading His people. That is an ever-present theme throughout the Bible. God is leader; we are His followers.

That truth is certainly true in the Sermon on the Mount. We may be walking with Jesus on the Mount of Blessing, but He is definitely in front of this grand tour of Christian principles. He is the guide; we are the guided.

Progression is evident even in the last three petitions of the Lord's Prayer. For example, the petition for bread is a prayer for the present, the petition for forgiveness is for the removal of a bad past, and the petition for God's leading is a prayer for a good future. God is always concerned with where we are heading. Like a good shepherd, He seeks to guide His sheep into healthy pastures.

The petitions regarding not being led into temptation and being delivered from evil follow naturally from the prayer for forgiveness. After all, when we ask for forgiveness, it is our built-in desire to want to be kept from the very temptations that make forgiveness necessary. True repentance leads to a turning away from the old life and the old ways that were destructive. It is a turning toward the things of God. Thus we pray not only for forgiveness but also to be kept from evil.

There is a final point of progressive development in the Lord's Prayer. It begins with the Father and ends with a warning against the evil one. That is particularly evident in those Bible versions that translate "evil" as "evil one." The prayer provides a tour from heaven to hell, from God to Satan. And in between those polar positions we are provided with the seven brief petitions that cover everything of importance in life.

We have now studied the Lord's Prayer for almost a month. And at the end we have the same request as the disciples had at the beginning. Lord, continue to teach us to pray.

POINT OF EMPHASIS

For if ye forgive men their trespasses, your heavenly Father will also for-give you: but if ye forgive not men their trespasses, neither will your Father forgive your trespasses. Matt. 6:14, 15.

The great prayer is over, but not the commentary on the prayer. It is significant that the only petition of the prayer on which Jesus offers commentary is the fifth. He undoubtedly knew how difficult it is for most of us to genuinely forgive other people. Thus He comes back to that point to provide special emphasis on its cruciality.

Matthew 6:12, 14, 15 are not the only places in the first Gospel where the lesson of our passing on God's forgiveness is emphasized. The most vivid and complete treatment of the topic is found in Matthew 18:21-35. Take time to read those verses carefully.

That passage begins with Peter asking an interesting question. He wants to know how often he should forgive others.

Interestingly enough, Peter also supplies an answer to his question. He suggests seven forgivenesses.

When you think of it, seven forgivenesses is quite a few. It certainly is if it has to do with you backing into my car on successive days. Think about it.

Peter also thought he was being generous. After all, the rabbis of the day suggested that it was wrong to forgive more than three times, since they had deduced from the book of Amos that God forgives only three times. And certainly one shouldn't be more gracious than God.

But Peter doubled the rabbinical three and added one for good mea-sure. He must have thought that is a pile of forgiveness, and wondered how generous a man could be. He undoubtedly expected commenda-tion from Jesus. Maybe Jesus would even say he was too soft and gener-ous. "After all, Peter, you can't let people take advantage of you."

Peter must have been shocked out of his skull when Jesus said that we should forgive 70 times seven.

Can you do that? Should you?

There is something important here. We will return to Jesus' point of emphasis tomorrow.

WHAT PETER REALLY WANTED TO KNOW

Then Peter came up and said to him, "Lord, how often shall my brother sin against me, and I forgive him? As many as seven times?" Jesus said to him, "I do not say to you seven times, but seventy times seven." Matt. 18:21, 22, RSV.

Yesterday we noted that Jesus went out of His way to make the passing on of forgiveness a point of emphasis in His teaching in the Sermon on the Mount. We also noted that Jesus raises the same lesson in Matthew 18.

There Peter is outwardly asking how many times he should forgive another person. But is that his real point? Is that what he really wants to know?

Those questions drive us to the heart of the problem of human nature, the heart of the reason as to why Jesus three times in the first Gospel emphasized the issue of passing on to others the forgiveness God extends to us. The fact is that Peter is not nearly so concerned with the extension of forgiveness as he is with its limits.

Peter was really asking about the limits of Christian love and forbearance. After all, it is reassuring to know at what point I can with a good conscience stop loving my neighbor. I want to know when I have fulfilled my moral quota of love and forgiveness so that I can with a clear conscience let people have what they deserve. The all-too-human questions underlying Peter's query are "When can I let go? When do I have a right to explode? When can I give you what you deserve?"

Jesus' reply is frustrating to all such questions. His answer is not seven forgivenesses, but 70 times seven, or 490. The plain fact is that there is no limit to forgiveness for the Christian.

The good news is that God's forgiveness toward me is limitless. The other side is that I am expected to be just as forgiving to you as God is to me. Now, that is a hard saying. But it is an important one. Thus Jesus gives us a vivid parable, as we shall see tomorrow, to underline and drive home His point.

Jesus really seems to be serious about this passing on of forgiveness.

A FURTHER ILLUSTRATION
OF THE LESSON

*Then his lord summoned him and said to him, "You wicked servant! I for-
gave you all that debt because you besought me; and should not you have
had mercy on your fellow servant, as I had mercy on you?" And in anger
his lord delivered him to the jailers, till he should pay all his debt. So also
my heavenly Father will do to every one of you, if you do not forgive your
brother from your heart. Matt. 18:32-35, RSV.*

The parable of Matthew 18:21-35 builds upon the fifth petition
of the Lord's Prayer (that we should forgive others in the same
proportion that God has forgiven us) and the question in
Matthew 18:21 regarding the extent of forgiveness.

Like most of Jesus' parables, this one is a model of simplicity. It is
built around three main characters: the king (God), a servant forgiven
an unbelievably large debt (you and me), and a servant (our neighbor)
who owes the first servant (you and me) a relatively insignificant sum.

The parable also has three rapidly flowing scenes. In scene 1, the
first servant is in the king's audience chamber, where he is forgiven a
large debt. Note how pitiful and sincere are his pleadings for forgiveness. Note how desperate he is. I have been in that position. So have
you. What a wave of joy comes over us when we are at last forgiven.
How we want to praise God.

Scene 2 shows the recently forgiven servant out on the street, where
he meets a neighbor who owes him a relatively small debt. The parable
treats us to an exact rendition of the pitiful and sincere and desperate
pleadings of the first servant. But the mercy is not passed on. To the
contrary, the first servant calls for justice.

He gets justice, but not the way he expected. In scene 3 the unmer-
ciful servant is thrown into jail (hell) until he pays his impossible debt.

The moral of the story: We need to be just as forgiving to others as
God has been to us (verse 33). We need to learn how to forgive others
from our heart.

That takes grace, transforming grace, empowering grace.

THE BIG CONTRAST

"Therefore, I tell you, her many sins have been forgiven—for she loved much. But he who has been forgiven little loves little." Then Jesus said to her, "Your sins are forgiven." Luke 7:47, 48, NIV.

The past few days we have been studying forgiveness in the Sermon on the Mount and in the parable of Matthew 18:21-35. One of the most important things to note about that parable is the tremendous contrast between the debts.

The 10,000-talent debt (verse 24) was impossibly large. A talent equaled 6,000 denarii, or 6,000 days' wages (see Matt. 20:2). At today's minimum wage of $4.25 per hour and calculated on an eight-hour day, one talent would be worth $204,000. Ten thousand talents would be worth the incredible sum of $2,040,000,000. By contrast, the 100-denarii debt would be 100 days' wages, or $3,400.

To put the matter another way, it would take 100 days to work off the 100-denarii debt, but (at seven days per week) 164,384 years to work off the 10,000 talents.

One writer has suggested that if each denarii were a penny, the 100 denarii could be carried in one pocket. On the other hand, the 10,000-talent debt would need an army of 8,600 people to carry it. Each carrier would have a 60-pound bag full of pennies, and, if spaced a yard apart, they would form a line nearly five miles long.

Jesus went out of His way to present us with a staggering contrast. Why?

William Barclay sums up the meaning of the contrast nicely when he pens these words: "The point is that nothing that man can do to us can in any way compare with what we have done to God; and if God has forgiven us the debt we owe Him, we must forgive our fellowmen the debts they owe us."

Thus we are left without excuse if we fail to pass on the forgiveness that God has so graciously extended to us.

Jesus went out of His way to emphasize the lesson of passing on forgiveness because it is one of the most difficult for us to practice in daily life.

Lord, help me today to be more like You in forgiveness.

MISGUIDED FASTING

And when you fast, do not look dismal, like the hypocrites, for they disfigure their faces that their fasting may be seen by men. Truly, I say to you, they have received their reward. Matt. 6:16, RSV.

Matthew 6:16 picks up a thread dropped in verse 6. In verses 2 through 4 Jesus warned against ostentatious giving, and in verses 5 and 6 He did the same for prayer. He provided some very important instruction on prayer in verses 7 and 8, and provided a sample prayer in verses 9 through 13. He is now ready in verse 16 to return to His major theme of proper piety (see verse 1). This time His instruction has to do with fasting.

Verses 16 through 18 are Jesus' only instruction on the topic, and it should be pointed out, His purpose is to warn against abuses rather than to tell us how and when it should be done.

Fasting was important to the saints of both the Old and the New Testaments. The only commanded fast in the Old Testament was the annual Day of Atonement, but by the time of Jesus the Pharisees were fasting two days a week—Mondays and Thursdays.

It just so happens that those days were also market days. Thus large numbers of people arrived in the towns and villages on the weekly fast days.

This proved to be a temptation to some of the Jews who appreciated the larger audience for their displays of holiness. There were many who took deliberate steps so that others could not miss the fact that they were fasting. Some walked through the streets with their hair deliberately uncombed and with clothes deliberately soiled and disarrayed.

While such displays may have fooled the common people, they certainly didn't mislead the wiser rabbis and Jesus. Jesus let them know that their fasting was a deliberate act of spiritual pride rather than an act of humility.

Well, you may be thinking, no one would do that today.

Wrong! I have more than one acquaintance who routinely let it be known to certain of their friends in straight-faced piety that they are fasting.

Human nature doesn't change across time. But today God wants to take your human nature and make it be like His. Will you let Him?

PROPER FASTING

But when you fast, anoint your head and wash your face, that your fasting may not be seen by men but by your Father who is in secret; and your Father who sees in secret will reward you. Matt. 6:17, 18, RSV.

Perhaps the most remarkable thing in this passage to most evangelical Christians is that Jesus recommended fasting at all. After all, it is one of the easiest things to pervert. Look at the mechanical way many Jews went at it. And those problems were "reinvented" in the medieval church.

Note that Jesus didn't say don't fast, but "when you fast." He expects His disciples to fast just as He expects them to give alms and pray. Fasting was certainly carried out by the early church, often in connection with prayer and important decisions. The answer to a practice that has been misused in the church is not to cast it out and go to the other extreme, but to modify the practice and carry it out in a manner that leads to spiritual results.

Considering the times in which we live, perhaps Adventists should look anew at the practice of fasting. Perhaps those who seek revival and reawakening and reform should reexamine the issue of fasting.

Fasting is not to be a routine, mechanical event that we perform periodically. To the contrary, its primary use is for those exceptional situations in which we need to have clear minds and clean hearts as we seek God with all our soul.

Fasting should not be viewed as a "penny in the slot" avenue to divine rewards. Nor is it an end in itself. Rather, fasting is a physical means to spiritual ends as the soul wrestles with itself and God. Fasting generally has to do with the giving up of food or certain types of foods for a day, but true fasting can also entail the giving up of other things or activities for spiritual purposes. Part of the purpose of fasting is to clear out the channels of our lives so that we can more effectively meet God in prayer and meditation. God wants us to come and meet with Him at crucial and critical points in our lives.

JUST LOOK NORMAL

Is this the kind of fast I have chosen, only a day for a man to humble himself? Is it only for bowing one's head like a reed and for lying on sackcloth and ashes? Is that what you call a fast, a day acceptable to the Lord?

Is not this the kind of fasting I have chosen: to loose the chains of injustice and untie the cords of the yoke, to set the oppressed free and break every yoke? Is it not to share your food with the hungry and to provide the poor wanderer with shelter—when you see the naked, to clothe him, and not to turn away from your own flesh and blood? Isa. 58:5-7, NIV.

I t is easier to look pious than to be pious. It is easier to put on outward appearances than it is to be a genuine Christian in daily life. It is easier to fast than it is to love one's neighbor in a concrete way.

God is not against fasting, but if one must choose between fasting and loving one's neighbor, fasting should go. That is the message of Isaiah 58 (our scripture for today) and the Sermon on the Mount. Heart religion is the crucial element, not outward show.

In fact, in Matthew 6:16-18 Jesus is against all forms of outward show while fasting. He not only tells us not to look dismal, but He says that we should wash our face and comb our hair and look normal so that no one will even know we are having a special day with God.

That does not mean that on fast days I have to go out of my way to be extra "sweet and happy." There is nothing worse than those who go to the opposite extreme from being dismal when they are having a fast. You know the type. They can be sickeningly sweet and unnaturally happy when being pious. They may be at the opposite extreme from the Jews, but they share the same pit. They are still, by their unnatural actions, showing that they are "being with Jesus."

Just be normal when you are being with Jesus. It is between the two of you.

YET ANOTHER TRIP TO THE BEATITUDES

He said, I am the God of thy father, the God of Abraham, the God of Isaac, and the God of Jacob. And Moses hid his face; for he was afraid to look upon God. Ex. 3:6.

I don't know how you feel as you walk with Jesus on the Mount of Blessing, but I feel humbled again and again. As I see God's ideal for me I realize afresh my weaknesses and shortcomings; I realize how much I fall short of God's ideal.

For the past few weeks we have been looking at purity of heart in worship. We have been brought face-to-face with the fact that even in worship our motives are sometimes less than pure. We realize that there are times we give or pray or perform some other religious devotion partly for the effect on others, partly because we desire to look good and right in their eyes.

How would I pray, give, or act if no one was watching? That is the question that needs to be answered. Do I like it when people see me up front, when they hear my "beautiful" prayer and say so, when they think my talk or sermon was the "best" ever?

Suddenly I am driven back to the foot of the cross as I realize that Jesus' words aren't just for the Pharisees of old. They are for me, also.

Suddenly I once again am driven back to the Beatitudes. I realize afresh my poverty of spirit (Matt. 5:3) as I see myself as I really am. Once again I hunger and thirst after righteousness (verse 6) because I realize that my righteousness does not exceed that of the scribes and Pharisees (verse 20), because I am not yet as much like the Father (verses 43, 48) as I should and can be.

When I see the standard of Jesus in character, in witnessing, in relating to the true meaning of the law, and even in worshiping, I realize my need anew. My first reaction is to hide my face from Him. But then I realize that the life of Jesus makes it possible for me to come boldly before His throne and find His grace again. Suddenly I realize what a wonderful God I serve.

TAKING A FIFTH STEP
IN OUR WALK WITH JESUS

Lay not up for yourselves treasures upon earth, where moth and rust doth corrupt, and where thieves break through and steal. Matt. 6:19.

Suddenly we have fallen from heaven to earth, from worship to possessions. With Matthew 6:19, Jesus' great sermon makes another radical shift in its focus. And in the new focus we will see in a fresh way the wideness of God's interest in His earthly children. He is interested not only in our attitude toward heavenly things but also toward earthly things. The Sermon on the Mount really covers every area of life. It is truly God's ideal for His people.

Let's step back for a moment and review our walk with Jesus on the Mount of Blessing so far this year. We first walked with Him through the Beatitudes, His ideal for Christian character (Matt. 5:3-12). We next walked with Him through the responsibility for Christians to witness to His love (verses 13-16). Then Jesus gave us a grand tour through the depth and breadth of the law as we learned that a Christian's righteousness must exceed that of the scribes and Pharisees (verses 17-48).

That brought us to chapter 6. In the first 18 verses we learned that not only must a Christian's righteous actions exceed those of the scribes and Pharisees (see Matt. 5:21-48) but so also must his or her piety (Matt. 6:1-18). Now with verses 19-34 we are going to find out that even a Christian's goals and priorities in the things of this world need to be different from the values of the larger culture. Jesus began chapter 6 with a focus on the Pharisees; He ends it with telling us that we need to renounce the value system of the Gentiles.

The message is that to be a disciple of Jesus is to be radical. We can be church members without being radical, but not disciples. That is a crucial difference.

Today Jesus is calling me to be more like Him, not only in the way I live and worship but even in the way I think about material possessions.

HEAVEN VERSUS THE WORLD

But lay up for yourselves treasures in heaven, where neither moth nor rust [or worm] consumes and where thieves do not break in and steal. Matt. 6:20, RSV.

In Matthew 6:19-24 Jesus presents us with three sets of antitheses: earth versus heaven (verses 19-21), darkness versus light (verses 22, 23), and money versus God (verse 24). The first antithesis presents us with two treasures, the second with two eyes, and the third with two lords. All three deal with goals and priorities. All three deal with the "stuff" of everyday life. All three deal with heaven and the world.

The world in the New Testament is not the physical universe. Rather, the world is an outlook, a mentality, a way of looking at things, a way of evaluating the whole of life, a way of selecting goals and priorities.

One of the most significant problems that Christians have to face is their relationship to the world. It is Satan's strategy to get us to give ourselves over to the world, that anti-God orientation.

In order to achieve his ends, the adversary presents us with both internal and external temptations, private and public allurements.

In Matthew 6 Jesus is arming us for combat against the devil. In the first part of the chapter He suggests that we prepare ourselves through prayer and fasting. And now in the second half He is providing us with strategies to do combat with the evil one in the theater of daily affairs.

And in the affairs of daily life He prepares us for two types of temptations, both equally destructive. The first is the positive love of the world and the things of the world (Matt. 6:19-24), while the second is anxiety in respect to the world (verses 20-34).

Jesus' solution is not for us to replicate the monastic error of removing ourselves from the world so that we can live a holy life, but to live as Christians in the larger society, as He did. Thus He shows us how to overcome the world while living in the midst of it.

Our God is a God of this earth, but He is also the God of heaven. He wants each of us to live in this earth according to the principles of heaven.

TRANSITORY WEALTH

The kingdom of heaven is like treasure hidden in a field. When a man found it, he hid it again, and then in his joy went and sold all he had and bought that field. Matt. 13:44, NIV.

The preservation of wealth has always been a problem. That was especially so in the ancient world, where banks were not dependable and storage facilities were less than adequate. Some, as in the parable quoted above, buried their gold in the ground, only to die without anyone else knowing of its whereabouts.

Jesus highlights the transitoriness of wealth in Matthew 6:19, 20. In doing so, He comments on the three great sources of wealth in Palestine.

First, He tells us not to put our trust in those things that moths can destroy. In ancient Palestine a person's wealth often consisted in expensive clothing. Thus when Gehazi, Elisha's servant, wished to make some profit on the side from Naaman, after he had been cured of leprosy, he asked him for a talent of silver and two changes of garments (2 Kings 5:22). And one of the things that tempted Achan was "a beautiful robe from Babylonia" (Joshua 7:21, NIV). But, warns Jesus, such things hold no security because moths eat at them even while stored away.

Second, Jesus warns us to avoid those things that can be destroyed by rust or worms (Matt. 6:19, margin, RSV). Wealth can be eaten by either rust or worms, or even by rats and mice. The latter pests made stored food a dubious source of long-term wealth in the ancient world.

Third, Jesus suggests that if the moths and rust and so on don't get your wealth, a thief might. Thievery was an ever-present problem in Palestine, where the walls of most homes were made of baked clay. A burglar had only to dig through the wall. Imagine the surprise of the householder returning to find not only an extra hole in the wall, but his small hoard of treasure gone.

Today we have developed a million better ways to protect our wealth. But they are still not good enough. And if our wealth doesn't pass away, we will. Jesus' counsel is just as meaningful for us today as it was 2,000 years ago.

LIFE IS A DEATH SENTENCE

Love not the world, neither the things that are in the world. . . . The world passeth away, and the lust thereof: but he that doeth the will of God abideth for ever. 1 John 2:15-17.

No matter how happy you are with life today, things will get worse. Think about it. Let's say that you have a beautiful home on a tropical island paradise, with the surf to its front and a beautiful clear stream with a waterfall to its immediate left. All around are palm trees, lawn, flowering shrubs, and an abundance of birds, butterflies, and flowers.

It's heaven on earth, right? Not exactly. Even though it may be perfect today, some tomorrow will bring crippling or terminal accident or illness to one of the inmates of this earthly paradise. Earthly heavens sooner or later come crashing to the ground. None of us are immortal. Life is a death sentence. We are each subject to death from the time we are born. The question is not *if* we will be gone, but *when*.

It is that truth that Jesus is driving at in Matthew 6:19-21. Thus He warns us against those pleasures that will wear out like a suit of clothes. The most beautiful garment in the world, even without the help of moths, will eventually disintegrate. All earthly pleasures have a way of wearing out. And for the thrill of such pleasures we need larger and larger doses to get the same effect. People are foolish to put their hope in things that are bound to offer diminishing returns.

Jesus also warns against those pleasures that can be eroded away like iron in salt spray, or like grain in the path of marauding rodents. There are certain pleasures that lose their attraction as people grow older. Jesus suggests that we should trust in those things that time is powerless to erode.

Jesus also warns against those things that can be stolen away, even by such an impersonal thing as a stock market crash.

True happiness comes from putting our trust in the eternal. What is it that I have put my trust in?

IT'S IN YOUR HEAD

The love of money is the root of all evils; it is through this craving that some have wandered away from the faith and pierced their hearts with many pangs. 1 Tim. 6:10, RSV.

Tell me, what exactly is the root of the problem?

Paul makes it clear that the root of all evil is *not* money. Rather, it is the love of money. Some people will do anything for money, but it is the human heart and mind that are at fault, not the money itself.

With that teaching we are back to the old problem of sin as misdirected love, of sin as a problem of heart and mind rather than a mere problem of this or that behavior.

Jesus is making the same essential point in Matthew 6:19-21. We get into trouble when we love the wrong things.

But don't get confused. Jesus is not so much concerned with our treasures as with our attitude toward them. It is not what a person may possess, but what he or she thinks of wealth. It is a matter of attitude that Jesus is aiming at primarily.

Another point of confusion arises over the idea of "treasures." We should not limit the "treasures" that Jesus is talking about to money or financial wealth. *Treasure* is a very broad term that includes money but extends way beyond it. The transitory treasures Jesus is thinking of are anything that we love more than God and those things that belong to His eternal kingdom.

For some of us the treasure may indeed be money or a house or a car. But for others it may be love of honor, love of position, love of status, love of one's work, or a host of other things.

Our treasure is that which we live for, that which is closest to our heart, that which we spend our spare time thinking about. This is the point of Jesus' remarks. He wants our treasure to be of eternal value.

He is speaking to you, my friend. He is speaking to me. Take a moment and evaluate your *real* goals and priorities. Is a change needed? What is it?

REAL TREASURE

Fear not, little flock, for it is your Father's good pleasure to give you the kingdom. Sell your possessions, and give alms; provide yourselves with purses that do not grow old, with a treasure in the heavens that does not fail, where no thief approaches and no moth destroys. Luke 12:32, 33, RSV.

What is the real treasure that Jesus is talking about? What is the treasure that we are to store up?

Some have interpreted this passage in such a way as to imply that Jesus was teaching that we can earn our own salvation. "Treasure in heaven" they interpret as a person's salvation and eternal destiny. That interpretation contradicts the rest of the Bible and is obviously incorrect.

Luke's parallel passage is helpful here. In Luke it is clear that Jesus speaks of the kingdom as a gift. He goes on to imply that the treasures are those characteristics and actions that have eternal value.

The Jews were quite familiar with the phrase "treasure in heaven." They identified such treasure specifically with two things. The first was kindness. They said that the deeds of kindness done by a person upon earth became treasure in heaven. Such deeds had eternal value and eternal consequences.

The principle of kindness also found root in the early Christian church. Caring for the poor and the sick was a characteristic of the early church. Christians cared for those for whom no one else cared.

The story is told that during the brutal persecution of Decius in Rome the authorities broke into a Christian church. They sought the treasures that they believed the church to possess. "Show me your treasures," demanded the Roman leader. The deacon pointed to the widows and orphans who were being fed and the sick being nursed. "These," he replied, "are the treasures of the church."

Kindness has eternal results. The church at its best has always believed that "what we keep, we lose, and what we spend, we have."

The results of kindness never end. Such are the eternal treasures of the kingdom of God, the kind of treasures that Jesus is asking us to invest in.

ANOTHER REAL TREASURE

There is great gain in godliness with contentment; for we brought nothing into the world, and we cannot take anything out of the world. 1 Tim. 6:6, 7, RSV.

A Spanish proverb has it that there are no pockets in a shroud. That proverb is driving at the same truth as Paul in 1 Timothy. But think about it for a moment. Is there really nothing we take with us when we depart this world? Has nothing happened of eternal consequence during our years here? Is everything about us just wiped out so that every person starts over at the resurrection as a neutral zero? Take a few moments to discuss or think about these questions before reading further.

I would like to suggest that there is something that we take from this life to the next. Of course, it is not silver or gold or possessions. Paul and the Spanish proverb are quite correct on that count. But what we can take and must take is the treasure of character—something that can't be carried in a pocket, but something that every person develops in one direction or another.

On this earth we are forming characters. These characters are who we are. They are our identity. And they have eternal consequences. Only those with characters like Jesus' character will be happy in God's kingdom; only they will be in the first resurrection.

Outside of accepting Jesus, character building is life's most important task. Character is the one thing that we take to heaven. Character has eternal consequences. That is why Ellen White can write that "character building is the most important work ever entrusted to human beings" (*Education*, p. 225). Developing a Christlike character is laying up "treasures in heaven, where neither moth nor rust doth corrupt, and where thieves do not break through nor steal" (Matt. 6:20).

Heavenly treasure, of course, has earthly value. Every day women and men of good (or bad) character influence their children and other people with whom they come in contact.

Today my life can make a difference. And what I am today is a sure foreshadowing of what I will be tomorrow.

YET ANOTHER REAL TREASURE

Dear brother Christians, I love you and long to see you, for you are my joy and my reward for my work. My beloved friends, stay true to the Lord. Phil. 4:1, TLB.

A third type of treasure that cannot be eaten by moths or stolen by thieves is souls saved for the kingdom of heaven. In today's scripture Paul calls them his "reward." In the King James Version the translation is "crown." People won to Jesus are eternal treasure.

"At the final day," we read in *Thoughts From the Mount of Blessing*, "When the wealth of earth shall perish, he who has laid up treasure in heaven will behold that which his life has gained. If we have given heed to the words of Christ, then, as we gather around the great white throne, we shall see souls who have been saved through our agency, and shall know that one has saved others, and these still others—a large company brought into the haven of rest as the result of our labors, there to lay their crowns at Jesus' feet, and praise Him through the ceaseless ages of eternity. With what joy will the worker for Christ behold these redeemed ones, who share the glory of the Redeemer! How precious will heaven be to those who have been faithful in the work of saving souls!" (pp. 90, 91).

Treasure in heaven. What a thought! What a privilege to be able to participate in the process of helping others know Jesus better.

That thought brings us back to Matthew 5:13-16 and the evangelistic function of every Christian. Remember that each of us is to be both salt and light. Each of us is to have a daily ministry of just letting our Christian love permeate those around us (the salt function), and also of consciously witnessing evangelistically (the light function). We need to take advantage of the opportunities that God brings us each day.

And as we are being salt and light to others, it impacts on our own lives as our characters continue to develop to be more and more like the character of Jesus.

Treasure in heaven yields compound interest.

A FINAL LOOK AT TREASURE

Train up a child in the way he should go: and when he is old, he will not depart from it. Prov. 22:6.

Children. All of us have been children, and most of us have at least one child. How precious they are, but at times how discouraging, how frustrating.

As a parent and a teacher I have found great encouragement from the book *Education*. In that book Mrs. White tells us that our guardian angel will be the first to greet us on the resurrection morning. Our angel will bring us up-to-date on our life's work. Then, we read, "all the perplexities of life's experience will . . . be made plain. Where to us have appeared only confusion and disappointment, broken purposes and thwarted plans, will be seen a grand, overruling, victorious purpose, a divine harmony."

At that time, she continues, "all who have wrought with unselfish spirit will behold the fruit of their labors. The outworking of every right principle and noble deed will be seen. Something of this we see here. But how little of the result of the world's noblest work is in this life manifest to the doer! How many toil unselfishly and unweariedly for those who pass beyond their reach and knowledge! Parents and teachers lie down in their last sleep, their lifework seeming to have been wrought in vain; they know not that their faithfulness has unsealed springs of blessing that can never cease to flow; only by faith they see the children they have trained become a benediction and an inspiration to their fellow men, and the influence repeat itself a thousandfold. . . . Men [and women] sow the seed from which, above their graves, others reap blessed harvests. They plant trees, that others may eat the fruit. They are content here to know that they have set in motion agencies for good. In the hereafter the action and reaction of all these will be seen" (pp. 305, 306).

Children are treasures. More than that, they are dynamic treasures that extend blessings to other people.

We need to take our stewardship for the young seriously, even if they are not our personal offspring. We are all parents in Israel to all of God's little ones.

A LOOK AT THE FIRST COMMANDMENT

Where your treasure is, there will your heart be also. Matt. 6:21.

The first commandment reads "Thou shalt have no other gods before me" (Ex. 20:3). That command is basic to the Old Testament. It shapes Old Testament theology, history, and ethics.

It has also shaped the New Testament. In Matthew 6:19-24, for example, we find the first commandment illustrated several times. Perhaps we can get at Jesus' intent a little more clearly if we paraphrase the commandment to say: "Thou shalt have no other goals before me." Then, suggests F. D. Bruner, we can paraphrase the intent of Matthew 6:21 to be: "Where your goal is, there will your heart be also."

That is a crucial insight, because our goals determine our actions. Our goals determine everything else in our life. Thus where our heart is, or that which we have set our hearts on, is all-important. Whatever it is will determine both how we live our lives and where we will spend eternity.

What is it that I love? What is it that truly captivates my imagination, my spare time, my highest allegiance? These questions can help me determine both the location of my heart and the shape of my goals. They are questions that we ought to meditate upon today as we complete our devotions.

In John 3:19 we read: "This is the condemnation, that light is come into the world, and men loved darkness rather than light, because their deeds were evil."

They "loved" darkness. Love is an affair of the heart. All of us will choose to love something. Fortunately, we are offered a choice in the matter. We are not predestined.

Today Jesus is offering me a choice. Today He is appealing to my heart, my affections, my allegiance.

He is appealing to me in the very context of Matthew 6:21 to love those things that have eternal value rather than those things and ways of life that are transitory. He desires me to love "real" treasure.

What is my response? How shall I answer Him this day?

PUTTING PRIORITIES INTO ACTION

These all died in faith, not having received what was promised, but having seen it and greeted it from afar, and having acknowledged that they were strangers and exiles on the earth. . . . They desire a better country, that is, a heavenly one. Heb. 11:13-16, RSV.

It is one thing to have correct goals and priorities, it is quite another to put them into action.

Perhaps the most important thing in putting our priorities into practice is the realization that we are but pilgrims in this life, transients on this earth. Like the heroes of Hebrews 11, we are "strangers and exiles on the earth," we "desire a better country." One of my favorite hymns in the *Seventh-day Adventist Hymnal* is based on that thought:

> I'm a pilgrim, and I'm a stranger;
> I can tarry, I can tarry but a night;
> Do not detain me, for I am going
> To where the fountains are ever flowing.

> There's the city to which I journey;
> My Redeemer, my Redeemer is its light!
> There is no sorrow, nor any sighing,
> Nor any tears there, or any dying.

In the most literal sense of the word, this earth is not our home. We are walking on this earth under the eye of God and in the direction of God toward our everlasting hope.

That perspective enables us to put everything else in its proper place in our lives, including our possessions. Suddenly we realize that we are not the permanent holders of our possessions or our talents. To the contrary, the Christian realizes that all she or he is and has belongs to God and that we are but His stewards for a short time.

The non-Christian believes that he or she owns those things. Non-Christians can put their priority on things because of that belief. But as Christians we realize that God has loaned us our talents and possessions to be used in His service.

Because of that worldview, things are not at the center of our existence. We can move forward, asking daily how we can be used in the service of God.

An "Eye" Lesson

The light of the body is the eye: if therefore thine eye be single, thy whole body shall be full of light. But if thine eye be evil, thy whole body shall be full of darkness. If therefore the light that is in thee be darkness, how great is that darkness! Matt. 6:22, 23.

In these verses the eye is likened to a window that lets light into the whole body. The color or state of such a window determines what kind of light and how much light gets into a room.

If the window is clean and clear, the light will be able to flood the room and illumine its every corner. On the other hand, if the window glass is dirty or frosted, the entrance of light will be hindered. Thus the amount and quality of light that gets into a room depends on the state of the window through which it enters.

Jesus applies this concept to the human eye. The amount of light that gets into a person's heart and mind depends upon the spiritual state of one's eye, since the eye is the window for the entire body.

In the context of Matthew 6:19-24, this teaching on the eye has to do with our goals and priorities. If our spiritual perceptions and understandings are correct, we will have a correct view of both earthly and heavenly treasures; we will have a correct view of which master we should serve (verse 24). But if our spiritual eye is out of kilter, so will be our priorities.

Most of us value our physical eyes very much. We realize that without them no light can enter our bodies. We cherish our eyes and go out of our way to protect them. In the pursuit of clear vision, many people wear glasses or contact lenses.

Unfortunately, modern people are much less concerned with their spiritual eyesight. Some run around completely blind, while claiming all the while to be seeing perfectly. Others see things through distorted lenses. Their whole lives are shaped by those distortions.

God wants us to have good spiritual eyesight. The Sermon on the Mount is a corrective for poor eyes.

AVOIDING SPIRITUAL SCHIZOPHRENIA

One thing I do, forgetting what lies behind and straining forward to what lies ahead, I press on toward the goal for the prize of the upward call of God in Christ Jesus. Phil. 3:13, 14, RSV.

I'm not all that excited about spectator sports, but I do like to watch the Olympics from time to time. In our scripture for today Paul pictures a runner straining toward the finish line. At full stride the lead runner dare not look behind lest that edge of speed that makes the difference between being the winner and a runner-up be lost. To the contrary, all the runner's mental and physical energy is focused on the goal ahead.

Paul compares that experience with that of the Christian. Christians also must keep their attention and priorities focused on their one and only goal.

Jesus expressed much the same idea in Matthew 6:22, 23, when He talked about the Christian's eye being "single." As Ellen White puts it, "Singleness of purpose, wholehearted devotion to God, is the condition pointed out by the Saviour's words. Let the purpose be sincere and unwavering to discern the truth and to obey it at whatever cost, and you will receive divine enlightenment. Real piety begins when all compromise with sin is at an end" *(Thoughts From the Mount of Blessing*, p. 91).

Paul had that kind of devotion in mind when he said, "I count everything as loss because of the surpassing worth of knowing Christ Jesus my Lord. For his sake I have suffered the loss of all things, and count them as refuse, in order that I may gain Christ and be found in him" (Phil. 3:8, 9, RSV).

Paul is the opposite of the doubting, double-minded man described by James. Such a one is "like a wave of the sea that is driven and tossed by the wind" (James 1:6, RSV).

Lord, today I come to You in humbleness. I know that my goals and priorities need to be more consistently lived out in my daily life. I confess to being double-minded at times. Lord, help my vision to clear up, help my focus to be single to Your glory and to the true treasure that has enduring value. Thank You, Father.

DISTORTED VISION

Take heed to yourselves, lest at any time your hearts be overcharged with surfeiting [dissipation, RSV], and drunkenness, and cares of this life, and so that day come upon you unawares. Luke 21:34.

Demas hath forsaken me, having loved this present world. 2 Tim. 4:10.

It's a disease that generally comes with age. The problem centers on a clouding up of the eye's lens. As the lens becomes opaque, total or partial blindness is the result. Such is the quite common affliction known as cataract.

While we know cataracts as a physical disease, there is a parallel dynamic in the spiritual world that also clouds our vision and leads to progressive blindness. Distorted spiritual vision has many causes. One of them is self-conceit or self-love. Persons who do not have a balanced and correct view of self are incapable of self-criticism. And those incapable of self-criticism are also incapable of self-improvement. Neither can such persons see others as they really are. Thus the light in which they live has become darkness.

Prejudice also distorts our spiritual vision. Nothing destroys judgment as effectively as does prejudice. It prevents the forming of clear and logical judgments. It blinds us to the facts and the significance of the facts. Thus our light becomes darkness.

A third distorting factor is jealousy. The jealous person has lost the ability to coolly weigh the facts. Jealous persons are incapable of correct evaluations because their vision is impaired. They often see red when they should see white. They live in fading light.

And the cares of this world, as we noted in our scripture reading today, also turn our light into darkness. Thus it was with Demas, a man who had been at the core of Paul's evangelistic team. He began to love the wrong things; he lost his vision and eventually became bereft of faith itself.

The Great Physician calls all those suffering from spiritual cataracts to come to Him for corrective surgery.

DARK LIGHT

The god of this age has blinded the minds of unbelievers, so that they cannot see the light of the gospel of the glory of Christ, who is the image of God. 2 Cor. 4:4, NIV.

God is light, and in him is no darkness at all. 1 John 1:5.

God is light! Sin blinds! The god of this age (Satan) is an agent of blindness! These are basic facts that stand near the center of the great controversy between good and evil.

Satan's aim is to blind us in certain vital respects closely related to Matthew 6:19-24. First, he seeks to blind us to our own mortality. When we are young it seems that we have forever to live, to be healthy, to be beautiful or handsome. The world puts great value on those attributes. So much so that we on the downward side of life sometimes try to prop up our physiques or facial characteristics in unnatural ways in an attempt to provide ourselves with the illusion that we really look young. But we fool no one but ourselves. The plain fact is that we grow old, and we might as well face it in a healthy manner.

Our beauty fades, our strength dribbles away, and too many of our muscles head south for something more than the winter. In the long run, we die. That is a truth that should put other truths into perspective.

A second point in which Satan seeks to blind us is the relative value of time. It is his aim to get us to live for time and to forget eternity. The wisdom of the world is that it is foolish to live for the coming kingdom. Rather, people should do all they can and get all they can in the present world.

But the light of God helps us clearly see through such darkness. He helps us see that there is no comparison between the relative importance of time and eternity.

In the Sermon on the Mount, Jesus brings us face-to-face with these truths. He does so because each of us must make a choice as to what we will live for. Each of us must choose blindness or sight, God or Satan.

THE CASE OF LAZARUS

"Then I beg you, father, to send [Lazarus] to my father's house, for I have five brothers, so that he may warn them, lest they also come into this place of torment." But Abraham said, "They have Moses and the prophets; let them hear them." And he said, "No, father Abraham; but if some one goes to them from the dead, they will repent." He said to him, "If they do not hear Moses and the prophets, neither will they be convinced if some one should rise from the dead." Luke 16:27-31, RSV.

Here is Jesus' priceless parable about a man whose light had become darkness. The rich man (generally known as Dives) had swallowed the philosophy of the world hook, line and sinker. He had gobbled down the whole nine yards of Satan's deception.

Dives lived for this world and did quite well at it. Just look at him, all decked out in purple and fine linen. Ate well, too. And his house was something to behold. He had made it in this world. He was top dog, or nearly top dog, in his social circle.

Then there was poor old Lazarus, a man who was apparently faithful to his God, but dirt poor and covered with sores. He was so poor that he would have been happy to eat Dives's garbage. Even the despised dogs of the ancient world had it better than Lazarus—they licked his sores.

What a contrast!

But the story isn't ended. Playing on popular imagery, Jesus presents Lazarus as going to heaven and Dives to hell.

Now the devil's curtain that masks the most important priorities, goals, and values is torn aside. The light shines forth, and even Dives sees the truth at last.

He begs that Lazarus be sent to warn his brothers so they won't be deceived. But he is told that they already have the source of light and truth. They already have the Bible, the Book that tells the true story of values and goals.

The problem is that they don't read the Bible; they don't want its truth. But that light, my friends, is the only light. We ignore it to our eternal peril. It is God's word to us.

THE NATURE OF SLAVERY

No man can serve two masters: for either he will hate the one, and love the other; or else he will hold to the one, and despise the other. Ye cannot serve God and mammon. Matt. 6:24.

This verse was undoubtedly more forceful in the ancient world than it is to us. The verb translated as "serve" is from *doulos*, which is our word for "slave." The word translated as "master" is *kurios*, a word that denotes absolute ownership and is nearly always rendered as "lord" in the New Testament. Thus the idea of Matthew 6:24 is that no one can be enslaved to two owners or lords at the same time.

To catch the full impact of this statement we need to realize that in the ancient world a slave was not regarded as a person but as a living tool. Slaves had no rights of their own. They were completely under the control of their masters, who could do with them as they wanted. Masters could sell slaves, beat them, throw them out, or even kill them.

A second thing to note is that in the ancient world slaves had no time of their own. All their time belonged to their master. In modern culture each worker has time off for his or her personal needs. During that time workers can have hobbies or even hold a second job. But that was not so in the ancient world of slavery. A slave's time belonged wholly to the master.

Jesus is saying that Christians must let God be the undisputed master of their lives. Paul makes the same point in Romans 6, where he says we are slaves of either sin or righteousness, Satan or Christ.

Thus Christians, being enslaved to Jesus, always take God's will into consideration in all they do. They daily ask themselves, "What does God wish me to do?" Every moment of every day they live for God. God has no part-time devotees who largely serve Him but then moonlight for some other master in their time off.

When Jesus said no person can serve two masters, He meant it.

Think about it. Are you trying to serve two masters? Are you seeking to accomplish the impossible?

SLAVERY REVERSED

Do you not know that if you yield yourselves to any one as obedient slaves, you are slaves of the one whom you obey, either of sin, which leads to death, or of obedience, which leads to righteousness? But thanks be to God, that you who were once slaves of sin have become obedient from the heart to the standard of teaching to which you were committed, and, having been set free from sin, have become slaves of righteousness. Rom. 6:16-18, RSV.

It's just not true that no person can serve two masters. The truth is that people can't serve two masters at the same time. On the other hand, two masters can be served sequentially, one after the other.

In fact, that's how it is with Christians. Every person, according to the Bible, is born with a bent toward evil. Now, it's true that not all of us are tempted to evil of the same sort. Many "nice" church members think of sin in only its more outward forms. They think of sin in terms of such things as adultery, murder, theft, blatant dishonesty, and so on.

But that is only half the picture. Such "nice" church members too often forget such "vegetarian" sins as pride, self-sufficiency, and unsanctified goodness. They forget the sins that stand closest to the heart of the real problem of sin. "Nice" people (even people inside the church) are quite often the hardest to reach with the converting, saving message of Jesus, because nice people feel no need of forgiveness.

But according to the Bible, every person needs to be converted. Every person needs to meet Jesus and discover the sad truth that even pride in our goodness needs to be repented of.

The concepts of repentance and conversion have in them the idea of a complete turnaround, a reversal of direction. That is what happens to people when they meet Jesus. They may be heading one direction, but then they head in the other. They discover they have been serving the wrong master. That discovery leads them to choose Jesus as the Lord of their lives. Praise God for miracles of grace.

YOU "CANNOT"

Then saith Jesus unto him, Get thee hence, Satan: for it is written, Thou shalt worship the Lord thy God, and him only shalt thou serve. Matt. 4:10.

Perhaps the word "cannot" is the most forceful word in Matthew 6:24. No one can serve two masters. He or she *"cannot."*

The verse does not say "may not" or "shall not," but "cannot." It is impossible. And Jesus is so concerned about getting that point across that He says it two times in the same verse. Chrysostom, the great preacher of the early church, commented on this text by noting that when God has said it is impossible, don't say it is possible. It isn't.

But why? we must ask. Why can't we serve more than one at a time?

Ellen White has suggested that the reason is that "no one can occupy a neutral position; there is no middle class, who neither love God nor serve the enemy of righteousness. Christ is to live in His human agents and work through their faculties and act through their capabilities. . . . He who does not give himself wholly to God is under the control of another power, listening to another voice, whose suggestions are of an entirely different character. Half-and-half service places the human agent on the side of the enemy as a successful ally of the host of darkness" *(Thoughts From the Mount of Blessing*, p. 94).

Just think of World War II. A soldier couldn't be just "a little bit" on the side of the United States and "a little bit" on the side of Hitler. It was one or the other. So it is in the great galactic war between Christ and Satan. Those who claim to serve with Christ but are "part-time" agents for Satan are the equivalent of spies.

Along that line we read that "the strongest bulwark of vice in our world is not the iniquitous life of the abandoned sinner or the degraded outcast; it is that life which otherwise appears virtuous, honorable, and noble, but in which one sin is fostered, one vice indulged" *(ibid.)*. The presence of spies is confusing to any army. It is so in Christ's army. The only way to serve Him at all is to do so wholeheartedly. You *cannot* serve both God and mammon.

JESUS THE TOTALITARIAN

"If you would be perfect, go, sell what you possess and give to the poor, and you will have treasure in heaven; and come, follow me." When the young man heard this he went away sorrowful; for he had great possessions. Matt. 19:21, 22, RSV.

Jesus doesn't beat around the bush. Sell *everything* and give it to the poor. That is a very dramatic statement, a very demanding statement.

But so is the statement that "he who loves father or mother more than me is not worthy of me; and he who loves son or daughter more than me is not worthy of me; and he who does not take his cross and follow me is not worthy of me. He who finds his life will lose it, and he who loses his life for my sake will find it" (Matt. 10:37-39, RSV). There is nothing very subtle about all this. Jesus is making absolutist demands.

But, if we begin to think about it, such demands are not new with Jesus. The Ten Commandments say "Thou shalt have no other gods before me" (Ex. 20:3). God demanded all from His people in the Old Testament. He was a "jealous God" who brooked no competition.

That concept of the worship of God and no other is carried over into the New Testament, where we are commanded to love God with all our heart, soul, and mind.

Christianity is not a halfway religion. It is a religion of *total* dedication. This is one of the things that makes Christianity different from most of the other great religions of the world.

I remember how frustrated I was the first time I confronted Hinduism, a religion of hundreds of millions of deities. A Hindu has no problem accepting Christ as one God among the millions of others. But it is quite another thing for a Hindu to accept Jesus as the *one and only* God and Saviour. That's radical—too radical for most.

But it's what Jesus demands. One either belongs to Christ or does not. This is a serious choice. It is a choice that knows no compromise. Christianity is a radical faith.

CHRISTIANS ARE ATHEISTS

*Our God whom we serve is able to deliver us from the burning fiery fur-
nace; and he will deliver us out of your hand, O king. But if not, be it
known to you, O king, that we will not serve your gods or worship the
golden image which you have set up. Dan. 3:17, 18, RSV.*

C hristians have died for the strangest reasons. In the early persecution by the Roman Empire, for example, they were killed because
they were presumed to be cannibalistic, immoral, and atheistic.

They were viewed as cannibalistic by the larger public because they
ate the flesh and drank the blood of someone called Jesus. They were
seen as immoral because their "love feasts" were held in secret. And
given what happened at Greek and Roman feasts, it took only a small
stretch of the imagination to come up with conclusions of immorality,
especially since they were already eating human flesh and drinking
blood in their secret "orgies."

Interestingly enough, early Christians were also thought of as being
atheists. You may wonder how that could be. Hadn't these people given
all for their religious beliefs?

That is true, but they didn't honor the deities of Greece and Rome,
including the emperor. Thus they were atheists in terms of the cultures
in which they lived. Not only were they atheists but they were considered haters of humanity, because their failure to worship the civil gods
meant that the community could not be fully blessed by the deities.

Christians today should be thought of as atheists, also. The gods of
modern culture are material wealth and positions of prestige and power.
These are of supreme value for most people. Many will do anything to
get them, and few are those who don't worship at their altars and show
deference to their high priests.

True Christians refuse to play this game. Like Daniel's friends of old
and like the early Christians, they worship a strange God; they worship
Yahweh, the invisible God who demands their total allegiance.

Christians are different from their larger culture. They serve a different master.

THE PLACE OF MATERIAL POSSESSIONS

And if you obey the voice of the Lord your God, being careful to do all his commandments which I command you this day, the Lord your God will set you high above all the nations of the earth. Deut. 28:1, RSV.

Jesus is not telling us in Matthew 6 that there is anything wrong with material possessions, or "mammon." What He is telling us is that those blessings need to have their proper place in our lives. Rather than being of supreme importance, they are to be seen in relation to the God who gave them. They are not to be our master. Rather, we are to be the master of material blessings for the service of God.

There are several things that we need to remember about material blessings and our relation to them. The first is that they belong to God. "The earth is the Lord's, and the fulness thereof; the world, and they that dwell therein," says the psalmist (Ps. 24:1). "For every beast of the forest is mine, and the cattle upon a thousand hills. . . . If I were hungry, I would not tell thee: for the world is mine, and the fulness thereof" (Ps. 50:10-12).

The story is told of a city schoolgirl on a field trip to the country. For the first time she saw the spring abundance of wildflowers that covered the hills. Turning to her teacher, she asked, "Do you think God would mind if I picked one of His flowers?"

She had it right. All that is belongs to God.

A second thing that we as Christians should note is that we are God's stewards. He entrusts us with material goods so that we can share them with others. To some we are spiritual stewards, but to the homeless and the hungry we are called upon from time to time to share the material blessings God has given us. The stewardship principle holds not only for money, but also for our gifts and talents.

In Jesus' parable, it was the master who gave out the talents to be used till he returned. So it is in real life. We are the stewards, not the owners, of wealth. We are God's agents.

WHY IS IT ALWAYS
THE LORD'S CALF THAT DIES?

He that is faithful in that which is least is faithful also in much: and he that is unjust in the least is unjust also in much. If therefore ye have not been faithful in the unrighteous mammon, who will commit to your trust the true riches? Luke 16:10, 11.

The story is told of a farmer who happily reported to his wife and children that their best cow had given birth to twin calves, one brown and one white. He said that he was so grateful that he had decided to dedicate one of the calves to the Lord. "We will bring them up together, and when the time comes we will sell one and keep the proceeds, and we will sell the other and give the proceeds to the Lord's work."

"But which one is the Lord's?" queried his wife.

"There is no need to bother with that now," he replied. "We will raise them the same way until they are ready for market."

A few months later the farmer came home looking very miserable and unhappy. When his wife asked him the reason for his discouragement, he told her that the Lord's calf had died.

"But," she said, "you hadn't decided which was to be the Lord's."

"Oh, yes," said he, "I had decided some time back that it was the white one, and it is the white one that died."

Now, we may smile at that simple story. But don't smile too broadly, or else you may be smiling at yourself. For too many of us it is always the Lord's calf that dies. When things become difficult, one of the first places we choose to economize is in our contributions to the Lord's work. The Lord's calf is always the first to go.

Why? we are constrained to ask. Because we still struggle with the god mammon. We still struggle with the direction of our allegiances. Our giving patterns speak loudly about what is important in our lives.

We need to constantly remember that we can't serve both God and mammon. We need to get our financial priorities straight. That is not so difficult once the heart is facing toward the right deity.

A PROGRESSIVE ARGUMENT

May God himself, the God of peace, sanctify you through and through. May your whole spirit, soul and body be kept blameless at the coming of our Lord Jesus Christ. The one who calls you is faithful and he will do it. 1 Thess. 5:23, 24, NIV.

The God of our salvation is eager to save us entirely. He wants as many as possible to be in His kingdom. When Paul talks about God wanting to save spirit, soul, and body, he is telling us that God wants to save the whole person, not just the body, not just the mind, and not just our spiritual side. There will be no bodiless spirits in the kingdom, nor any mindless bodies.

Jesus has been dealing with the whole person in Matthew 6:19-24 in a progressive sort of way. At the end of His first illustration in verse 21 He deals with our heart, the seat of our attitudes. He knows that it is crucial to warn us first of the importance of problems of the heart. It is the heart that inclines us toward choosing one way of life or the other. Thus, in the saying of the two treasures He begins with our hearts.

Then verses 22 and 23 have the saying of the two eyes. Jesus moves quickly to our visual organs, the part of our selves that supplies our minds with a large amount of data on which we make decisions. If our eyes and minds provide us with biased data, we have little hope of making correct choices.

Next He moves to our whole being and our ultimate allegiances in the saying of the two masters. Here Jesus reaches the climax that He has been driving at since verse 19. The ultimate fruitage of our attitudes and mental outlooks is a life that will be either with God or against Him.

These three sayings leave us with no middle ground. Our treasure is *either* in heaven *or* on earth. Our eyes are providing us with *either* light *or* darkness. We are serving *either* God *or* mammon.

Jesus couldn't have put it in plainer language. But He leaves the final decision with you and me. Which master shall I serve *today*?

A Case of Priorities

He who believes in the Son has eternal life; he who does not obey the Son shall not see life, but the wrath of God rests upon him. John 3:36, RSV.

J enny Lind (1820-1887) was perhaps the greatest female operatic singer of her day. Fame and fortune were at her command. Yet she left her career while she was still singing at her best, and never returned to it.

She must have missed the applause of the countless thousands who had admired her. She must have felt the absence of the constant attention and fame, and perhaps even the money. Yet she chose to live out the rest of her life in privacy.

Once a British friend found her sitting on the beach, Bible in hand, staring into the sunset. They talked, and as they did so the conversation came to the inevitable question: "How is it that you came to abandon the stage at the very height of your success?"

"When every day," she answered, "it made me think less and less of this [laying her hand upon the Bible] and nothing at all of that [pointing to the sunset], what else could I do?"

Of course, she could have done many things. She certainly could have stayed in her profession. That was a valid choice.

We are faced with critical choices every day. The most important choice that we will ever make has been touched upon by Jesus in Matthew 6:24. Daily we must choose to let Jesus be our master. Daily we must commit ourselves to being His servant.

Our scripture for today reminds us that that choice is not a meaningless one. Choosing Jesus means choosing life eternal. Rejecting Jesus means remaining under the wrath of God, remaining under His holy and loving anger at the destructive results of sin.

The heart of God appeals to me today to come to Him, to give my heart to Him, to truly make Him the Lord of my life. Those who do so already have eternal life. They are already a part of the kingdom.

WE LOVE TO WORRY

Therefore I tell you, do not worry about your life, what you will eat or drink; or about your body, what you will wear. Is not life more important than food, and the body more important than clothes? Matt. 6:25, NIV.

"My life has been full of terrible misfortunes—most of which have never happened." These words of philosopher Montaigne express the human predicament. We love to worry. In fact, if we don't have anything significant to worry about, it seems that we usually manage to be anxious concerning the insignificant. All too often we are like the little lady who declared, "I always feel bad when I feel good, for I know that I will feel bad after a while."

Unfortunately, worry exacts a heavy toll from its participants. The ancient Chinese warlords had a special form of torture for their prisoners. They would tie them hand and foot and put them under a bag of water that constantly dripped . . . dripped . . . dripped, day and night. Those drops of water incessantly falling on the head finally became like the sound of hammer blows and drove men insane.

Worry is like the constant drip, drip, drip of water. The constant dripping of worry weakens the vital energies of men and women and leads to such consequences as ulcers, heart disease, insanity, and suicide. Hospitals are filled with people who have collapsed under the crushing burden of worry and anxiety. Worry is a killer, both directly and indirectly.

The Sermon on the Mount meets the problem of worry head-on, and its advice still forms the foundation for some of the most helpful psychological, medical, and spiritual counsel on the topic. Jesus tackled this problem in Matthew 6:25-34. In the next few days we will examine His counsel and seek to apply it to our lives.

As we examine that advice we need to keep in mind the fact that God is interested in our daily lives. He is interested in the quality of those lives. He wants them to be fuller because of our faith.

Thank You, God, for caring today about me. Thank You for wanting not just the good for me, but the very best. I love You, God.

"TAKE NO THOUGHT"

Be careful for nothing; but in every thing by prayer and supplication with thanksgiving let your requests be made known unto God. And the peace of God, which passeth all understanding, shall keep your hearts and minds through Christ Jesus. Phil. 4:6, 7.

B e careful for nothing," we read in today's Bible verse. What does it mean to "be careful for nothing"? Does it mean that we shouldn't care?

That phrase is just as confusing as the King James Version's rendering of Matthew 6:25, where we read: "Take no thought for your life, what ye shall eat, or what ye shall drink; nor yet for your body." The phrase "take no thought" is repeated again in verses 31 and 34. Whatever Jesus was driving at must have been very important to Him, since He says it three times in nine verses.

Several English translations of the Bible that were published prior to the King James Version translate the phrase "take no thought for your life" as "be not careful for your life." They use the word "careful" in the literal sense of full of care. That is a more helpful translation than that of the KJV. It is not ordinary, prudent foresight that Jesus is condemning; it is worry.

And worry or anxiety is the translation given by most modern translations. Jesus is telling us repeatedly that Christians are not to worry about life, or be anxious about what they should wear or eat.

The Jews of Christ's day were quite familiar with the attitudes being set forth by Jesus. The great rabbis taught that a person should meet life with a combination of sensibility in practical matters on the one hand and serenity on the other. Thus they taught that a person should plan carefully but also trust in God. For them the two went hand in hand.

We shall see in the next few days that Jesus and the New Testament teach the same combination of virtues. Taking no thought and being careful for nothing should be thought of as "Don't be anxious or worried all the time." Why should we? Isn't God our Father? Doesn't He care for us?

A Bit More
About Not Being "Careful"

Jesus answered and said unto her, Martha, Martha, thou art careful and troubled about many things: But one thing is needful: and Mary hath chosen that good part, which shall not be taken away from her. Luke 10:41, 42.

Two of my favorite New Testament characters are Mary and Martha, the two sisters of Lazarus of Bethany. How different they were. Martha was a faithful plodder. She was full of care about each of the duties and details of daily life. She worried about everything being done and done right—that the meals would be fit for guests, that they would be on time, that the house would be clean, that the clothes would be washed, that everything would work out right. She was concerned about these things; she was full of care. To put it in more modern terms, she was anxious and worried.

Then there was Mary. Mary, as I picture her in my mind's eye, was like a butterfly flitting from flower to flower. She spent a lot of time smelling the roses of life. She was more interested in the beauty of things and in relationships than she was in getting things done on time.

And that's where the rub came between the two sisters. Jesus had come to Bethany, and Martha had invited Him to dinner. That invitation put her in a real tizzy. After all, the beds needed to be made, the floor needed to be swept, the food had to be purchased and prepared, and . . . Choleric Martha was in high gear.

But where's Mary? There she is! Doing nothing! Just sitting at Jesus' feet, listening and smiling! Doesn't she know that things need to be done? Doesn't she care?

Martha was worried; she was full of care. Too full. Too full even to take time with Jesus.

Jesus gives her a mild rebuke and plainly tells her that Mary had made the more important decision. He didn't tell Martha not to clean and cook, but He did tell her to get her priorities straight.

The characteristics of both Mary and Martha are needed. Workers are needed, but at their best, workers take time to be with Jesus first.

THE PLACE OF WORK

By the sweat of your brow you will eat your food until you return to the ground, since from it you were taken; for dust you are and to dust you will return. Gen. 3:19, NIV.

Some people have taken Jesus' words in Matthew 6:25 about taking no thought about life, food, and clothing to mean that they must not think about such things. Such zealous but misguided people have forgotten the lesson that we need to recognize all that the Bible says on a topic and not regulate our lives by isolated passages taken out of context.

The Bible command is not just to "live by faith" while having no care for our temporal needs. Far from it. At the time of the Fall in Eden, God set up a work program for Adam and Eve. It was God's command that humans after the Fall should work by the sweat of their brow. In Matthew, Jesus is not condemning farmers for plowing and harrowing and sowing and reaping and gathering into barns.

The apostle Paul put it quite explicitly in his second letter to the Thessalonians when he said that if a person "would not work, neither should he eat." Even in Paul's day there were fanatical elements in the church who argued that since the Lord is going to return very soon, we must not work, we must live by faith and spend our time studying the Bible as we prepare for the Second Coming. So they ceased working and imagined themselves to be exceptionally spiritual. Thus Paul's rebuke.

In Matthew 6 Jesus is seeking to get us to set our priorities straight. While we are to work with diligence, Christians are not to be workaholics. Neither are we to be so concerned with the material side of life that we are filled with care and anxiety. The material side of life is important, but not all-important. Work is important, but not what life is all about.

As Christians we have a heavenly Father who cares for us. We don't need to worry or be full of care. Because we trust in God we are freed to live life more abundantly in every part of our lives.

WE HAVE A SNEAKY DEVIL

Cast all your anxieties on him, for he cares about you. Be sober, be watchful. Your adversary the devil prowls around like a roaring lion, seeking some one to devour. 1 Peter 5:7, 8, RSV.

The devil's not picky. He doesn't care which way he trips you up. The main thing for him is that you trip and fall. For some of us he uses one temptation, for others another ploy. Success is all that counts with him. He can use opposite tactics to reach the same goal.

Thus we may think that we have won the battle against Satan because we have met him and fended him off when he came in at the front door of our life. But before we know it we find that he has sneaked in through the back door. There is no end of his methods. He can even appear as an angel of light.

Those thoughts speak directly to the teachings of Jesus in the last half of Matthew 6. Take time to read verses 19 through 34 again. What verse sets those verses off into two parts? What is the common thread that holds the two parts together? How do the two parts differ?

The turning point in those verses is verse 25. Up to this point in the passage Jesus has been telling His hearers not to make possessions and success their goal, not to make them all-important. But in verse 25 there is a definite shift. Now the topic is not to worry about possessions or even the necessities of life.

The common thread running throughout verses 19 to 34 is material possessions. The verses differ in that the first part deals with acquiring possessions, while the latter part focuses on worrying about them.

But the devil's strategy is the same all the way through. He wants the material side of life to be the focal point of our thoughts. He wants the material to dominate the spiritual. He has gained his goal as long as he can get our priorities out of order.

Jesus speaks to both sides of the common temptation to materialism in Matthew 6. He has a message deeply needed in our times. He has a message especially needed by me.

ARGUMENT NO. 1 AGAINST WORRY

He that spared not his own Son, but delivered him up for us all, how shall he not with him also freely give us all things? Rom. 8:32.

What does our Scripture verse for today have in common with Matthew 6:25: "Do not be anxious about your life, what you shall eat or what you shall drink, nor about your body, what you shall put on. Is not life more than food, and the body more than clothing?" (RSV)? Think through your answer before reading further. If you are reading this devotional with other people, take time to discuss the similarity and its meaning.

The answer is that both passages argue from the greater to the lesser. Romans 8:32 argues that since God gave His Son (the greater), He will certainly give us what we need. We find the same thing in Matthew 6:25.

Thus a first reason not to worry in Matthew 6:25-34 is that life is based on trust in and dependence on God for its most essential properties. Every person has life and a body. We never received these by being anxious. They came as gifts from our loving Creator. Therefore, says Jesus, if God provided us with such marvelous attributes, why worry about such mediocre things as food, clothing, and shelter?

He who provided the greater—life itself—is certainly capable and willing to provide the lesser—material goods—without our constant fretting. We need to learn to trust. We need to take our eyes off our selves and off our lives and put them on the God who cares for us.

Jesus will go on to illustrate His point about trusting God by having us contemplate the birds and the flowers. But before moving into that, we should note that the things Jesus told us not to worry about are the most important of life's essentials. Food, drink, and clothing are at the center of existence. They are necessary commodities. Without food and drink (and even clothing, in most climates) we will cease to be. These are at the foundation of survival. Now, if we are told not to worry about these most important items, it seems even more logical not to worry about the luxuries of life.

THANKING GOD FOR THE OBVIOUS

And one of them, when he saw that he was healed, turned back, and with a loud voice glorified God, and fell down on his face at his [Jesus'] feet, giving him thanks; and he was a Samaritan. And Jesus answering said, Were there not ten cleansed? but where are the nine? Luke 17:15-17.

I have only one back. Until I was in my early 40s I was largely unconscious of that back. I never got up in the morning and thanked God for a strong, painless back. I took it for granted and went my way.

Then it happened. Disaster. I was helping my son unload the trunk of my car as I visited him at Mount Pisgah Academy in North Carolina. I don't know what I lifted, but it couldn't have weighed more than 10 pounds. It wasn't heavy, but as I bent down something happened to my back.

For the next few days I walked around like a hairless orangutan. Whenever I straightened up, I knew I had a back. In fact, even when I didn't straighten up, I knew I had a back. It had become the center of my life.

Suddenly I began to pray about a back—not backs in general, but my back.

Now, many of you can tell me a similar story. For others, it would be stories about arms or eyes or stomachs, or even life. The stories are similar. We begin to pray about this or that part when things go wrong.

My question is Why do we wait? Why do things have to get bad before we pray about them? Wouldn't it be better to live in a state of thankfulness to our Maker, who has made us wonderfully?

God gave us life, God gave us bodies. They are marvelously made. Today I want to thank Him for two eyes that function so well (although not perfectly), for two arms that are helpful and pain-free, and even for a back that is fine (as long as I do my part and exercise it each day).

Be thankful now. Don't wait for something to go wrong before you pray. Praise God right now for your body and life itself.

BIRD LESSONS

Look at the birds of the air: they neither sow nor reap nor gather into barns, and yet your heavenly Father feeds them. Are you not of more value than they? Matt. 6:26, RSV.

S ome years ago the United States Public Health Service issued a statement in connection with the prevalence of nervous disease and the tendency of worry to weaken and shorten life. In this statement was the following observation (no doubt suggested by the words of Jesus): "So far as is known, no bird ever tried to build more nests than its neighbor. No fox ever fretted because he had only one hole in which to hide. No squirrel ever died of anxiety lest he should not lay by enough for two winters instead of one, and no dog ever lost any sleep over the fact that he had not enough bones laid aside for his declining years."

The point that Jesus made in reference to God's care of the birds was not that they don't work. No one works harder to make a living than the sparrows. They certainly don't sit around on fence posts, waiting for someone to drop food into their mouths. The proposition that Jesus put forth is that they don't worry. They don't strain to see a future that they cannot see, or seek security in things stored up and accumulated.

Obviously, claimed Jesus, persons are of more value than birds. If the Creator cares for them, you can trust that He will care for you.

The beautiful, delicate, but short-lived flowers are used in verse 28 to illustrate a similar insight.

Today, my Father, I want to thank You for the lessons of nature, lessons that confront us each day. Help me, Lord, to be in tune with what You want to tell me. Help me to learn not to fret but just to trust in Your care. Help me to find peace in Your love.

LOOKING AT

I pray also that the eyes of your heart may be enlightened in order that you may know the hope to which he has called you, the riches of his glorious inheritance in the saints, and his incomparably great power for us who believe. Eph. 1:18, 19, NIV.

God wants us to look at those things that will lead us to understand Him and His loving care for us better. The first words in the Revised Standard Version's rendering of Matthew 6:26 are "look at." They are translated as "behold" in the King James Version. God wants us to get our eyes off our selves and our worries. He wants us to see beyond our needs and desires. He wants us to focus above our fears.

Thus He says "look at" the birds of the air. They have a lesson for us. Paul puts it nicely in our Bible passage for today when he says that the eyes of our hearts need to be enlightened concerning the greatness of God's love and plan for us. He has higher plans for us than we do for ourselves.

In order to see the breadth and depth of God's love for us, we need to "look at" Him in both His Word and in the book of nature.

Our passage takes us a step further in understanding Matthew 6:28, where we are commanded to "consider" the lesson of the lilies. The word "consider" is a stronger, more forceful word than the words "look at." It implies meditation, a consideration of the things of God on a deeper level.

God wants us to understand Him better. He wants us to more fully comprehend His great love and care for us. He desires to move each of us beyond anxiousness and worry to faith. Thus He commands us to "look at" and "consider" His lessons in nature and in the Bible.

"Be still, and know that I am God," the Lord says through the psalmist (Ps. 46:10). How still have you been lately? What do you spend the most time looking at?

The answer to those questions will say much about your goals and priorities; the answer says much about the quality of your faith.

WORRY IS BLIND

My soul is cast down within me, therefore I remember thee from the land of Jordan and of Hermon, from Mount Mizar. Ps. 42:6, RSV.

Yesterday we saw that Jesus told us to "look at" the birds and "consider" the lilies. He told us that if we looked at and considered them, we could learn priceless lessons of trust in God's watchcare. But worry is blind. It has no eyes for the birds that it might find peace; it has no mind for the flowers that it might discover trust. Worry refuses to learn the lessons of nature.

Beyond that, worry refuses to learn the lessons of history. That is where our Scripture text for today comes in. The psalmist cheered himself with the memory of history, with the memory of the land of Jordan and Hermon. These places brought to his mind the covenant and its promises. His soul may have been cast down, but he could remember God's promise of a better tomorrow; he could remember God's leading in past history. He could hope for the future because he remembered what God had done in the past.

That thought brings to remembrance the lesson that God's leading in the past had for Ellen White. "In reviewing our past history, having traveled over every step of advance to our present standing, I can say, Praise God! As I see what the Lord has wrought, I am filled with astonishment, and with confidence in Christ our leader. We have nothing to fear for the future, except as we shall forget the way the Lord has led us, and His teaching in our past history" (*Life Sketches*, p. 196).

Worry is not only blind to the lessons of nature and the lessons of history, it is also blind to the lessons of life. Let's face it, we are still here; we have made it thus far in life, past some obstacles that appeared to be insurmountable. With God's help, we have borne the unbearable, done the undoable. The God who helped us yesterday will be there for us tomorrow.

The main difference between faith and worry is that the first has eyes, while the second doesn't.

YOUR FATHER

You have received the spirit of sonship. When we cry, "Abba! Father!" it is the Spirit himself bearing witness with our spirit that we are children of God, and if children, then heirs, heirs of God and fellow heirs with Christ. Rom. 8:15-17, RSV.

God is your Father, "your heavenly Father," we are told in Matthew 6:26. That is exciting. The fatherhood of God to each Christian is one of the great repeated themes of the Sermon on the Mount.

All who have been born again have been adopted into the family of God. They have given up their old father and his way of sin and accepted God as Father. They have joined the great family of the redeemed. Thus they can call God "Abba! Father!" That cannot be done by those who still have the devil as their father. "Abba" is a term of endearment, much like the expression "Daddy" in English. What a wonder. The God of the universe is my Abba. No wonder I don't have to worry. No wonder I don't have to fear. God is Abba to me. That fact provides the basis of confidence.

However, God has not only the closeness of a daddy, but also the power of a Creator. He is the one who spoke the worlds into existence. "By the word of the Lord were the heavens made; and all the host of them by the breath of his mouth" (Ps. 33:6). "For he spake, and it was done; he commanded and it stood fast" (verse 9). Our Abba is also the powerful Creator of the birds and the flowers.

That's why I don't have to worry. He has the closeness of a daddy and the power of the galactic God. What a Lord.

But that's not all. Our Abba Creator also has the heart of a redeemer. He loved us so much that He gave His Son to die in our place that we might have eternal life.

This is the God we serve. He is Daddy, Creator, and Redeemer, all at once. He cares for us—not only for our spiritual side, but also for our daily sustenance and our clothing. Who can be anxious with such a Lord as their friend?

THE APEX OF CREATION

Are not two sparrows sold for a farthing? and one of them shall not fall on the ground without your Father. But the very hairs of your head are all numbered. Fear ye not therefore, ye are of more value than many sparrows. Matt. 10:29-31.

Human greatness. That's a topic that we hear a lot about these days. It is trumpeted in the newspapers, by authors of books, and by the newscasters of radio and television.

Yet it is in the Bible that we get the fullest view of human greatness. In Psalm 8 we find that God made us "a little lower than the angels" and "crowned" us "with glory and honour." We were made to have dominion over all the other creatures that God had made (see verses 5-8). And in Genesis 1:26, 27 we find that we were made in the image and likeness of God. Human beings are the acme of creation, the most precious of all God's creatures.

Perhaps the greatest compliment ever paid to human nature was the incarnation of the second person of the Trinity as Jesus of Nazareth. Just think of it. God became a human being. God became one of us, one with us.

All other views of human dignity pale into insignificance in the face of the light that shines from the Bible on the topic. By way of comparison, the world's visions of human greatness are shabby and false.

It is from the perspective of the Bible's view of human dignity and value that we need to realize the depth and breadth of God's care for us. If God cares so much for even lowly sparrows, Jesus is telling us in today's Bible reading, just think of how much He cares for the most important part of His creation. As Jesus asked in Matthew 6:26: "Are ye not much better than they?"

His point is an important one. If the birds are cared for without their worrying from day to day, won't God care just as much and even more for the crown of creation?

Christian friend, today is the day to trust God more; today is the day to learn the lesson of God's care ever more fully.

ARGUMENT NO. 2 AGAINST WORRY

Which of you by taking thought can add one cubit unto his stature?
Matt. 6:27.

Jesus' second argument against worry is that it is useless. Worry accomplishes nothing.

A French soldier in World War I carried with him the following recipe for worry: "Of two things, one is certain. Either you are at the front or you are behind the lines. If you are at the front, of two things one is certain. Either you are exposed to danger or you are in a safe place. If you are exposed to danger, of two things one is certain. Either you are wounded or you are not wounded. If you are wounded, of two things one is certain. Either you recover or you die. If you recover, there is no need to worry. If you die, you can't worry. So why worry?"

Another person has suggested that there are at least two things about which we should never worry. First, the things we can't help. If we can't help them, worrying is certainly most foolish and useless. Second, the things we can do something about. If we can do something about them, let's get on with it and not weaken our powers through worry.

Jesus illustrated the uselessness of worry by declaring that no person could add a cubit (about 18 inches) to his or her stature through anxiety. I once had a late-developing teenage friend who fretted constantly about being too short. Charles worried day and night about the problem. He eventually grew to be almost six feet tall, but it was quite evident that something besides worry had started his belated growth spurt.

The word translated as "cubit" in the King James Version is also translated in terms of time ("hour" [Goodspeed] and "moment" [TCNT]). But it should be obvious that worry about adding time to one's life is even more foolish than worry about adding to one's height. Worry tends to shorten life, not lengthen it.

Jesus pointed out the uselessness of worry, which not only prostrates our energies but also diverts us from the field of action.

FLOWER LESSONS

And why be anxious about clothes? Consider how the lilies grow in the fields; they do not work, they do not spin; yet I tell you, even Solomon in all his splendor was not attired like one of them. Matt. 6:28, 29, REB.

In Matthew 6:26 Jesus said we could learn a lesson about worry from watching the birds. Now in verses 28-30 He points us to the flowers for a similar lesson.

One of the focal points of Jesus' teaching about the flowers is the oven, in verse 30. The Palestinian oven was made of clay. It was like a box, set on bricks over the fire. When the cook desired to raise the temperature rapidly, she would throw handfuls of dried grasses and wildflowers into the oven and set them on fire.

The flowers had had but a short period of life before they were tossed into the oven so that the baking could be hurried on its way. The dried flowers had no better use than to be burned up for the making of bread, yet God clothed them with a beauty that even Solomon couldn't imitate.

Jesus' point is this: If God gives such beauty to a short-lived flower, how much more will He care for His human children? Certainly the generosity that lavished beauty on a flower would not forget us humans, the crown of God's creation.

Of course, most of us don't use dry grass and flowers in our ovens. But most of us in the twentieth century still admire the beauty of flowers. We admire them so much that we spend a great deal of money to buy them for weddings, Valentine's Day, and so on.

But we can't make them last. The very moment we cut them they begin to fade and die. We take them home in all their exquisite beauty, but they are gone with the trash in a few days.

But people are not for time. We are for eternity. When we realize the fact that God has already given every Christian eternal life (see John 3:36; 5:24), we can begin to grasp why we have so little reason for worry.

A SOLOMON SIDE LESSON

And when the queen of Sheba had seen all the wisdom of Solomon, the house that he had built, the food of his table, the seating of his officials, and the attendance of his servants, their clothing, his cupbearers, and his burnt offerings which he offered at the house of the Lord, there was no more spirit in her. And she said to the king, "The report was true which I heard in my own land of your affairs and of your wisdom, but I did not believe the reports until I came and my own eyes had seen it; and, behold, the half was not told me; your wisdom and prosperity surpass the report which I heard." 1 Kings 10:4-7, RSV.

The glory of Solomon was proverbial among the Jews. One can read of his magnificence in the Old Testament. His marvelous clothing; his palaces of cedarwood, with their furniture overlaid with gold and beautified with precious stones. And yet, says Jesus, all that glory pales into insignificance in comparison to the world of flowers with all their colorful array.

I can say amen to that thought. Recently I had the privilege of spending a week on Upper Michigan's wild Lake Superior shoreline. There it was my privilege to walk among the colorful and ornately crafted columbines. From time to time I was overjoyed to discover a lady slipper orchid. The variety of shape, pattern, and color of June's wildflowers seem to be endless. God is a lover of beauty.

That is an important thought. It is also a side lesson that we gain from Jesus' lesson about the flowers. God loves beauty. It was so in Creation. It was so in the earthly tabernacle built by Moses and in the Temple later constructed by Solomon.

Some misguided Christians would have us believe that God would be happy if our clothing, homes, and churches were devoid of beauty. But that is not the message of the Bible. The God who created the colorful flowers, birds, and tropical fishes is an aesthetic God; He is a lover of beauty, not only in color but also in sound and shape. God loves the beautiful, and He wants us to be like Him.

LITTLE FAITH

Wherefore, if God so clothe the grass of the field, which to day is, and to morrow is cast into the oven, shall he not much more clothe you, O ye of little faith? Matt. 6:30.

With the words "O ye of little faith" Jesus sums up the argument He has been working on since Matthew 6:25. The conclusion of His detailed argument worked out through appeals to the birds and the flowers is that His hearers had not drawn the obvious deductions from the created world around them. As a result, they lacked faith—they had "little faith."

Note that Jesus did not say they had no faith. They had some faith. These are believers who are being addressed in the Sermon on the Mount. Those addressed are those of whom the Beatitudes are true. Those addressed are those who are poor in spirit, those who mourn because of their sense of guilt, those who have seen themselves as lost and helpless and who have hungered and thirsted after true righteousness. Those addressed are those who love God as their Father.

Their problem is not that they have no faith, but that they possess "little faith." That is, their faith is inadequate; it is immature. It is insufficient faith. The phrase "little faith" is used five times in the Gospels, and each time it is used in relation to the disciples. They had faith, but that faith was insufficient.

What is "little faith"? Some have suggested, given the context here in Matthew 6:30 and other places, that "little faith" is a faith that grasps the fact that Jesus is a Saviour from sin but fails to apply that belief to other aspects of life. These people have saving faith, but stop at that. Their faith does not extend to the affairs of daily life. It fails to grasp the fact that God has an interest in all the affairs of our lives. It fails to recognize that because of God's interest in every aspect of our lives, we have no need to worry. "Little faith" fails to grasp that God is with us in the workplace just as much as in the place of worship.

"LITTLE FAITH" IN ACTION

And behold, there arose a great storm in the sea, so that the boat was covered with the waves; but He Himself was asleep. And they came to Him, and awoke Him, saying, "Save us, Lord; we are perishing!" And He said to them, "Why are you timid, you men of little faith?" Matt. 8:24-26, NASB.

What a contrast! Jesus asleep, and the disciples at their wit's end with fear. But perhaps more important than the size of the contrast is the reason for it. Why were the disciples so fearful, while Jesus slept in perfect peace?

This is one of those passages where it is helpful to compare the readings in the various Gospels. Take a few moments to read and compare Matthew 8:23-27 with Mark 4:36-41 and Luke 8:22-25. What does each passage have to say about faith? What are the implications of the variations of the questions asked by both Jesus and the disciples in each Gospel?

Note that whereas in Matthew, Jesus merely called the disciples "men of little faith," in Luke He asks them a penetrating question: "Where is your faith?"

"Where is your faith" when things get tough? "Where is your faith" when the storms of life come? All of us know that it is not difficult to have what we call faith when things are going well for us, when our boat of life is sailing on calm seas. But where is our faith when things get tough? That is the test to see if we have little faith or mature faith.

The question of the disciples in Mark 4:37 also helps us flesh out this incident: "Teacher, do you not care if we perish?" (RSV).

Of course He cares. These men were the core of His future church. He cared very much. The problem was in them, not in Him. They lacked trust that God cared for them in every aspect of their lives. Thus Jesus asked them: "Why are you afraid? Have you no faith?" (verse 40, RSV).

Where is my faith? Where is it when I face genuine threats and crises? Am I one of "little faith," or do I see that God cares for me in every circumstance and that I am under His watchcare?

LITTLE FAITH REVISITED

Whereby are given unto us exceeding great and precious promises: that by these ye might be partakers of the divine nature, having escaped the corruption that is in the world through lust. 2 Peter 1:4.

The past two days we have examined what it means to have "little faith," what it means to have a faith that grasps the fact that God will be there for our salvation but fails to understand that He is active in caring for us in all aspects of our daily lives.

The result: little faith worries; little faith does not know how to trust in the Father. The person of little faith is controlled by worries and fears. Such a person's mind goes round and round in circles without coming to trusting solutions. Such persons lie awake for hours at night while their minds are anguishing over the same miserable details about some person or thing. In such situations people are no longer in control of their thought processes. To the contrary, they are being controlled by something, and that something, if the process continues, will lead them into a state of worry. Little faith is a condition that allows circumstances to control us, to master us. But God wants us to have the sort of faith that masters situations, that puts anxiety behind and moves on to constructive action on the basis of its trust in the God who cares.

At its foundation, little faith is a failure to take God and His word seriously; it is a failure to believe His "exceeding great and precious promises." We have much to learn from the promises of God. We have much to learn from those Bible characters who took God's promises seriously, those who had great faith. We need to learn from such flawed but heroic believers as Abraham, David, Daniel, Peter, and Paul.

With Paul, we need to remember that our God can "do exceeding abundantly above all that we ask or think, according to the power that worketh in us" (Eph. 3:20). We need to realize "the exceeding greatness of his power" (Eph. 1:19). In the light of such statements, all worry seems foolish.

TRANSFORMING LITTLE FAITH INTO GREAT FAITH

Therefore do not be anxious, saying, "What shall we eat?" or "What shall we drink?" or "What shall we wear?" Matt. 6:31, RSV.

"Therefore" is the key word in our Scripture verse for today. "Therefore" ties together what has gone before in verses 25 through 30 and what follows in verse 31. "Therefore" implies that if we have really thought about the wonders of nature, the beauty of nature, the way God cares for nature in terms of such things as birds and flowers, we will have no occasion to worry about such things as food, drink, and clothing. In fact, we won't be able to worry.

"Therefore" implies that if we have really begun to grapple with what it means for God to be our Father, we will have no place for worry about the means of continued existence. The trouble with many Christians is that we do not realize what we are as children of God; we do not see His gracious purposes in respect to our lives. Worry becomes impossible when we truly grasp God as our personal Father.

"Therefore" further implies that little faith can be transformed into great faith when we learn the lessons that Jesus has set forth for us in regard to both the place of material possessions in our lives (verses 19-24) and the lack of any need to worry over any such things (verses 25-34).

Great faith is the ideal for each of Jesus' followers. Great faith is built upon the promises of the Bible and the application of those promises to every aspect of our lives. Great faith is a part of the "therefore" of verse 31. Even though we as Christians will have to face trials, problems, distress, and sorrow, we have no need to fear because "in all these things we are more than conquerors through him that loved us." Nothing "shall be able to separate us from the love of God, which is in Christ Jesus our Lord" (Rom. 8:37, 39).

Lord, help me today to become a person of great faith. Through Your power, let me put little faith behind me forever. Thank You for fulfilling Your promise to me.

283

ARGUMENT NO. 3 AGAINST WORRY

For the Gentiles seek all these things; and your heavenly Father knows that you need them all. Matt. 6:32, RSV.

Jesus' third argument against worry is that it is paganistic, if not atheistic. To worry about material goods, reputation, or even salvation is to act like those who have no faith or trust. A characteristic of many Gentiles or nonbelievers is that their whole life centers around their possessions. They are made happy or unhappy by their gain or loss of things.

The heathen are those who have no faith in God and are therefore given over to worry. They don't understand that "God so loved the world, that he gave his only begotten Son, that whosoever believeth in him should not perish, but have everlasting life" (John 3:16). They haven't comprehended the actuality that the Creator is a loving Father who cares for each person with a love far exceeding human love (Luke 15:11-32). They have not yet grasped the fact that Jesus is coming back to this earth to put an end to the problem of sin and to prepare for His people a new earth, where there will be no more pain, illness, destruction, and death—a place where the sources of human worry will no longer exist (John 14:1-3; Rev. 21:1-4).

Worry is essentially distrust in God. The worried Christian is a contradiction. The believer cannot be overcome with worry because he or she knows and believes in the love of God.

When we really understand our God, we will not be able to worry. When we come to grips with His love for us, our anxiety will dissipate like the dew when it is hit by the warm rays of the morning sun.

With the suggestion that to worry is to act like one who doesn't know God, Jesus has put the capstone on His arguments against worry. Worry has failed to learn the lesson of nature that God cares for His creation; it is not only useless but also heathenish. In the next two verses Jesus will turn to suggestions for overcoming worry.

SPIRITUAL WORLDLINGS

And he said to them, "Take heed, and beware of all covetousness; for a man's life does not consist in the abundance of his possessions." Luke 12:15, RSV.

Spiritual worldlings! The world is full of them. The church is full of them.

But who are they? What is a spiritual worldling?

Perhaps the best definition is that they are persons who have a correct view of salvation, but are worldlings in their thoughts about life in general. That is, they have it straight when they speak of salvation, but when they talk about daily life they sound like the heathen—they have a worldly philosophy. They are worried about houses, clothes, and cars. They are always talking about wealth and possessions and position. These are the things that really control them. They are made happy or unhappy by such things. They are always thinking about them. That, says Jesus, is to be like the Gentiles, to be like those who don't know Jesus as Lord, and God as Father.

Christians are not controlled by things. Their central happiness does not come from possessing things, and their central unhappiness does not stem from losing them.

Being a spiritual worldling is obviously a serious situation, from the perspective of the New Testament. But how do people tell if they are suffering from this illness?

Certain questions can help us determine the issue. Where, for example, are my thoughts when I have free time? What do I emphasize most in my talking? What makes me happy and unhappy? When something happens to upset me, is my reaction essentially different from what it would be if I were not a Christian?

The plain truth is that the only things of true value are those things that will be of value 10,000 years from now. The Christian perspective on life is at the opposite end of the spectrum from that of both worldlings and spiritual worldlings.

Lord, You know how easy it is for me to get my priorities wrong. Help me today to move beyond all forms of worldliness and into the realm of genuine Christianity.

THE FATHER KNOWETH

But my God shall supply all your need according to his riches in glory by Jesus Christ. Phil. 4:19.

Matthew 6:32 does not say that God knows that we have no need of earthly things. To the contrary, it says that "your heavenly Father knoweth that ye have need of all these things"—that is, food, drink, and clothing. Likewise, in verse 8 we read that "your Father knoweth what things ye have need of, before ye ask him."

We have a Father who "knoweth" our needs. Furthermore, we know that we have such a Father. Those are points on which we differ from the Gentiles.

We need to remember that we are never in any situation or position outside of God's knowledge and care. He not only knows of our physical needs, but He is concerned with our entire life. He is willing to lead us day by day. We read in *The Desire of Ages* that "God never leads His children otherwise than they would choose to be led, if they could see the end from the beginning, and discern the glory of the purpose which they are fulfilling as coworkers with Him" (pp. 224, 225).

What a Father. What a God. No wonder Christians can't worry. They are never outside the watchcare of God. He is always with them, no matter how dark the outward circumstances may appear at the time. He always anticipates their needs.

And He has a heart to match His knowledge. God cares for us even more than we care for our children. "Can a woman forget her sucking child," God queries in Isaiah, "that she should have no compassion on the son of her womb?" The rather startling reply is "Even these may forget. Yet," says God, "I will not forget you. Behold, I have graven you on the palms of my hands" (Isa. 49:15, 16, RSV).

Our Father knows. That is one of the most comforting thoughts of Scripture. He knows all my needs, all my desires, and all my potentials, and He wants those needs and potentials to be filled even more than I care for my own children's needs. I am so thankful that I know that He knows.

STRATEGY NO. 1
FOR OVERCOMING WORRY

But seek ye first the kingdom of God, and his righteousness; and all these things shall be added unto you. Matt. 6:33.

Jesus did not come to condemn us for worrying. Rather He came to show us the way out of the problem so that we can be healthier and happier. He put forth two simple, yet profound, suggestions for conquering this crippling habit.

His first suggestion is "seek ye first the kingdom of God, and his righteousness." Most of our worries stem from the fact that we are all too often heading in the opposite direction from that indicated by Jesus. We seek and worry about material things, and hope that God will somehow slip us into His kingdom. On the other hand, says Jesus, for true success we must put first things first.

Only as we seek and understand the lovingness, caringness, and righteousness of God will worry be dispelled. When we really see what God is like, we will not be able to worry. That is the crux of the matter.

In effect, Jesus is saying that if you must worry about something, then be concerned about your relationship to God. Perhaps you are seeking the wrong thing in life. If you put the most important thing first, the lesser things will follow as natural by-products. It was Jesus' conviction that when we really trust, love, and understand God, anxious worry can have no place in our lives.

Dear Father, today I am concerned about my personal priorities. I know that I love You. And I know that I give You some of my time every day. After all, I am reading this devotional book.

But Father, I feel a deeper need, a need to put You and Your kingdom at the real center of my life, not just at the edge of the center. Today I give myself anew to You. Please come in not only as Saviour but also as Lord of all my thoughts and actions. Give me the grace to put You first, even ahead of myself.

ANOTHER LOOK AT PRIORITIES

If ye then be risen with Christ, seek those things which are above, where Christ sitteth on the right hand of God. Set your affections on things above, not on things on the earth. For ye are dead, and your life is hid with Christ in God. Col. 3:1-3.

In commanding us to seek first God and His righteousness, Jesus is telling us to turn our backs on the gods of this earth (possessions and position) and to turn our primary attention to the quest of spiritual things. That command focuses on the word "his." We are not to seek our righteousness or to build up our type of kingdom. Far from it. We are to seek His righteousness and kingdom.

The command to seek His righteousness is a return to the fourth beatitude: "Blessed are they which do hunger and thirst after righteousness: for they shall be filled" (Matt. 5:6). We noted that the fourth beatitude is first of all a heartfelt cry to be covered with Christ's righteousness because we have seen our spiritual poverty, mourned over our shortcomings, and hungered and thirsted for forgiveness.

But we noted that the fourth beatitude also implied the birth and growth of God's holiness in us. Thus the outgrowth of His righteousness in us would bear fruit in such virtues as mercy, purity, and peacefulness (the fifth, sixth, and seventh beatitudes).

Holiness or holy living is a part of our seeking God's righteousness. The more we let Him live out His character in us, the more fully we shall know Him and be able to trust Him. We shall more adequately know Him as faithful Father when we become faithful sons and daughters.

We have only so much energy in life. There are only so many things we can seek each day. What we are dealing with in this part of the Sermon on the Mount is a matter of priorities. What is it that is our *real* priority in life? Is it all those things, or is it God, His kingdom, and His righteousness? By the very nature of things, everything can't be a priority. Slowly but surely Jesus is bringing us to the point of decision.

ANOTHER SOLOMON SIDE LESSON

I give you also what you have not asked, both riches and honor, so that no other king shall compare with you, all your days. And if you will walk in my ways, keeping my statutes and my commandments, as your father David walked, then I will lengthen your days. 1 Kings 3:13, 14, RSV.

What would you ask for if God said "What shall I give you?" God said that to Solomon. We don't know exactly what thoughts went through Solomon's mind before he responded, but we can certainly think about what our personal answer might be. What would you ask for? A perpetual vacation in some delightful paradise? Good looks and/or a powerful physique? A new car or house, or both? A position of power second to none? What if this were really a blank check from God? How would you fill it in?

Solomon had just such a blank check. Fortunately, God's question found the young king in one of his wiser moments. He humbly noted his lack of wisdom and his inability to lead God's people. As a result, he prayed, "Give thy servant therefore an understanding mind to govern thy people, that I may discern between good and evil" (1 Kings 3:9, RSV).

That was the right kind of request. It was not a selfish request, but a request to further the kingdom of God on earth. God was pleased. "Because you have asked this," He said, "and have not asked for yourself long life or riches or the life of your enemies, but have asked for yourself understanding to discern what is right, behold, I now do according to your word. Behold, I give you a wise and discerning mind, so that none like you has been before you and none like you shall arise after you." But Solomon not only got what he asked for. He would also receive "riches and honor" (1 Kings 3:10-13, RSV).

Solomon stands as an illustration of Jesus' command to seek first God's righteousness and kingdom. Solomon did so, and all the lesser things were added unto him. But note that all the other things came as a by-product and were not the primary goal. God wants to bless us far more than most of us ever hope for.

STRATEGY NO. 2
FOR OVERCOMING WORRY

Take therefore no thought for the morrow: for the morrow shall take thought for the things of itself. Sufficient unto the day is the evil thereof. Matt. 6:34.

Living one day at a time is Jesus' second suggestion for defeating worry. "Do not be anxious about tomorrow; tomorrow will look after itself. Each day has troubles enough of its own" (Matt. 6:34, NEB).

In the spring of 1871 a young man picked up a book and read 21 words that changed his life. A medical student in Montreal, he was worried—worried about passing his final examinations, worried about where to go after graduation, how to build up a practice, how to make a living, and on and on.

The 21 words that this young medical student read in 1871 helped him become the most famous physician of his generation. He later organized the Johns Hopkins University Medical School, received the highest medical honors of the British Empire, and was knighted by the king of England.

His name was Sir William Osler, and here are the 21 words that he read in the spring of 1871: "Our main business is not to see what lies dimly at a distance, but to do what lies clearly at hand." Those words from the pen of Thomas Carlyle helped Osler focus his energies on present tasks and freed him from the wearing burden of anxious care.

We are standing at the edges of two vast eternities—the past and the future. We live, however, only in the present. If we are going to live successfully in the present, then we must handle each moment and each day as it arrives. This is not to denigrate the value of intelligent planning for the future, but it does suggest the futility of worrying about events not under our control.

Living one day at a time is Jesus' second recommendation for overcoming worry.

The story is told of Abraham Lincoln and a traveling party approaching a flooded river. For days some in the party had been worried sick about the crossing. But Lincoln had the right idea. "I never cross a river until I get to it" were his words of wisdom on the topic.

ANOTHER MANNA LESSON

And the people of Israel ate the manna forty years, till they came to a habitable land; they ate the manna, till they came to the border of the land of Canaan. Ex. 16:35, RSV.

Manna was hardly the stuff of hog heaven. In fact, this bread from heaven could be downright frustrating. Just look at the way it came and how it had to be gathered.

The problem wasn't that there was a shortage of the flaky white stuff. To the contrary, there was plenty of it. It literally covered the ground six mornings a week. All you had to do was take a basket and scoop it up. Every person was to gather an omer (about two quarts) of it daily and twice that much on Friday so that there would be enough left over for Sabbath.

It is at this point that the stuff became problematic. Why not gather several omers per day as a hedge against illness or old age? After all, you know, troubles do come.

But that's not the way it worked. Strange stuff, that manna. Whereas it kept quite well from Friday to Sabbath, any stored up on any other day of the week bred worms and became foul by the next day. It didn't even last on the ground. Whatever was not gathered (even on Friday) melted when the sun grew hot each day. Weird stuff, at best. It kept on Friday in a basket for Sabbath, but melted if not collected. Thus those who didn't collect twice as much on Friday went hungry on Sabbath. The Israelites soon learned several lessons about Sabbath holiness and Sabbathkeeping from the manna.

But the manna also presents a lesson applicable to worry. Just as every day had its supply of manna, so every day has its supply of worry. And just as the manna became rotten for those who tried to store it up, so worry crushes and pollutes the lives of those who seek to gather more than their daily allotment.

Trusting God day by day is the only way with manna. And it is the only way with the cares of life.

AN "EVIL" LESSON

Brethren, do not be children in your thinking; be babes in evil, but in thinking be mature. 1 Cor. 14:20, RSV.

Matthew 6:34 says that "sufficient unto the day is the evil thereof." The word "evil" is the one we are interested in today. What conclusion should we draw from this King James rendering? Is it a command to sin, in the sense that I need to partake in my daily quota of evil deeds and experiences? What does this passage mean for Christians, since it is Christians who are the targets of Jesus' words on the Mount of Blessing?

To begin with, we should note that in the Lord's Prayer, Jesus told us to ask God for deliverance from evil (verse 13). One important point to recognize is that whereas both Matthew 6:13 and 6:34 use the word "evil" in the King James Version's English, the two verses actually use two different Greek words.

In verse 13 the word used is *ponēros*. *Ponēros* means wicked, bad, base, vicious, degenerate. Truly, God's children ought daily to pray to be delivered from such traits of character. *Ponēros* has no place in the Christian's life. Moral evil is not the stuff of Christian living.

Yet in verse 34 we are told that we as Christians will have our share of daily evil. The word translated as evil there is *kakia*. The New Testament tends to use *kakia* in the sense of trouble or misfortune. Thus many modern translations set forth *kakia* in verse 34 as "trouble."

What does this mean for me as a Christian? For one thing, it means that whereas I can expect to be delivered from the necessity of moral evil, I am not exempt from those sicknesses, natural disasters, and other problems that are built into the very nature of a sick planet.

Being a Christian does not mean we have an automatic exemption from the problems of life. But it does mean that we can trust in God as we undergo those problems. It means that we have a Father who will take care of us in a way not available to those who are not Christians.

A NEGATIVE LESSON

Cast thy burden upon the Lord, and he shall sustain thee: he shall never suffer the righteous to be moved. Ps. 55:22.

Jesus' discourse on worry has kind of a surprise ending. Read Matthew 6:25-33 again. Watch the flow of thought. Observe how the teaching comes to a perfect ending in verse 33. Nothing else is really needed. Jesus has made His major point.

When you think of verse 34 and its counsel to let each day take care of itself, it appears to be an afterthought. Jesus has ended His teaching on a positive note in verse 33. Then comes the negativity of verse 34, its rather disconcerting thoughts. Why the addition of verse 34?

The reason seems to be that whereas the teachings in verses 25 through 33 have helped us with present anxiety, verse 34 carries us into the future and extends the teaching to the whole of our lives.

Jesus realizes, in ways that most of us don't, the crippling effects of worry. Most of us seem to enjoy a little worry. I found in my earlier years that if I didn't have anything significant to worry about, I would become anxious about something insignificant. Most of us keep our "worry box" full. It is a way of life. And some of us act as if it is wrong to be relieved. For example, even after one of our friends spends hours helping us see that we have nothing to fear along a certain line, we are apt to say, "Yes, that is all right for now, but what about tomorrow? What about next week? What about next year?" And so it goes, as our imaginations conjure up all kinds of things to worry about.

The result is that worry controls us to a greater extent than we realize. It destroys our peace and blocks our current usefulness.

Jesus knows what we are too often unwilling or unable to recognize. He wants to free us from worry and anxiety both now and in the future. Thus the addition of verse 34.

Isn't it time we cast our burdens on the Lord? Isn't it time we stopped spending more time with anxious thoughts than we do thinking about our Lord and sharing His love? It's high time we junked our worry boxes.

BACK TO THE BEATITUDES

For I know that nothing good dwells in me—my unspiritual self, I mean—for though the will to do good is there, the ability to effect it is not. The good which I want to do, I fail to do; but what I do is the wrong which is against my will. Rom. 7:18, 19, REB.

W hat a mess! Lord, I've done it again!
As I read over Matthew 6 I am just as undone as when I read through chapter 5. It was bad enough to realize that I am not always the kind of salt and light I ought to be in my daily witness, that the law has depths of meaning that affect my thought life as well as my actions, and that I am not as perfect in loving other people as You are. But in chapter 6 You have humbled me anew.

I don't really like to show off, Lord. Well, I kind of like it, but I know it's wrong in both the spiritual realm and in the realm of daily life. Of course, after reading the sermon I realize the two can't be separated, but You know what I mean. Help me today to put self and self-display behind me. Help me to be poor in spirit, meek, and hungering and thirsting after righteousness. Help me not even to be proud of how spiritual I am in making this request.

And please forgive me for my failings in the area covered by the second half of chapter 6. You know how easy it has been for me to make things and position my goals. And You know better than anyone how I have struggled with anxieties and worries. It's not that I don't know that worry is counterproductive. It seems that I just can't help myself. I keep worrying about yesterday's mistakes and agonizing over tomorrow's negative possibilities instead of just living one day at a time in trust that You will work things out.

Today, my Father, help me to move beyond little faith to mature faith. Thank You for leading me once again back to the Beatitudes and Your saving righteousness. Truly, Father, I see my poverty and need. "Fill me today" is my prayer.

TAKING A SIXTH STEP
IN OUR WALK WITH JESUS

Judge not, that ye be not judged. Matt. 7:1.

We have come a long way in our yearlong walk with Jesus on the Mount of Blessing. First, we passed through Jesus' description of a Christian's character in the Beatitudes of Matthew 5:3-12. Then we examined Jesus' explanation of a Christian's influence in verses 13-16. We next moved on to a Christian's righteousness in Matthew 5:17-48. In Matthew 6 we walked with Jesus through His exposition of a Christian's piety (verses 1-18) and a Christian's goals and priorities (verses 19-34).

Christ's great sermon touches on nearly every aspect of a Christian's life. Now in the first half of Matthew 7 we are ready to look at a Christian's relationships to both other people (verses 1-6) and God (verses 7-12). We will then move on to Jesus' exposition of a Christian's commitment in verses 13-29.

The key word in our verse for today is "judge": "Judge not, that ye be not judged." That verse sets the tone for the entirety of Matthew 7. The underlying theme of the chapter is that of judgment—our judgment of others, God's judgment of us, and our judgment of the best way of life.

This is a chapter that brings us face-to-face with eternal realities—the realities connected with judgment. Here we need to remember that we are ever walking under the eye of God. Fortunately, as we saw in chapters 5 and 6, our God has a loving eye for us, but even love (or *especially* love) must finally bring an end to the sin problem. Thus the final judgment.

What matters for many people is what other people think of them, but what matters for Christians is what God thinks of them. From beginning to end in chapter 7, we are face-to-face with judgment; we are face-to-face with the eternal.

In these passages Jesus is not seeking to make us fearful. Rather, He wants us to be aware that our choices and the way we live do make a major difference. In terms of eternity, they make all the difference.

JUDGING NOT

Every one of us shall give account of himself to God. Rom. 14:2.

"Judge not." What did Jesus mean by that statement?

Like most Bible verses, Matthew 7:1 can be distorted and read in a wrong way. Some have held that the verse must be taken just as it reads. Thus a Christian person must never express an opinion about another person. Such people say we must be easy and tolerant and permit everybody to be what they want. Love and unity are what it is all about, the argument runs. Judge not anybody for anything. Such an interpretation is quite popular in a permissive culture, and even in permissive churches.

While that teaching may appear to be comfortable and Christian, it is certainly not biblical. For example, if we read down to verse 6 of Matthew 7, we will find that we are not to give that which is holy to the dogs or cast our pearls before swine. How can we follow that verse without exercising judgment? The plain fact is that we can't. In these six verses Jesus tells us not to judge (verse 1) and to judge (verse 6).

Beyond that, He tells us to beware of false prophets, in verse 15, and to evaluate fruit, in verses 19 and 20. And in various places in Paul's and John's Epistles we are told not to fellowship with those who are grossly immoral.

What are we to make of all this? We are not to judge, but we are also to judge.

The judgment we are asked to surrender is the judgment of condemnation. We are not to make final judgments on anyone; we are not to judge their motives, or speak as if we know their real character or God's final verdict on their lives.

On the other hand, we are definitely commanded to *discriminate* (on the basis of outward actions) those who are blatantly and openly rebellious against God. Along this line, Paul counseled the Corinthians not to tolerate the cohabitation of a man with his stepmother (1 Cor. 5:1-5).

Lord, help me today to have the power to know the difference between necessary discrimination and unlawful judgment.

THE SPIRIT OF JUDGMENTALISM

Judge not, and ye shall not be judged: condemn not, and ye shall not be condemned: forgive, and ye shall be forgiven. Luke 6:37.

Yesterday we noted that the "judge not" of Matthew 7:1 means not to condemn or seek to impute motives to others, but that it does not mean that Christians shouldn't discriminate.

Today we will examine the difference between what we will call constructive criticism and being hypercritical. True criticism, in the fullest sense of the word, is an excellent thing. While it does point out flaws, its major purpose is to make something better. It is primarily constructive rather than destructive. It stems from a desire to help another person. It is Christian in intent.

Jesus is not condemning constructive criticism in Matthew 7:1. Rather, His target is those who are hypercritical. Hypercriticism is negative in nature; it delights in criticism for its own sake. Hypercritical persons enjoy finding faults in others. They seem to hope they will find some fault. Their ears are open to the latest tidbits of gossip, which they promptly pass on to others. The hypercritical spirit is less than Christian. It is more akin to the spirit of Satan, "the accuser of our brethren" (Rev. 12:10).

One of the easiest ways to characterize the hypercritical spirit is to note that it is the opposite of love as defined in 1 Corinthians 13. It is unkind, jealous, boastful, rude, arrogant, resentful, rejoices in the wrongs of others. In short, it gets a malicious and twisted satisfaction in finding faults and blemishes. It is spiritually sick.

The spirit undergirding hypercritical judgmentalism is one that expresses a sensation of pleasure when it hears something unpleasant about another. It is an attitude that finds pleasure when a competitor makes a serious mistake. It is less than that love that stands at the center of Jesus' character.

We all struggle with these temptations. And we all need the power of Jesus to overcome them. We need His spirit today. I need His spirit today. I want to move beyond all forms of that judgmentalism that Jesus condemns.

PLAYING GOD

For God doth know that in the day ye eat thereof, then your eyes shall be opened, and ye shall be as gods, knowing good and evil. Gen. 3:5.

The Son of man is not come to destroy men's lives, but to save them. Luke 9:56.

B eing like God, usurping God's prerogatives, has been a temptation from humanity's Edenic beginning. When we judge another's motives or condemn, we are usurping God's place. We are taking to ourselves something that belongs to God.

It is one thing to express to another person a love-driven criticism of their theories, doctrines, or lifestyle, but it is quite another to condemn that person. The moment we become their judge is the moment that we have begun to play God. Jesus flatly tells us that that is beyond the role of acceptable behavior for Christians.

We need to realize our own weaknesses and that without God, we are totally lost. We can afford to be humble. It is God and God alone who has provided for us the way of life. If He gave us what we deserve, we would not be. But if that is so, then why are we so hell-bent on giving others what they deserve?

God doesn't give us what we deserve. He gives us what we need. He has given us salvation from sin, He has rescued us from the pit of hell, and He continues to rescue us and hold us up daily.

When we realize the magnitude of His grace, we begin to realize how thankful we should be. Being a Christian is passing on that thankfulness; it is being like God in giving our neighbors what they need rather than what they deserve.

When Jesus was rebuffed by the Samaritans in Luke 9, the disciples wanted to give them what they deserved—fire and brimstone. But Jesus said that "the Son of man is not come to destroy men's lives, but to save them" (verses 51-56).

An illegitimate way of playing God is to seek to become a judge of others. A more legitimate way is to become an agent of passing on His salvation to others on Planet Earth who don't deserve it any more than we do.

THE FLIP SIDE
OF THE FIFTH BEATITUDE

If ye had known what this meaneth, I will have mercy, and not sacrifice, ye would not have condemned the guiltless. Matt. 12:7.

B eing merciful is a big item in Matthew's understanding of the gospel message. One aspect of being merciful is not judging others, not condemning others, not being hypercritical of others' actions or motives.

Some have seen Matthew 7:1 ("Judge not, that ye be not judged") to be the fifth beatitude ("Blessed are the merciful") in reverse. Mercy is also at the heart of the fifth petition of the Lord's Prayer: "Forgive us our debts, as we forgive our debtors." And mercy is certainly at the heart of the command of Matthew 5:48, where we are told to be perfect in the same way that God is perfect. We noted some months ago that that statement comes in the context of God's merciful love for both His enemies and His friends. He gives His sunshine and His rain to all, irrespective of their personal merit or lack of merit. That connection is made explicit in Luke 6:36, which interprets Jesus' statement on being perfect, as the Father is, as being merciful, as the Father is.

Mercy is a factor all the way through the Sermon on the Mount, the first Gospel, and the entire New Testament. God's gift of Jesus is an act of mercy. And the final judgment, according to Matthew 25:31-46, is based upon whether we as believers in Jesus have internalized the merciful character of God.

Being judgmental and being merciful are at opposite ends of the spectrum. It is significant that both are repeatedly emphasized in the New Testament. These are central characteristics of the two sides in the great struggle between Christ and Satan. To be judgmental is to exhibit the very core character of Satan, while to be merciful is to be like God.

Our human problem is that we are tilted toward being judgmental by birth. We have a tilt toward evil. Jesus wants to come into our lives and tilt us toward the principles of God's kingdom. He desires mercy to become the central characteristic of our being, and He wants to eradicate all judgmentalism from us for both time and eternity.

ARGUMENT NO. 1 AGAINST JUDGING

*So when the plants came up and bore grain, then the weeds appeared also.
. . . The servants said to him, "Then do you want us to go and gather
them?" But he said, "No; lest in gathering the weeds you root up the
wheat along with them. Let both grow together until the harvest; and at
harvest time I will tell the reapers, Gather the weeds first and bind them
in bundles to be burned, but gather the wheat into my barn." Matt.
13:26, 28-30, RSV.*

Some church members are like the servants in Christ's parable.
They are jealous for the honor and purity of the church. As a result, they want to be quick in getting rid of those members who are
not "living up to the truth" as they see it. They want only good grain in
the Lord's garden. Of course, they view themselves as good grain.

In many cases, such a love for the church is commendable. In cases
of open, full-grown sin, weeding can and should take place. But that is
where the problem comes in. Most sins are neither open nor full-grown.
In these cases, elements of human judgment must feature large. In our
zeal, we are likely to think that all God's lines happen to lie exactly
where ours are. Thus the solution is simple—get rid of the rascals.

But Jesus pointed out a danger here. Because of our incomplete
knowledge of motives and circumstances, hasty weeding will of necessity take some of the grain with it.

What gardener hasn't pulled up some "weed," only to discover that
if it had come to maturity, it would have turned out to be a useful plant?
The only real way to tell a weed from a good plant in such cases is to let
the plant mature.

The history of the church is strewn with the wreckage of lives that
were "weeded out" prematurely. The problem is that human beings are
incapable of judging rightly. We do not fully understand the background factors in many cases, and we can never read motives. Thus we
are warned by Jesus not to judge, because we, unlike God, are incapable
of rendering accurate decisions.

ADVENTIST THOUGHT POLICE

I wouldn't dare say that I am as wonderful as these other men who tell you how good they are! Their trouble is that they are only comparing themselves with each other, and measuring themselves against their own little ideas. What stupidity! 2 Cor. 10:12, TLB.

It is all too easy for people who are serious about religion to judge their friends, relatives, and fellow church members who seem not to be quite as serious or zealous in their walk with God as they perceive themselves to be. That was the disease of the Pharisees, and the problem is certainly alive in the modern church.

Unfortunately, such an attitude is deadly for vital religion. Ellen White points out that people's satisfaction with their own definitions of religious orthodoxy and religious accomplishments creates an "atmosphere of selfish and narrow criticism [that] stifles the noble and generous emotions, and causes men to become self-centered judges and petty spies" *(Thoughts From the Mount of Blessing,* p. 123).

This is an easy pit to fall into, especially because those who do so are generally sincere in their beliefs and zealous in their religious life.

Part of the problem is that they seem to be more concerned with what others are doing or thinking or eating than they are with their own spiritual development. As a result, when they read the Bible or writings of Ellen White they find this passage for their husband or wife or that passage for their pastor, who obviously (from their viewpoint) isn't doing what is right. As Ellen White notes, their own attainments become the standard by which they judge others. "Putting on the robes of self-dignity," they mount "the judgment seat to criticize and condemn" *(ibid.).*

But such "thought police" or "petty spies" have failed to realize the truthfulness of Paul's argument in Romans 1 through 3. In chapter 1 the apostle notes that the Gentiles are sinners. All the self-righteous Jews were quick to say amen to that. Then in chapter 2 Paul goes on to demonstrate how the Jews were in the same lost condition. In chapter 3 he notes that all have sinned and need the justifying blood of Jesus.

The moral of the story for all petty spies: Get busy cleaning up your own act.

ARGUMENT NO. 2 AGAINST JUDGING

You, therefore, have no excuse, you who pass judgment on someone else, for at whatever point you judge the other, you are condemning yourself, because you who pass judgment do the same things. Rom. 2:1, NIV.

The story is told of a Persian judge who gave a biased verdict under the influence of a sizable bribe. When the king discovered what had happened, he ordered the judge executed. He then had the skin taken from the dead judge's body and preserved. With that same human skin he covered the seat of the chair on which judges sat when passing judgment, that it might be a grim reminder to them never to allow prejudice to affect their verdicts.

While that story is as gruesome as it is forceful, at best it only highlights an unobtainable human ideal. The simple fact is that no human being is ever completely impartial. Impartiality is beyond us. Only God is truly impartial, thus only God can judge truly.

All of us finite human beings come to every decision loaded with preconceived opinions and unreasoned reactions that favor ourselves against other people. Thus we not only lack crucial knowledge to be adequate judges of others (argument No. 1 against judging), but what knowledge we do have is partial and biased (argument No. 2 against judging).

With this in mind, it is easy to see why we receive the following warning in *Thoughts From the Mount of Blessing*: "Do not set yourself up as a standard. Do not make your opinions, your views of duty, your interpretations of Scripture, a criterion for others and in your heart condemn them if they do not come up to your ideal. Do not criticize others, conjecturing as to their motives and passing judgment upon them" (p. 124).

Lord, today help me to realize my own frailty and faults. More than that, help me honestly come to grips with them as I seek to relate to both You and other people. I have been impressed with the seriousness of judgment. Help me to avoid a task that You have never given to me or any other human being.

On Your Own Head

For with what judgment ye judge, ye shall be judged: and with what measure ye mete, it shall be measured to you again. Matt. 7:2.

In the preceding verse Jesus set forth the maxim that we should judge not. In this verse He provides us with a very practical reason why we shouldn't judge others. In short, the way we treat others in terms of judgment will eventually come back onto our own head.

Now, that is about as personal a consequence as one could find. But what does it mean?

Some have suggested that those people who are always censorious and critical of others bring criticism on themselves by other people who tend to give them a dose of their own medicine. The converse also is generally true. Those who are less critical of others are, generally, more appreciated and less often attacked. So there is a temporal meaning to our text. But that meaning is not all there is to Matthew 7:2.

The more significant implication of our being judged according to the judgment we give to others should be seen in terms of God's final judgment. The implications of this are rather frightful when we sit down and think it through.

Many of us give very little thought to our critical remarks about family members, church leaders, colleagues at work, or neighbors. We just open our mouths and out they come as an automatic action.

We give even less thought to what God thinks of our unkind and judgmental attitudes and actions. Jesus is telling us in no uncertain terms that we ought to be giving a great deal of thought to God's thoughts on the topic. They are fraught with eternal consequences.

The plain and repeated teaching of the Bible is that in the final judgment, God will give us what we give others. God gives us grace, and He expects us to pass it on to others. God gives us mercy, and He expects us to pass it on. If we refuse, if we pass on only condemnation and harshness, we can expect condemnation in the judgment. All who will be in the eternal kingdom will have internalized God's loving character.

But I Thought Christians Were Beyond the Judgment

Truly, truly, I say to you, he who hears my word and believes him who sent me, has eternal life; he does not come into judgment, but has passed from death to life. John 5:24, RSV.

How, some ask, can we as Christians come into final judgment when John 5:24 plainly states that we already have eternal life and do not come into judgment? And what about Romans 8:1, which claims that there is "no condemnation to them which are in Christ Jesus"? Don't these texts prove that we already have final assurance of salvation?

Some interpreters have held that these texts prove the doctrine of eternal assurance. That is, once people have come to Jesus and been justified, they are safe in Him for eternity. There is no future judgment for them because they have already been judged.

That belief is true to the extent that they maintain their belief in Jesus. But salvation is a continuing process rather than a once-saved-always-saved event that takes place at the point of initial justification. The Bible teaches that people can fall out of grace, that people can turn their backs on Christ, that they can go back to the world. To retain the assurance of salvation, therefore, people must remain in covenant relationship with God through Christ.

It is one of the most emphasized teachings of Jesus in the Sermon on the Mount and elsewhere that there will be a final judgment, even for those who say "Lord, Lord" and do many works in His name (see Matt. 7:21, 22).

Those who negate the necessity and reality of a final, end-time judgment of humanity have made the mistake of emphasizing some Bible teachings while neglecting others. The counsel of Paul is that we pay heed to all the Bible's teachings. When we do, we see that they fit together.

Genuine Christians have nothing to fear from the final judgment. Its purpose is to confirm for the universe that they are "in Christ," that they have accepted His blood, and that they therefore love God with all their heart. There is truly "no condemnation to them which are in Christ Jesus."

ARGUMENT NO. 3 AGAINST JUDGING

And why beholdest thou the mote that is in thy brother's eye, but consider-
est not the beam that is in thine own eye? Or how wilt thou say to thy
brother, Let me pull out the mote out of thine eye; and, behold, a beam is
in thine own eye? Matt. 7:3, 4.

The supreme reason Jesus said that no one should judge another person is that no person is good enough. To illustrate His point, Jesus presented a vivid picture of a man with a 2" x 4" plank sticking out of his eye, trying to find a speck of sawdust in a friend's eye and extract it.

Talk about humor! Jesus wasn't afraid to use humor to get across a serious point. In my opinion, if you let the cartoonist side of your brain conjure up this picture, it is second only to Jesus' statement about straining out the gnat and swallowing the camel. These are powerful images that not only drive their point home but also are easy to remember and leave one chuckling over the foolishness of our blind oculist. Jesus wasn't against the use of humor in a sermon. And my guess is that He even smiled in church.

But what makes His illustrations powerful and memorable is that they are all so true to life. Who hasn't had the dubious "privilege" of receiving advice from some person who has the problem 10 times worse?

In physical reality it is almost impossible to help anybody get anything out of their eye when we are troubled by something in our own, whether our problem be a speck or a plank. It is unfortunate that our spiritual faculties aren't as sensitive as our eyes. None of us is without specks and planks. None of us is good enough to judge other people. Once again, only God is good enough. That is why He must be the ultimate judge of every one of us.

Lord, today I pray that You will give me a sensitivity to my own faults and a patience with the faults of others. Help me to see myself more clearly in spite of my problems.

THE LAW OF THE LOG

He lifted up himself, and said unto them, He that is without sin among you, let him first cast a stone at her. John 8:7.

Here is a familiar Bible story. The scribes and Pharisees drag in a woman caught in the "very act" of adultery and want to know if Jesus is in harmony with Moses' command that adulterers should be stoned to death.

If Jesus said no, they could present Him to the people as unfaithful to Moses. On the other hand, if He agreed to her stoning, He could be reported to the Roman authorities, since the Jews had no right to judge capital cases. The scribes and Pharisees had Jesus where they wanted Him. Any answer would destroy His influence. It was a high day for these protectors of "righteousness."

Yet something is missing! Where is the man? Didn't they say she was caught in the "very act"? It is a well-known fact that it takes two to perform such an act. This is obviously a put-up job, and Jesus sees through it.

Jesus doesn't respond directly; He just kneels down and writes His thoughts in the sand. One by one the Jews realize they have been discovered. Here they are plotting Jesus' death and using this woman to accomplish their object. They are blatantly transgressing God's law in several respects, and Jesus knows it. He next says that the one without sin should throw the first stone. Then He continues writing as the Jews slink off one by one, convicted by their own conscience.

What a story! What an illustration of the law of the log (trying to remove a speck from the eye of another when we have a log in our own eye). Why is it that we are so anxious about the shortcomings of others and so oblivious to our own? How can it be that we are so hard on other people but so soft on ourselves?

Don't back away from these questions. Jesus is talking to you. He is talking to me. Don't just put down this devotional book and run off to hide in some pious prayer. No! Don't! Jesus is calling us to account right now. Let Him talk to you. You and I both need it.

A DISEASE OF THE SPIRIT

But why dost thou judge thy brother? or why dost thou set at nought thy brother? for we shall all stand before the judgment seat of Christ. Rom. 14:10.

Judgmentalism," claims Douglas Hare, "is the habit of constantly finding fault with what others say and do. It is a disease of the spirit" in which "the critic arrogantly assumes a superiority that entitles him or her to assess the failings of others."

In Jesus' sayings in Matthew 7:1-5 about judging others, He is declaring that the higher righteousness of His kingdom (see Matt. 5:20) involves the resolute renunciation of the temptation to judge others more harshly than we judge ourselves.

And yet how easy it is to hold a higher standard for others. I remember my wife helping me with a typing project when I was a college student. We had two typewriters and were working as fast as we could to meet my deadline.

Then a problem came up. Her work, I pointed out, wasn't up to snuff. It had this problem and that. I grew quite indignant. But that attitude was forced to a screeching halt when she pointed out that my pages were more error-strewn than hers.

Help me, Lord, to overcome my disease of the spirit.

Despite Jesus' injunction *to be* perfect (Matt. 5:48), no one *is* perfect. We need to work on cleaning up our own lives before we are in a position to give kindly advice to others. And even then that kindly advice will always be given within the context of the gentle mercy that God has given to us.

In the light of Jesus' words, I am always wary of those who major in being critical of others, especially when the critic's attitude is arrogant and/or sarcastic.

The attitude of the Pharisees lives on in those self-righteous individuals who, in their *own* eyes, have tried harder and gone further than others in their Christian walk. Such an attitude overlooks both the weakness of human nature and the abundant mercy of God. All of us have room for humility. All of us have diseases of the spirit. All of us will stand as equals before the judgment seat of Christ.

SANCTIFIED PERVERSION

Let us no more pass judgment on one another, but rather decide never to put a stumbling block or hindrance in the way of a brother. Rom. 14:13, RSV.

Oh, how we love to pass judgment on others. First we draw God's line of orthodoxy for Him and then we apply that line to others. If they don't fall into place, it is because they are not faithful, they don't believe the "straight testimony," and so on.

Of course, we are always careful to base our judgments on Bible texts or quotations from Ellen White. Interestingly enough, this approach was practiced in her day, as well. Fortunately, she addressed the issue more than once. We will look at one illustration today.

She pointed out that some were taking her remarks on health reform and making them a "test." "They select statements made in regard to some articles of diet that are presented as objectionable. . . . They dwell on these things and make them as strong as possible, weaving their own peculiar, objectionable traits of character in with these statements and carry them with great force, thus making them a test, and driving them where they do only harm. . . .

"We see those who will select from the testimonies the strongest expressions and, without bringing in or making any account of the circumstances under which the cautions and warnings are given, make them of force in every case. . . . There are always those who are ready to grasp anything of a character which they can use to rein up people to a close, severe test. . . . Picking out some things in the testimonies they drive them upon every one, and disgust rather than win souls. . . .

"Let not individuals gather up the very strongest statements, given for individuals and families, and drive these things because they want to use the whip and to have something to drive" *(Selected Messages,* book 3, pp. 285-287).

One of the great tragedies of Adventism is that we have used our personal compilations from Ellen White's writings to form "religious" tests by which to judge others. We have used her writings to transgress the teachings of Jesus on the Mount of Blessing.

Lord, forgive us and help us to be more Christian.

MISREPRESENTING THE GOSPEL

Judge nothing before the appointed time; wait till the Lord comes. He will bring to light what is hidden in darkness and will expose the motives of men's hearts. 1 Cor. 4:5, NIV.

W e can afford to be patient. The Lord knows what He is doing. The salvation of the world (or of my soul) does not depend on everyone's living up to my ideas of right and wrong. Yet that was the perspective of the ancient Pharisees, and it is alive and well in Adventism today.

The Pharisees of old had a burden to multiply rules, regulations, and tests of fellowship by which faithfulness might be judged. The same is true of modern Pharisees. I have in my files an article from a zealous group of "reformed" Adventists in which they have listed a dozen or so things that Ellen White said should not be considered tests. The article faithfully outlines each nontest issue and then concludes that all are tests today because we live at the end of time.

Will we never learn? Will we never come to grips with the sin of pharisaism?

The problem with too many of those who have a burden to correct others is not only their message but their spirit. According to *Thoughts From the Mount of Blessing*, "it is one's own lack of the spirit of forbearance and love that leads [a person] to make a world out of an atom. Those who have never experienced the contrition of an entire surrender to Christ do not in their life make manifest the softening influence of the Saviour's love. They misrepresent the gentle, courteous spirit of the gospel and wound precious souls, for whom Christ died. According to the figure that our Saviour uses [when talking about the mote and the beam], he who indulges a censorious spirit is guilty of greater sin than is the one he accuses, for he not only commits the same sin, but adds to it conceit and censoriousness" (p. 125).

Why don't we give God a chance to be God, so that we will have time and energy to do what He has asked us to do in the Sermon on the Mount?

SPECK EXTRACTING
VERSUS SPECK IMPLANTING

You hypocrite! Take the plank out of your own eye first, and then you can see clearly enough to remove your brother's speck of dust. Matt. 7:5, Phillips.

W hen all is said and done about specks and beams, it is important to note that we really do have a responsibility to help our neighbor with his or her genuine speck (rather than some speck that is based upon our biased thinking).

But never forget that we are not commanded to be speck removers until after we have become successful beam extractors. In other words, "you must *be* good before you can *do* good. You cannot exert an influence that will transform others until your own heart has been humbled and refined and made tender by the grace of Christ. When this change has been wrought in you, it will be as natural for you to live to bless others as it is for the rosebush to yield the fragrant bloom or the vine its purple clusters" *(Thoughts From the Mount of Blessing*, p. 128).

It is unfortunate that many are at their worst when they are trying (often sincerely) to help others. Their judgmental, "pious," and censorious manner becomes the most important beam that blocks their vision and spiritual discernment. Their work with others tends to implant more specks in their eyes, rather than removing them.

If we really want to be speck removers rather than implanters, then we need to have the mind of Jesus in regard to others.

We read in the book *Education* that even though "Christ was a faithful reprover," He still saw hope in every person no matter how fallen. Not only did He see hope, He met people needing help in a positive, buoyant spirit that "inspired hope." By way of contrast, speck implanters inspire hopelessness.

"Looking upon men in their suffering and degradation, Christ perceived ground for hope where appeared only despair and ruin. Wherever there existed a sense of need, there He saw opportunity for uplifting. Souls tempted, defeated, feeling themselves lost, ready to perish, He met, not with denunciation, but with blessing. . . . In every human being He discerned infinite possibilities. He saw men as they might be, transfigured by His grace" (pp. 79, 80).

Go thou and do likewise.

SO YOU REALLY WANT TO HELP PEOPLE

Speaking the truth in love, we will in all things grow up into him who is the Head, that is, Christ. Eph. 4:15, NIV.

Christians ought to have a desire to help people, but any such "helping" must be from a pure motive and a correct spirit. All desire to find fault, any gloating over another's misfortune, and all censoriousness are out of place. We must always remember that there is no sin more serious than that of having a judging spirit.

Well, you may be asking, how may we put our helping into practice in such a way that it is really helping? D. Martyn Lloyd-Jones offers several suggestions. First, he asks us to read 1 Corinthians 13 (the great love chapter) every day. Why not do it right now? Think for a moment as to what specific counsel from that chapter you can apply to your life today.

Second, recall the statements you make about other people. Sit down and analyze those statements and ask yourself what you really mean. In times past I have found this step to be very painful. In dealing with another colleague, I had made statements that were less than Christian in spirit and content. That doesn't mean that that person didn't have some glaring faults, but when I sat down and thought through my tactic, I came to realize that my whole approach contradicted the very gospel I thought I was standing for. That is frightening. There are beams at every turn in our lives.

Third, remember that getting something out of one's eye is a very difficult operation. No bodily organ is more sensitive than the eye. In dealing with an eye we need to use sympathy, patience, calmness, and coolness. Those qualities need to be transferred to the spiritual realm as we deal with other people. As Paul put it, we need to learn to speak the truth in love. I have actually thanked people who have approached me that way when they needed to confront me. That feeling is in contrast to those who have come at me like the proverbial bull in the china shop.

Thank You today, Lord, for gentle spirits. May mine increase.

OF HOGS AND DOGS

Do not give dogs what is holy; and do not throw your pearls before swine, lest they trample them under foot and turn to attack you. Matt. 7:6, RSV.

Surprise!

After five verses of telling us in a most forceful way not to judge, Jesus now tells us that we need to judge. And He tells us that we can judge adequately, that we can tell swine and dogs from more worthy creatures.

Before examining the meaning of this passage, we need to look at the meaning of dogs and pigs from a Jewish perspective. To us, a dog is seen as a cute little pet that we often hug and adore. A dog, to many, is "man's best friend." But that was not so in the ancient world. Dogs were half-wild scavengers. Their very name was a term of distaste and dishonor. In a similar manner, to the Jewish mind swine stood for all that was unclean and forbidden.

Thus we are not dealing with fine-line judgments in this passage, but discrimination based on outward attributes. Anybody could tell the difference between a hog and a sheep. Thus, Christians must also judge in the sense of discrimination on the basis of outward actions of a "hoggish" sort.

It is fortunate that Matthew 7:6 is included in our Bible. If we had only the first five verses of the chapter, we would have only half the picture. The only conclusion that would have been justified is that it is wrong to judge others in any way. But verse 6 brings balance. Without its sentiments, there would be no basis for discipline in the church or for discriminating true from false teachings.

There is a lesson in Bible reading here. We need to take the whole counsel of God's Word. Christians get into problems because they take this and that text or quotation, but fail to read the balancing information. When we take one side of an issue and run with it, we open ourselves to that extremism and fanaticism that has plagued Christianity from its inception. We are called to be a people of the whole Book, not just part of it.

HOGS AND DOGS AGAIN

And Paul and Barnabas spoke out boldly, saying, "It was necessary that the word of God should be spoken first to you. Since you thrust it from you, and judge yourselves unworthy of eternal life, behold, we turn to the Gentiles." Acts 13:46, RSV.

The fundamental idea undergirding that which is "holy" in the Bible is that of being set apart for the service of God. And what is set apart must be used only for holy purposes. Since dogs were regarded as unclean, it is only logical that they should not be the recipients of holy things. In a similar manner, things of beauty will not be appreciated by pigs. Hogs are not noted for their aesthetic sensitivity.

Now, you may still be wondering what Jesus meant in Matthew 7:6 about not giving the dogs that which is holy and not throwing our pearls before swine.

In answer, we need to remember that nothing is more holy than the gospel message. That message is to be preached to every nation. It is to be preached to prostitutes, mobsters, the common people, and even hard-bitten religionists.

The precious message is to be freely offered to all, but when it is repeatedly ignored or derided by those who have no desire to escape from slavery to sin, we are to move on to more fruitful ground with the message of the Saviour. That is part of what Jesus meant when He instructed the disciples to shake the dust from their feet and move on when their message was not received (see Matt. 10:14).

Paul took similar measures at Antioch (see today's scripture) and toward the Jews at Corinth. Concerning his experience in Corinth we read: "And when they opposed themselves, and blasphemed, he shook his raiment, and said unto them, Your blood be upon your own heads; I am clean: from henceforth I will go unto the Gentiles" (Acts 18:6).

The gospel task is large and the laborers are few. God doesn't expect us to continue forever to try to force the message on the scornful, but He does command us to witness with sincerity in ever-widening spheres. Remember, we are salt and light.

PRAYER AS A BLANK CHECK

Ask, and it shall be given you; seek, and ye shall find; knock, and it shall be opened unto you. Matt. 7:7.

Is this really true? Is prayer a blank check? Does God give believers everything they ask for?

Be careful here. We get into a great deal of trouble by proof-texting, by taking statements out of context and then generalizing them in irresponsible ways.

Let's be honest here. Has God given you everything you asked for? Why not? How has that affected your faith?

This statement on prayer is an absolute promise of what God will do for us, but it has a very definite context. That context is one of judgment—the theme that runs throughout Matthew 7. We need to see our earthly life as a school in which we build character for the life beyond. God wants us to be prepared for eternal life. Thus He is willing to give us everything we need for well-rounded Christian development.

The first six verses of Matthew 7 have dealt with the problem of judging other people and thinking of them more harshly than we think of ourselves. We are told that we will get unjust judgments back in full measure. Realizing our weaknesses, we cry out, "Who is sufficient for these things? How can I live up to such a standard?" Christ's answer is that He will give us what we need if we ask, seek, and knock.

What is true of Matthew 7:1-6 is true of the entire Sermon on the Mount. We feel hopeless when we see the demands of true righteousness. It is in the context of those demands that Christ offers us His grace to overcome so that we can live the Christian life. "Ask, and it shall be given you; seek, and ye shall find; knock, and it shall be opened unto you."

We do indeed have a blank check in Matthew 7:7 for God's grace. Christ's imperatives are humanly impossible to fulfill. Those who take seriously the terrifying demands of the Sermon on the Mount must also take seriously God's willingness to assist them. Those who ask, seek, and knock for such assistance will not be turned away.

WHO IS SEEKING WHOM?

Behold, I stand at the door, and knock: if any man hear my voice, and open the door, I will come in to him, and will sup with him, and he with me. Rev. 3:20.

There is something we should never forget about Jesus' command to seek Him. That is that He gave it because He was already seeking us. That was the purpose of His incarnation. He came "to seek and to save that which was lost" (Luke 19:10). Just as God sought sin-laden Adam in Eden, so Jesus came seeking us. He is still seeking us, He still stands at the doors of our hearts seeking entrance. The big question is Will we choose to let Him in?

The condition on which we come to Christ and let Him in is not our worthiness, but our lostness. It is our need to be cleansed and purified from all iniquity that leads us to respond to His initiative, that leads us to ask, seek, and knock for God's forgiveness.

We are commanded to ask, and it shall be given to us. Ellen White has penned that "if you come with true contrition you need not feel that you are presumptuous in asking for what the Lord has promised. When you ask for the blessing you need, that you may perfect a character after Christ's likeness, the Lord assures you that you are asking according to a promise that will be verified. That you feel and know you are a sinner is sufficient ground for asking for His mercy and compassion" *(Thoughts From the Mount of Blessing*, pp. 130, 131).

Seeking and knocking mean that we go on asking. We noted in studying the fourth beatitude that our hungering and thirsting after righteousness is not a onetime event. To the contrary, the Christian constantly feels his or her shortcomings and hungers and thirsts after that righteousness that only God can provide. The asking, seeking, and knocking are parallel to that continuous hungering and thirsting. God is constantly answering the prayer of faith and giving us what we have asked for. His supply of grace is unlimited.

Lord, help me learn to seek after those things that are most important. Help me to long for Your grace.

PAUL'S UNANSWERED PRAYER

For every one that asketh receiveth; and he that seeketh findeth; and to him that knocketh it shall be opened. Matt. 7:8.

Now, that is a nice saying, a nice promise, but the plain truth is, people don't receive or find everything that they ask for and seek. Take the apostle Paul, for example. He repeatedly asked for healing, but to no avail. God's word to Paul was, "My grace is sufficient for thee: for my strength is made perfect in weakness" (2 Cor. 12:8, 9). In a similar manner, Jesus prayed three times that the cup of His crucifixion might be removed from Him, but was crucified anyway (Matt. 26:36-46).

Neither Jesus nor Paul put up a fuss over their "unanswered" prayers. They didn't accuse God of making promises He didn't keep. They never lost faith. To the contrary, Jesus merely said, "Thy will be done," and Paul said, "I will boast all the more gladly about my weaknesses, so that Christ's power may rest on me" (2 Cor. 12:9, NIV).

Neither Jesus nor Paul had taken Matthew 7:7 as a blank check for anything they might ask. Both seem to have interpreted it in the sense that God would give them grace to do whatever they needed to do. Thus they interpreted the command to ask, knock, and seek in its context in the Sermon on the Mount—that God would give them power to live the Beatitudes, love their enemies, and live a life of trust in the face of anxiety-producing crises. The lives of both Jesus and Paul are a witness that God did indeed fulfill the promise of asking, knocking, and seeking for the purpose for which it was intended. They did have grace to live exemplary lives.

We may have that same grace. In fact, without it we will be the same self-centered, judgmental people we were before we met Jesus.

- Praise God today that He is gracious.
- Praise God today that He is more than willing to enable us to live the Christian life.
- Praise God today that His promises never fail.
- Praise God today that if we ask, He will give; if we seek, we will find; if we knock, He will open.

HAVE A SERPENT, SONNY

Or what man is there of you, whom if his son ask bread, will he give him a stone? Or if he ask a fish, will he give him a serpent? Matt. 7:9, 10.

Many people who are reading this devotional are parents. We love our children, and they know it. They feel free to come to us and ask us for this or that favor. They trust us, and rightly so.

Jesus' illustrations in today's Bible verse are of interest because of their commonality. Even the stingiest of parents feel compelled to supply some food for their children. None would give a stone for bread. Why? Because a stone is absolutely useless when it comes to eating.

The case of the serpent for a fish is not nearly so clear at first glance. While there is some difference of opinion as to the exact nature of the serpent, with many seeing it as an eel, the point is clear that such a creature, having no fins or scales, would be unclean. Thus it would be useless as food for Jewish children.

Luke brings us a third illustration at this point in his narrative. He adds that no father would give his son a scorpion if he asked for an egg. The scorpion, of course, is a highly poisonous little beast that appears to be useless for food or anything else. None of the items in the contrasts provided by Jesus were fit for food. None of them could be seen as a gracious, loving gift.

The point of verses 9 and 10 really comes in verse 11, where Jesus concludes that if even earthly parents love their children enough to give them what they need, just think of the kind of giving God is capable of.

That is an important thought. Perhaps we think too lowly of God's willingness to give, to provide us with what we need for both our temporal and our eternal lives.

The point of Matthew 7:7-11 is that God will never turn away our prayer. Above all things, God desires us to be happy and healthy and whole. He asks us to come to Him for our needs. What an opportunity.

PRAISE GOD FOR "UNANSWERED" PRAYER

Father, if thou art willing, remove this cup from me; nevertheless not my will, but thine, be done. Luke 22:42, RSV.

I still remember the day. My 14-year-old son had wanted a motorized dirt bike for some time. I had done my best to discourage him, but had finally come to the conclusion that if he had to have one, it should be a good one. But good ones cost money. That would certainly slow down the process of acquisition, I hoped.

Within a few days, however, Jeff came home with the report of a really cheap dirt bike. Under his urging, I went to look at it. To put it bluntly, it was a real dog. It was not only ugly but almost useless. I told him so in no uncertain terms. It would be a mistake to spend good money on garbage.

But he kept begging me to let him buy it. It was, he claimed, just what he wanted.

At last, against my better judgment, I gave in. How excited he was. The first day, he zipped and roared with abandon through the neighboring fields. But the first day was also the last. It never ran again. The money paid was money lost.

We may smile at such youthful desire. But don't smile too broadly. Haven't you prayed (even begged) to God to give you this or that, only to discover later that what you had once desired so desperately really wasn't what you needed? I have. And in those cases I am glad that God didn't answer my prayer.

At this point I should ask if it is accurate to say that He didn't answer. Perhaps He did, but the answer was no. Many times no is the best answer to our prayers.

Think of the prayer of Jesus in Gethsemane that He not have to drink the cup of the cross. God's answer to His request was no. Jesus accepted that answer. The result: He went to Calvary for you and me; He died for each of us so that we might have eternal life; He secured our salvation.

Praise God for "unanswered" prayer. In His wisdom God gives us what we need, not what we want.

PRAYERS THAT
GOD WILL ALWAYS ANSWER

If you then, who are evil, know how to give good gifts to your children, how much more will your Father who is in heaven give good things to those who ask him! Matt. 7:11, RSV.

According to our text for today, God works to give us "good things." That is wonderful, because we like good things.

In the verses we have been studying (Matt. 7:7-11), Jesus lays down no conditions for prayer, such as faith or asking in accordance with the will of God. Such things are made clear elsewhere and appear to be assumed here in Matthew 7. Here He concentrates on the wonderful truth that the Father gives freely to those who ask Him.

In spite of the fact that there are conditions to answered prayer, there are some requests that God will always answer because they are *always* His will and they can *only* be asked for in faith.

Among the prayers that God will always answer is the sincere request for forgiveness. "If we confess our sins, he is faithful and just to forgive us our sins, and to cleanse us from all unrighteousness" (1 John 1:9). God is not stingy on forgiveness. He always honors the heartfelt prayer of one who is burdened with guilt and seeks pardon.

A second prayer that God will always answer is a request for the power of His Spirit so that we can become more loving, so that we may more perfectly reproduce the character of Jesus. Becoming more loving is what sanctification is all about. It is the central characteristic of those who will be in the kingdom for all eternity. God may allow some stressful things or people to be placed in our path for the development of that love, but the aim is always to help us grow in love.

A third prayer that God will always answer is for peace in our hearts and minds. Even though we may be in an atmosphere of strife, God will always give peace to trusting Christians. Look at Jesus as He went to the cross. Look at Stephen as he was stoned. They could endure because of the Father's peace in their hearts.

WHAT KIND OF GOD?

Every good gift and every perfect gift is from above, and cometh down from the Father of lights, with whom is no variableness, neither shadow of turning. James 1:17.

It's only natural to want to know the One we are praying to. We want to know the kind of atmosphere our prayer will be heard in. Are we praying to a God out of whom every gift has to be coerced? Are we praying to a God whose anger must be appeased? Or are we praying to a God whose heart is so kind that He is more than willing to give more than we ask?

Jesus is seeking to set us straight on these issues. Not only is He describing God in Matthew 7:7-11 as one who is more than willing to answer our prayers with "good things," but His whole life was a revelation of the loving character of God. We see God most clearly through the lens of Jesus' life and teachings.

All of us, in a sense, are in an insecure situation in our daily life. We never know for certain what bad or good things might come our way.

In that sense we are like Abraham, who was called from his ancestral home to Canaan. When Abraham started out he didn't know exactly where he was going, but he did know who was going with him. And that knowledge made all the difference in the world to him. That knowledge gave him courage and peace; it gave him hope and direction; it gave him assurance and comfort.

That God who was Father to Abraham wants to be Father to me. He wants to guide my life just as He guided Abraham as he left Ur of the Chaldees. He loves me just as much as He loved Abraham, Daniel, Peter, John, Paul, Martin Luther, John Wesley, and Joseph Bates.

That is a wonderful thought. The God of the universe is a personal Father to me. No wonder I can kneel in faith before His throne. Those in need He will in no wise cast out. He gives every good gift to those who ask of Him.

WHAT KIND OF PEOPLE?

For all have sinned, and come short of the glory of God. Rom. 3:23.

In Matthew 7:11 the contrast couldn't be greater than that between the good Father and humans, who are evil. Of course, the sinful nature of humanity is not Jesus' main point in that text, but it is all the more forceful because the truth of His statement is so self-evident to Him that He is able to use it in an offhand comparison. Jesus' belief that humanity is evil and sinful stands against all forms of humanism.

I remember how excited I was to do my doctoral dissertation. My field of study was the philosophy of revolution. At the time, I was in rebellion against God and the church and wanted nothing more than to find a new explanation for life that made sense.

How thrilled I was with the revolutionary schemes set forth by some who essentially claimed that humans could create heaven on earth by creating new and just economic and political systems. It sounded so nice to say that everyone should contribute what they can to society and only take out what they need.

It was all great in theory. But then I was forced to ask the hard question as to why such good ideas never work in real life, why history is a catalog of one utopian failure after another. I was driven back to the fact that human nature is essentially selfish and sinful, that Christianity holds the answer, after all.

We should notice that Jesus did not include Himself in the description of sinful humanity. "Ye then, being evil" are His words. Jesus was not evil. He had the heart and mind of God. In that, He is different from us.

But He wants us to become like Him. That is what conversion and the new birth are all about. God wants to change us to be like Him.

Thank You, Father, for not giving up on me. Thank You for caring enough to risk Your Son in a world of sin that I might have life eternal.

LOVE BEYOND LAW

So in everything, do to others what you would have them do to you, for this sums up the Law and the Prophets. Matt. 7:12, NIV.

With this verse we have come to the high point of Christian ethics. Here is the central characteristic of what it means to act like a Christian.

Yet, we might ask, what is so special about this statement? Haven't other great thinkers said similar things?

Yes, you're right. Let's look at a couple of them. Rabbi Hillel said, "Whatsoever thou wouldst that men should not do to thee, do not do that to them. This is the whole Law. The rest is only explanation." Even non-Jews had a similar saying. The Stoics, for example, held that "what you do not wish to be done to you, do not do to anyone else."

So, what is so different about what Jesus said? Very much, because He put the saying in positive form rather than negative.

When put in the negative, the saying is a simple, commonsense statement that makes social intercourse a possibility. The negative form does not go out of its way to give anything extra. A person can perform the negative form of the rule by merely remaining inactive, by doing nothing.

But the positive form of the golden rule as set forth by Jesus implies a new attitude toward other people. It does not say I must not do to others what I would object to their doing to me, but I must go out of my way to help other people and be kind to them, even as I would wish them to help and be kind to me.

One man has illustrated the difference this way: The law can compel a person with an automobile to drive in such a way as not to injure other people, but no law can compel that person to stop and, out of love, give help to someone who is in trouble.

Christians living the golden rule treat others not as the law allows but as love demands. And no one can do that without having heart surgery, without having the old selfish heart removed and a heart filled with the love of God put in its place.

ANOTHER LOOK
AT CHARACTER PERFECTION

"Teacher, which is the great commandment in the law?" And he said to him, "You shall love the Lord your God with all your heart, and with all your soul, and with all your mind. This is the great and first commandment. And a second is like it, You shall love your neighbor as yourself. On these two commandments depend all the law and the prophets." Matt. 22:36-40, RSV.

With the golden rule of Matthew 7:12 we have come to the acme of Christian conduct, a key element in the biblical definition of character perfection, an essential element of the scriptural presentation of what it means to be like Jesus.

Commenting on this text, *Thoughts From the Mount of Blessing* suggests that "no man who has the true ideal of what constitutes a perfect character will fail to manifest the sympathy and tenderness of Christ. The influence of grace is to soften the heart, to refine and purify the feelings, giving a heaven-born delicacy and sense of propriety" (p. 135).

In the same book we read that "the standard of the golden rule is the true standard of Christianity; anything short of it is a deception. A religion that leads men to place a low estimate upon human beings, whom Christ has esteemed of such value as to give Himself for them; a religion that would lead us to be careless of human needs, sufferings, or rights, is a spurious religion. . . . It is because men take upon themselves the name of Christ, while in life they deny His character, that Christianity has so little power in the world" (pp. 136, 137).

With Christ's positive portrayal of the golden rule we have come to the heart of Jesus' definition of character perfection. One of the great pities in some Adventist circles is that character perfection has come to be identified with such things as diet, Sabbathkeeping, and doing (or not doing) this thing or that.

What confusion! Diet and other elements of Adventist lifestyle are means to an end rather than the end itself. God wants us in good health so that we can be more loving, not so that we can merely be better rulekeepers.

PRACTICING THE GOLDEN RULE

And as you wish that men would do to you, do so to them. Luke 6:31, RSV.

For the past two days we have been examining the golden rule. We have noted that this rule is at the very heart of what it means to be a Christian, the very apex of what it means to be perfect in character, as Jesus is perfect.

But one may wonder how that can be put into practice. It can't be done consistently under our own steam. Our selfishness gets in the way, our laziness propels us to do the minimum for others. We are not bent toward the golden rule. In fact, our characters are bent away from it. Even when doing good for others, we generally expect some kind of recognition and reward. Thus, we are really doing it for ourselves.

The plain truth is that to do genuinely unto others as we want them to do to us can't be done under human power. It takes the dynamic, transforming impulsion and propulsion of the Holy Spirit. To consistently live the rule is to live a Spirit-filled life.

With that understanding, we need to move into some very practical suggestions on how to put the golden rule into practice. Perhaps one of the first things that I can do is to make a list of all the things I like people to do for me. Don't start with the other person. Start with yourself. List all those things that you would like others to do for you.

But don't stop there. Take that list and begin to do those things for other people. Do you like to be spoken to with kindness and respect? Then do so to other people. Do you like to have someone give you a hand when you are overburdened? Then that's what you need to do for others. By now, you have the idea.

Next, make a list of all the things that you don't like. Then apply that list to your daily life. Avoid those actions in your relationship with others.

Lord, I need help! Help me today to make Your rule the rule for my life.

WHY I DON'T LIKE THE GOLDEN RULE

The old sinful nature within us is against God. It never did obey God's laws and it never will. That's why those who are still under the control of their old sinful selves, bent on following their old evil desires, can never please God. Rom. 8:7, 8, TLB.

We don't like the golden rule, because it interferes with the way we run our lives. And that's irritating!

Behind our dislike of the golden rule is our dislike of God's law, which plainly states that love to God and others is what true living is all about. And behind our dislike of the law is a dislike of the God who gave it. Why doesn't He just mind His own business and let us do our thing?

That question brings us to the real root of the issue. The reason we don't like the golden rule, the law, and even God, is that they interfere with the natural course of our self life, our sinful life outside of Christ. We must never forget that love of self is the center of sin. The sinful nature is entirely self-centered, whereas the golden rule and the law and God are others-centered. These things interfere with our self-centered life. And that interference puts us at enmity with them.

The self-centered life says if you like something, take it; if you desire someone else's husband or wife, use their body for your own gratification; if it serves your purpose to tell a lie, do it. Then along come God and Jesus and Their meddlesome law and rule to frustrate our natural selves. Makes us feel downright hateful at times.

That's what Jesus wants to put an end to. He wants to transform our hearts and minds so that we will be in harmony with God, His law, and His rule. He wants to write the principles of His kingdom on our hearts. Then we will love the golden rule.

Help me today, Lord, to see more clearly. Help me today to want to see, help me to want Your help. Help me to love Your golden rule and to put it into practice.

BACK TO THE LAW AND THE PROPHETS

If ye fulfil the royal law according to the scripture, Thou shalt love thy neighbor as thyself, ye do well. James 2:8.

With Matthew 7:12—"All things whatsoever ye would that men should do to you, do ye even so to them: for this is the law and the prophets"—we have come full circle from Matthew 5:17: "Think not that I am come to destroy the law, or the prophets: I am not come to destroy [them], but to fulfil [them]."

Both Matthew 5:17 and 7:12 highlight the law and the prophets. Their mention of the law and the prophets bracket the central core of the Sermon on the Mount. As a result, the golden rule must be viewed as a summary of Christ's interpretation of the law of the prophets, with 5:21-7:11 being His expansion or filling out of several principles inherent in that summary.

After Matthew 7:12 we come to a major shift in the sermon. The principles have been laid out; now we are ready for Christ's presentation of the judgment that is to be based upon those principles.

We can be thankful that Jesus spent so much time on filling out the principles of the law and the prophets, because we as humans seem bound and determined to misunderstand their intent. Even after Jesus illustrated over and over that the principles of the Old Testament law were not to be seen as rules related only to action, we find people using His very words to create merely more rules of outward action.

Will we never catch the real import of His teaching? Will we never understand that His law is a way of living and thinking rather than a list of prohibitions?

And we need to realize that the eternal law, in its essence, is something positive rather than something negative. It is doing unto others; it is loving God and others with all our heart and mind and soul.

Thank You, Jesus, for making plain for us the spiritual nature of the law. Thank You for not only doing so in words, but in Your daily actions. Help us to desire to be like You.

BACK TO THE BEATITUDES AGAIN

And the son said unto him, Father, I have sinned against heaven, and in thy sight, and am no more worthy to be called thy son. But the father said to his servants, Bring forth the best robe, and put it on him; and put a ring on his hand, and shoes on his feet: and bring hither the fatted calf, and kill it; and let us eat, and be merry: for this my son was dead, and is alive again; he was lost, and is found. And they began to be merry. Luke 15:21-24.

Father, is there no end to the number of times that I will have to return to the Beatitudes? Is there no end to my failures? As I look at my temptation not only to judge others, but to be harder on them than I am on myself; as I look at my failure to seek You and Your power as I ought; and as I fail to live out Your golden rule fully, I feel anew my poverty of spirit. Once again I am led to mourn because of my shortcomings, and again I am filled with meekness in Your presence. Once again I come to You, hungering and thirsting after righteousness.

Father, don't You ever get tired of my coming to You in failure? I praise You that You don't. I praise You for the story of the prodigal son. I thank You that there is a party in heaven every time someone comes to You in repentance.

Thank You for Your willingness to hear my asking, seeking, knocking prayer; for Your willingness to fill my continuous need for grace; for Your willingness to get me started on the right path again.

Father, in one sense I have come a long way with You in our walk on the Mount of Blessing. My knowledge of You is greater, and my ability to follow You has grown. But there is another sense in which I have not progressed since January 1. I still need just as much of Your power, just as much of Your forgiveness. Please fill my hungering and thirsting, but please also keep me hungry and thirsty for Your righteousness.

TAKING A SEVENTH STEP IN OUR WALK WITH JESUS

Enter by the narrow gate; for the gate is wide and the way is easy, that leads to destruction, and those who enter by it are many. Matt. 7:13, RSV.

Father, it is hard to believe that we have been walking so many months with You on the Mount of Blessing. Here we are in the tail end of the year, and our journey is almost completed.

We remember that statement in *Life Sketches* that says that we have nothing to fear for the future, except as we should forget the way that You have led us in the past (p. 196). We realize that that passage is primarily a statement of how You have led Your last-day church in its history, but we also see that its sentiments apply to our personal lives.

Help us not to forget how You led us through the Beatitudes as You explained to us the essential elements that *must* be found in *every* Christian's character. And help us to remember the glorious opportunity that You have given us to witness in our daily lives as permeating salt and shining light.

How can we ever forget Your great explanation of the depth of the law as You described a Christian's righteousness? And thanks again for Your counsel on piety as we think of prayer, giving, fasting, and other acts of worship. We are also thankful that You think of us in our material struggles as we read Your unmatchable counsel regarding our priorities and the senselessness of worry. And last, we want to thank You for Your counsel on our relationships with others.

Our walk has been a blessing. It hasn't been painless, but it has been a walk in which we have grown to be more like You in character.

We are now ready for Your conclusion, Lord. We realize that You want to talk to us about our ultimate commitments as You conclude Your message. Our ears are open for Your words. We realize that judgment of those commitments is a reality that is yet to come. We want to be ready in every way for Your approval of our choices.

END-TIME JUDGMENT IS PERVASIVE

The kingdom of heaven is like a net which was thrown into the sea and gathered fish of every kind; when it was full, men drew it ashore and sat down and sorted the good into vessels but threw away the bad. So it will be at the close of the age. The angels will come out and separate the evil from the righteous, and throw them into the furnace of fire; these men will weep and gnash their teeth. Matt. 13:47-50, RSV.

F. D. Bruner points out that "Jesus began His sermon with unqualified tenderness" but "concludes it with unqualified toughness." After opening with the manifold blessing of the Beatitudes, the sermon moves to repeat judgment scenes in its closing verses. It is as if Jesus is telling us that His message is not an intellectual option or one philosophy among several that we might choose from.

The Sermon on the Mount concludes in Matthew 7 with three forceful eschatological (end-time) illustrations related to judgment and Christian commitment: the two ways (verses 13, 14), the two trees (verses 15-20), and the two builders (verses 24-27).

Judgment scenes are not unique to the Sermon on the Mount in Matthew's Gospel. Matthew gives us five of Jesus' sermons, and four of them each end with three judgment scenes. Thus the three final units of chapter 10's missionary discourse (verses 32, 33; 34-39; 40-42) have to do with end-time rewards and punishments. That also is true of the last three units in chapter 13's parables of the kingdom (verses 44; 45, 46; 47-50) and the last three parables of Jesus' end-time sermon in Matthew 24 and 25 (25:1-13, 14-30, 31-46). The one major teaching sermon of Jesus in Matthew that does not follow the pattern of three end-time warnings breaks only the threefold aspect, not the end-time reward-and-punishment element. Thus, the sermon on forgiveness in Matthew 18 closes with a parable of punishment for those who refuse to forgive their neighbors.

This repeated teaching of final judgment in all five of Jesus' sermons in Matthew, and the tying of those judgment scenes to Christian conduct, is important. Jesus tells us repeatedly that how we live our life and treat other people is important to God. Therefore, how we live each day must be important as well.

LEAVE YOUR JUNK BEHIND

Make every effort to enter through the narrow door, because many, I tell you, will try to enter and will not be able to. Luke 13:24, NIV.

Life outside of loyalty to Jesus is broad in what it permits. You can do or be what you like. The moral boundaries are wide open. If it feels good, do it. If it gives you a high, drink it.

The way of Jesus, on the other hand, is marked with restrictions. It is narrow because it respects the rights of others, because it is based upon love to God and His principles, and because it leads people to treat their bodies with respect. The way of Jesus is narrow because it forbids retaliation, hate, lust, and judgmentalism. It is narrow because it commands its advocates to be merciful and peacemakers.

Evangelism ought to be honest; Jesus was. He plainly taught that you can't get into the kingdom with your arms full of the baggage of this world. The Bible knows of no easy religion that says only believe and be saved. To the contrary, the religion of Jesus says "Believe, be transformed, live the principles of the Sermon on the Mount, and be saved." That message will get even stronger and more straightforward as we move into the next two judgment scenes of Matthew 7—the tree producing fruit, and those who say "Lord, Lord," but are lost anyway.

Christianity is not all fun and games, and Jesus never pretended that it would be. The way is hard.

And, as Luke tells us in today's Bible reading, the gate isn't all that easy to get into. Now, watch out here. The problem is not that salvation is difficult. Jesus stands with open arms and bids us all to come to Him. The real problem is that some of us try to enter the gate carrying the baggage of the world. Not that we carry it openly. Some have dropped off the outward symbols of worldliness, but are seeking entrance with the same pride and love of position—only now these things have been attached to religious symbols. That's not radical enough for Jesus. He wants you to drop all your "junk." Take Him seriously.

LIFE'S GREATEST BATTLE

But as for you, man of God, shun all this; aim at righteousness, godliness, faith, love, steadfastness, gentleness. Fight the good fight of the faith; take hold of the eternal life to which you were called when you made the good confession in the presence of many witnesses. 1 Tim. 6:11, 12, RSV.

Yesterday we noted that to enter the narrow way we need to leave our junk behind. But that's easier said than done. After all, we like our junk. We lust after it; we dream about it; we desire it. Becoming like Jesus goes against our natural inclination. It involves a struggle, a fight against both the external powers of evil and our own selves.

Ellen White echoes Paul when she claims that "the Christian life is a battle and a march" *(Thoughts From the Mount of Blessing,* p. 141). Fortunately, we are not left alone in the struggle. God offers us the Holy Spirit and the ministry of angels. The battlefield is each individual human heart. Each person has to choose to enter the narrow gate. We aren't saved by nations, tribes, families, or groups.

But surrender is a struggle. Ellen White says that the greatest battle ever fought "is the surrender of self to the will of God, the yielding of the heart to the sovereignty of love. The old nature, born of blood and of the will of the flesh, cannot inherit the kingdom of God. The hereditary tendencies, the former habits, must be given up" *(ibid.).*

But, as noted earlier, we can't do this ourselves. We need God's help. Fortunately, He stands poised to give us every bit of help that we desire. Here is one of those prayers that God will always answer as we ask, seek, and knock. We will find ourselves back on His doorstep day after day, hat in hand, doing more asking, but He knows both our weaknesses and the intensity of the battle. He is willing to forgive us and help us more than we can ever imagine.

The way may be narrow, and the battle may be hard, but all who truly desire to enter can and will when they surrender their wills and hearts to Jesus.

OF GATES AND WAYS

"I am the door; if any one enters by me, he will be saved, and will go in and out and find pasture." John 10:9, RSV.

The two main symbols in Matthew 7:13 are the gate and the way. Of course, as Jesus sees it, there is more than one gate and more than one way. There are two, but not more than two. We are either with Christ or against Him. We either have God for our Father or we have the devil as our parent. There are no other options.

The gate may be thought of as our decision to follow Jesus. As He says in John 10, He is the door. And in Acts 4:12 we read that "there is no other name under heaven given to men by which we must be saved" (NIV). Entering the gate is our decision to follow Jesus.

It is of interest to notice that in Matthew 7:13, 14 there is no mention of anyone entering the wide gate. Why? Because we are born in the broad way that leads to destruction. That is a fact of birth, not a conscious decision. We make a decision to leave the broad way but not to enter it.

If the gate symbolizes our initial acceptance of Jesus as Saviour, then the way signifies our Christian life subsequent to that acceptance.

Matthew's own life is an illustration of the gate and the way. In Matthew 9 we find him sitting in his tax office. At that point Jesus enters the picture and says, "Follow Me." Matthew drops his business and his old ways and begins a new way of life. He leaves behind his unjust ways as a publican, his old friends, and his old goals and commitments. Matthew now has a new Master. That means that he also has new values, new friends, and new goals.

Christianity is not a flash of light or a warm fuzzy feeling. Those things may (or may not) take place, but the main point of the illustration of the way is that Christianity is a lifelong commitment to Jesus and the manner of life set forth in the Sermon on the Mount. Genuine Christianity dominates everything we do. It is truly a "way" of life.

THE MORAL MINORITY

The gate is narrow and the way is hard, that leads to life, and those who find it are few. Matt. 7:14, RSV.

If democracy were the way to arrive at truth, the devil would win every time. He has the votes. It is easy to follow Satan and his ways. In fact, it is natural.

I remember when I became a member of the church. Numbers meant a lot to me. How could this little Adventist church have the truth when all the big churches did not believe the same things? They didn't keep the seventh-day Sabbath, they didn't believe that people slept in their graves until the resurrection, they didn't emphasize Christ's ministry in the heavenly sanctuary, and so on. How could the Adventists be right?

It took me time to realize that only one vote counts when it comes to establishing ethical and spiritual truths. That vote is carried by God's word in the Bible. The moral minority follow that Word as their guide to life. The maxim "Everybody is doing it, so it's OK" doesn't move them. They have chosen to follow the Bible for guidance. They are on the narrow way.

Our text for today says that those who find the narrow gate are few. That appears to be true, but that statement does not mean that the number must be few. By way of contrast, we read in Matthew 8:11 that "many will come from east and west and sit at table with Abraham, Isaac, and Jacob in the kingdom of heaven" (RSV). And Revelation 7:9 describes the saved as "a great multitude which no man could number" (RSV).

The "few" in Matthew 7:14 appears to be a comparative term signifying that the saved will be few in proportion to the many more who will be lost.

And why will they be lost? That is the point of the judgment scene of the two gates in Matthew 7:13, 14. They have failed to commit their lives to Jesus; they have failed to enter the narrow gate, to journey on the narrow way.

How is it with you this morning? Where are your commitments? Who has your affections? How do you know your answer to those questions is correct?

THE MEANING OF "EASY"

There is a way which seemeth right unto a man, but the end thereof are the ways of death. Prov. 14:12.

One of the significant contrasts between the two ways of Matthew 7:13 and 14 is that the broad way is "easy" and the narrow way is "hard."

"Easy." That is a nice word, a pleasant word. I wonder what it means.

I remember a few years ago when I was backpacking in the Wind River Range of the Wyoming Rockies. I had struggled all day up an extremely steep trail and had finally reached a plateau that ran parallel to Lizardhead Peak. I was dead tired. Carrying my 65-pound pack the next seven or eight miles to the next valley seemed almost more than I could bear.

At that point I met another hiker, who told me of a shortcut that would save me several hours. It was much "easier." The so-called shortcut may have been shorter, but it was not easier. I struggled for a day and a half over terrain that I didn't think could be crossed with a full pack.

The moral: Things aren't always what they seem. The easy way is sometimes the hard way in the end.

That's the way it is for many on the broad way. Hangovers, AIDS, and a host of other diseases that stem from life on the fast track make life more difficult than it would have been had they been more temperate.

But let's face it. Many people on the broad way don't face those difficulties. Their lives are moderate and even moral, in the secular sense of the term. Their way really does seem easy. They are just doing what comes naturally.

But that is where the other great contrast of the two ways comes in. The broad way, Jesus tells us, leads to destruction, while the narrow way leads to life. And once again, there are no alternatives. Everyone will someday either go to their heavenly reward or be eternally destroyed.

Each of us has a choice in this matter. Would we rather have it easy now and hard later, or hard now and easy later?

CHOICES

*This day I call heaven and earth as witnesses against you that I have set
before you life and death, blessings and curses. Now choose life, so that you
and your children may live. Deut. 30:19, NIV.*

M oses had come to the end of his days. In the book of
Deuteronomy he rehearsed the way God had led Israel out of
Egypt, through the wilderness, and to the very borders of the
Promised Land. In chapters 28 and 29 he summed up the covenant
promises and obligations. The two always go together. They can never
be separated. The obligation of obedience and allegiance to God is
always connected to the covenant promise.

Moses is ready to climb Nebo for what will be a one-way trip. But
before turning over the reins of leadership to Joshua, he calls upon his
people to choose whether they will walk in the way of life or the way
of death.

Choices are the stuff of life. Each of us is at a crossroads every day.
The decisions we make determine not only the events of that day but
also our eternal destiny.

That theme is found throughout the Bible as well as in Moses' and
Jesus' teachings of the two ways. Thus we find Joshua appealing to the
Israelites, "Choose for yourselves this day whom you will serve, whether
the gods your forefathers served beyond the River, or the god of the
Amorites, in whose land you are living." Joshua concluded by expressing his personal decision: "As for me and my household, we will serve
the Lord" (Joshua 24:15, NIV). Jeremiah made a similar statement
when he said "Behold, I set before you the way of life, and the way of
death" (Jer. 21:8).

Which way will your soul go? That is the question underlying
Jesus' teaching of the two gates. It is the most important question that
can be asked.

A PROGRESSIVE LINE OF JUDGMENT

Beware of false prophets, which come to you in sheep's clothing, but inwardly they are ravening wolves. Matt. 7:15.

Jesus is finished with gates and ways. Now He is ready for false prophets who come in deceptive garb. There is a progression between these two judgment scenes that should not escape our notice.

The illustration of the two gates and the two paths separates the many from the few, those who enter the broad gate from those who enter the narrow. To be more explicit, the first illustration deals with the separation of Christians from the world, those who are heading for life eternal from those who are traveling the path to eternal destruction.

But in verse 15 the scene has shifted. Here we see for the first time in this sequence that there are problems even in the church, among those who profess to be on the narrow way. Jesus was no utopian dreamer. He knew there would be problems in the church, even among those who claimed to be teachers and leaders of the flock. Thus here He tells us that we must beware of false prophets. The assumption undergirding that warning is that we need to be judges of these people, in spite of His admonition in verse 1 for us not to judge. But once again Jesus warns us against judging motives. He says that we should examine the fruit these people produce. If we are patient, every teacher, every leader, will bear fruit. Then and only then will we be able to tell the true from the false.

The third illustration in this judgment sequence will take us one step beyond the false-prophet illustration. In verses 21 to 23 Jesus will tell us that we need to judge even those things inside of our own selves that incline us to hear His words while leading us away from doing them. It is a call to self-examination. We need to pass judgment even on ourselves.

Jesus takes us and our professions of belief seriously. And He wants us to take our professions just as seriously as He does. He wants us to see that religion is a serious matter.

OF WOLVES AND SHEEP

And the Lord said to Moses, "See, I make you as God to Pharaoh; and Aaron your brother shall be your prophet. You shall speak all that I command you; and Aaron your brother shall tell Pharaoh to let the people of Israel go out of his land." Ex. 7:1, 2, RSV.

A prophet is one who speaks for God. Prophecy, if you think about it for a moment, is one of the great wonders of the universe. In prophecy the Creator of all humbles Himself to speak to the dust, to speak to wayward humans. Since the Genesis fall of Adam and Eve, God no longer generally speaks directly to men and women. Since that time He has selected individuals to speak for Him. As today's scripture indicates, the ideas that a true prophet speaks are the ideas of God given through a human intermediary.

To speak for God. What a privilege, what an awesome responsibility. Prophets have rightly had an honored place in the history of Israel and the church.

But there is a problem. Not all prophets are straight; not all are who they claim to be; not all are sent by God. Some of them, in fact, appear in sheep's clothing, even though on the inside they are ravenous wolves.

Sheep and wolves make a nice contrast. Sheep are among the most harmless of animals, whereas wolves sometimes have the reputation of being ruthless and bloodthirsty. Now, it's not hard to distinguish a wolf from a sheep. But that's not the problem here. The situation Jesus is describing is one in which the wolves arrive at church masquerading as sheep. That is, while they claim to be speaking for Jesus, they are actually under the employ of the devil.

Here is a problem that arises because of the subtlety of the situation. They are only inwardly wolves. To all outward appearances, these men and women are true prophets. Where they are accepted as such, they prey upon the souls and pocketbooks of the believers.

That and related problems have plagued Christianity from the beginning. Jesus is trying to tell us that we must beware of being gullible.

OF GOOD FRUIT AND BAD

Ye shall know them by their fruits. Do men gather grapes of thorns, or figs of thistles? Matt. 7:16.

By their fruits ye shall know them." Because of the subtlety of false prophets, you can't always tell them by outward appearance. You need to check out their fruit.

It's a law of nature that apple trees produce apples and coconut palms produce coconuts. You don't get coconuts off a poison ivy vine, and you don't harvest apples from a thistle. Nature is consistent and predictable. So are people. If you give them enough time and space, their true character will show through. Thus it is with prophets and other religious leaders. They also can be tested by their fruit.

But what did Jesus mean by fruit in Matthew 7?

Interpreters differ. The first group says that a prophet's fruit is his or her teachings. A true prophet will have correct doctrine. Some interpreters claim that having correct doctrine is the sole meaning of good fruit.

But others are just as adamant that good fruit has to do with a prophet's character. Good fruit, they argue, is solely the kind of life that they live. This interpretation is paraphrased by *The Message*: "Be wary of false preachers who smile a lot, dripping with practiced sincerity. Chances are they are out to rip you off some way or other. Don't be impressed with charisma; look for character. Who preachers *are* is the main thing, not what they say."

It seems that both groups of interpreters are probably right and wrong. They are wrong in saying that fruit must be either teaching or character. They are correct in what they affirm. It is wrong to draw too firm a line between teachings and character, since people's teachings generally flow out into their daily lives.

The main thing is that we keep our eyes open. On the one hand, we don't want to be so naive that we are taken in by religious shysters. But on the other, we don't want to become so skeptical that we miss God's blessings.

Help us, Father, to have a spirit of discernment as we seek to hear Your voice.

FRUIT INSPECTION

Quench not the Spirit. Despise not prophesyings. Prove all things; hold fast that which is good. 1 Thess. 5:19-21.

A few weeks ago a man arranged a visit with me so that he could share some "new light." He was an impressive person to listen to. He had studied extensively his Bible and the writings of Ellen White. I was also impressed with his sincerity, even though I had to conclude he was sincerely wrong.

On what basis, you may be asking, did I make my decision that this man was wrong? Isn't sincerity everything? Isn't motive the entire basis of God's judgment? No, it's not. Truth is also important. I have no doubt as to the devil's sincerity, but I am just as certain that he is wrong. Doctrinal truth isn't everything, but the Bible holds it to be important as a guide for our lives.

My visitor had come with what he believed to be the truth of God. One aspect of that "truth" was that there is no judgment in the sense that God actually destroys people. Since God is love, destruction of human life for any reason is beyond Him.

I pointed out to my visitor that the deaths of such people as Korah and Abiram in the Old Testament were obviously an act of God. The response was that such Old Testament stories are primitive, and not to be accepted at face value. I next went to the sequential deaths of Ananias and Sapphira in Acts 5. But that also was merely the natural result of their own wrong actions. God had nothing directly to do with it. God never takes life, even in the final executive judgment.

By the time we were finished, my visitor had done away with most of the Old Testament and all that he didn't like in Paul. So I finally indicated that Jesus Himself probably taught the final destruction of the wicked more than anyone in the New Testament. To this he replied that he didn't accept all of Jesus' teachings, either.

This man had come to my office purporting to be a messenger of light, but by the time he left I had concluded that he was a wolf in sheep's clothing.

THE DOCTRINAL TEST

To the law and to the testimony: if they speak not according to this word, it is because there is no light in them. Isa. 8:20.

All religious teachers, whether they are laypersons or clergy, need to be brought to the test of God's Word. We need to listen with both ears open to what is being said and what is not being said.

Most of us can spot rank heresy when we hear it. But that's not how wolves in sheep's clothing operate. They come to us with a whole raft of Bible quotations and perhaps large numbers of passages from Ellen White. Look at what I'm teaching you, they say. It's biblical. We're impressed. They know their stuff.

But wait a minute. These people seem to be saying correct things, but do they have these things in balance? Are they preaching the whole Word of God or only what agrees with what they believe? What are they leaving out? What Bible teachings are they avoiding?

The subtleness in false teaching isn't always in what people teach. It is often rooted in those invisible things that they don't mention.

For example, while false teachers may have a great deal to say about this and that specific sin, they may fail altogether to talk about the power of sin that enslaves us. Thus they leave the impression, through the use of selective Bible verses, that if we just try hard enough, we can overcome. They fail to preach the total helplessness of each of us and our utter hopelessness. The result of such teaching is a theological orientation that leads to a solution through human effort.

Others emphasize the love of God to the extent that His justice is neglected, while still others downplay either law or grace.

Those who speak for God need to be straight on doctrine. The doctrinal test is one way in which we can apply Jesus' admonition to test prophets by their fruit.

Help us, Father, to become better Bible students so that we might be able to detect truth and error.

END-TIME WOLVES

For there shall arise false Christs, and false prophets, and shall shew great signs and wonders; insomuch that, if it were possible, they shall deceive the very elect. Matt. 24:24.

The crisis of the ages takes place right before the second coming of Christ. Satan will pull out all stops in his one last attempt to win. We can expect to see a great outpouring of signs and wonders, and wolves in sheep's clothing will arise in every circle.

Speaking of that time, John says that the lamblike beast of Revelation 13 will work "great signs, even making fire come down from heaven to earth in the sight of men; and by the signs which it is allowed to work in the presence of the beast, it deceives those who dwell on earth, bidding them make an image for the beast" (Rev. 13:13, RSV).

I am not sure what it means when it says that the lamblike beast will have power to make fire come down from heaven, but it is clear that it will succeed where the priests of Baal failed in the time of Elijah. End-time deceptions will be the most powerful that have ever taken place. Multitudes, including large numbers of Adventists, will be taken in.

How can we stand in such a time? In *The Great Controversy* we read that "only those who have been diligent students of the Scriptures and who have received the love of the truth will be shielded from the powerful delusion that takes the world captive. By the Bible testimony these will detect the deceiver in his disguise. To all the testing time will come. . . . Are the people of God now so firmly established upon His Word that they would not yield to the evidence of their senses? Would they, in such a crisis, cling to the Bible and the Bible only? Satan will, if possible, prevent them from obtaining a preparation to stand in that day. He will so arrange affairs as to hedge up their way, entangle them with earthly treasures, . . . [that] the day of trial may come on them as a thief" (pp. 625, 626).

Today is the day to set aside more time for Bible study. Why put it off?

WOLVES ON THE LEFT AND WOLVES ON THE RIGHT

For I know this, that after my departing shall grievous wolves enter in among you, not sparing the flock. Acts 20:29.

The words of Paul in today's Bible verse were addressed to the Ephesians of his day, but unfortunately they have been applicable to the church in every age. Christianity has not been short on wolves in sheep's clothing.

Wolves are mentioned a remarkable number of times in Scripture, and never in flattering terms. The Bible knows nothing of the nice wolf.

In the biblical accounts, wolves are found both inside (Eze. 22:27; Zeph. 3:3) and outside (Matt. 10:16; John 10:12) the sheepfold. In Paul's counsel to the Ephesians in today's scripture, we find that they are in the inside.

Every church, including the Adventist, has had its share of wolves. Most of us have been warned about the wolves masquerading as sheep on the left (liberal) side of the fold. We have heard that they downplay the authority of the Bible and the gift of prophecy, the substitutionary atonement of Jesus on the cross, and the role of God as Creator.

But few of us are nearly as aware of wolves that enter on the right (conservative) side of the fold. These look so much more Christian because they look so much more faithful and biblical, and they often wave around large collections of Ellen White quotations. But their errors are just as serious as those on the left. They are especially liable to be deceptive in their nonbiblical definitions of perfection, tendencies to make more use of Ellen White than the Bible, fanaticism in health reform, and a proneness toward verbal rather than thought inspiration.

Watch out! Wolves are wolves no matter what their orientation. Heresy on the right is still heresy; it is just as dangerous as heresy on the left, but much more subtle.

Help us, Lord, to keep our eyes open. Help us to have balance in all things, especially in our understanding of Your Word. Help protect us, both as individuals and as a church, from all forms of error.

CORRUPT FRUITS

Even so every good tree bringeth forth good fruit; but a corrupt tree bringeth forth evil fruit. A good tree cannot bring forth evil fruit, neither can a corrupt tree bring forth good fruit. Matt. 7:17, 18.

What is a "corrupt," or "bad" (RSV), tree? Have you ever seen one? How did you know it was corrupt or bad?

"Corrupt" doesn't mean rotten or decayed, because trees in that condition don't bring forth fruit at all. That is an important point, since Jesus is once again pointing to the subtlety of the false prophets. Not only are they wolves masquerading as sheep, but they are apparently good-looking trees that are bad on the inside. For the purpose of this illustration, the good and the bad trees resemble each other. Both are good, to all appearances. But their fruit is different.

But even the fruit isn't defined as rotten. It is called "evil," but it is still fruit. Once again we are faced with a subtle difference. Once again, it seems, we are dealing with a situation in which outward appearances can mislead.

The danger that Jesus seems to be driving at with both the corrupt-tree and the evil-fruit illustrations is that of appearing to be Christian without really being so.

You may wonder how that can be. Can there be such a thing as an "evil Christian"? Isn't that a contradiction in terms? Yes, it is, but that's what the illustration is all about. Jesus is talking about people who claim to be Christians but aren't.

How can that be? Think about it for a minute. Christians are those who are born again of God. They have been transformed from the inside out. They live for Jesus because the principle of God's law (love) is written on their hearts. Thus they act like Christians. They walk the Christian walk.

But there are others who merely drop certain things off of their old selfish life and add on new behaviors. But they aren't converted. They just look like the real thing.

Help me, Lord, to give myself every day to You so that my fruit might be the real thing.

A Nice Young Man in Jail

And many false prophets shall rise, and shall deceive many. Matt. 24:11.

Today my young friend resides in the St. Joseph County Jail. He seemed like such a nice young Christian, so vibrant and sincere in his witness. I enjoyed spending a Sabbath with him three weeks ago and hearing him tell how he had been dramatically won to Christ after a life of crime and drugs. He spoke lovingly of the local Adventist who had studied the Bible with him in jail, and of his baptism. He knew his Bible well. He even claimed he wanted to go into the ministry. What a joy it was to be with him. His charismatic personality took us all in.

Then it happened. On an excellent pretense, he talked one of my friends out of a few hundred dollars. It soon came out that he had done the same with several others in town who were impressed with this young "hero for the Lord." He was arrested the day before yesterday. Today he is awaiting trial.

Here is a budding young false prophet; here is a wolf in sheep's clothing; here is a corrupt tree with evil fruit. It is all so vivid in my mind. And I, of all people, after having unmasked several deceivers in the past, was totally taken in.

Are we never safe from such people? Not according to Jesus. False prophets will be with us till the end of time.

How can we protect ourselves from deception? Not by automatically turning away from everyone we don't know. By that method we would miss blessings that God has for us, and we would miss the blessing of helping genuine Christians in distress.

The Bible answer is to test the prophets, to test those who claim to be Christians. We do that by testing their teachings to see if they line up with the Word of God and by testing the fruits of their lives. Here is where my young friend failed.

Thank You, God, for giving us both open minds and discerning spirits.

FRUIT-TESTING IN THE EARLY CHURCH

Beloved, believe not every spirit, but try the spirits whether they are of God: because many false prophets are gone out into the world. 1 John 4:1.

The early Christian church had many traveling preachers who claimed the prophetic gift. At their best, such people inspired the church and gave it direction in the same way that true prophets have always passed on God's word to His people. But the office was subject to abuse. That abuse and the ways to handle it are found in the earliest surviving church manual—the Didache.

The teachings in the Didache were probably formulated soon after Matthew wrote his caution about false prophets. In chapters 11 and 12 it says that a traveling prophet should "be received as the Lord." But, claims the Didache, a prophet is to be tested. How? Here the manual gets quite practical. "Not everyone who speaks in a spirit is a prophet, except if he have the behaviour of the Lord. From his behaviour, then, the false prophet and the true prophet shall be known." At that point the document gets even more specific: "No prophet who orders a meal in a spirit shall eat of it; otherwise he is a false prophet. And every prophet who teaches the truth, if he do not what he teaches, is a false prophet. . . . But whosoever shall say in a spirit 'Give me money,' or anything else, you shall not listen to him; but if he tell you to give on behalf of others in want, let none judge him."

That sounds like good counsel for people in our day. There are many today proclaiming to have the word of God. We see some of them on TV and hear them on radio. But some of their messages will not pass the tests of the Didache. This is practical counsel. A few years ago one of America's most popular TV programs was *PTL*. The official name was *Praise the Lord*, but before the arrest of its "star prophet," many had begun to call it *Pass the Loot*.

We still need to be careful. In giving, there is a blessing, but God expects us to be careful in that giving.

THE SPIRIT TEST

If anyone says, "I love God," yet hates his brother, he is a liar. For anyone who does not love his brother, whom he has seen, cannot love God, whom he has not seen. And he has given us this command: Whoever loves God must also love his brother. 1 John 4:20, 21, NIV.

Whom shall we listen to? Who has the truth? Who has the Word of God?

Those are crucial questions for Christians, because on every side we are beset by those who claim to be speaking for God. They are also tricky questions, because people can have correct doctrine but still not be Christians. People can even have good moral standards and not be Christians.

You may be wondering at this point how it is that a person who is straight on doctrine and lives a good moral life can be a false prophet.

The answer is that Christianity is much more than doctrine and ethics. Some people like correct theology because theology is a game for them, kind of like doing a jigsaw puzzle in which you have to fit in all the parts correctly. And some people are even born with a quiet manner and a desire for the less visible and less offensive sins. Thus they look good and proper.

Correct doctrine and good conduct are important, but the ultimate test of a prophet (or any Christian) has to do with the fruit of the Spirit that we find in Galatians 5:22, 23. Is the person loving in the biblical sense of the term, joyful, peaceful, longsuffering, gentle, good, faithful, meek, and temperate? Jesus put the spirit test about as straightforwardly as anyone could make it when He said, "By this all men will know that you are my disciples, if you have love for one another" (John 13:35, RSV).

Here is the ultimate test, the test of 1 Corinthians 13 in daily action. Here is the way not only to test "prophets" but to test ourselves.

Are we daily growing more like Jesus in how we relate to others in our family, church, and workplace? Have we grasped the idea of what it means to reflect His character, to have the fruit of the Spirit?

HELL AND OTHER INTERESTING PLACES

Every tree that bringeth not forth good fruit is hewn down, and cast into the fire. Matt. 7:19.

Hell is not a very popular topic in the twentieth century. Most Christians think it is not in good taste to bring up the topic. But Jesus didn't have any such qualms. In fact, He may have had more to say on the topic than any other person in the Bible.

Of course, when one thinks about the history of hell, it is not hard to discover why the doctrine fell out of favor. One only has to recall the teaching of the medieval church, of endless torture in a never-consuming fire, to quickly develop a distaste for the topic. Such inhumane torture makes Hitler and Stalin look like pikers.

With that picture in mind, it is little wonder that Ellen White wrote that "it is beyond the power of the human mind to estimate the evil which has been wrought by the heresy of eternal torment. . . . The appalling views of God which have spread over the world from the teachings of the pulpit have made thousands, yes, millions, of skeptics and infidels" *(The Great Controversy*, p. 536).

However, false teaching on a topic should not lead us to throw out the truth on the matter. The facts of the case are that God is love and that all who eventually are in His eternal kingdom will live by that principle. Yet, He won't force anyone to be loving.

As a result, God is forced to make a decision. Either He can let sinners continue to exist in endless unhappiness, or He can mercifully put them out of their self-chosen misery. There are no other choices. God opts for the latter.

But the wages of sin is death, not immortality in hell (Rom. 6:23). Thus Revelation 20:9 makes it explicit that hellfire "consumes" the wicked. The results are eternal. Those consumed will be burned up; they will be as if they had never been (Mal. 4:1). Thus, strange as it may sound at first, God demonstrates His mercy even in the final destruction of the wicked.

The alternative to hell, of course, is heaven. God wants as many as will be happy in heaven to be there.

THE FRUITS OF FALSENESS

Wherefore by their fruits ye shall know them. Matt. 7:20.

Repetition is a law of learning. Jesus had no aversion to that law. So He again pounds home in verse 20 the lesson of the fruit that He has just set forth in verse 16. He wants us to catch the message.

William Barclay suggests that there are five fruits of falseness. First, teaching is false when it produces a religion that consists solely or mainly in the observance of externals. That was what was wrong with the religion of the scribes and Pharisees. That was the error that Jesus has been arguing against all through the Sermon on the Mount. Religion is not merely what you do—whether it's carrying no more than the weight of two figs on the Sabbath day or being a vegetarian. Religion is a matter of the heart that flows out into everyday life.

Second, teaching is false if it produces a religion that consists primarily of prohibitions. It can never be said enough that no one will ever be saved by what he or she did not do. The core of Christianity is positive. It is a reaching out to God and other people in loving kindness.

Third, teaching is false if it produces an easy religion. We must never forget that the narrow way is far from easy. In Romans 6 Paul flatly rejected the formula that we should sin all the more that God's grace might abound. The religion of Jesus helps us overcome our natural inclinations toward evil.

Fourth, teaching is false if it divorces religion from life. The way of the monastery is not the way of Jesus, whether that monastic order be one of the Catholics in the Middle Ages or an Adventist ghetto of the present. Like salt and light, Jesus mixed with the people.

Fifth, teaching is false if it makes us arrogant and proud of our "spiritual superiority." The religion of Jesus is always one of humility.

Think about it: What is your religion doing to you? Does it have the attributes of soundness, or are there adjustments that need to be made?

SINCERELY DECEIVED

Not every one that saith unto me, Lord, Lord, shall enter into the kingdom of heaven; but he that doeth the will of my Father which is in heaven. Matt. 7:21.

Today's verse is one of the most frightening in the New Testament. It flatly states that I can be lost while claiming Jesus is my Saviour; that I can be sincerely deceived; that I can think that all is well with my religious life when all is wrong.

Today's text is also one of the most serious in all of God's Word. Jesus is not playing games. He has spent a large portion of His sermon on the mount telling us how the scribes and Pharisees had deceived themselves. Now He is pointing at me and you. We can be just as confused and deceived as the scribes and Pharisees unless we pay heed to Jesus' words. There is nothing more serious in all the words of Jesus than those in Matthew 7:21-23. He is speaking to us with all the earnestness of His soul. It behooves us to listen carefully.

Not all who claim to be a believer in Jesus as Lord and Saviour will be saved, even though they make that plea in the judgment itself. That is the message of verse 21. That is an amazing thought, given the fact that so many say that the totality of salvation is claiming Jesus as Saviour. Jesus is warning us that there is more to being saved than merely making such claims. He is not saying that claiming Him as Lord is a wrong thing to do, but rather that there is more to salvation than merely making such a claim.

For Jesus really to be Lord means that He must be our Master and that we must be His disciples. A disciple is one who follows his or her master. A lord is one who has complete control of a person's life. A disciple's life is totally committed to his or her lord, not for the perks or recognition that the disciple may receive, but for the glory of the master.

Father, help us to have understanding and self-understanding as we study these all-important verses. Help us to be totally committed to You.

DOING GOD'S WILL

He who says "I know him" but disobeys his commandments is a liar, and the truth is not in him; but whoever keeps his word, in him truly love for God is perfected. By this we may be sure that we are in him: he who says he abides in him ought to walk in the same way in which he walked. 1 John 2:4-6, RSV.

After reading that frightful text in Matthew 7:21 about being lost even while crying "Lord, Lord" in the face of judgment, we naturally want to know how we can avoid self-deception. Jesus answers our question in that same text, when He says that we must be doers and not just hearers of His Father's will. And John reinforces that point when he says "we may be sure that we are in him" if we keep His commandments and walk as Jesus walked.

That's good news. That's true assurance of salvation. We can know! Praise God!

But what is doing the Father's will? That is an important question. Before answering it, we need to remember that every Bible passage needs to be read in its own context. We also need to remember that the context of Matthew 7:21-23 is the Sermon on the Mount.

Thus *doing* God's will in this great judgment scene is living the Beatitudes; it is feeling sorrow for our sin and going to God as starving men and women to be filled with His righteousness; it is allowing God to transform us into merciful peacemakers. Doing God's will is being salt and light as we witness for Him. Doing God's will is letting Him live out the height and depth and width of His law of love in us; it is loving even our enemies and thus being like God Himself. Doing God's will means having a sincere and active prayer life and being a joyful steward of His money. Doing God's will means having our priorities right and trusting in Him, rather than living lives focused on materialism and worry. Doing God's will means avoiding judging the motivations and destinies of others, but at the same time it means discriminating outward good from evil on the basis of His Word.

Doing God's will is being like Jesus.

DOING THE WILL ILLUSTRATED

By this we may be sure that we know him, if we keep his commandments.
1 John 2:3, RSV.

Doing God's will. It is easier said than done; it is easier pledged than fulfilled. But nice words are never a substitute for good actions.

The Bible knows of only one proof of love, and that is obedience. It is hypocritical to say we love a person and then turn around and do things that break that person's heart.

Many of us in our younger days said to our mothers from time to time, "I love you." And sometimes our mothers must have smiled and whispered to themselves, "I wish you would show it a little more in the way you behave."

So it is in our walk with God. Too often we confess Him with our lips but deny Him by our lives. One insightful author has written that "it is not difficult to recite a creed, but it is difficult to live the Christian life. Faith without practice is a contradiction in terms, and love without obedience is an impossibility."

One of my favorite Bible stories along this line is the parable of the two sons. Today we will read it from *The Message* paraphrase:

"'A man had two sons. He went up to the first and said, "Son, go out for the day and work in the vineyard."

"'The son answered, "I don't want to." Later on he thought better of it and went.

"'The father gave the same command to the second son. He answered, "Sure, glad to." But he never went.

"'Which of the two sons did what the father asked?'"

"They said, 'The first.'

"Jesus said, 'Yes, and I tell you that crooks and whores are going to precede you into God's kingdom. John came to you showing you the right road. You turned up your noses at him, but the crooks and whores believed him. Even when you saw their changed lives, you didn't care enough to change and believe him'" (Matt. 21:28-32).

"Not every one that saith, 'Lord, Lord,' shall enter into the kingdom of heaven; but he that *doeth* the will of my Father" (Matt. 8:21).

REALLY DOING JESUS' COMMANDMENTS

If ye love me, keep my commandments. John 14:15.

For too long we Adventists have glibly quoted today's Bible verse out of context and applied it to the Ten Commandments in our Bible studies and evangelistic sermons. Now, I know that Jesus as the "I AM" gave the Ten Commandments to Moses on Sinai and that "my commandments" could possibly mean the Decalogue.

But that is not what we find in the context of John 14:15. We find something deeper, something more basic. A careful study of John 13 through 15 is needed before the exact definition of "my commandments" can be determined. Let's take a few minutes to look at the context.

A first hint at Jesus' definition is found in John 13:34, 35: "A new commandment I give to you, that you love one another; even as I have loved you, that you also love one another. By this all men will know that you are my disciples, if you have love for one another" (RSV).

Another helpful contextual passage in our quest for a definition is John 15:12-14: "This is my commandment, that you love one another as I have loved you. Greater love has no man than this, that a man lay down his life for his friends. You are my friends if you do what I command you" (RSV). And what does Jesus command us? The answer is found in verse 17: "This I command you, to love one another" (RSV).

Thus John's Gospel is in harmony with Jesus in the Sermon on the Mount when He talked about being like God and being as perfect as the Father. John's Gospel is also in harmony with those beatitudes that command us to be merciful and peacemakers.

Doing the will of the Father is to be like Jesus; it is to love like the Father loves.

Keeping the Ten Commandments is included in those injunctions, but only as a by-product of a heart infused with love for God and other people. One can keep the letter of the Ten Commandments without being loving, but a person can never be loving without keeping the Decalogue as he or she understands it.

Jesus is taking us to the basics. He wants us to really do the Father's will.

"That Day" Again

Many will say to me in that day, Lord, Lord, have we not prophesied in thy name? and in thy name have cast out devils? and in thy name done many wonderful works? Matt. 7:22.

"That day," we saw some months ago, is the day of judgment, the day when all accounts are settled, the day when the rewards and punishments are passed out.

The story is told of a young boy who was given the task of planting string beans in his mother's garden. The job started out quite well. It was cool, the birds were singing, and the morning sun felt good on his back.

First came the spading, then the breaking up of the clods with a hoe, then the raking, and then the making of the rows. Finally, there was the planting of each seed, two inches apart.

In spite of a good start, as the sun got hotter, the job began to look less and less attractive. *Whoever,* he thought, *would want so many string beans? What a waste of a summer day. All my friends are down at the swimming hole, having fun and eating watermelon.*

Such thoughts put an end to persevering faithfulness. But our friend knew he had to plant all the seeds. So he planted a few more in the proper way. But then he dumped the rest of the seeds in the middle of a row and covered them up.

His mother was pleased with what she supposed to be a job well done. But then "that day" arrived. That day was the day the seeds sprouted. It was quite plain to her what had happened. The day of reckoning had arrived.

"That day" will also arrive for the entire world. Then our faithfulness will be evident to all. How we have lived our lives will make a difference. Our present is a part of our future. Our present, according to Jesus, will determine our future.

Father, as we contemplate the words of Jesus, we realize that even though judgment may be an unpopular topic, it is a reality that needs to be taken into consideration.

THE FRIGHTENING PART
OF MATTHEW 7:22

They also will answer, "Lord, when did we see thee hungry or thirsty or a stranger or naked or sick or in prison, and did not minister to thee?" Then he will answer them, "Truly, I say to you, as you did it not to one of the least of these, you did it not to me." Matt. 25:44, 45, RSV.

The frightening part of Matthew 7:22 is who is left on the outside of the kingdom. How can we who have been such great workers, who have done so many things in Your name, be left out? is their questioning cry.

This passage is not the only one in which questions arise over God's final decision in the judgment. Another is the parable of the sheep and goats in Matthew 25:31-46.

To one group Jesus says, "Enter into My kingdom." They reply, "But how did we make it? We're not like those Pharisees who spent their entire lives seeking to live out the multitude of do's and don'ts."

Jesus replies, "You don't understand. When I was hungry, you fed Me. When I was in prison, you visited Me."

They query in return, "Wait a minute. How can that be? We never saw You or fed You."

"But," Jesus answers, "if you did it to one of the least of these, you did it to Me."

About this time the other group is getting excited. There are quite a few Pharisees in this group. "Wait a second, Lord," they cry out, "we kept the Sabbath. We kept all of our 1,500 rules regarding the Sabbath. We also paid tithe rigorously—even to the extent of every tenth leaf of our mint plants. And we had a good diet. Lord, You have to save us. We deserve it."

"Well," replies Jesus, "there is only one problem. When I was in prison and thirsty, you didn't seem to care."

"Lord," they shoot back, "if we had known it was You, we would have been right down."

"But," Jesus responds, "you haven't gotten the point. You haven't internalized the great principle of My kingdom—love. And if you don't have that, you won't be happy there."

THE BASIS OF THE GREAT SURPRISE

And these shall go away into everlasting punishment: but the righteous into life eternal. Matt. 25:46.

Yesterday we looked at the frightening reality of who was left outside of the kingdom in the final judgment of Matthew 7:22 and 25:31-46. We found out that some of them were "good Adventists." They not only claimed Jesus as their Lord, but had done many mighty works in His name, and had even kept the Sabbath meticulously, paid an exact tithe, and been scrupulous in health reform. Yet they were profoundly shocked at the verdict of Christ on judgment day.

We ended by noting that according to Matthew 25, the deciding factor in the judgment is whether people have internalized and acted out the kingdom principle of love. Ellen White makes that point explicit. "Thus," she writes, "Christ on the Mount of Olives pictured to His disciples the scene of the great judgment day. And He represented its decision as turning upon one point. When the nations are gathered before Him, there will be but two classes, and their eternal destiny will be determined by what they have done or neglected to do for Him in the person of the poor and the suffering" *(The Desire of Ages, p. 637).*

If people are not passing on the love of God to their neighbors, it's because they don't have it. If people have God's love in their hearts, there is no way it can be kept corked up.

God wants everyone to be in heaven who will be happy there. And those who will be happy will be those who have given up the principle of self-love (sin) and have let God infuse the great principle of His law into their hearts and lives.

The new birth includes this shift from selfishness to living the life of love (the principle of the law). Sanctification is merely the process of becoming more loving. The biblical picture of perfection is one of becoming mature in expressing God's love. Such people are forming characters like Christ's, for "God is love" (1 John 4:8). Such people are safe to save for eternity.

Lord, thank You for instructing us so that we won't be surprised in the judgment. Now help us to live what we know.

GOD'S KIND OF SOMETHING

If I have prophetic powers, and understand all mysteries and all knowledge, and if I have all faith, so as to remove mountains, but have not love, I am nothing. 1 Cor. 13:2, RSV.

The staggering aspect of Matthew 7:21, 22 is the impressive credentials of the petitioners. They are obviously pious. "Lord, Lord" is constantly on their lips. And they are truly zealous workers. Just look at the list of their accomplishments. They have prophesied, they have cast out demons, and they have done many mighty works. And it was all done in His name.

We need to face it. We need to admit it. These people are impressive workers. They would probably even be cited for merit by the General Conference and have their exploits written up for all to see in the *Adventist Review*.

But God doesn't see it that way. He sees behind the scenes. Even on the surface, these workers were a bit too conscious of their own goodness and accomplishments. "Look at all we have done; look at what superior believers we are" is their appeal. Where is that humility and poverty of spirit that characterizes true believers?

At a deeper level, we need to ask why they were doing all these things. Was it to get recognition as a super soul winner, giver of Bible studies, or Ingatherer? What is the motivation behind their actions? That is the heart of the matter. And why is it that some of these "super Christians" are so good at doing visible things that impress others, but have no delight in the less visible things, such as spending time with their spouse or their children? To God, the invisible is more important than the visible.

Paul accomplished a lot, yet he had things straight in his mind. Listen to him: "If I speak in the tongues of men and of angels, but have not love, I am a noisy gong or a clanging cymbal. . . . If I give away all I have, and if I deliver my body to be burned, but have not love, I gain nothing" (1 Cor. 13:1, 2, RSV).

I don't know about you, but I want to rededicate my life to being God's kind of something.

HARD WORDS FOR JESUS

And then will I profess unto them, I never knew you: depart from me, ye that work iniquity. Matt. 7:23.

The words of this verse must be the hardest Jesus will ever have to say. Some people have the idea that the final judgment is so that God can weed as many people out of heaven as possible. But that is Satan's version of the purpose of the judgment. He has been God's accuser from the beginning. From the beginning, he has brought God's love and justice into question.

The opposite position is where the truth lies. God and Christ want to see as many people in heaven as possible. The judgment is not to keep them out, but to get them in. The judgment is to certify before the universe that they have indeed accepted the sacrifice of Jesus on the cross as the atonement for their sins, and that they have allowed God to fill them with the principle of His love.

God has done all He can to prepare the way for as many as possible to pass the judgment and enter the kingdom. God sent His Son to live and die for us; He accepts the blood of Jesus in our place; He accepts Christ's ministry on our behalf in the heavenly sanctuary; and He is preparing a place for us in His everlasting kingdom.

After all that has been done, it is a heartbreaking thing for Jesus to have to say "I don't know you, depart from me." If He had tears at His rejection by Jerusalem in Matthew 23, He will certainly have tears as He utters those fateful words. But utter them He will on "that day."

God and Christ have done their part to avoid those words. The question is: Have we done our part? Have we repented of our sins and accepted Jesus as our Saviour? Have we allowed Him to infuse us with His love and let Him live out that love in our daily lives? Have we allowed Him to fill us with His Spirit and transform us?

If not, why not? If not, why not do so today? Today is the day to commit your life to Him.

"EVILDOERS" OF GOOD THINGS

For [Christ's] sake I have suffered the loss of all things, and count them as refuse, in order that I may gain Christ and be found in him. Phil. 3:8, RSV.

One day William Wilberforce, the Christian who led out in the battle against slavery in the British Empire, was accosted by a woman who said, "Mr. Wilberforce, what about your soul?" He turned to the woman and said, "Madam, I had almost forgotten that I had a soul."

Like many Christian warriors in the heat of battle, the intense philanthropist had begun to lose perspective on what the struggle was all about. It is all too easy to lose our way while being involved in the midst of "good" activities. The "evildoers" of Matthew 7:23 (RSV) were not doing bad things. To the contrary, they were doing "good" things.

What are some of these good things that can lead us astray, in terms of salvation? One might be going to church. Now, going to church sounds harmless enough. There are some people who love to go to church. The doors never open without their being there. But that going never seems to do anything for them. It never inspires them to help others or share their talents. They just sit there and take it all in. Churchgoing becomes an end in itself.

The same can be said about those who take a delight in studying the Bible. For some people, Bible study is as fascinating as watching a TV program. It absorbs their time, but fails to inspire changes in their lives.

Others are led astray defending denominational doctrines. They love to battle over the defense of the Sabbath and creationism. Talk to them on these topics, and they have a world to say. But ask them what Jesus means to them, and they are silent.

These are all good things that can be put to bad use. We need to stand with Paul, whose primary aim was to know Jesus and be found in Him. We need to do these good things, but with proper Christian perspective.

AVOIDING SELF-DECEPTION

Let a man examine himself, and so eat of the bread and drink of the cup. For any one who eats and drinks without discerning the body eats and drinks judgment upon himself. 1 Cor. 11:28, 29, RSV.

Those condemned by Jesus in Matthew 7:21-23 are suffering from self-deception. They thought they were right, but they were wrong—seriously wrong.

This is frightful. You may be wondering how you can know you are not deceived about your own standing with God.

For one thing, it is important to avoid false doctrines of assurance. There are some who would have us believe that justification is to be equated with salvation. Just believe, and it is OK. Just say "Lord, Lord," and you will be all right. That is the very doctrine that Jesus is warning against in Matthew 7:21.

Christian assurance of salvation is a Bible doctrine, but it is based on holy living by those who have been justified and born again. Assurance, according to Jesus in Matthew 7, belongs to the "doers" of the Father's will.

A second thing we can do to avoid self-deception regarding our standing with God is to examine ourselves. Paul tells us to examine ourselves as to whether we are in the faith (2 Cor. 13:5). That examination needs to take place in the full light of Scripture. We must honestly ask ourselves why we are doing certain things and what the motives are behind our words and actions. We need to honestly face up to the truth if we are doing good things for self-interest.

A third thing we can do to avoid self-deception is to get our priorities straight. First and foremost, God wants our hearts; He wants us to have a loving relationship with Him that leads to obedience in all things. And here it is important to be honest. Some of us are ready to be obedient in those areas we like, but avoid faithfulness in other areas. God wants us to take the whole Bible and put it into balanced practice.

Deception is a real danger, but we never need to be deceived. God has plainly laid out a clear path before us if we are willing to follow without reservation.

WORKING THROUGH INSECURITY

And this is life eternal, that they might know thee the only true God, and Jesus Christ, whom thou hast sent. John 17:3.

Life eternal. That's what we have been dealing with the past few days and months. That is what we desire with all our hearts. We hunger and thirst for it, and yet we may be filled with doubts as to where we stand with God, especially after reading Matthew 7:21-23.

We need not be insecure, even in the midst of a passage on judgment and self-deception. Jesus has made the way plain for us, even if He has had to say it a bit harder than we like. His purpose is to wake us up to the seriousness of the matter. But once we are wakened, our task is to follow His counsel in the Sermon on the Mount. The study of that sermon and how Jesus put its principles into practice in daily life changes us. By beholding Him we become changed. That is why we need to behold Him more often.

Today I would like you not only to recommit all you are and all you have to Jesus, but also to set aside time each day for walking with your Lord. Let's be concrete here. Commit yourself to spending daily a specified amount of time carefully and slowly reading through the four Gospels. And when you are finished, do it again in a different translation. Eventually you may want to study the Gospels in connection with the suggested Bible readings at the beginning of each chapter of *The Desire of Ages*. That kind of study always brings me closer to Him and softens my character.

Invite Jesus into your heart each day, and ask Him to live out His life through you. Walk with Him whom to know is life eternal. Believe His word, accept His grace, and do His will.

And when you slip and fall, remember that Jesus said that him "that cometh to me I will in no wise cast out" (John 6:37). He will forgive any and every sin repented of. In spite of our weaknesses, we can have assurance that we are safe in Him when we are doing His will.

FOUNDATIONS ARE ALL-IMPORTANT

Every one then who hears these words of mine and does them will be like a wise man who built his house upon the rock. Matt. 7:24, RSV.

It was my first church in my first district as a pastor. It wasn't the largest of my three churches, but it was the first that I preached in. It had an attractive and functional little building. But that building had a major problem; it was cracking badly. From the slab to the rafters were cracks that were getting larger by the month.

Fortunately for my small congregation, the bank note on the church had been paid up a few months after my arrival. That left us free to think about the cracks. We soon discovered the problem. The church had been built on land from which underground water was being pumped faster than it could be replaced. Our property was literally sinking.

The solution was to hire a company to dig down 10 feet to the clay every yard or so around the periphery of the building (clay was the closest thing to rock in that part of the state), and put in pillars to buttress the building. It was an expensive task, but we had no choice. Foundations are all-important. We either had to do the job or lose the building.

What is true in the physical realm is also true in the spiritual. Foundations are everything to the life of a Christian and to the health of the church. And the foundation of both must be none other than Jesus Himself. Paul says that "other foundation can no man lay than that is laid, which is Jesus Christ" (1 Cor. 3:11). Again, Paul wrote to the Ephesians that they were citizens "of the household of God; and are built upon the foundation of the apostles and prophets, Jesus Christ himself being the chief corner stone; in whom all the building fitly framed together groweth unto an holy temple in the Lord; in whom ye also are builded together for an habitation of God through the Spirit" (Eph. 2:19-22).

Jesus means everything to the health of our religious experience. He is not an optional aspect of our faith and church, but their very foundation. Without Him we have nothing; we are nothing.

ACTING RATIONALLY

Be ye doers of the word, and not hearers only, deceiving yourselves.
James 1:22.

J esus implies in Matthew 7:24 that we must do two things if we are to build upon the foundation He has laid. The first is to be a hearer of His words; the second is to be a doer.

As both Jesus and James (in today's Bible verse) point out, hearing is important, even though it is not everything. Let's face it: one can't do His will if one hasn't heard. That's where the first problem comes in. A significant fact is that too many are not listening to the Lord. We have our ears tuned more to the popular media and to sports and the news than we do to the Word of God. We are listening, all right, but not always to the right things. And when we do listen, we want to tune in to only those parts of the Bible that please us. And so begins the deception that Jesus is talking about. We need to recommit ourselves today to listening more carefully, to hearing the whole counsel of God.

When we have listened carefully and have heard all God wants to say to us, we are ready to be doers. Jesus has already emphasized in Matthew 7:21-23 that the final test in the judgment is doing His will. Now in verses 24 to 27 He rams that important truth into our resistant minds again. He obviously believes that His point is important, or He wouldn't be repeating it with such enthusiasm.

And if you think about it for a minute, you will see why. Let's take going to the doctor as an example. It's foolish to go to her office for an examination if you fail to listen to the diagnosis. After all, that's what you went for. But it's just as foolish to hire the time of a physician and not follow her advice.

Now, you are probably thinking that that is obvious. Yet there are countless thousands of people who go to church weekly, who have an excellent knowledge of what Jesus said, yet fail to put it into practice.

If you are one of those people, today is the very best time to begin acting rationally.

AND THE STORMS CAME

And the rain fell, and the floods came, and the winds blew and beat upon that house, but it did not fall, because it had been founded on the rock. Matt. 7:25, RSV.

And the storms came. An important point to notice in this verse is that the storms come on both the good and the evil, those who have built on the rock and those who have built on sand. Building on the rock doesn't help us avoid the storms of life, but it does help us successfully withstand those storms.

But what are the storms of life? Some hold that the storm that separates those who build on the rock from those who build on sand is exclusively the final judgment. It seems to me that that interpretation is too restrictive. While the judgment is certainly a major emphasis in the storm metaphor, we need to see it as also including those daily troubles that hit us from every side. Thus building on the rock not only helps us at the end of time, our faith also helps us weather daily difficulties.

There is a sense in which it would be wonderful if nothing but good things happened to people after they were baptized. Suddenly they would have no more illnesses; tornadoes would never hit their homes; their cars would never get a flat tire; their cupboards would never be empty; their well would never go dry; and insects would never infest their crops. That would indeed be glorious.

But it would have some less-than-good by-products. The most serious would be that multitudes would flock into the church, not from a conviction of sin and the need of forgiveness, but in order to escape flat tires, moths, rust, sore throats, and a host of other things.

God in His wisdom realized that such a course would not be good for the church. So He lets the ills of life fall on His saints, just as He lets the sun shine and the rain fall on sinners. This gives the saints the opportunity to demonstrate that their faith indeed sustains them through all crises, that they are firmly anchored to the rock.

AND WHAT ABOUT THE ROCK?

Simon Peter replied, "You are the Christ, the Son of the living God." And Jesus answered him, "Blessed are you, Simon Bar-Jona! For flesh and blood has not revealed this to you, but my Father who is in heaven. And I tell you, you are Peter, and on this rock I will build my church, and the powers of death shall not prevail against it. Matt. 16:16-18, RSV.

Matthew 7:25 explicitly states that the house built upon the rock stands firm because it is founded on the rock. Being built on the rock makes all the difference in the world. But what is the rock that upholds the faith of the church and its members?

In our Scripture passage for today, Jesus identifies the rock undergirding the church. But that passage has been the basis of a debate that has raged across the course of church history. Does Jesus mean that Peter is the rock on which the church is founded, or does He mean that Peter's confession that Jesus is "the Christ, the Son of the living God" is the foundation of the church?

Given the teaching of the rest of the New Testament, it is safe to conclude that it is Peter's confession in Christ as the Son of God that is the rock. Paul definitely identifies Jesus as the only foundation of the church (see 1 Cor. 3:11; Eph. 2:20), and Peter himself sets forth Jesus as "the living Stone . . . a chosen and precious cornerstone," upon which the church is built (1 Peter 2:4-7, NIV).

It is Jesus as the crucified Lamb and our confession of Him that stands at the foundation of the Christian faith. Of course, the primary way to know Jesus is through the Bible's testimony of Him. Building on the rock means not only having a faith relationship to Jesus but also heeding the injunctions of the Bible. That aspect of building on the rock is especially clear in Matthew 7:24, where Jesus talks about hearing and doing "these sayings of mine." Given its context, it seems that part of what Jesus meant by building on the rock was giving heed to the teachings of the Sermon on the Mount in our daily lives.

AND WHAT OF THE SAND?

And every one who hears these words of mine and does not do them will be like a foolish man who built his house upon the sand. Matt. 7:26, RSV.

Jesus doesn't leave us with a whole lot of options. We must either build on the rock or build upon sand. Like the two ways in Matthew 7:13, 14, and like the trees of verses 16-20, there is no middle ground. We can't "kind of" accept Jesus. We are either with Him or against Him. He brooks no competition and no time-share arrangements.

Now, if those who build upon the rock build upon faith in Jesus and fidelity to His Word, what is it that those building on the sand are using as a foundation? If it isn't the Word of God and faith in Jesus, then it must be faith in humanity and human ideas.

The decision not to follow Jesus' words, for whatever reason, is already a decision to do a great deal. It is a decision to live by someone else's words and ideas, because all of us live by someone's words, someone's ideas, someone's philosophy of life.

If we don't live by the commandments of God, we will find ourselves living by the commandments of people. Their standards, their rules, their faith will set the direction of our lives.

The world is full of philosophies and schemes concerning the meaning of life and how to solve the problems of the universe. But these schemes are piles of sand. They may look good, but they won't stand up to the pressures of time and reality. They make an unstable foundation for life.

We read in *Thoughts From the Mount of Blessing* that "every building erected on other foundation than God's Word will fall. He who, like the Jews in Christ's day, builds on the foundation of human ideas and opinions, of forms and ceremonies of man's invention, or on any works that he can do independently of the grace of Christ, is erecting his structure of character upon the shifting sand" (p. 150).

Help us, Father, to be able to appreciate the difference between sand and rock. Help us to commit ourselves to rock-only construction.

A FOOL'S PARADISE

And the rain fell, and the floods came, and the winds blew, and beat upon that house; and it fell: and great was the fall of it. Matt. 7:27.

This verse took on new meaning for me a few years back. I live about 10 miles from Lake Michigan, and one of my favorite forms of exercise is walking on the beach.

It was on one such walk that I graphically saw what Jesus meant. A home that a few days earlier had been "safely" nestled on a bank 40 feet above the beach was now suspended between beach and sky. The sandbank upon which it had been built 30 years before had been eaten up by the pounding waves, and now the house was teetering on only one half of its foundation. The other half of the house was hanging over a newly widened beach. A few days later it fell, and great was the fall thereof.

The great certainty for both houses in Matthew 7 is that the floods will come. We are not faced with options for escaping floods, but we do have the option of building wisely.

Building wisely may take more planning and forethought than meets the eye. I was raised in the Russian River country of northern California. In the summer, in a land that never sees rain in that season, the river falls to a gentle trickle as it meanders through pleasant redwood valleys. It is tempting in the summer to build a house close to the river, especially if one hasn't seen the river at flood stage. But periodically the winter rains create muddy torrents that flood the towns built high above the riverbed. Those foolish enough to have built too close to the river have seen their houses floating downstream toward the Pacific.

Beware of how you build and where you build. What might look nice in time of peace could turn out to be a fool's paradise in times of storm. And remember, the storms of life *will* come. The only question is whether we will be ready for them.

TWO BUILDERS

But this is the covenant which I will make with the house of Israel after those days, says the Lord: I will put my law within them, and I will write it upon their hearts; and I will be their God, and they shall be my people. Jer. 31:33, RSV.

We have not only two houses and two types of building places in the saying of Jesus, but two builders, two types of people. These men are important because they represent personality profiles that can belong to you and me. Let's look at them.

First, we will look at how they are alike. To begin with, they both had the same desire to build a house in which they could live and enjoy themselves. A second point of similarity is that they apparently chose locations in close proximity to each other, since the houses were subject to precisely the same tests and stresses. A third point of similarity is that they seem to have liked the same style of house. As far as Jesus' parable is concerned, the two houses looked essentially the same. The only place they differed seems to be their beneath-the-surface foundation.

These similarities are impressive, but they are important also because they have meaning for our spiritual lives. For too long have we clung to the idea that the difference between the true Christian and the pseudo-Christian is obvious, that it is an external matter. But that all-too-easy conclusion misses Jesus' point that we are dealing with something much more subtle. The difference is not obvious in the two men or the two houses, nor is it always obvious between two church members. The whole difficulty with false prophets, we noted a few days ago, is that on the surface they look so much like true prophets. The same thing holds true for the two trees.

Genuine Christianity is not a matter of mere externals. It is an affair of the heart. Two people can do the same good things for very different reasons. The wise man in our story not only does the right things; he does them because of his heart relationship with Jesus.

TWO BUILDERS AGAIN

He is like a man which built an house, and digged deep, and laid the foundation on a rock. . . . But he that heareth, and doeth not, is like a man that without a foundation built an house upon the earth. Luke 6:48, 49.

Yesterday we looked at the similarities between the two builders of Matthew 7:24-27. We discovered that on the surface they were similar. Both, to put it in spiritual terms, appeared to be good Christians.

Today we want to examine the ways they differ. In undertaking that task, we are greatly aided by Luke's version of this story. He provides information not found in Matthew. Luke tells us, as we saw in today's Scripture reading, that the wise man dug deep and went to the trouble of laying a foundation for his house. By way of contrast, the foolish man did not dig at all. He didn't even go to the trouble of laying a foundation.

The key to understanding the man whose house had no foundation is the word "foolish." The foolish man was in a hurry. Why not, he thinks, take a shortcut if you get the same results? After all, no one will know the difference, since foundations are beneath the surface. So why waste time building a foundation?

The foolish man also appears to be a know-it-all. He knows how to build a house without following the rules that govern the construction business. He doesn't need or heed the advice of architects or other experts.

Beyond those attributes, the foolish man is one who doesn't plan ahead. He wants a house, not a surveying expedition. Why not build it right near the river, where it is so pleasant? And he is smart enough to know that it is easier and quicker to build on sand than on stone.

All of these attributes carry over into our spiritual lives. Foolish Christians are interested only in surface religion; since they know it all, they don't need to take counsel from their fellow church members; and they live for today rather than for the future.

It all looks good. There is only one problem. Their building doesn't make it through the storms of life and judgment.

DIFFERENT KINDS OF GREATNESS

And an argument arose among them as to which of them was the greatest. But when Jesus perceived the thought of their hearts, he took a child and put him by his side, and said to them, "Whoever receives this child in my name receives me, and whoever receives me receives him who sent me; for he who is least among you all is the one who is great." Luke 9:46-48, RSV.

It is interesting that the last word of the Sermon on the Mount is "great." That does not show up in the King James Version of Matthew 7:27, but it is the last word in the Greek and also in Luke's version of the story of the two builders, which reads: "And the ruin of that house was great" (Luke 6:49). It was a great fall, a great collapse, a great ruin.

What is most interesting is that it is that same word that was most cherished by those who failed to understand Jesus' message, among both those who were Jesus' enemies and those who were His friends.

A desire for greatness was the problem of Satan, who wanted to be like God. It was the problem of the scribes and Pharisees, who wanted the best seats at dinner parties, since seating was according to rank. They also desired to be seen as great men in prayer and fasting.

Even the disciples had a desire to be great. They incessantly argued as to which of them was the greatest. That discussion preoccupied them even as Jesus moved toward the cross.

From the beginning of His ministry Jesus declared war on the desire to be great, and He never ceased warning against it. Why? Because the desire for human greatness stands at the center of the sin problem. One writer has suggested that Jesus' concluding word of the Sermon on the Mount suggests that "the only finally great thing about greatness-seeking Christians is the greatness of their fall."

In Christ's eyes, the way of service and humility, the way of poverty of spirit and hungering and thirsting, is the way to greatness. Thus the sermon ends with the same thought with which it began.

THE CRY OF GOD'S HEART

Say to them, As I live, says the Lord God, I have no pleasure in the death
of the wicked, but that the wicked turn from his way and live; turn back,
turn back from your evil ways; for why will you die, O house of Israel.
Eze. 33:11, RSV.

It may seem strange for a sermon that started out with so much blessing and hope to end up with one judgment scene after another. I
would suppose that judgment was not Jesus' favorite topic, but then,
He didn't come to earth to talk about only those things He liked most.
To the contrary, He came to give us the message that we, as sinful humans, most need to hear.

And while we need large doses of hope, we also need to be awakened; we need messages of thunder and lightning to jolt us into reality;
we need messages of judgment. Thus it should not be too astonishing to
us that a fairly large portion of the New Testament is given over to
warnings. The last half of the third chapter of the Sermon on the Mount
is one string of judgment scenes and warnings.

Hopefully, these warnings will wake us up and send us to the
Beatitudes in poverty of spirit, humility, and hungering and thirsting
after God's righteousness.

Jesus knows our temptations. He knows that we like to listen to
beautiful sermons. But He also knows that we don't always put them
into practice. Here in the final scenes of the Sermon on the Mount He
tells us in no uncertain terms that to have life is to walk in His ways, to
have life is to live out the principles that He has been talking about in
the Sermon on the Mount.

He is telling us that this business of choosing kingdoms, of choosing
fathers, of choosing principles, and of choosing to practice those principles, is what life is all about. It is those things that will determine
where we spend eternity.

Jesus wants us to find life, not death. He has poured out His heart.
Have you heard Him?

AND WHO IS THIS MAN?

And when Jesus finished these sayings, the crowds were astonished at his teaching. Matt. 7:28, RSV.

A nd why shouldn't they be astonished? Have you ever stopped to think of their perceptions of Jesus and the kinds of things He said that were not only astonishing, but shocking in the extreme? We have become so familiar with Jesus and history's interpretation of Him that we forget how He must have appeared to His contemporaries.

And how did His contemporaries see Him? For what He was: an unlearned carpenter from a little village called Nazareth in Galilee. He was not a scribe or a Pharisee, but a common man, a laborer. He had not sat at the feet of Gamaliel or any of the other learned teachers. He was nothing but a rustic and lowly carpenter.

But suddenly He bursts onto the scene of Jewish life with a popular and extraordinary ministry. He doesn't beat around the bush. From the very beginning He teaches the most astounding things in the most authoritative manner. His arrival is a shock to the Jewish body politic.

Look at His audacity in the manner of His teaching. The scribes, the religious Ph.D.s of the day, were not noted for original thinking. Their method of teaching was to rely on the authority of others. Their learning was extensive, and they could quote this and that authority with great ease and showmanship. They argued by amassing long lists of quotations.

Jesus didn't even give lip service to the scribal methodology. He needed no other authorities. He was The Authority. "I say unto you" was His style, not "So-and-so has said."

Beyond that, He spoke with utter authority as He made pronouncements. He had no hesitation in telling His hearers what would bring them blessings. And He was not bashful about promising others the kingdom of heaven.

The lowly Carpenter hit Palestine like a wave of surprises. It was difficult not to give Him attention. It still is today. He is still speaking with authority, even to you and me.

AND WHAT KIND OF MAN IS HE?

For he taught them as one having authority, and not as the scribes.
Matt. 7:29.

The ultimate authority of the Sermon on the Mount stems from the Preacher who presented it. That is why Matthew gives us the message found in chapter 7, verses 28 and 29. Having heard the sermon, Matthew wants us to take a look at its Preacher—the One who so astonished the crowds because He taught with authority. Who delivered the sermon is just as important as its contents, if not more so.

And who was it that preached the Sermon on the Mount? Listen to Him. He claims to be much more than a carpenter from Nazareth.

Jesus begins making claims to His identity as early as Matthew 5:11, where He says, "Blessed are you when men revile you and persecute you and utter all kinds of evil against you falsely on *my* account" (RSV). He doesn't say on account of God, but on account of Me.

Then in verse 17 He says, "Think not that I am come to destroy the law, or the prophets." "I am come," not "I was born." And where has He come from? From the One He so very personally calls "My Father." He is the incarnate One who comes from the bosom of the Father.

But perhaps the most profound statement in the Sermon on the Mount regarding Jesus' personal sense of identity is found in Matthew 7:21, where He says, "Many will say to me in that day, Lord, Lord, have we not prophesied in thy name?" He does not hesitate to say that people will address Him as Lord, as a divine person.

And note that He claims that people would be making their petitions to Him on that day, rather than to the Father. Even more astounding is that, in verse 22, it is this Carpenter from Nazareth who pronounces judgment on men and women.

It is little wonder that the Jews were astonished at the authority of Jesus. Not only did He teach in an authoritative manner, but by claiming the prerogative of God He claimed to be God.

This Jesus-Carpenter, this Jesus-God, still speaks with authority. The question is: What are we going to do about it? What are we going to do about Him?

AUTHORITY BEYOND WORDS

When he came down from the mountain, great crowds followed him; and behold, a leper came to him and knelt before him, saying, "Lord, if you will, you can make me clean." And he stretched out his hand and touched him, saying, "I will; be clean." And immediately his leprosy was cleansed. Matt. 8:1-3, RSV.

Words are cheap. Anyone can make great statements. A couple years ago a minister came through town preaching that if people had the right kind of faith they could leave his meeting and never sin again. I had heard that one before. There was a time I used to teach it. I would have been more impressed if brother John had said that he had enough faith to leave the auditorium, go down to the lake, and walk on water. Real authority has demonstrable action, not mere verbiage.

Jesus has real authority not only in His words but also in what He is able to do. That is what Matthew 8 and 9 are all about. Chapters 5-7 set forth Jesus as an authoritative teacher, then come two chapters demonstrating that Jesus has authority in deeds and not merely in words.

Between Matthew 8:1 and 9:33, Matthew has Jesus performing nine miracles that demonstrate His authority in a way that leaves no doubt about who He is. The first miracle finds Jesus healing a leper. Leprosy was the most dreaded disease in the ancient world. Beyond the slow physical deterioration of the leper was the social ostracism. Lepers were banished from human society immediately upon diagnosis. They had to leave family and friends, cover their faces, and cry "Unclean" wherever they went.

Yet Jesus could heal even a leper. He has authority even over such a dreaded disease. The eight subsequent miracles demonstrate that Jesus has authority not only over disease but also over the forces of nature and the demonic world. At the end of the nine miracles, Matthew notes that "the crowds marveled, saying, 'Never was anything like this seen in Israel'" (Matt. 9:33, RSV).

Jesus not only speaks as God, He acts as God. He has authority. And that authority is meant for our cleansing just as much as it was for the cleansing of the Jews 2,000 years ago.

AUTHORITY PASSED ON

He called his twelve disciples to him and gave them authority to drive out evil spirits and to heal every disease and sickness. Matt. 10:1, NIV.

Authority. That is the closing note of Matthew 7. Jesus finished the Sermon on the Mount in Matthew 7:27. Matthew spends the next two verses saying how the crowds were astonished at Jesus' teaching because He taught with authority.

Then, as we saw yesterday, Matthew immediately presents nine miracles in chapters 8 and 9 and concludes that once again the crowds were impressed with Jesus' authority to do things in the real world.

Authority in words and actions has been the theme of Matthew 5 through 9. In the first Gospel these chapters are really a literary unit. But the unit does not end with 9:33. To the contrary, the topic of authority flows right on into Matthew 10, except now it is not Jesus' use of His authority, but the delegation of that authority to His followers.

As Christians we share in the authority of Jesus. He has given us not only His words and example but also the Holy Spirit to empower us to speak words for God and to do good for others whom God puts in our path.

The use of that authority is a God-given right and responsibility. Matthew closes his Gospel on that note. "All authority," said Jesus, "in heaven and earth has been given to me. Therefore go and make disciples of all nations, baptizing them in the name of the Father and of the Son and of the Holy Spirit, and teaching them to obey everything I have commanded you. And surely I am with you, always, to the very end of the age" (Matt. 28:18-20, NIV).

So the message of Jesus in His great sermon goes on and on. We are not only to be hearers and doers of the words of Jesus in the Sermon on the Mount, but we are commanded to help others hear and obey. Jesus is sharing His authority with us.

Lord, help us this day to be faithful to You as stewards of Your authority.

AND HOW SHOULD WE RESPOND?

And Pilate again said to them, "Then what shall I do with the man whom you call the King of the Jews?" Mark 15:12, RSV.

We have come to the end of our year of walking with Jesus on the Mount of Blessing. In some ways it seems our journey has been but a few days, but in others it seems it has been much longer than a year.

Our perceptions of time really matter very little. The fact is that the year is over today, and we start a new one tomorrow. The real question is whether we will end our walk with Jesus or continue on.

This past year we have been confronted with some of the most powerful teaching ever given. We are each faced in the end with the question that Pilate put to the Jews: "What shall I do with the man whom you call the King of the Jews?"

I see you squirming over there. But let's face up to it, squirming doesn't solve the issue. What are you going to do with the Jesus of the Sermon on the Mount? What am I going to do with His teachings?

The answer of the Jews to Pilate was loud and clear: "Crucify Him! Crucify Him!" And Pilate did so.

That is still a live option for us. The other option is that we will let Him crucify us and resurrect us to a new way of life. That's where we began our walk this year. We began with Jews who felt their poverty of spirit and mourned over their sins and hungered and thirsted after righteousness and let God not only forgive them but transform them into being merciful and peaceful.

We are still there. We still need the same experience. Oh, it's true that we are a little wiser after our walk with Jesus, but we are still just as dependent.

Today, Father, we want to thank You for the journey. But more than that, we want to recommit our lives to walking with You on the mount in the coming year. We need the blessing, we need the help, we need the guidance, we need You.

Scripture Index

Also by
George R. Knight

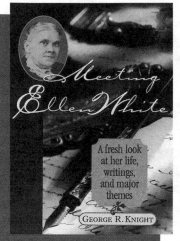

Meeting Ellen White

George R. Knight helps readers understand and appreciate the fascinating life and role of Ellen White. Part one presents a concise biographical overview of her life. Part two introduces you to both her published and unpublished writings, showing the major categories of her counsel to the church. Part three explores seven major themes that run through everything she wrote. Paper, 127 pages. US$8.99, Cdn$12.99.

Reading Ellen White

At long last we have a book that helps readers understand the principles that Ellen White indicated should be used in the reading and application of her writings. Rich in illustrations from her own works and from the Bible, *Reading Ellen White* is must reading for every student of the writings of God's special messenger to His last-day people. Paper, 128 pages. Coming spring 1997.

The Gospel According to Matthew Videos
Word for word from the NIV text

Journey with Matthew as he leads you through 3½ years that changed the world. Told entirely in the trusted words of the New International Version, this unique presentation brings to the screen a divine yet warmly human Jesus.

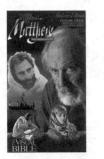 

The entire story of Jesus in four one-hour videos:

volume 1:	Matthew 1:1-9:1
volume 2:	Matthew 9:2-14:36
volume 3:	Matthew 15:1-23:39
volume 4:	Matthew 24:1-28:20

Four-volume set with slipcover, US$99.95, Cdn$144.95

Distributed by Review and Herald Publishing.

Available at all ABC Christian bookstores (**1-800-765-6955**) and other Christian bookstores. Prices and availability subject to change. Add GST in Canada.

To Help You Grow Spiritually

Sunday's Coming!
Eye-opening evidence that these are the very last days. G. Edward Reid reports how U.S.-Vatican activities and the work of the Christian Coalition, Catholic Alliance, and Catholic Campaign for America are fulfilling Revelation 13 and other Bible prophecies. Distributed by Review and Herald. Paper, 250 pages. US$14.99, Cdn$21.49.

On Wings of Praise
Kay Rizzo shares how praise to God lifted her from her "spiritual winter" and filled her life with a joy and power she had never known. "Prayer combined with praise changed my heart," Rizzo writes. Here she shows how it can change yours too. Paper, 171 pages. US$12.99, Cdn$18.99.

The Appearing
Four lives hang in the balance in the chaotic months before the Second Coming. An inspiring story of the end-time by *Women of Spirit* editor Penny Estes Wheeler. Back by popular demand. An expanded edition. Paper, 224 pages. US$10.99, Cdn$15.99.

Meet Ellen White Video
Documentary and drama help viewers get to know Ellen White better both on a personal level and in her role as messenger in the early history of the Adventist Church. Selected from *Keepers of the Flame*. Distributed by Review and Herald. 90 minutes. US$19.95, Cdn$28.95.

The Seventh-day Adventist Bible Commentary for Windows on CD-Rom

The Seventh-day Adventist Bible Commentary is now teamed up with the acclaimed Logos Bible Software 2.0 that turns any IBM-compatible computer into a complete Bible reference library.

Includes the complete text of *The Seventh-day Adventist Bible Commentary,* the King James and New International versions of the Bible, and *Strong's Concordance,* together with an illustrated Bible dictionary and full-color historical atlas, for a complete Bible study reference tool.

- More than 100 interactive illustrations
- More than 160 fully rendered 3-D landscape maps with interactive links to Bible texts
- More than 400 full-color photographs of biblical sites, artifacts, scenery, and rare aerial photography of ancient landscapes

US$389.99, Cdn$565.49
